The Politics of
Global Governance

FOURTH EDITION

The Politics of

Global

Governance

International Organizations in an Interdependent World

edited by
Paul F. Diehl and
Brian Frederking

LYNNE
RIENNER
PUBLISHERS

BOULDER
LONDON

Published in the United States of America in 2010 by
Lynne Rienner Publishers, Inc.
1800 30th Street, Boulder, Colorado 80301
www.rienner.com

and in the United Kingdom by
Lynne Rienner Publishers, Inc.
3 Henrietta Street, Covent Garden, London WC2E 8LU

Library of Congress Cataloging-in-Publication Data
The politics of global governance : international organizations in an interdependent world /
edited by Paul F. Diehl and Brian Frederking. — 4th ed.
   p. cm.
  Includes index.
  ISBN 978-1-58826-711-5 (pb : alk. paper)
  1. International organization. 2. International agencies. 3. Non-governmental
organizations. I. Diehl, Paul F. (Paul Francis) II. Frederking, Brian.
  JZ5566.P65 2010
  341.2—dc22
                                2010011075

British Cataloguing in Publication Data
A Cataloguing in Publication record for this book
is available from the British Library.

Printed and bound in the United States of America

The paper used in this publication meets the requirements
of the American National Standard for Permanence of
Paper for Printed Library Materials Z39.48-1992.

5 4 3 2 1

Contents

1

Introduction

Paul F. Diehl and Brian Frederking

INTERNATIONAL ORGANIZATIONS ARE WORTH STUDYING because the most important issues in world politics today—poverty, terrorism, weapons proliferation, disease, regional conflict, economic stability, climate change, and many others—cannot be solved without multilateral cooperation. World politics is characterized by "security interdependence": no one state, not even the most powerful state, can manage these problems alone. Today's world requires both states and nonstate actors to coordinate action through international organizations to address these issues. Security interdependence, in short, requires global governance, and international organizations are a central component of global governance. This volume addresses the role of international organizations in contemporary global governance.

The chapters presented here provide a more nuanced view of international organizations than the two predominant views held among the general public. One is the realist notion that international organizations are relatively insignificant actors because they are unable to overcome the strong influences of conflict, national interests, and state sovereignty in world politics. The other is the idealist notion that international organizations are destined to solve common human problems. This book attempts to present a more balanced view, one that recognizes both the necessity of multilateral cooperation and the inherent limitations of international organizations. We hope to show that international organizations play an important role in world politics, but that their influence varies across issue areas.

In this introductory chapter we do not attempt to review the academic field of international organizations comprehensively.[1] Instead we provide a brief summary of both the history of international organizations and the academic study of those organizations from World War I to the contemporary world. We discuss the broad range of issues that constitute security interdependence in the post–Cold War world. We emphasize the inherent tensions between a world of sovereign nation-states and the creation of international organizations that can enable states to address contemporary issues adequately. We conclude with an overview of the sections and individual chapters in this book.

The Development of International Organizations

Early writings about the potential for international organizations to deal with common human problems include Jeremy Bentham's proposal for a "common legislature" and Immanuel Kant's advocacy of a "league of peace."[2] The academic study of international organizations began with the creation of the League of Nations after World War I, and was largely descriptive and legalistic. The League represented an attempt at international cooperation to prevent war. The breakdown of the League in the 1930s had many factors, including a lack of will by the major powers and the unwieldy requirements necessary for collective action. Although the League was unable to prevent World War II, it did provide a means of cooperation and consultation among states on a variety of issues beyond security matters.

World War II had a stimulating effect on the development of international organizations, and world leaders again sought to form another general international organization.[3] Much of the scholarship at the time was explicitly normative, calling for improvements to global institutions to promote world peace.[4] Perhaps surprisingly, the new United Nations had many similarities with the League.[5] The Security Council and the General Assembly of the United Nations had comparable predecessors in the League system. The UN was also predicated on the notion that continued cooperation among the victorious coalition in the previous war would ensure global stability.

With the emergence of the Cold War, it seemed quite possible that the United Nations might follow the path of the League. "Realist" scholars criticized earlier "idealists" and began to dominate the discipline of international relations. Realists emphasized the importance of state sovereignty, military power, and national interests in world politics and thus were less likely to expect states to delegate important powers to international organizations.[6] Realists argued that order could only be established by the enlightened use of diplomacy and force. The traditional route of alliances and the balance of power, not some potentially transformative international organizations, would maintain order.

Ultimately, the UN survived because it faced a radically different environment than the League. First, the Cold War bipolar alliance structure, while undoubtedly prohibiting superpower cooperation, also provided more stability than the rapid systemic upheavals that characterized the interwar period. Second, there was a greater recognition of a need for cooperation among states. The early stages of security interdependence occurred with the threat of global devastation from nuclear war or environmental disaster. Third, the UN acquired a symbolic importance and a legitimacy that the League of Nations lacked. States felt obligated to justify their actions before the UN even when they appeared contrary to UN Charter principles. The United States felt compelled to make its case to the UN at important times such as the Cuban Missile Crisis or prior to the invasion of Iraq because the UN can legitimize those actions.[7] Most important, a state does not even consider withdrawing its membership from the UN even when its actions appear contrary to its national interests. The loss of significant actors plagued the League during most of its existence.

The academic study of international organizations during the Cold War attempted to conceptualize what we now call global governance and tried to identify the role that IOs played in that process. Scholars began to study how IOs were part of larger patterns of world politics, particularly regarding conflict and peacekeeping.[8] A second approach was the neofunctionalist argument that the scope of international problems often overwhelmed the jurisdiction of both states and international organizations; this approach often advocated the emergence of political forms "beyond the nation state."[9] A third area included a wide variety of critical, neo-Marxist, and poststructuralist arguments about international organizations.[10]

A final area focused on international regimes, defined as "governing arrangements constructed by states to coordinate their expectations and organize aspects of international behavior in various issue-areas."[11] Regimes included principles, norms, rules, and decisionmaking procedures. Examples include the trade regime, the monetary regime, the oceans regime, and others. The concept of international regimes was the first systematic attempt to theorize "complex interdependence" and the existence of global governance without global government. It challenged the realist notion of a world dominated by nation-states, emphasizing that economic, energy, and environmental issues could not easily be understood by referring to states with a particular distribution of power.[12] It also emphasized the role of nongovernmental organizations in influencing the beliefs, norms, rules, and procedures of evolving regimes. Realists incorporated this approach with "hegemonic stability theory," arguing that any stability brought about by regimes is associated with a concentration or preponderance of power in one state. That "hegemon" achieved multilateral cooperation, according to this approach, through a combination of coercive threats and positive rewards.[13]

The end of the Cold War signaled a new era for the UN and international organizations in general as the superpower rivalry had established many of the barriers that had prevented UN action in the security area. The UN authorized the use of force against Iraq in the First Gulf War, the first such collective enforcement authorization since the Korean War. The UN also authorized far more peacekeeping operations in the two decades after the Cold War than in the forty-five years that preceded it. Those peacekeeping operations took on a wider scope of functions, including humanitarian assistance, nation building, and election supervision. Other international organizations also increased in scope. The European Union took further steps toward complete economic integration, and other regional economic blocs such as the Asia Pacific Economic Cooperation and the North American Free Trade Agreement took shape.

The Cold War's demise thus brought about greater prospects for expanding the roles, functions, and powers of international organizations in global governance. Nevertheless, a series of events underscored the limitations of international organizations in the contemporary era. The greater number of peacekeeping operations did not necessarily translate into greater effectiveness in halting armed conflict or promoting conflict resolution. The UN was extremely slow to stop the fighting in Bosnia, could not produce a political settlement in Somalia, and did not prevent the genocide in Rwanda. With the United States under the Bush administration at best ambivalent about the UN, the organization played little or no role in the US invasion of Iraq, both during and afterward. Despite its successes, the European Union stumbled badly in its peace efforts toward Bosnia, and attempts at further integration and expanded membership have produced significant domestic and foreign controversies. The North Atlantic Treaty Organization has struggled with the redefinition of its role as the new environment significantly altered its original purposes. While international organizations continue to play a greater role than they ever have, state sovereignty and lack of political will continue to inhibit the long-term prospects of those organizations for creating effective structures of global governance.

The academic field of international organizations has more explicitly theorized "global governance" in the post–Cold War era.[14] The dominant trends of this era—particularly increased economic globalization and an emerging global civil society—suggest that the state is no longer the only source of authority for global governance. The rules of world politics are now generated through the interaction of international governmental organizations, nongovernmental organizations, norms, regimes, international law, and even private-public governance structures. Increasingly, the functions of governance—defining standards of behavior, allocating resources, monitoring compliance with rules, adjudicating disputes, enforcement measures—occur at a global level to deal with common security concerns and transnational issues.[15]

The dominant theoretical approaches in international relations explain these changes and the contemporary role of international organizations in different ways. Liberalism argues that international organizations provide an arena in which states can interact, develop shared norms, and cooperate to solve common problems. International organizations also coordinate action by providing information, monitoring behavior, punishing defectors, and facilitating transparency at a reduced cost to states.[16] They are also indispensable actors in the provision of public goods (for example, clean air and water) and protecting the "global commons" (for example, oceans and polar regions).[17] Liberals also continue to emphasize regime theory and apply that concept to an increasing number of issue areas.[18]

Realists continue to argue that international organizations have little power over states because states can always leave those organizations.[19] To the extent that international organizations are important, it is because they are used as tools by great powers to pursue their interests. They argue that deterrence systems, alliance mechanisms, and the overall balance of power are more effective at maintaining peace than international organizations. They caution against great powers like the United States relying on such institutions to further their own interests.[20] While realists generally dismiss the importance of nongovernmental organizations, international law, and transnational corporations to explain world politics, some aspects of the realist tradition (for example, hegemonic stability theory and alliances) continue to inform the study of international organizations.

A great variety of approaches to international organizations exists beyond the classic debate between liberals and realists. Critical theorists and neo-Marxists continue to argue that global governance is dominated by the logic of industrial capitalism, which in turn generates opposition from environmental, feminist, and other social movements.[21] Other analysts emphasize rational design, organizational processes (including the study of social networks), organizational culture, and principal-agent interactions.[22] A more recent approach is social constructivism, which emphasizes the role of social structure—norms, identities, and beliefs—in world politics. Constructivists have analyzed the potential for international organizations to socialize policymakers and states to embrace certain norms, identities, and beliefs.[23]

Overview of the Book

The chapters in this volume address a wide variety of issues regarding international organizations and global governance. Part 1 offers an overview of international organizations. In Chapter 1, Thomas Volgy and his colleagues attempt to define and identify international organizations to determine the extent to which a "new world order" is being created after the end of the Cold War. Using a variety of measures and comparing their results to others, they conclude that states have been less willing and/or able to create new organizations to meet post–Cold War challenges. In Chapter 2, Kenneth Abbott and Duncan Snidal provide the classic argument about why states create international organizations rather than pursue other approaches such as bilateral agreements. They argue that two characteristics of international organizations—centralization and independence—allow them to perform various functions more efficiently, including norm creation and the arbitration of disputes. Together these two chapters illustrate the overall argument that world politics is often not organized in a way that enables states to address contemporary issues effectively.

Part 2 details the decisionmaking processes of international organizations. The range of activities and the processes that are often hidden from public view or receive little media attention are revealed in these selections. Furthermore, proposals to change the most visible aspect of decisionmaking—voting—are considered.

From these first two parts, the reader will gain a broad view of the place of international organizations in the world system and the patterns of their activities. Armed with this understanding, the reader is directed to the actions of international organizations in three major issue areas: peace and security, economic, and social and humanitarian. In Parts 3

' through 5, one can appreciate the number of organizations involved, the scope of activities undertaken, and the variation in effectiveness across organizations and issue areas. While the first two parts highlight common patterns in international organizations, the next three parts provide more details and reveal the diversity of these bodies.

Part 3 explores the effectiveness of peacekeeping operations and the prospects for humanitarian military intervention, but also considers the changes that the end of the Cold War has wrought. That series of events has led to a redefinition of security threats from traditional military attacks to include threats from nonstate actors including terrorists.

The economic issue area, addressed in Part 4, is one of great importance especially to many underdeveloped countries. Chapters on the World Trade Organization and the international monetary system illustrate how international institutions have played a role in creating the structure of international finance, trade, and development, how they have adapted (or not) to changing demands, and perhaps how they paradoxically might both enhance and mitigate the dependence of poorer countries on their wealthier counterparts.

Part 5, on social and humanitarian activities, shows the interface of many organizations in a variety of important concerns, including human rights, public health, genocide, and international crimes.

Part 6 returns to the more general concerns addressed at the outset of the book: What roles can international organizations play in global governance? The first chapter in this section addresses the kinds of reforms that might be possible in the UN system given its seemingly continuous focus on reform proposals and actual implementations that fall short. The collection concludes with a brief analysis of perhaps the most radical reform proposal in global governance—the creation of a world government.

Notes

1. Few reviews of the field or international organizations exist. Two early reviews are John Gerard Ruggie and Friederich Kratochwil, "International Organization: A State of the Art on the Art of the State," *International Organization* 40 (1986): 753–775; and J. Martin Rochester, "The Rise and Fall of International Organizations as a Field of Study," *International Organization* 40 (1986): 777–813. See also Lisa Martin and Beth Simmons, "Theories and Empirical Studies of International Institutions," *International Organization* 52 (1998): 729–757.

2. Jeremy Bentham, *Plan for a Universal and Perpetual Peace* (London: Grotius Society, 1927); Immanuel Kant, *Eternal Peace and Other International Essays* (Boston: World Peace Foundation, 1914).

3. J. David Singer and Michael Wallace, "International Government Organizations and the Preservation of Peace, 1816–1964," *International Organization* 24 (1970): 520–547.

4. David Mitrany, *A Working Peace System* (London: Royal Institute of International Affairs, 1943).

5. Leland Goodrich, "From League of Nations to United Nations," *International Organization* 1 (1947): 3–21.

6. E. H. Carr, *The Twenty Years' Crisis, 1919–1939* (London: Macmillan, 1939); John H. Herz, *Political Realism and Political Idealism* (Chicago: University of Chicago Press, 1951); Hans J. Morgenthau, *Politics Among Nations* (New York: Knopf, 1948).

7. Ernst Haas, "Collective Legitimation as a Political Function of the United Nations," *International Organization* 20 (1966): 360–379.

8. Inis L. Claude, *Swords into Plowshares* (New York: Random House, 1959); Ernst B. Haas, "Types of Collective Security: An Examination of Operational Concepts," *American Political Science Review* 49 (March 1955): 40–62; Karl W. Deutsch et al., *Political Community and the North Atlantic Area* (Princeton: Princeton University Press, 1957).

9. Ernst B. Haas, *Beyond the Nation State: Functionalism and International Organization* (Stanford: Stanford University Press, 1964).

10. Immanuel Wallerstein, "The Rise and Future Demise of the World Capitalist System: Concepts for Comparative Analysis," *Comparative Studies in Society and History* 16 (September 1974); Richard K. Ashley, "The Poverty of Neorealism," *International Organization* 38 (Spring 1984); Robert W. Cox, "Social Forces, States, and World Orders: Beyond International Relations Theory," in Robert O. Keohane, ed., *Neorealism and Its Critics* (New York: Columbia University Press, 1986).

11. Stephen D. Krasner, ed., *International Regimes* (Ithaca, NY: Cornell University Press, 1983); Robert O. Keohane, "Theory of Hegemonic Stability and Changes in International Economic Regimes," in Ole Holsti et al., eds., *Change in the International System* (Boulder: Westview, 1980); Duncan Snidal, "The Limits of Hegemonic Stability Theory," *International Organization* 39 (Autumn 1985).

12. Robert O. Keohane and Joseph S. Nye, *Power and Interdependence* (Boston: Little, Brown, 1977).

13. Robert O. Keohane, *After Hegemony: Cooperation and Discord in the World Political Economy* (Princeton: Princeton University Press, 1984), 57–60; Robert Gilpin, *US Power and the Multinational Corporation* (New York: Basic, 1975).

14. James N. Rosenau, *Along the Domestic-Foreign Frontier: Exploring Governance in a Turbulent World* (Cambridge: Cambridge University Press, 1997); Anne-Marie Slaughter, *A New World Order* (Princeton: Princeton University Press, 2004); Michael Barnett and Raymond Duvall, eds., *Power in Global Governance* (New York: Cambridge University Press, 2005).

15. Joseph S. Nye and John D. Donahue, *Governance in a Globalizing World* (Washington, DC: Brookings Institution, 2000).

16. Robert Keohane and Lisa Martin, "The Promise of Institutionalist Theory," *International Security* 20, no. 1 (Summer 1995): 39–51.

17. Elinor Ostrum, *Governing the Commons: The Evolution of Institutions for Collective Action* (Cambridge: Cambridge University Press, 1990).

18. Volker Rittberger and Peter Mayer, eds., *Regime Theory and International Relations* (Oxford: Clarendon, 1993).

19. Lloyd Gruber, *Ruling the World: Power Politics and the Rise of Supranational Institutions* (Princeton: Princeton University Press, 2000).

20. John J. Mearsheimer, "The False Promise of International Institutions," *International Security* 19, no. 3 (1994–1995): 5–49.

21. Craig Murphy, "Global Governance: Poorly Done and Poorly Understood," *International Affairs* 75, no. 4 (2000): 789–803.

22. Margaret Keck and Kathryn Sikkink, *Activists Beyond Borders: Advocacy Networks in International Politics* (Ithaca: Cornell University Press, 1998); Darren Hawkins, David A. Lake, Daniel L. Nelson, and Michael J. Tierney, eds., *Delegation and Agency in International Organizations* (Cambridge: Cambridge University Press, 2006); Barbara Koremenos, Charles Lipson, and Duncan Snidal, *The Rational Design of International Institutions* (New York: Cambridge University Press, 2004).

23. Michael Barnett and Martha Finnemore, *Rules for the World: International Organizations in World Politics* (Ithaca: Cornell University Press, 2004); Jeffrey Checkel, "International Institutions and Socialization in Europe," *International Organization* 59, no. 4 (2005): 801–826.

PART 1
Overview

2

Identifying Formal Intergovernmental Organizations

Thomas J. Volgy, Elizabeth Fausett,
Keith A. Grant, and Stuart Rodgers

IN THIS EFFORT, WE PROBE CONCEPTUAL AND EMPIRICAL dimensions for identifying the existence of intergovernmental organizations (IGOs) in international affairs and create a new database of IGOs. We do so because we are interested in two major research questions that we believe are not usefully addressed by existing data on IGOs. First, we wish to ascertain the extent to which a formal, institutional dimension of a "new world order" is being created after the end of the Cold War. From a theoretical standpoint, we see the possibility of such new institutional creation partly as a function of the strength possessed by the lead global power in the international system (the USA) and partly as a function of the capacity of other powers and the extent of their dissatisfaction with the dominant state's leadership. We assume that creating IGOs with little bureaucratic organization and very limited autonomy is less useful in stabilizing a new world order than a network of organizations that are significantly organized and autonomous. Additionally, it may be far easier to construct organizations that have neither of these characteristics than ones that do. By including in our analysis IGOs that are easy to assemble but produce little autonomous capability, we would distort responses to research queries regarding the importance of great-power strength in formal institutional construction.

Our second research concern is about patterns of joining and participation by states in these IGOs. We wish to uncover whether or not states

Reprinted from *Journal of Peace Research* 45, no. 6 (2008): 837–850. © 2008 Sage Publications. Reprinted by permission of the publisher.

participate in these organizations for reasons similar to, or different from, factors correlated with their participation during the Cold War. We assume that joining organizations that lack bureaucratic organization and offer little capacity to execute the collective will of members requires much less from states in terms of the costs of joining such organizations. Therefore, analyzing patterns of participation by states in such organizations may distort our understanding of the conditions under which states may invest resources in joining IGOs, including possibly confusing membership in minimalist organizations with the willingness of state policymakers to potentially surrender some of their sovereignty as a trade-off for their participation in more autonomous organizations.

We assume, too, that joining organizations is based both on opportunity and willingness. Measures of organizational participation based on simple counts of number of organizations joined fail to take into account the numbers of organizations a state is qualified to join. Since a simple count may distort the opportunities states have to join, we develop a denominator which allows us to factor in this dimension of participation.

Clearly, alternative definitions of IGOs have substantial impacts on their empirical enumeration. As Jacobson, Reisinger & Mathers note (1986: 144), different "reasonable" definitions yield population estimates that vary by as much as 300%. Below, we discuss previous efforts to enumerate systematically the population of IGOs in international relations, identify our conceptually based definition of an IGO and compare it with previous efforts, provide a series of criteria with which to identify an IGO, illustrate some of the empirical results, and compare the database with the most recent systematic data on IGO population.

The literature in international relations offers three major efforts that provide overlapping empirical criteria and quantify systematically—and longitudinally—the number of IGOs in the international system. None of the three, however, focuses explicitly on the broader conceptual meaning of an IGO that is associated with our research concerns, and therefore these efforts create both coding rules and empirical enumerations that differ substantially from those we identify below.

The earliest effort is by Wallace & Singer (1970), who posited four empirical criteria for identifying the existence of an intergovernmental organization: a minimum membership of two states; regular plenary sessions; a permanent headquarters arrangement; and independence from other IGOs (Wallace & Singer, 1970: 245–248). A second effort (Jacobson, Reisinger & Mathers, 1986; Shanks, Jacobson & Kaplan,

1996) provides a similar set of empirical criteria: intergovernmental organizations are "associations established by governments or their representatives that are sufficiently institutionalized to require regular meetings, rules governing decision making, a permanent staff, and a headquarters" (Shanks, Jacobson & Kaplan, 1996: 593). Further, these authors define and identify separately emanations as "second-order IGOs created through action of other IGOs" (Shanks, Jacobson & Kaplan, 1996: 594).

Finally, Pevehouse, Nordstrom & Warnke (2003, 2005) represent the most recent and most comprehensive effort to measure annually the number of IGOs in the international system. They define an IGO as an organization with the following attributes: "(1) is a formal entity; (2) has [three or more] [sovereign] states as members; and (3) possesses a permanent secretariat or other indication of institutionalization such as headquarters and/or permanent staff" (Pevehouse, Nordstrom & Warnke, 2005: 9–10).

Defining IGOs

Taken together, the empirical criteria noted above share critical characteristics related to the institutionalization of enduring multilateral relationships: routinized interactions by state members, explicit methods of decision making within organizations, enduring bureaucratic structures, and evidence of organizational independence from other IGOs. These approaches seek to distinguish between IGOs and other types of cooperative arrangements, such as ad hoc agreements, ongoing but uninstitutionalized meetings between states, sub-units of other IGOs, or institutions controlled not by member states but by other entities (e.g., IGOs or NGOs).

While these authors provide essentially empirical measures, the indicators hint at a broader conceptual view of an IGO. That broader conceptual view is our starting point. We define intergovernmental organizations as *entities created with sufficient organizational structure and autonomy to provide formal, ongoing, multilateral processes of decision making between states, along with the capacity to execute the collective will of their members (states).* This definition highlights both the process of interactions within IGOs and the possibility of collective outcomes from them, even though collective outcomes are contested among realist conceptions of international politics.

Furthermore, formal, ongoing processes of interaction within an organization and collective action require ongoing administration and organization. We concur with Abbott & Snidal (Chapter 3 of this volume) that the two primary functions of formal organizations are a stable organizational structure and some amount of autonomy in a defined sphere. Stability of organizational structure (in terms of routine interactions by states along with an administrative apparatus to ensure both institutionalized interactions and stability of organization) and autonomy are also critical for institutional conceptions of power (Barnett & Duvall, 2005), for assessing both global governance and hegemony.

This conceptual approach suggests that IGOs evidence attributes that (1) institutionalize state decision making and oversight in governance, (2) provide sufficient bureaucratic organization to assure some stability of management, and (3) demonstrate autonomy in organizational operation and in the execution of the collective will of the membership. All the operational definitions above seem to address some of the conditions under which these criteria can be observed. However, each of these criteria represents a continuum and suggests a *threshold*, below which institutionalization may not be in evidence, and for our theoretical concerns, an entity is not classified as an IGO. For instance, it is a rare IGO (perhaps not even the European Union) that exhibits fully autonomous characteristics in the execution of the collective will of the organization. Requiring absolute autonomy in a decentralized international system would, at that end of the continuum, leave virtually no empirical cases of formal organizations. At the same time, an IGO that relies completely on its members to carry out voluntarily the collective decisions made by the organization, without a secretariat that at least monitors and reports on the actions of its members, would represent the other end of the autonomy continuum, and it would be more realistic to view a structure of this type as a "discussion forum" rather than a viable, formal IGO. Somewhere between these two extremes exists some threshold, above which an organization qualifies as an IGO.

Where is that threshold? We turn now to the task of identifying thresholds below which an IGO loses one or more of its three qualifying characteristics.

Membership, Decision Making, and Oversight

First, we concur that the threshold for membership is one that consists of an IGO that contains three or more member states, consistent with the multilateral idea associated with IGOs. While it is plausible that an organization containing two members can be of theoretical interest, it falls within the area of bilateral relationships, and virtually all of the literature in the area focuses on multilateral dynamics effecting cooperation between states.

Second, we require that the membership be composed overwhelmingly of states and governed by them without a veto by non-state members. We recognize that some forms of cooperative arrangements have integrated into their deliberations non-state actors, including other IGOs and NGOs, and we have conceptualized IGOs, first and foremost, as mechanisms of cooperation between states. We are reluctant to exclude institutions that may contain non-state actors, but we require that decision making and oversight must reside overwhelmingly among states.

Third, we require that state membership entail representation by individuals or groups acting on behalf of the state, as individuals who are either directly part of the central governmental machinery of a state, or are temporarily (albeit primarily) acting in that capacity. If the individuals who represent their states are not expected to represent the preferences of their policymakers, then the state membership threshold is not reached. This would be the case if an organization's membership is designated for states, but each state appoints a citizen who is acting as an expert rather than in the role of government representative.

Fourth, we require that collective decision making and oversight be routinized: there are clear procedures governing the timing of meetings and decision making, and members meet routinely to make decisions and to exercise oversight over organizational operations. Procedural requirements are typically set out in the charters/constitutions/treaties of organizations and are easy to uncover. There is, however, much variation in the frequency with which organizational plenums are held, and a threshold value establishing a minimum is somewhat arbitrary. Ideally, meetings would occur on an annual basis. Recent efforts seem to have relied on the UIA definition of inactivity: the lack of reported meetings for four or more years. We reluctantly accept the four-year threshold for regular meetings, although most viable organizations appear to hold annual meetings of their members.

Bureaucratic Organization and Autonomy

While conceptually distinct criteria, in practice, the empirical correlates of collective decision making, bureaucratic organization, and autonomy within an IGO may be difficult to separate, especially with respect to the last two dimensions. Viable administration requires professional staffing on a permanent basis; we anticipate the same for the execution of collective decisions, even if such staffing is only for the coordination or reporting on efforts of member states. Furthermore, permanent professional staffing is not feasible without a permanent source of funding.

Autonomy requires that both staffing and funding be relatively immune from control by either a single member state or outside forces (e.g., another IGO). Staffing that is not controlled by members of the organization and may not report primarily to the organization (e.g., the Andean Parliament initially was staffed by Colombia's foreign ministry) does not meet the staffing autonomy threshold. Likewise, if the primary funding for administration is provided by another IGO or overwhelmingly by one state—as is the case with some organizations—then it fails to meet the autonomous resources threshold.

Thus, we require evidence of the following thresholds for an IGO to have sufficient bureaucratic organization and autonomy. First, an IGO must demonstrate the existence of a *permanent headquarters and non-symbolic, professional staffing, independent* of other IGOs and/or one single state. Typically, the issue of a permanent headquarters is relatively unambiguous. Such headquarters may move periodically but is usually required within the charter of an IGO and specified as its address. By non-symbolic staffing, we are referring to an actual group of people who administer the organization. There are a few organizations that indicate a staff of one or two, which we assume to be either symbolic of an administration, or of a minor, clerical function, and does not represent an administration needed for a complex organization. By professional staffing, we are referring to people who administer the organization as their livelihood and are paid to do so (some organizations report a staff of volunteers). By independence of staffing, we are referring to an administration that is paid by, reports only to, and holds as its permanent assignment, the IGO in question.

Finally, we require that a majority of the funding for the ongoing operations of the IGO be *non-symbolic, systematically available, and independent* of any one state or another IGO. Extensive budgetary data are difficult to obtain for many IGOs, especially on an annual basis. Therefore, we settle for a relatively low set of thresholds. By non-symbolic, we require that the available funding is minimally sufficient to support staffing beyond one or two individuals. Funding that is systematically available requires provisions in the charter/constitution of the organization for a routine, recurring method of funding. Finally, independence of funding requires that a majority of the organization's budget is independent of any one member or other IGO(s).

Thus, we identify 11 threshold values as operational criteria for designating an entity as a formal intergovernmental organization (FIGO). The most consistent pattern of differences between our empirical criteria and those of other efforts relates to the nature of staffing and funding within FIGOs.

Constructing the Database

We create the FIGO database for three points in time: 1975, 1989, and 2004. These years are of interest to us for ascertaining changes to the web of organizations in the post–Cold War environment (2004), changes that require comparison with the two time periods that represent some mid-point during the Cold War (1975) and one that is directly at the end of the Cold War (1989). The three time points represent relatively equidistant intervals and the 1989–2004 period offers a 15-year time span in the development of post-Cold War institutional formation; 2004 is the most current point for reliable information on FIGOs.

Our compilation of FIGOs, similar to other efforts, starts with the UIA *Yearbook of International Organizations*. We use the online version and supplement it with the hardbound yearbooks as needed. In addition, we check our compilation against both the Jacobson database, *International Governmental Organizations: Membership and Characteristics, 1981 and 1992* (ICPSR 6737), and the Pevehouse and Nordstrom update of the COW IGO database: *Correlates of War 2 International Governmental Organizations Data Set*, Version 2.1. We supplement these sources with additional sources when information is insufficient: reading the websites of IGOs;[1] corresponding with the headquarters and/or executive committees of IGOs; reading the treaties and/or charters of the organizations; querying *Europa World Plus* online edition; and searching news sources and scholarly materials (Buzan & Waever, 2004; Grant & Soderbaum, 2003; Katzenstein, 2005; Pempel, 2005; Solingen, 1998, 2005).

The FIGO database yields 265 IGOs that are alive in 2004. Several patterns are worth noting regarding our concerns about new institutional world order construction, great-power contestation, and state membership. First, the dominant mode for FIGOs is a combination of regional and sub-regional organizations (accounting for nearly half of all FIGOs), consistent with earlier findings (Shanks, Jacobson & Kaplan, 1996); global FIGOs constitute approximately 26% of the overall FIGO population. At the same time, there is considerable variation in the number of

FIGOs within regions (Figure 2.1). Africa and Europe—the poorest and richest regions—contain the largest number of FIGOs. By contrast, Asia has very few regional organizations. This is a region where the USA has worked to substitute bilateral mechanisms of coordination and cooperation, in lieu of multilateral arrangements from which it may be excluded or which it may not be able to control (Rapkin, 2001; Goh, 2004), and where there has been a culture of informal arrangements between state and non-state actors (Katzenstein, 2005).

Second, a decade and a half after the end of the Cold War, nearly two-thirds of all FIGOs are institutions that were created during the 1945–89 period. The number of FIGOs created during the 1970s alone accounts for approximately one-quarter of all FIGOs still alive in 2004, a number larger than all the FIGOs created since the end of the Cold War.

Third, classifying FIGOs by their primary original mandate indicates that approximately two-thirds of the organizations alive in 2004 have an economic mandate as their primary mission. Considerable variation exists, however, depending on when the organizations were created: 72% created prior to 1990 and surviving through 2004 have an economic mandate, compared with less than 50% of those created after the Cold War. Whether or not this is due to the higher survivability rate of economic FIGOs, or due to other factors, is not readily observable from the data.

Fourth, factoring in "opportunity" to join FIGOs should make a difference in assessing state membership. The average number of organizations joined by any one of the leading EU states (Germany, France, and the UK) is substantially higher than the membership rate of other major powers (Figure 2.2). This differential in membership is due, in part, to the opportunities for European states to join a large constella-

Figure 2.1   FIGO Population, by Region, 2004

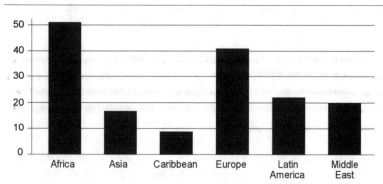

tion of regional FIGOs; Japan and China are "penalized" by the virtual absence of a major network of regional FIGOs in Asia. At the same time, the differential between Japan and China indicates additional forces at work, beyond simple opportunity to join available FIGOs.

An additional example may indicate further the differences between a simple count of memberships versus a measure based on "opportunity" to join. Sudan actually has more memberships in FIGOs than does Australia. However, once we factor in the opportunity to join certain organizations, it appears that Sudan's joining rate is actually 15% below that of Australia, due in part to the much larger constellation of regional FIGOs in Africa compared with Oceania. Unsurprisingly, but masked by a simple frequency count, Australia's membership rate in global organizations (78%) significantly surpasses Sudan's membership rate (54%).

Comparing FIGO with COW IGO

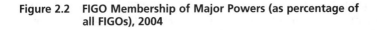

In order to gauge the effects of our threshold criteria on the population of IGOs, we compare the FIGO population with the COW IGO series (Table 2.1). We do so for a number of reasons. Most important, the COW IGO effort is the current benchmark for IGOs, representing a careful process of data collection (meeting scientific standards for validity and reliability) and most current assessment (up through 2000) of the IGO population. A second reason is its wide utilization (see Volgy et al., 2006, for a sampling of literature) in quantitative analyses.

We compare the FIGO data with the COW IGO series in two ways: first, we update the number of COW IGOs formed between 2000 and 2004, in order to be able to make comparisons at the aggregate level

Figure 2.2   FIGO Membership of Major Powers (as percentage of all FIGOs), 2004

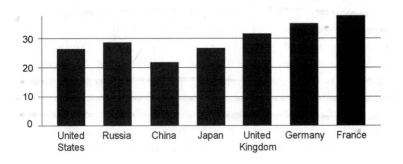

Table 2.1   Comparison of Changes in Numbers of FIGOs and COW IGOs, 1975–2004 (as percentage change)

Year	FIGO	COW IGO
1975–89	+26.4	+25.0
1989–2004	−2.9	+6.1
1975–2004	+23.6	+32.5

between the two datasets for the years 1975, 1989, and 2004. Second, we compare state membership between the two datasets, using the existing COW IGO data and eliminating from FIGO the last four years uncovered in COW IGO.

The COW IGO database contains 340 IGOs classified as "live" for the year 2004. Of these, 105 organizations (30.9%) fail to meet one or more of our criteria. Clearly, the dominant reason for exclusion occurs as a result of issues related to autonomy and/or the bureaucratic organization capabilities of these IGOs, although 29 cases also violate some provisions related to collective decision making and oversight by states.

Can we note significant differences as a result of these exclusions? Comparing the two sets of data yields substantial differences regarding both the population of IGOs and state membership in them. First, and at the macro level, the two populations are substantially different in size, in rates of growth over time, especially during the post–Cold War era. For example, the FIGO population in all time periods is substantially smaller (e.g., 28% smaller in 2004) than the COW IGO population. There are also significant differences between the two databases regarding rates of growth. While both populations show vigorous growth in the 1975–89 period, the net growth rate for FIGOs in the post–Cold War era is negative (reversing a long-term trend toward increased organizational development). The cumulative effect of these differences demonstrates a more modest net growth of FIGOs than COW IGO growth over a quarter of a century.

Second, the frequency of state memberships differs between the two databases: US membership in the FIGO web is roughly 20% smaller than in COW IGO; China's is approximately 18% smaller; for the three major states of the EU (combined)—the UK, Germany, and France—it is 13% smaller. As these differences suggest, the effects of differential IGO selection on membership frequency is not uniform across states, a point illustrated by considering that membership is nearly identical for Russia across the two sets of data and only minimally different for Japan. Apparently, a stricter definition of IGOs, requiring more states, may alter the enumeration of state membership in the web of intergovernmental organizations.

Do these differences matter? We believe they do, at both the macro and micro levels of analysis. With respect to the distinction between FIGOs, IGOs, and the Kantian peace, replicating Russett, Oneal & Davis (1998), we find that generic IGO membership underestimates the importance of membership effects on conflict, with FIGOs demonstrating a stronger effect. The IGO variable yields a positive and significant effect when both measures are included in the same model (Volgy et al., 2006). The reversal in directionality of the IGO variable may be indicative of the aggregation of two distinct populations of organizations, with FIGOs reducing the likelihood of interstate dispute, while non-FIGOs possibly increase it. Future research will investigate further the dynamics underlying these relationships (Volgy et al., 2008).

At the macro level, a focus on IGOs substantially overestimates the ability of major powers to restructure the institutional dimension of the new world order (Volgy et al., 2008). Focusing on FIGOs and constellations of organizations created since 1989 indicates a substantial diminution in the capacity and/or willingness of global states to fashion new organizations to meet the challenges of the post–Cold War international system.

Conclusion

We conceptualized a FIGO as constituting three dimensions: (1) institutionalization of state decision making and oversight in governance, (2) bureaucratic organization allowing for stability of management, and (3) evidence of autonomy in organization and in the execution of collective decisions. Based on these dimensions, we identified 11 threshold criteria with which to mark an organization as being a FIGO. Comparing the resulting database with the COW IGO database, we found, as expected, significant differences in the size of the IGO population, changes in the growth of IGOs over time, and differences in state membership in the constellation of IGOs in international affairs.

It is important to note that data on all IGOs are both more "squishy" and "dynamic" than they appear on the surface. By "squishy," we mean that the disparate sources needed to trace their activities and membership make changes difficult to pinpoint. For example, while we are able to ascertain procedural requirements for organizational funding and can trace some amount of funding being spent, we are loath to estimate the exact size of FIGO budgets and the extent to which those budgets are resupplied annually. This is not a problem for many organizations, but it is probably so for a substantial number of them. A similar problem occurs with data on state membership, which is relatively accessible for organizations operating currently. But, when such membership changed over time, there are more formidable problems in pinpointing the exact year of the change. This issue is especially problematic for research based on annual observations of state membership in IGOs.

There is also the issue of "dynamism": organizations may acquire additional attributes (or lose some) over time, either lifting them across the minimum threshold to qualify as a FIGO, or drop them below the threshold. Detecting the precise time when such changes occur is difficult through self-reporting, especially in the case of lost attributes. Just as important, institutional design characteristics may change over time, and some of these structural changes may not be reported for several years. Again, research based on annual observations may be more susceptible to this problem.

Researchers working in this field may gain more valid observations through aggregating observations over periods larger than one year. This is the strategy we adopt by sampling three time frames—15 years apart—with the hope that we are able to minimize errors that we would likely generate utilizing annual observations.

Note

1. From this point forward, IGOs refer to the generic classification of intergovernmental organizations, while FIGOs refer to formal intergovernmental organizations.

References

Abbott, Kenneth & Duncan Snidal, 1998. "Why States Act Through Formal International Organizations," *Journal of Conflict Resolution* 52(1): 3–32.
Barnett, Michael & Raymond Duvall, 2005. "Power in International Politics," *International Organization* 59(1): 39–79.
Buzan, Barry & Ole Waever, 2004. *Regions and Powers: The Structures of International Security*. Cambridge: Cambridge University Press.
Goh, Evelyn, 2004. "The ASEAN Regional Forum in United States East Asian Strategy," *Pacific Review* 17(1): 47–69.

Grant, Andrew J. & Fredrik Soderbaum, 2003. *The New Regionalism in Africa*. Aldershot: Ashgate.

Jacobson, Harold K.; William R. Reisinger & Todd Mathers, 1986. "National Entanglements in International Governmental Organizations," *American Political Science Review* 80(1): 141–159.

Katzenstein, Peter J., 2005. *A World of Regions: Asia and Europe in the American Imperium*. Ithaca, NY: Cornell University Press.

Pempel, T. J., 2005. *Remapping East Asia: The Construction of a Region*. Ithaca, NY: Cornell University Press.

Pevehouse, Jon; Timothy Nordstrom & Kevin Warnke, 2003. "Intergovernmental Organizations, 1815–2000: A New Correlates of War Data Set" (http://cow2.la.psu.edu/).

Pevehouse, Jon; Timothy Nordstrom & Kevin Warnke, 2005. "Intergovernmental Organizations," in Paul F. Diehl, ed., *The Politics of Global Governance*. Boulder, CO: Lynne Rienner (9–24).

Rapkin, David P., 2001. "The United States, Japan, and the Power to Block: The APEC and AMF Case," *Pacific Review* 14(3): 373–410.

Russett, Bruce; John R. Oneal & David R. Davis, 1998. "The Third Leg of the Kantian Tripod for Peace: International Organizations and Militarized Disputes, 1950–85," *International Organization* 52(3): 441–467.

Shanks, Cheryl; Harold K. Jacobson & Jeffrey H. Kaplan, 1996. "Inertia and Change in the Constellation of International Governmental Organizations, 1981–1992," *International Organization* 50(4): 593–627.

Solingen, Etel, 1998. *Regional Orders at Century's Dawn: Global and Domestic Influences on Grand Strategy*. Princeton, NJ: Princeton University Press.

Solingen, Etel, 2005. "East Asian Regional Institutions: Characteristics, Sources, Distinctiveness," in T. J. Pempel, ed., *Remapping East Asia: The Construction of a Region*. Ithaca, NY: Cornell University Press (31–53).

Union of International Associations (UIA), Various Years. *Yearbook of International Organizations*. New York: K. G. Saur (and online edition at https://www.diversitas.org/).

Volgy, Thomas J.; Elizabeth Fausett, Keith A. Grant & Stuart Rodgers, 2006. "Ergo FIGO: Identifying Formal Intergovernmental Organizations," Working Papers Series in International Politics: Department of Political Science, University of Arizona (October).

Volgy, Thomas J.; Zlatko Sabic, Petra Roter, Andrea Gerlak, Elizabeth Fausett, Keith A. Grant & Stuart Rodgers, 2009. *Searching for a New World Order*. Oxford: Blackwell.

Wallace, Michael & J. David Singer, 1970. "Intergovernmental Organizations in the Global System, 1816–1964: A Quantitative Description," *International Organization* 24(2): 239–257.

3

Why States Act Through Formal International Organizations

Kenneth W. Abbott and Duncan Snidal

- When the United States decided to reverse the Iraqi invasion of Kuwait, it did not act unilaterally (although it often does). It turned to the United Nations (UN) Security Council.
- When the Security Council sought to learn the extent of chemical, biological, and nuclear arms in Iraq, it did not rely on US forces. It dispatched inspectors from the International Atomic Energy Agency (IAEA).
- When the international community sought to maintain the suspension of combat in Bosnia, it did not rely only on national efforts. It sent in peacekeeping units under the aegis of the UN and North Atlantic Treaty Organization (NATO).
- When states liberalized trade in services and strengthened intellectual property protection in the Uruguay Round, they were not content to draft rules. They created the World Trade Organization (WTO) and a highly institutionalized dispute settlement mechanism.

Formal international organizations (IOs) are prominent (if not always successful) participants in many critical episodes in international politics. Examples in addition to those above include the following: Security Council sanctions on Libya, IAEA inspectors in North Korea, UN peacekeepers in the Middle East, and so forth. The UN secretary-general's 1992 Agenda for Peace sets out an even broader range of current and proposed UN functions in situations of international conflict:

Reprinted from *Journal of Conflict Resolution* 42, no. 1 (February 1998): 3–32. © 1998 Sage Publications. Reprinted by permission of the publisher.

fact finding, early warning, and preventive deployment; mediation, adjudication, and other forms of dispute resolution; peacekeeping; sanctions and military force; impartial humanitarian assistance; and postconflict rebuilding. But IO influence is not confined to dramatic interventions like these. On an ongoing basis, formal organizations help manage many significant areas of interstate relations, from global health policy (the WHO) to European security (OSCE and NATO) to international monetary policy (IMF). What is more, participation in such organizations appears to reduce the likelihood of violent conflict among member states (Russett, Oneal, and Davis 1998).

IOs range from simple entities like the APEC secretariat, with an initial budget of $2 million, to formidable organizations like the European Union (EU)[1] and the World Bank, which has thousands of employees and multiple affiliates and lends billions of dollars each year. Specialized agencies like the ILO, ICAO, and FAO play key roles in technical issue areas. New organizations like UNEP, the EBRD, and the International Tribunal for the former Yugoslavia are regularly created. Older IOs like NATO and the Security Council are rethought and sometimes restructured to meet new circumstances.[2] As the examples illustrate, moreover, even the most powerful states often act through IOs. In short, "it is impossible to imagine contemporary international life" without formal organizations (Schermers and Blokker 1995: 3).

Why do states so frequently use IOs as vehicles of cooperation? What attributes account for their use, and how do these characteristics set formal organizations apart from alternative arrangements, such as decentralized cooperation, informal consultation, and treaty rules? Surprisingly, contemporary international scholarship has no clear theoretical answers to such questions and thus offers limited practical advice to policy makers.

We answer these questions by identifying the functional attributes of IOs across a range of issue areas. Although we are concerned with the concrete structure and operations of particular organizations, we also see IOs as complex phenomena that implicate several lines of international relations (IR) theory. From this vantage point, we identify two functional characteristics that lead states, in appropriate circumstances, to prefer IOs to alternate forms of institutionalization. These are centralization and independence.

IOs allow for the centralization of collective activities through a concrete and stable organizational structure and a supportive administrative apparatus. These increase the efficiency of collective activities and enhance the organization's ability to affect the understandings, environment, and interests of states. Independence means the ability to act with a degree of autonomy within defined spheres. It often entails the capacity to operate as a neutral in managing interstate disputes and conflicts. IO independence is highly constrained: member states, especially the powerful, can limit the autonomy of IOs, interfere with their operations, ignore their dictates, or restructure and dissolve them. But as in many private transactions, participation by even a partially autonomous, neutral actor can increase efficiency and affect the legitimacy of individual and collective actions. This provides even powerful states with incentives to grant IOs substantial independence.

The broad categories of centralization and independence encompass numerous specific functions. Most IOs perform more than one, though each has its own unique combination. We do not enumerate every such function or provide a comprehensive typology. Instead, we highlight several of the most important. We focus especially on the active functions of IOs—facilitating the negotiation and implementation of agreements, resolving disputes, managing conflicts, carrying out operational activities like technical assistance, elaborating norms, shaping international discourse, and the like—that IR theory has only sparingly addressed. Rational states will use or create a formal IO when the value of these functions outweighs the costs, notably the resulting limits on unilateral action.

Distinguishing formal IOs from alternative forms of organization is important from several perspectives. For IR scholars, who largely abandoned the study of formal IOs in the move from the legal-descriptive tradition to more theoretical approaches, developing such distinctions should "open up a large and important research agenda" with institutional form and structure as central dependent variables (Young 1994: 4; see also Koremenos et al. 1997). This will complement emerging work on international legalization, a closely related form of institutionalization (Burley and Mattli 1993; Abbott and Snidal 1997; Keohane, Moravcsik, and Slaughter 1997). Such research will also benefit practitioners of conflict management and regime design (Mitchell 1994). The policy implications of our analysis are significant as well. Many states, notably the United States, now resist the creation of IOs and hesitate to support those already in operation, citing the shortcomings of international bureaucracy, the costs of formal organization, and the irritations of IO autonomy. This is an ideal time for students of international governance to focus on the other side of the ledger.

The next section spells out our theoretical approach, drawing lessons from the ways in which different schools of theory have dealt with (or have failed to deal with) the questions posed above. It is followed by an analysis of the organizational attributes of centralization and independence and the functions they make possible—especially in contexts of cooperation and nonviolent conflict. The final section explores two composite functions that challenge conventional views of IO capabilities and demonstrate the complementarity of prevailing theories: developing, expressing, and carrying out community norms and aspirations and enforcing rules and commitments. We conclude with the example of the Security Council in the Gulf War, which draws together these themes in the context of violent conflict.

Putting IOs into Theory and Theory into IOs

Our primary approach is rationalist and institutionalist. We assume, for simplicity, that states are the principal actors in world politics and that they use IOs to create social orderings appropriate to their pursuit of shared goals: producing collective goods, collaborating in prisoner's dilemma settings, solving coordination problems, and the like. We start with the pursuit of efficiency and employ the logic of transaction costs, economics, and rational choice (Snidal 1996), using analogies with business firms and medieval trading institutions. Decentralized cooperation theory and, especially, regime theory provide a strong deductive basis for this analysis.

Regime theory (Krasner 1983; Keohane 1984) represents a major advance in understanding international cooperation. It is self-consciously theoretical and focuses directly on the institutional organization of international cooperation. But it has several shortcomings. Most important, regime scholars embrace an earlier turn in IR, which unnecessarily coupled a move to theory with a move away from consideration of IOs themselves. This resulted in "the steady disengagement of international organization scholars from the study of organizations, to the point that today one must question whether such a field even exists any longer except in name only" (Rochester 1986: 783–84). Indeed, regime theory deals with institutions at such a general level that it has little to say about the particular institutional arrangements that organize international politics. Our focus on the concrete operations of formal IOs not only brings them into regime theory but also provides a broader opportunity for IR theory to differentiate among institutional forms and recapture institutional details. We draw on the legal-descriptive literature to accomplish this.

Furthermore, regime theory has been rightly criticized for paying insufficient attention to issues of power and distribution in international politics. We draw on realist considerations to supplement our institutionalist approach in this regard. Finally, although regime theory has paid increasing attention to the role of ideas and norms in international politics (Goldstein and Keohane 1993), it has only begun to incorporate these important considerations. Here, we draw on constructivist theory for guidance. In sum, we enrich our primarily rationalist approach with important insights from several different traditions, which we see as complementary rather than competitive.

Decentralized cooperation theory takes as the problematic of international governance the existence of coordination and collaboration problems requiring collective action (Oye 1986; Stein 1983; Snidal 1985a). It assumes anarchy, often depicted in game models, and analyzes how states cooperate in that spare context through strategies of reciprocity and other forms of self-help. The dependent variable is typically cooperation in the abstract, and much of the research in this tradition has been directed to disproving the realist assertion that cooperation in anarchy is unlikely. There is no nuanced account of the forms of cooperation because the anarchy assumption makes IOs and other institutions largely irrelevant. However, the strong assumptions that underlie the theory, such as the need for high-quality information, suggest that cooperation is unlikely without an adequate institutional context although the theory is only beginning to analyze that context (Morrow 1994). For our purposes, however, it performs a useful service by emphasizing that institutional capacities other than centralized enforcement are crucial in mediating interstate relations.

Regime theory, in contrast, deals explicitly with institutional factors affecting cooperation, and regime scholars frequently mention IOs. But they downplay the distinctive institutional role(s) of IOs, perhaps in continued reaction against the earlier preoccupation with formal organizations. For example, Martin (1992) depicts the European Economic Community (EEC) and the Coordinating Committee for Export Controls (COCOM) as important but nevertheless quite rudimentary forums for intergovernmental bargaining; Weber (1994) emphasizes the broad political and symbolic goals of the EBRD. Neither discusses the organizations' primary operational roles. Keohane's (1984) *After Hegemony* also emphasizes intergovernmental bargaining, arguing that regimes help states reach specific agreements by reducing transaction costs, improving information, and raising the costs of violations. But this valuable analysis also excludes many significant operational activities of IOs.[3] In all these works, furthermore, regime scholars treat international institutions as passive. Regimes are seen, for example, as embodying norms and rules or clarifying expectations (Keohane 1984; Yarbrough and Yarbrough 1992; Garrett and Weingast 1993), functions also performed by treaties and informal agreements. Regimes are also seen as forums in which states can interact more efficiently: like Keohane and Martin, Moravcsik's (1991) analysis of the Single European Act treats IOs as sites of, but not as agents in, cooperation. Indeed, the canonical definition of regime (Krasner 1983) encompasses only norms and collective choice procedures, making no provision for the active and independent IO functions—and the corresponding institutional forms that we emphasize below.

Legal scholarship continues to offer descriptive accounts of the history and institutional architecture of IOs, as well as doctrinal analysis of norms and texts, especially the normative output of organizations such as ILO treaties or General Agreement on Tariffs and Trade (GATT)/WTO panel decisions (Bowett 1982; Kirgis 1993). More important for present purposes, another strand of doctrinal theory addresses the constitutional law of IOs, including membership and voting rules, external relations, finance, and the authority of specific organs (Amerasinghe 1994; Sohn 1950, 1967; Dupuy 1988; Shihata 1991, 1995). The best of this work is comparative, examining how common problems of organization and operation are addressed in the constitutive documents and practices of various IOs (Schermers and Blokker 1995; Chayes and Chayes 1995). Unfortunately, "in the land of legal science, there is no strongly established tradition of developing theories on IOs" (Schermers and Blokker 1995: 8; see also Brownlie 1990: 679). Nevertheless, legal scholarship, like some earlier work in IR, notably Cox and Jacobson (1973), carefully differentiates among institutional forms and emphasizes institutional details, an important contribution that we use in our analysis.

Realist theory finds both legal and regime scholarship naive in treating IOs as serious political entities. Realists believe states would never cede to supranational institutions the strong enforcement capacities necessary to overcome international anarchy. Consequently, IOs and similar institutions are of little interest; they merely reflect national interests and power and do not constrain powerful states (Mearsheimer

1995; Strange 1983; for a more nuanced view, see Glaser 1995). We accept the realist point that states are jealous of their power and deeply concerned with the distributive consequences of their interactions. Yet, realists underestimate the utility of IOs, even to the powerful. The United States, at the peak of its hegemony, sponsored numerous IOs, including GATT, IMF, and NATO; these organizations have provided "continuing utility . . . as instruments . . . for regime and rule creation" (Karns and Mingst 1990: 29). Even the Soviet Union, the very model of a modern repressive hegemony, used the Council for Mutual Economic Assistance to organize economic relations within the Eastern bloc. We argue that powerful states structure such organizations to further their own interests but must do so in a way that induces weaker states to participate. This interplay is embedded in IO structure and operations.

Finally, Kratochwil and Ruggie (1986) argue that only constructivist (interpretivist) theory focusing on norms, beliefs, knowledge, and understandings can satisfactorily explain formal organizations. We accept the insight that social constructions are fundamental elements of international politics (Wendt 1992, 1995; Barnett 1993) and agree that IOs are—in part—both reflections of and participants in ongoing social processes and prevailing ideas (Finnemore 1996; Kennedy 1987). But the role of IOs is best understood through a synthesis of rationalist (including realist) and constructivist approaches. States consciously use IOs both to reduce transaction costs in the narrow sense and, more broadly, to create information, ideas, norms, and expectations; to carry out and encourage specific activities; to legitimate or delegitimate particular ideas and practices; and to enhance their capacities and power. These functions constitute IOs as agents, which, in turn, influence the interests, intersubjective understandings, and environment of states (McNeely 1995). Potentially, these roles give IOs an influence well beyond their material power, which is trivial on conventional measures. Indeed, IO activities may lead to unintended consequences for member states, a fear often expressed by US politicians. Yet, IO autonomy remains highly constrained by state interests, especially those of the powerful, a fact often demonstrated by US politicians.

Although we adopt a predominantly rationalist theoretical approach, we are concerned with highlighting the importance of formal IOs as empirical phenomena rather than with maintaining a particular theoretical dogma. None of the individual approaches mentioned adequately explains why states use formal IOs; each holds key insights. In identifying formal IOs as an important category of institutionalization to be explained, therefore, we proceed in a more interpretive mode, drawing on different strands of argumentation to highlight ways in which formal IOs function to manage interstate cooperation and conflict.[4]

The Functions of IOs: Centralization and Independence

Two characteristics distinguish IOs from other international institutions: centralization (a concrete and stable organizational structure and an administrative apparatus managing collective activities) and independence (the authority to act with a degree of autonomy, and often with neutrality, in defined spheres).[5] The very existence of a centralized secretariat implies some operational autonomy, but this is often limited to administrative and technical matters and subject to close supervision by governments. In other situations sometimes involving the same organizations, substantive autonomy and neutrality are essential. The range and potential importance of these activities lead us to treat independence as a separate category.

Centralization and independence enhance efficiency. An analogy to private business firms is instructive. The firm replaces contractual relations among suppliers, workers, and managers; it substitutes a centralized, hierarchical organization for the horizontal, negotiated relations of contract. In Coase's (1937) theory, firms are formed when the transaction costs of direct contracting are too high for efficient operation. Similarly, the move from decentralized cooperation to IOs occurs when the costs of direct state interaction outweigh the costs of international organization, including consequent constraints on unilateral action (Trachtman 1996).

Centralization and independence represent different forms of transaction cost economizing. Small businesses draw mainly on the centralization benefits of formal organization, interposing a legal entity with the ability to manage employees hierarchically and the capacity to contract, sue, and be sued. The owners still manage the business directly, though their interactions are more highly structured. Investors in larger firms additionally benefit by granting autonomy and supervisory authority to professional managers; in Berle and Means's (1968: 5) famous phrase, there is a "separation of ownership and control." The situation is similar in complex IOs, in which member states grant some authority to IO organs and personnel but supervise them through structures resembling the corporate shareholders meeting, board of directors, and executive committee. Introducing these new actors changes the relations among states and allows them to achieve goals unattainable in a decentralized setting.

Centralization and independence produce political effects beyond mere efficiency. In these respects, IOs resemble governments and private associations more than business firms. Independence, in particular, enables IOs to shape understandings, influence the terms of state interactions, elaborate norms, and mediate or resolve member states' disputes. The acts of independent IOs may be accorded special legitimacy, and they affect the legitimacy of members' actions. Even centralization, seemingly more mechanical, can alter states' perceptions and the context of their interactions.

Centralization

It is no great theoretical insight that an established organizational structure and centralized administrative support can render collective activities more efficient: even students of international governance are not content to communicate by e-mail; they form the International Studies Association and the International Law Association. This simple insight goes far to explain the proliferation of IOs in the twentieth century in a period of increasing issue complexity and a growing number of states. The (inter)subjective effects of centralization are less apparent, though equally important. We consider the benefits of centralization under two headings—support for direct state interaction (the principal focus of regime theory) and operational activities (the traditional focus of IO studies). Here, we emphasize concrete activities in which governments remain closely involved; the following section introduces broader functions also requiring IO autonomy.

Support for State Interactions

The organizational structure of IOs enhances even the passive virtues recognized by regime theory. An established organization provides a stable negotiating forum, enhancing iteration and reputational effects. Such a stable forum also allows for a fast response to sudden developments. The Security Council, for example, is organized so that it can function on short notice, with each member required to maintain continuous representation at UN headquarters. A permanent organization also reinforces accepted norms: the most favored nation (MFN) principle instantiated in the WTO provides a sounder basis for state expectations than any informal arrangement.

In other ways too, centralization shapes the political context of state interactions. IOs provide neutral, depoliticized, or specialized forums more effectively than almost any informal or decentralized arrangement. This enables a broader range of behavior: the superpowers could discuss technical nuclear issues within the IAEA without the intrusion of high politics, even at the height of the cold war. IOs also serve as partisan forums for political coalitions: the United Nations Conference on Trade and Development (UNCTAD) for developing countries, the Organization for Economic Cooperation and Development (OECD) for industrialized states. Finally, IOs strengthen issue linkages by situating them within common organizational structures, as the WTO has done for goods, services, and intellectual property rights.

Formal organizations further embody the precise terms of state interaction. Representation and voting rules "constitutionalize" balances among states having different levels of power, interest, or knowledge. States with advanced nuclear technology and large supplies of nuclear raw material are guaranteed seats on the IAEA Board of Governors; states with major shipping and carrier interests have equal representation on the International Maritime Organization (IMO) Council. Such decision structures frequently guarantee disproportionate influence for powerful states. Yet, they may also constitutionalize protection for weaker states and hold the powerful accountable to fixed rules and procedures. For example, both the Security Council and the EU Council are structured so that the most powerful members can block affirmative actions but, even if united, cannot approve actions without support from smaller powers.

Such considerations often lead to elaborate organizational structures. The substantive work of many IOs takes place in specialized committees staffed by their secretariats. The OECD uses more than 200 committees and working groups; the IMO prepares treaties in substantive groupings like the maritime safety and marine environmental protection committees. Such committees are often formally open to all members, but specialization occurs naturally because of differences in interest, expertise, and resources. Delegation can also be encouraged institutionally: in the third UN Law of the Sea Conference (UNCLOS III), the chairs of open-ended committees sometimes scheduled meetings in rooms capable of holding only 30 people![6]

Organizational structure influences the evolution of interstate cooperation as conditions change. For example, several environmental agreements were facilitated by appointing UNEP as secretariat and the World Bank as financial administrator, obviating the need for new institutions. These institutional links are often contested because of their distributional implications. The advanced countries fought to locate new intellectual property rules in the WTO (rather than in the World Intellectual Property Organization [WIPO]) so they could enforce their rights more effectively. In other cases, organizational structures create vested interests that impede change or politicize issues, as in the United Nations Education, Scientific, and Cultural Organization (UNESCO) during the 1970s. More generally, because IOs are designed for stability, they may not adapt smoothly to changing power conditions, as the continuing makeup of the Security Council attests. Yet, the gradual reduction of US voting power in the IMF, mandated by its declining share of capital contributions, illustrates how organizational structure can facilitate such adaptation.

Most IOs include a secretariat or similar administrative apparatus. In simple consultative organizations, the secretariat need only assist with the mechanics of decentralized interaction. The 1985 Vienna Ozone Convention assigned the following functions to its secretariat: "(a) To arrange for and service meetings . . . ; (b) To prepare and transmit reports based upon information received . . . ; (d) To prepare reports on its activities . . . ; (e) To ensure the necessary coordination with other relevant international bodies . . . ; (f) To perform such other functions as may be determined" ("Vienna Convention" 1985: 1532). The secretariat for the Convention on Long Range Transboundary Air Pollution (LRTAP) performed similar functions with only five professionals. Levy (1993: 84) notes that the staff had "little time to do anything else but keep the meetings running smoothly."

Even such modest activities can strengthen international cooperation. Here, we draw on the analogy to the medieval law merchant and the corresponding theoretical literature (Milgrom, North, and Weingast 1990; Calvert 1995; Morrow 1994). Informal consultations produced sufficient information on the identity of untrustworthy traders to support a substantial volume of trade. Yet, modest efforts by central administrators at commercial fairs to collect and relay additional information created a new equilibrium at a higher level of exchange.

Most IOs perform more extensive supportive functions. Law-making conferences like UNCLOS III or the Rio conference on the environment

and development rely heavily on their secretariats. IO personnel coordinate and structure agendas, provide background research, and promote
successful negotiations. They keep track of agreements on particular
issues, trade-offs, and areas of disagreement, periodically producing texts
that consolidate the current state of play. They also transmit private offers
or assurances, improving the flow of information.

IO staffs support decentralized cooperation between major conferences. The large, expert OECD secretariat collects, produces, and publishes information relevant to national economic policy coordination.
The WTO secretariat assists in numerous negotiations, from the settlement of disputes to sectoral talks under the services agreement. IO staffs
also support the decentralized implementation of norms. UNEP, secretariat for the Basel convention on the transboundary movement of haz-
ardous wastes, provides information states need to manage activities
under the treaty; the ILO receives, summarizes, and circulates national
reports on treaty implementation.

Experience under the international trade regime testifies to the
importance of organizational structure and administrative support. The
original GATT was a normative and consultative arrangement; almost
all organizational features were removed at the insistence of the United
States. Yet, member states soon needed more extensive organizational
structure and support. As membership expanded and complex new
issues appeared on the agenda, GATT began its metamorphosis into the
WTO, a true IO.

Managing Substantive Operations

IOs do more than support intergovernmental negotiations; they manage
a variety of operational activities. A prototypical operational organization is the World Bank, which finances massive development projects,
borrows on world capital markets, reviews state investment proposals,
provides technical assistance and training in many disciplines, generates extensive research and publications, and performs other substantive
activities. Operational organizations normally have sizable budgets and
bureaucracies, complex organizational structures, and substantial operational autonomy.[7]

Member states of an IO like the World Bank use the institution as an
agent, taking advantage of its centralized organization and staff to carry
out collective activities. The analogy of the large business corporation,
with its dispersed owner-investors and professional managers, is apt.
Compared with a decentralized approach based on ad hoc contracting, a

formal organization provides efficiency gains that outweigh the accompanying costs in terms of money, human resources, and constraints on unilateral action. Especially when participating states differ in power, centralized operations will have significant distributional consequences.

IO operations also significantly influence the capabilities, understandings, and interests of states. This is most apparent with outputs such as information and rules. But it is also true of more material activities like technical assistance and joint production. Indeed, virtually all of the activities discussed below promote certain norms and practices among states, often in unanticipated ways.

Pooling

Many IOs are vehicles for pooling activities, assets, or risks. Some pooling can be accomplished on a decentralized basis, as in a business partnership, but a separate entity with a stable organizational structure and specialized staff can greatly reduce transaction costs while providing additional advantages.

Consider the World Bank again. As in other international financial institutions (IFIs), members pool financial resources through capital contributions and commitments. Pooling provides a solid cushion of capital that enables the World Bank to make credible financial commitments to borrowers, who rely on them for costly planning and investment decisions, and to world capital markets, in which the bank borrows at advantageous rates. In addition, this common effort promotes burden sharing in providing a collective good and may limit the competition for influence that characterizes some bilateral assistance. Similarly, by combining development loans in a common portfolio, bank members pool, and thereby reduce, their individual risk.

Pooling enables the World Bank to achieve economies of scale by carrying out a large volume of activities, establishing uniform procedures and building up a common body of data. These economies allow it to develop greater technical expertise on various aspects of country and project assessment than could most states and to innovate in emerging areas like "basic needs." Finally, the bank's broad jurisdiction creates a horizontal advantage akin to economies of scope: by dealing with virtually all needy countries, the bank can target global priorities while avoiding duplication and gaps in coverage.[8]

The largest states, especially the United States, could mobilize sufficient capital to accomplish their international financial objectives unilaterally.[9] They are unwilling to do so, however, for international and domestic political reasons and because of competing priorities. Indeed, the United States is actively working to strengthen the IFIs, in part because their broad membership and assessment structures encourage wide cost sharing.[10] In the meantime, although the G-7 countries bear most of the costs of the IFIs, they also retain the greatest share of voting power and influence on management. During the cold war, they successfully excluded the Soviet bloc and the People's Republic of China. Yet, the United States has been unable consistently to dictate IFI decisions on specific transactions.

Nonfinancial IOs provide similar advantages. The public health activities of WHO, like other UN-specialized agencies, are based on the pooling of national contributions and cost sharing (though the industrialized countries bear the bulk of the costs); economies of scale provide operational efficiencies. The WHO smallpox campaign illustrates the horizontal benefits of centralization: a single global campaign against a contagious disease is more effective than decentralized efforts because global scope avoids gaps in coverage. (The IAEA nuclear safeguards system offers a similar advantage.) In addition, the stable organizational structure of WHO and the reputation-staking effect of membership encourage participation. Free-rider problems remain, but the organization can alleviate them by using its own resources. WHO also provides effective technical assistance by pooling financial and technical resources and accumulating expertise; its global scope diffuses new technologies and allows rational prioritization of needs. By enhancing the development and transmission of ideas, technical activities of specialized organizations have significantly shaped the interests and identities of states. At the same time, they have helped less developed states acquire capacities essential to both national policy making and international activity.

An example of the limits of pooling illustrates these effects and the importance of realist and constructivist considerations. UNESCO's scientific arm was intended to promote the public goods aspects of scientific research by pooling international scientific facilities and creating a central clearinghouse. The organization was initially oriented toward the needs of scientists: executive board members did not represent governments. With the cold war, however, state interests asserted themselves. The board was reorganized to represent states, and UNESCO's orientation shifted to national science. Finemore (1996) documents how UNESCO technical assistance subsequently promoted national science programs even in states where there was little need for them. Thus,

UNESCO helped shape states' identities, interests, and capabilities in the area of science policy even though its initial global objectives were frustrated by interstate rivalries.

Joint Production

Alchian and Demsetz's (1972) theory of the firm suggests that a centralized organization is particularly important when workers, managers, and other "inputs" must work in teams, producing a joint output. In these situations, the hierarchical organization of the firm makes it easier for managers, themselves beholden to the owners ("residual claimants"), to monitor, reward, and discipline employees. IO personnel engage in similar teamwork and thus are typically organized hierarchically, with supervision by and on behalf of member states.

Beyond this, states themselves sometimes form multinational "teams" to engage in production activities. Experts from several European states cooperate in subatomic research through the European Organization for Nuclear Research (CERN), an IO that operates a nuclear laboratory; the Airbus project is a similar example. In addition to holding participants responsible, these organizations pool resources and risks, achieve economies of scale, avoid duplication and unproductive competition, and ensure that the outputs, including technological externalities, are shared. Projects like CERN and Airbus resemble business firms even more than the typical IO. Indeed, Airbus, originally created as a partnership under French law, is being transformed into a private corporation to better coordinate the participants.

Perhaps the best example of interstate joint production is the NATO military alliance. Common war plans, specialization of military tasks, joint exercises, common equipment and interchangeable parts, and, of course, the conduct of battle are examples of teamwork par excellence. NATO's integrated command—operating hierarchically on behalf of member states as residual claimants—organizes, monitors, and disciplines participants in the joint activities of the alliance, probably the most successful in history.[11]

Norm Elaboration and Coordination

States arrange cooperative relationships through agreements. As Williamson (1985, 1994) and others have pointed out, bounded rationality and high transaction and information costs make it difficult for states—like the parties to any contract—to anticipate and provide for all possible contingencies. The longer and more complex the relationship, the more significant the contingencies; the greater the investment in specific assets, the greater the uncertainty and risk of opportunism. The domestic legal system helps alleviate these problems by supplying missing terms and decision rules, but the international institutional context is comparatively thin. "First, in international law, there is not a very complete body of law that can be applied to supply missing terms. . . . Second . . . there is generally no dispute resolution tribunal with mandatory jurisdiction. . . . The alternative, of course, is to write comprehensive contracts" (Trachtman 1996: 51–54).

There is another alternative: to create procedures for the elaboration of norms within an IO. Decentralized procedures do not address the problems of transaction costs and opportunism. Even with coordination issues in which equilibria can sometimes be reached without communication, these problems can stymie cooperation when there are many actors, complex problems, and distributive conflicts. The stable organizational structure of IOs addresses both issues. Established procedures for elaborating rules, standards, and specifications enhance cooperation even when member states retain the power to reject or opt out—as they do even in IOs with relatively advanced legislative procedures, like the ILO. Nonbinding recommendations can become de facto coordination equilibria, relied on by states and other international actors. This gives IOs some power to affect international norms and state behavior and potentially much greater power with the backing of key states.

As always, powerful states exert disproportionate influence over norm elaboration and structure legislative processes to ensure their influence. Here, too, however, protection for weaker states may be the price of their participation, and the effectiveness of an established rule-making procedure requires that powerful states respect those arrangements. For example, powerful states often limit IO jurisdiction to technical areas with limited distributional impact; as a result, IO legislative procedures may go forward—up to a point, at least—less influenced by narrow national interests and differential power than direct intergovernmental bargaining.

Many IOs engage in norm elaboration, especially of a technical kind. The EU, most notably, has issued a huge number of directives, regulations, and other legislative acts—affecting everything from franchise agreements to telecommunication interconnectivity standards to tax policy—though many important issues have been addressed through interstate agreements and mutual recognition. The preparation of proposed legislation is housed exclusively in the commission to facilitate a depoliticized and expert approach.

Many other IOs carry out extensive legislative programs, frequently focusing on coordination rules. The ICAO promulgates international "rules of the air"; the International Telecommunications Union (ITU) coordinates national broadcasting standards; the Customs Cooperation Council implements common customs rules; and the Codex Alimentarius Commission harmonizes food standards. Although technical, these standards have important effects on (and within) states, as the concern over privileging Codex standards under the North American Free Trade Agreement (NAFTA) demonstrated. Although the associated IOs are quite weak, their influence is strengthened by the self-enforcing nature of coordination equilibria.

Independence

Although centralization often requires some operational autonomy, many valuable IO functions require more substantive independence. The participation of an IO as an independent, neutral actor can transform relations among states, enhancing the efficiency and legitimacy of collective and individual actions. These functions require a delicate balance among short- and long-term collective and distributional interests. Powerful states will not enter an organization they cannot influence, yet undermining the independence of an organization performing the functions discussed here will simultaneously reduce its effectiveness and their own ability to achieve valued ends.

Analogies from the business firm and the law merchant illustrate the point. Shareholders in a large corporation must monitor managers to limit agency costs. Yet, if major shareholders cause managers to favor their interests unduly, others may refuse to invest. If shareholders generally assert excessive control, moreover, they lose the advantages of professional management. The law merchant analogy is even sharper. Powerful princes granted monopoly privileges to independent guilds of foreign merchants, enabling them to embargo the princes themselves if they took advantage of the merchants (Grief, Milgrom, and Weingast 1994). By eliminating princes' incentives to cheat, these arrangements enabled them to make the binding commitments necessary to induce mutually beneficial trade. The princes could withdraw the guilds' privileges, of course, but were constrained from doing so by the resulting loss of trade.

Support for Direct State Interaction

Independent IOs promote intergovernmental cooperation in more proactive ways than those discussed earlier; they are *initiating* as well as supportive organizations. The governing body is often authorized to call together member states to consider current problems. IO personnel also influence negotiation agendas. On a high political plane, UNEP kept ozone protection alive when interstate negotiations deadlocked and built support for the Montreal Protocol. The UN secretary-general may put before the Security Council any matter that, in his opinion, threatens international peace and security. At the administrative level, the ILO governing body sets the General Conference agenda with assistance from the International Labor Office. At the technical level, IO and conference officials advance specific proposals and suggest linkages or trade-offs: the president of UNCLOS III was authorized to defer contentious votes to forge a consensus during deferment; the negotiating text advanced by GATT Director General Dunkel during the Uruguay Round catalyzed the faltering negotiations and helped bridge substantive differences.

IO officials are also prominent members of the epistemic communities that develop and transmit new ideas for international governance (Haas 1992). Drake and Nicolaidis (1992: 76) document the role of IOs in developing the concepts behind the liberalization of trade in services: a "comparatively small number of experts in the GNS [Group on Negotiation in Services] and on the GATT, UNCTAD and OECD staffs [were] the main source of the specific kinds of new ideas needed to carry the policy project to a conclusion." The UN Economic Commission on Latin America is well known as the source of many ideas regarding economic development that rallied the Group of 77. Such autonomous efforts can modify the political, normative, and intellectual context of interstate interactions. These factors are not purely exogenous, as in structural theories or constructivist approaches that locate them in general societal trends, but are tied to the agency and interests of IOs (Ness and Brechin 1988; Scott 1992).

Independence is equally important in implementation. The ILO committee of experts—a group of private individuals—comments on national reports. Some ILO organs use these comments to highlight noncompliance with ILO conventions and recommendations and to invite governments to submit additional information. Other IOs report on state compliance in addition to, or in lieu of, national reports. IO officials further monitor state conduct, in more or less intrusive ways, although enforcement remains decentralized. For example, the WTO regularly reviews the general effects of national trade policies.

Managing Substantive Operations

In the above examples, IOs facilitate interstate collaboration by pushing negotiations forward. This role could be played by, say, a dominant state, but suspicions of bias might impede cooperation; an independent IO may be more acceptable because it is neutral. For many substantive IO operations, however, it is the existence of a truly independent third party, not the absence of bias per se, that enables states to achieve their ends.

Laundering. Laundering has a negative connotation from its association with running ill-gotten gains through seemingly independent financial institutions until they come out clean, having lost their original character and taint. Without necessarily adopting that connotation, we use the term advisedly because the process at work in IOs is similar: activities that might be unacceptable in their original state-to-state form become acceptable when run through an independent, or seemingly independent, IO. The concept should be familiar to IR scholars who are reluctant to accept Central Intelligence Agency funds but eagerly accept National Science Foundation grants overseen by independent academic panels.

Appropriately enough, the World Bank, IMF, and other IFIs provide clear examples. States may prefer development assistance from an independent financial institution over direct aid from another state, especially a former colonial power or one seeking political influence. IFI restrictions on national autonomy (e.g., on project design or broader economic policies) may not carry the same domestic political implications of dependence and inferiority as would conditions imposed directly by, say, the United States or France. These considerations may make IFI conditions a superior means of promoting domestic reforms.

IFIs equally serve a laundering function for donor states seeking to avoid domestic and international controversies. The World Bank's charter requires, for example, that development loans be made without regard for the "political character" of the recipient; disregard of this factor is difficult within the United States, where financial assistance budgets require congressional approval. The United States called on the IMF to manage the 1980s debt crisis, keeping the issue less politicized and more technical. Similarly, the Soviet Union laundered subsidies to subordinate states in Eastern Europe through Council for Mutual Economic Assistance (CMEA) trading practices, muting domestic opposition to these political and economic arrangements both at home and in recipient states (Marreese 1986). IFIs also inhibit domestic special interests from distorting policy for other purposes, as in the case of tied aid.

Although the obligation to participate in IFIs may be strong, doing so helps donor states curtail aid recipients' expectations, thus preserving flexibility. Although international intermediaries diminish a donor state's leverage over recipient states, this factor is offset by decreases in other states' leverage and in competition for leverage among donors. Donor states as a group, of course, retain control over the IFIs. But it is the fund, not the United States or Germany, that imposes austerity on borrowers.

The autonomy needed for successful laundering gives IOs influence over the substance of their activities. For example, IFI staff have significant input into lending criteria and adjustment policies and, increasingly, into social, environmental, and other related policies. Robert McNamara was able to broaden development discourse beyond economic growth to include social factors and to reorient World Bank policy (Finnemore 1996; Sanford 1989). The point should not be overstated. McNamara's reforms were hardly radical, and Western countries were largely receptive. Subsequently, the Reagan administration pushed the World Bank partially back toward market policies. Thus, IO autonomy remains bounded by state interests and power, as reflected in institutional arrangements.

Such interventions can cause IOs to be perceived as politicized, responding to the interests of certain states or to issues beyond their regular purview. This occurred in the 1960s and 1970s, when the World Bank withheld loans from states that expropriated foreign property without compensation (Lipson 1985: 138–39); recently, the United States linked support for World Bank lending to human rights in cases, including China and Malawi (Kirgis 1993: 572–75). Whatever their justification, such measures reflect a partial failure we label dirty laundering. Powerful states face a tension between the immediate advantages of dirty laundering versus the long-run costs of jeopardizing IO independence.

Laundering is not limited to financial organizations. UN peace-keeping allows powerful states to support conflict reduction without being drawn into regional conflicts and discourages other powers from taking advantage of their inaction. This simultaneously reassures small countries that the conflict will not be enlarged. The IAEA performs two different laundering functions. First, recipients may prefer technical assistance from an independent agency rather than a particular nuclear state, even though nuclear states as a group dominate the agency. Direct assistance may create dependence, reduce policy flexibility, and be domestically controversial. IAEA technical assistance programs also distance provider states from recipient nuclear programs and inhibit the commercial rivalry among suppliers that otherwise facilitates proliferation. Second, states subject to nuclear safeguards may be more willing to admit independent international monitors into sensitive nuclear facilities than to permit entry by representatives of another state. Interestingly, when the United States transferred bilateral safeguard responsibilities to the IAEA in 1962, some recipients resisted the new arrangement, fearing that nationals of various states on the IAEA staff would conduct covert intelligence missions. This suggests, however, not that the logic of laundering is false but that it turns on the perceived independence of the organization.

Laundering thus has significant implications for the constitutive rules of IOs. Although member states retain ultimate control, organizations must be structured from their organs of governance down to their personnel policies—to create sufficient independence for laundering to succeed. A failing of the UN secretariat is that its personnel are viewed as retaining their national identities; by contrast, the "Eurocrat" is seen as having loyalties beyond his or her individual state.

Neutrality. Neutrality adds impartiality to independence. It enables IOs to mediate among states in contested interactions, including disputes and allocation decisions. UN neutrality underlies most of the functions discussed in the secretary-general's Agenda for Peace, from fact-finding and other forms of preventive diplomacy through dispute resolution and peacekeeping to postconflict consolidation of peace. Even more than laundering, neutrality demands that institutions be buffered from direct pressures of states.

IO as neutral information provider. Regime theory recognizes the importance of information but does not emphasize differences in its quality. Information created or verified by an independent, neutral IO is more reliable than that provided by states because it is free of national biases. Consider the air pollution monitoring stations established in Europe under LRTAP. Data supplied by Sweden or Russia could be perceived as biased, but a neutral source of information was more credible and could support greater cooperation. The convention protecting Antarctic seals incorporated an existing institution, the Scientific Commission on Antarctic Research, as a neutral source and verifier of information on the status of seals and state activities. Based on this information, the parties attained a rather high degree of cooperation. Similar conventions without neutral sources of information, such as that concerning Antarctic marine living resources, have been less successful. Finally, the 1991 General Assembly declaration on fact finding strengthens the UN secretary-general's role as a neutral information source in politically charged situations; the General Assembly has similarly encouraged the secretary-general to develop early warning systems for international disputes and humanitarian crises.

International monitoring organizations, notably those operating under multilateral arms control treaties, provide outstanding examples of neutral information production. From the perspective of many participants, the neutrality of these organizations is their most important feature. Impartial information not only deters cheating by others but also helps states assure others of their own compliance (Abbott 1993). Although the literature on informal cooperation and the US-Soviet arms control experience suggest that states can perform these functions on their own (Glaser 1995), the widespread use of IOs testifies to the advantages of third-party neutrals.

IO as trustee. In private commercial dealings, neutral parties often hold assets belonging to persons who cannot be trusted with possession until a transaction is completed. The "escrow agent," for example, protects assets until all elements of the transaction are ready for closing, while the trustee holds assets on behalf of owners who cannot take title immediately.

Such arrangements are not common in IR, but notable examples exist. The Security Council held Iraq responsible for losses caused by its invasion of Kuwait. It required Iraq to contribute a percentage of its oil export revenues to a UN compensation fund from which payments would be made. A compensation commission (whose governing council includes representatives of Security Council members) administers the fund as trustee for claimants. Subsequently, concerned about humanitarian needs in Iraq, the council authorized states to import limited amounts of Iraqi oil with payments to be made directly into a special escrow account for purchases of food and medicine. Similarly, an international oil pollution compensation fund is part of the IMO regime governing oil spills in territorial waters.

Building on the League of Nations mandate system, the UN charter established an international trusteeship system. Individual states were typically designated as trustees for various territories, with mixed results. But the charter did establish standards for trustees and a trusteeship council to monitor them. It even contemplated that the UN itself would perform the trustee function directly, an extraordinary example of the IO as a neutral party.

Traditional UN peacekeeping also illustrates the trustee function: UN forces patrol or even control territory to separate combatants, prevent conflict, and supervise negotiated cease-fires. UN neutrality also allows major powers to support peacekeeping without choosing sides among friendly states, as in Cyprus. Blue-helmet neutrality is crucial and guaranteed in multiple ways: operations are voluntary and require continuing consent of all parties, peacekeepers are from countries with no stake in the conflict and under UN command, operations are financed through general assessments, and troops are unarmed (observers) or lightly armed for self-defense to prevent uses of force inconsistent with neutrality. But these restrictions can limit the effectiveness of peacekeeping operations in some conflictual environments—as has been evident in Bosnia. To deal with these limitations, the secretary-general's Agenda for Peace proposes a preventive trustee function: UN-administered demilitarized zones, established in advance of actual conflict to separate contending parties and remove any pretext for attack.

Neutral activities must be keenly attuned to the realities of international power. U Thant's quick withdrawal of the United Nations Emergency Force (UNEF) at Egypt's request in 1967 was based on the legal principle requiring consent for UN operations but equally reflected the reality that two contributing countries had threatened to withdraw troops if Egyptian wishes were not respected. Nevertheless, like an escrow agent, peacekeeping is effective when it furthers state interests in limiting conflict.

The Acheson-Lilienthal (Baruch) Plan would have created an international agency to manage fissile material, contributed by the United States and the United Kingdom, the existing nuclear powers. This institutional arrangement (which was not, of course, adopted) resembled a trusteeship with the world community as beneficiary. It reflected the vital interests of donor states in preventing destabilizing proliferation, but the plan required a neutral trustee. The sponsors would not have been trusted to hold the material themselves.

Similarly, under the "common heritage" principle of UNCLOS III, the convention declares that rights to seabed resources are "vested in mankind as a whole, on whose behalf the Authority shall act." The powers of the Seabed Authority were limited to accord better with market principles and US interests, but it retains its basic institutional structure, including important trustee characteristics that may evolve over time.

IO as allocator. A neutral party often allocates scarce resources among claimants to avoid paralyzing negotiating standoffs and lingering resentment: the parent, not the children, slices the birthday cake. IOs also serve this function.

The IAEA, for example, assists peaceful national nuclear programs. It necessarily evaluates proposed projects and allocates financial and personnel resources. Only a neutral body could be entrusted with such responsibility in a sensitive area. IFIs also allocate scarce resources according to project worthiness. The World Bank's charter tries to guarantee its neutrality by requiring that it ignore the political character of potential borrowers. The perception that the World Bank promotes pro-market policies on behalf of the Western powers and punishes governments that pursue other goals such as equity reduces its effectiveness. The World Bank defends its neutrality by presenting its policies as driven by technical analyses rather than value judgments. It has retained a sufficient aura of neutrality to be entrusted with allocating funds under the Global Environment Facility, the Ozone Trust Fund, and the climate change convention.

IO as arbiter. According to Morgenthau (1967: 272), "despite . . . deficiencies [in] . . . the legislative function [in international politics], a legal system might still be capable of holding in check the power aspirations of its subjects if there existed judicial agencies that could speak with authority whenever a dissension occurred with regard to the existence or the import of a legal rule." Few international institutions are truly designed to restrain state power, yet many help states resolve legal (and political) disputes. Neutrality is essential for such institutions, just as for a judge in the law merchant system (Milgrom, North, and Weingast 1990), the European Court, or a domestic court.

In *facilitative intervention,* an IO operates as "honest broker" to reduce transaction costs, improve information about preferences, transmit private offers, and overcome bargaining deadlocks. Chapter VI of the UN Charter requires states to use traditional measures—including good offices, mediation, conciliation and fact finding—to resolve disputes that threaten international peace and security. The secretary-general frequently provides these services. The Human Rights Committee provides its good offices in interstate disputes and may appoint ad hoc conciliation commissions to propose possible settlements. Numerous international conventions, from the Antarctic to the NATO treaties, provide for similar measures if direct negotiations fail. Even the highly legalized WTO understanding on dispute settlement allows members to request mediation or conciliation by the director-general.

In *binding intervention,* international institutions issue legally binding decisions with the consent of all parties. The mere possibility of binding external intervention may bring recalcitrant states to the bargaining table and make negotiating positions more reasonable. The most common dispute resolution mechanism of this kind is arbitration. Participating states agree on arbitrators, procedures, and jurisdiction and agree to be bound by the arbitrators' decision. When agreement on these matters cannot be reached, other neutral IOs sometimes fill the gap—as when the Permanent Court of Arbitration selected the president of the US-Iran claims tribunal.

Arbitral tribunals resolve disputes on an ad hoc basis, as in the 1941 US-Canada *Trail Smelter* arbitration, a leading precedent in international environmental law, or in the secretary-general's "Rainbow Warrior" arbitration between France and New Zealand. They also handle classes of disputes such as the famous Alabama Claims arbitration following the Civil War, the special claims commission for allied property claims following World War II, and the Iran-US claims tribunal. The following comment on the Rainbow Warrior dispute applies to most of these cases: "This solution is not without critics in both countries. . . . However, . . . the settlement proved much more acceptable— precisely because of its unimpeachable source—than would have been the same, or any other, solution arrived at solely by the parties themselves. Neither government . . . could be accused by its internal critics of having yielded to the other" (Franck and Nolte 1993: 166).

Many international agreements, from bilateral commercial treaties to the law of the sea convention, rely on arbitration through ad hoc panels or more permanent institutions. The GATT-WTO dispute resolution process is similar to arbitration. In the interest of neutrality, the director-general maintains a roster of qualified panelists, suggests panelists to disputants, and names the panel if the parties cannot agree. NAFTA incorporates several arbitration procedures, including an innovative one whereby arbitrators review national antidumping and countervailing duty decisions to ensure that national law was followed. The International Centre for the Settlement of Investment Disputes (ICSID), affiliated with the World Bank, provides neutral facilities for arbitrations between private investors and host governments.

The principal international judicial authority is the International Court of Justice (ICJ). Unlike domestic courts, it must be granted jurisdiction by parties to a dispute. Most cases have arisen under treaties that include submission to ICJ jurisdiction. The ICJ also issues advisory opinions to UN organs and specialized agencies. The court has issued a number of decisions of significance but has not been heavily used by states; GATT panels, for instance, have issued many more decisions than the ICJ. A relatively small number of states have accepted compulsory jurisdiction, and efforts to use the court during high-profile disputes led France and the United States to terminate their acceptance, although not without cost. The European Court of Justice and the European Court of Human Rights (which also requires acceptance of jurisdiction) have been more successful. Indeed, the former—whose judges are chosen "from persons whose independence is beyond doubt"—approaches the authority of the judicial institutions Morgenthau had in mind. Its judges have played a leading (independent) role in promoting European legal integration (Burley and Mattli 1993). Other international institutions, including the WTO appellate body, may also develop into successful judicial agencies.

IO as Community Representative and Enforcer

In this section, we consider broader and more controversial functions of formal IOs, some of which go beyond a simple state-centric approach. We examine how states structure and use formal organizations to create and implement community values and norms and to assist in the enforcement of international commitments. This discussion demonstrates further how the study of IOs forces different theoretical schools to engage one another. We discuss these two functions separately, then together in a brief examination of the role of the UN in the Gulf War—an example that also illustrates the significance of IOs in situations of violent conflict.

The IO as Community Representative

States establish IOs to act as a representative or embodiment of a community of states. This was a central aspiration in the postwar organizational boom and remains an important, if only partially fulfilled, aspect of IO operations today.

Community institutions take several forms. They may be inclusive bodies such as the General Assembly, the town square of international politics, created as a forum in which common issues can be addressed. Within such institutions, states work out and express their common interests and values. The process may be largely consensual, as when states consider some problem of common concern such as environmental change or the behavior of a rogue state, or it may entail one set of states pressuring another to accept new principles such as human rights, the oceans as a commons, or democracy. Other community institutions, such as the Security Council, are representative bodies. These incorporate the major actors (as realism would predict) as well as states representing other interests. These smaller bodies instantiate political bargains in their representation rules while providing a more efficient forum in which to deal with issues, especially those requiring operational responses. Finally, community institutions such as the ICJ are structured to promote independence and neutrality, their actions constrained by a charge to act in the common interest. All three types can advance community interests with special legitimacy.

The UN, established by the Allies when they had unchecked dominance, was undoubtedly intended to serve their own purposes. It was also based on a conception of shared interests and values that went well beyond laundering or even neutrality. The charter's broad goals presupposed a direct relation between national welfare, conditions around the globe, and the peaceful working of the international community as a whole. The principal goal was to maintain international peace and security, and UN organs were authorized to intervene, not just mediate in interstate disputes that threatened peace. Other goals were to develop friendly relations among states based on the principles of equal rights and self-determination, to promote fundamental freedoms, and to promote cooperation on a wide range of global problems. Shared interests in many of these areas—human rights, democracy, and liberal economic relations—are still developing.

Perhaps the most important function of community organizations is to develop and express community norms and aspirations. Although the General Assembly lacks the Security Council's power of action, it can have substantial impact on international politics by expressing shared values on issues like human rights, apartheid, decolonization, and environmental protection in ways that legitimate or delegitimate state conduct. The Universal Declaration of Human Rights is a striking example. Although the declaration cannot be enforced, its explicit and sweeping formulation of standards has significantly affected state behavior. Its norms have been included in binding treaties, and the declaration itself has been incorporated into some national constitutions, thereby influencing the character and preferences of states and, thus, of the international system itself. Although smaller states have been disproportionately held to account on this issue, even large states like the former Soviet Union and reputed nuclear states like South Africa have been affected.

Similarly, although GATT (unlike the WTO) was intentionally created with as few attributes of an independent IO as possible, its contracting parties and council have formulated important policies for the trading community, including "differential and more favorable treatment" for developing countries. Although contested, this principle has been reflected in subsequent trade negotiations and the generalized system of preferences.

Courts as independent institutions also formulate and express community policy. By enunciating, elaborating, and applying rules publicly, they educate the community and strengthen underlying norms (Abbott 1992). A highly unusual IO, the UN tribunal dealing with war crimes in the former Yugoslavia, combines these public judicial roles with the closely related public role of prosecutor. But states have not fully embraced the community functions of courts. Even the ICJ is structured to minimize its community role: its jurisdiction rests on party consent, and its decisions have no formal status as precedents. Yet, ICJ decisions are regularly relied on, and the court has on important occasions acted as expositor of fundamental community values, as in the Iranian hostages case and, many would say, Nicaragua's suit against the United States. These decisions have important moral authority even when they cannot be enforced in the traditional sense. Similar functions are performed by the European and Inter American Commissions and Courts of Human Rights, and even by quasi-judicial bodies like the ILO governing body.

The most controversial example of community representation is the Security Council's "primary responsibility for the maintenance of international peace and security." The council is empowered to investigate any situation that might lead to international friction and recommend means of resolving the conflict, including terms of settlement. It is further empowered under Chapter VII to "take action" against any threat to peace. When using armed force, however, the council has proceeded much as with economic sanctions, calling on members to give effect to measures it has approved.

An IO with these powers could overcome free-rider problems hampering decentralized efforts to maintain peace. But the Security Council has the deeper rationale of representing the community. Because local disputes might spill over and disrupt the larger community, they affect the general welfare. Such disputes should not be dealt with exclusively by the parties themselves, or by third states intervening for their own private interests, but by collective bodies that consider the effects of the dispute and of external intervention on the general welfare. Chapter VIII of the charter even authorizes regional organizations like the Organization of American States (OAS) to deal with local disputes, although they only take "enforcement action" with council approval, lest such action itself threaten the peace of the larger community. Finally, situating private disputes in terms of community interests and institutions brings a heightened level of political and moral pressure to bear on disputants and potential intervenors.

The creation and development of IOs often represent deliberate decisions by states to change their mutually constituted environment and, thus, themselves. IOs can affect the interests and values of states in ways that cannot be fully anticipated. Yet, it is important to stress that these processes are initiated and shaped by states. Furthermore, IOs are constrained by institutional procedures—including financial contributions and leadership appointments—that are controlled by states and, ultimately, by the ability of (some) states to withdraw, albeit at some cost. These possibilities and limitations make IOs an important window into the relation between rationalist and constructivist analysis.

IOs as Managers of Enforcement

The role of IOs in ensuring compliance with international commitments can best be understood by integrating managerial and enforcement views of the process. Observing high levels of compliance with international agreements, even though strong enforcement provisions are rarely included or used, the managerial school concludes that IR has focused too heavily on coercive enforcement. In this view, noncompliance typically results not from deliberate cheating but from ambiguity in agreements, insufficient state capacity, or changing international and domestic circumstances (Chayes and Chayes 1995; see also Mitchell 1994; Young 1994). Resolution of such problems lies not in stronger enforcement but in better management of compliance. Downs, Rocke, and Barsoorn (1996) counter that, without enforcement, states will cheat on agreements and that observed compliance levels largely reflect shallow agreements that require little change in state behavior.

An overly sharp distinction between managerial and enforcement functions is misleading. For many significant day-to-day activities— especially ones involving coordination—incentives to defect are relatively small compared with the benefits of cooperation; here, the managerial approach is sufficient. In other cases, some enforcement may be necessary, at least potentially. IOs support both kinds of activities. More important, the strictly decentralized models that underpin the enforcement view do not apply strictly to the richer environment of international politics, especially when states are numerous and face significant informational problems. In these more complex settings, IOs can manage enforcement activities to make them more effective and to limit their adverse side effects.

Many IO functions identified earlier are valuable in implementing the managerial approach. Ambiguity can be resolved through dispute resolution and other third-party procedures, including fact finding, good offices, interpretation of international agreements, and mediation. State incapacity is addressed directly by financial and technical assistance. Emerging compliance problems due to changing circumstances can be managed by IO political and judicial organs with authority to interpret and adapt agreements and elaborate norms.

When enforcement is needed, IOs can facilitate decentralized action. They increase the prospect of continued interaction, often across issues, and generalize reputational effects of reneging across members of the organization. Some IOs directly monitor state behavior, producing credible neutral information necessary for effective enforcement. IOs further provide forums in which suspicious actions can be explained, lowering the risk that misperceptions will upset cooperation, and in which pressure can be brought on transgressor states. In these ways, international legal discussions about "mobilization of shame" can be understood not in the moral sense of creating guilt among states but in an instrumental sense of enhancing reputational and other incentives to abide by commitments.

IOs also have some direct avenues of enforcement. These include requirements of national reporting—wherein failure to report itself indicates improper behavior—and the issuance of findings by the IO itself. The ILO has issued such reports with respect to labor practices, even in the case of powerful states such as the Soviet Union and Britain. A less frequent sanction occurs through resolutions criticizing state behavior. Such practices pressure states to change their behavior both by impairing their international standing and by empowering private groups to pressure national governments, thus increasing "audience costs" (Fearon 1994). The G-7 states are working to empower the IMF to make findings on national economic policies and to issue public criticism with precisely these goals in mind.

A second means of direct enforcement is withholding IO benefits, as the IAEA suspended technical assistance after Israel bombed an Iraqi nuclear reactor. The IMF's "conditionality" requirements and the World Bank's requirements on development loans have expanded over the postwar period, and these agencies have frequently had strong effects on the policies of member states.

Finally, IOs play an important role as managers of enforcement, authorizing and giving meaning to retaliation, thus ensuring that enforcement activities are not excessively disruptive to the larger international community. This possibility is differentially developed. The GATT only once authorized retaliation, whereas WTO practice is still emerging; the Security Council, by contrast, has authorized economic sanctions on numerous occasions. Martin (1992: 245) finds IOs important in managing economic sanctions because they provide a framework for side payments among retaliating states and increase incentives to cooperate in sanctions so as not to jeopardize the "broad functional benefits these organizations provided."[12] Furthermore, such validation is akin to laundering: when an IO legitimates retaliation, states are not vigilantes but upholders of community norms, values, and institutions. The IO imprimatur clarifies retaliatory behavior so that it will be seen by the target state for what it is, not as noncooperation by the retaliating state, while reassuring third parties that the retaliating state is acting appropriately. (Again, influential states might seek IO approval to disguise their noncooperative acts as retaliation, a form of dirty laundering, but this practice is limited by its self-defeating character and IO independence.) IO approval frequently limits the severity and duration of state retaliation, as the WTO does by limiting the amount of retaliation and the economic sectors targeted. Indeed, the IO may negotiate a response with the retaliating state to maximize third-party support for the action. Such managerial activities counteract "echo effects" and are improvements over strictly decentralized enforcement.

Chapter VII: The Uses and Limits of Direct Enforcement

The Security Council's experience with Chapter VII illuminates the role of the community representative in constructing interests, the possibility of more forcible methods of direct enforcement, and, equally important, their limitations. As noted above, the original conception of Chapter VII involved independent action by the Security Council on behalf of the community of states, using military units provided "on its call" by member states and guided by a military staff committee. This was direct enforcement except that the units to be deployed, even the members of the committee, were to be provided by states. This distinguishes Chapter VII from, say, the independent ability of the IMF to cut off funds to a country that violates its financial commitments. Moreover, Chapter VII has never operated as originally intended. In the two principal episodes in which military force has been used—Korea and the Gulf War—the council instead authorized national military actions, led in both cases by the United States. How are these episodes to be understood?

In the more cynical view, both are examples of dirty laundering. By obtaining Security Council approval, the United States cast essentially unilateral action as more legitimate collective action. The same interpretation can be applied to various OAS enforcement actions against Castro's Cuba. Arguably, the organizations were not sufficiently independent of US influence to convert the measures taken into genuine community action. In the Gulf War, these measures were transparently national: the council simply called on other states to cooperate with the United States, which was already operating in the Gulf theater, and coalition forces were visibly dominated by the United States, whose troops even retained their own uniforms and commanders.

Yet, these episodes can also be seen in a more affirmative light. The institutional underpinnings essential to the original vision of Chapter VII had never been put in place: there were no agreements for the provision of national forces, no emergency units standing by, no military staff committee. Lacking appropriate institutional arrangements, the council carried out its community responsibilities in the only practicable way, by shifting from direct to indirect enforcement, lending its institutional authority to legitimate action by willing nations. Its membership structure and voting rules made the council sufficiently independent and representative to perform a genuine laundering function.[13] The United States, after all, assiduously courted council approval (partly by moving more cautiously) for reasons of both domestic and international politics. The imprimatur of the council was essential to other participants: Middle Eastern states, for example, needed it to justify cooperation with the coalition. In this episode, just as Claude (1966: 74) put it more than 30 years ago, "proclamations of approval or disapproval by organs of the United Nations, deficient as they typically are in . . . effective supportive power, are really important. . . . Statesmen, by so obviously attaching importance to them, have made them important."[14]

The affirmative view sees the council, especially during the Gulf War, as representing the community of states. This representative status, not simply the formal procedures of Chapter VII, led the United States and other states to seek council action: Security Council resolutions on Iraq carried unique political weight because they came from the established community institution with primary responsibility for international peace and security. Resolutions condemning the Iraqi invasion of Kuwait as unlawful, declaring void the incorporation of Kuwaiti territory into Iraq, denouncing human rights and environmental abuses by Iraqi forces, authorizing member states to cooperate with US forces, forcing the destruction of Iraqi weapons, and holding Iraq financially responsible for its actions are clear expressions of the shared moral and legal sense of organized international society. The IO was the locus for giving meaning to state action. The United States, even as the clearly dominant power in coercive activity, had good reasons to act not simply from might but from persuasion.

Thus, realist, constructivist, and rational-regime arguments come together in consideration of the role of IOs in the Gulf crisis. Although some might prefer to find a singular "winner" among the three explanations, we believe each explains a significant part of the episode and that any unidimensional explanation would be incomplete. In any event, IOs provide an important laboratory in which to observe the operation of these different aspects of international politics.

Conclusion

For several decades, states have taken IOs more seriously than have scholars. Whereas formal IOs have been seriously neglected in the theoretical study of international regimes, they have played a major role in many, if not most, instances of interstate collaboration. By taking advantage of the centralization and independence of IOs, states are able to achieve goals that they cannot accomplish on a decentralized basis. In some circumstances, the role of IOs extends even further to include the development of common norms and practices that help define, or refine, states themselves. At the same time, because issues of power and distribution are pervasive, states are wary of allowing IOs too much autonomy. Thus, we do not claim that IOs are supplanting the states system. We do claim that IOs provide an important supplement to decentralized cooperation that affects the nature and performance of the international system. Scholars must take IOs more seriously if they are to understand interstate relations.

Although we have presented the case for the importance of formal institutions in international cooperation, the shortcomings of many actual organizations go without saying. In addition, in emphasizing the possibilities for formal organizations, we should not ignore the difficulty and even impossibility of some of the tasks that are presented to them. Despite these severe limitations, the fact that IOs have not been abandoned by states is testimony to both their actual value and their perhaps greater potential. A better theoretical and empirical understanding of formal organizations should help improve their performance.

Notes

1. Although we discuss certain of its operations, we deliberately de-emphasize the EU because some would regard it as an exceptional case of institutionalization.

2. A discussion of IOs is an exercise in acronyms. The ones not identified in the text, in order, are the World Health Organization (WHO), Organization for Security and Cooperation in Europe (OSCE), International Monetary Fund (IMF), Asia-Pacific Economic Cooperation forum (APEC), International Labour Organization (ILO), International Civil Aviation Organization (ICAO), Food and Agriculture Organization (FAO), United Nations Environment Programme (UNEP), and European Bank for Reconstruction and Development (EBRD).

3. Keohane (1984) does discuss monitoring, but Glaser (1995) argues that regime theorists do not explain why monitoring must be done centrally.

4. On the use of rational choice as an interpretive device, see Ferejohn (1991), Johnson (1991), and Snidal (1985b).

5. Centralization and independence are matters of degree, not only among IOs but even between IOs and related institutions. For example, the Group of Seven is not a formal IO but merely a negotiating forum. Its organizational

practices (e.g., a rotating chair) nevertheless provide some centralization bene-fits, and it partakes of some autonomy, as in legitimating members' actions.

6. Personal communication from Bernard Oxman, member of the US del-egation, 21 May 1997.

7. We reserve for the following section discussion of those functions that turn directly on independence and neutrality.

8. Of course, as Kratochwil (1996) notes, large-scale centralized opera-tions may not be necessary or desirable in all cases. The Maastricht Treaty's subsidiarity principle adopts this view, while authorizing supranational activity when the scale of the problem makes that appropriate.

9. The desire to benefit from pooling is nevertheless reflected in US Trea-sury Secretary Rubin's lament that the "United States cannot be the lender of last resort to the world" (quoted in Sanger 1995).

10. The G-7 countries also benefit from IFI independence, as discussed below.

11. The analogy is imperfect. NATO's organization differs from that of a firm. Nevertheless, team analysis suggests why a formal IO is valuable, whereas the standard public goods analogy reduces the problem simply to one of individual (under) provision. See Olson and Zeckhauser (1966).

12. Martin (1992: 245) also finds it important that the leading "sender" be willing to bear extra costs, suggesting a possible limitation to IO enforcement capacity in the absence of "leadership."

13. The current debate over the composition of the council reflects the idea that such an institution should be more representative of the community on behalf of which it acts.

14. See also Haas (1958) and, for a more skeptical view, see Slater (1969).

References

Abbott, Kenneth W. 1992. "GATT as a Public Institution: The Uruguay Round and Beyond." *Brooklyn Journal of International Law* 31:31–85.
———. 1993. "Trust but Verify: The Production of Information in Arms Control Treaties and Other International Agreements." *Cornell International Law Journal* 26:1–58.
Abbott, Kenneth W., and Duncan Snidal. 1997. "The Many Faces of Interna-tional Legalization." Draft paper presented at the Conference on Domestic Politics and International Law, June, Napa Valley, CA.
Alchian, Armen, and Harold Demsetz. 1972. "Production, Information Costs and Economic Organization." *American Economic Review* 62:777–95.
Amerasinghe, C. F. 1994. *The Law of the International Civil Service.* 2d rev. ed. Oxford, UK: Clarendon.
Barnett, Michael. 1993. "Institutions, Roles and Disorder: The Case of the Arab States System." *International Studies Quarterly* 37:271–96.
Bowett, D. W. 1982. *The Law of International Institutions.* 4th ed. London: Stevens.

Berle, Adolf A., and Gardiner C. Means. 1968. *The Modern Corporation and Private Property*. Rev. ed. New York: Harcourt, Brace & World.

Brownlie, Ian. 1990. *Principles of Public International Law*. 4th ed. New York: Oxford University Press.

Burley, Anne-Marie, and Walter Mattli. 1993. "Europe Before the Court: A Political Theory of Legal Integration." *International Organization* 47:41–76.

Calvert, Randall L. 1995. "Rational Actors, Equilibrium and Social Institutions." In *Explaining Social Institutions*, edited by Jack Knight and Itai Sened, 57–94. Ann Arbor: University of Michigan Press.

Chayes, Abraham, and Antonia Handler Chayes. 1995. *The New Sovereignty: Compliance with International Regulatory Agreements*. Cambridge, MA: Harvard University Press.

Claude, Inis Jr. 1966. "Collective Legitimization as a Political Function of the United Nations." *International Organization* 20:367–79.

Coase, R. H. 1937. "The Nature of the Firm." *Economica* 4:386–405.

Cox, Robert W., and Harold K. Jacobson, eds. 1973. *The Anatomy of Influence*. New Haven, CT: Yale University Press.

Downs, George W., David M. Rocke, and Peter N. Barsoom. 1996. "Is the Good News About Compliance Good News About Cooperation?" *International Organization* 50:379–406.

Drake, William, and Kalypso Nicolaidis. 1992. "Ideas, Interests and Institutionalization." *International Organization* 46:37–100.

Dupuy, Rene Jean, ed. 1988. *A Handbook on International Organizations*. Hingham, MA: Kluwer Academic.

Fearon, James. 1994. "Domestic Political Audiences and the Escalation of International Disputes." *American Political Science Review* 88:577–92.

Ferejohn, John. 1991. "Rationality and Interpretation: Parliamentary Elections in Early Stuart England." In *The Economic Approach to Politics*, edited by Kristen R. Monroe, 279–305. New York: HarperCollins.

Finnemore, Martha. 1996. *National Interests in International Society*. Ithaca, NY: Cornell University Press.

Franck, Thomas M., and Georg Nolte. 1993. "The Good Offices Function of the UN Secretary-General." In *United Nations, Divided World: The UN's Role in International Relations,* 2d ed., edited by Adam Roberts and Benedict Kingsbury, 143–82. Oxford, UK: Clarendon.

Garrett, Geoffrey, and Barry Weingast. 1993. "Ideas, Interests and Institutions: Constructing the European Community's Internal Market." In *Ideas and Foreign Policy: Beliefs, Institutions and Political Change*, edited by Judith Goldstein and Robert O. Keohane, 173–206. Ithaca, NY: Cornell University Press.

Glaser, Charles. 1995. "Realists as Optimists: Cooperation as Self-Help." *International Security* 19:50–93.

Goldstein, Judith, and Robert O. Keohane, eds. 1993. *Ideas and Foreign Policy: Beliefs, Institutions and Political Change*. Ithaca, NY: Cornell University Press.

Grief, Avner, Paul Milgrom, and Barry R. Weingast. 1994. "Merchant Guilds." *Journal of Political Economy* 102:745–76.

Haas, Ernst. 1959. *Beyond the Nation-State*. Stanford, CA: Stanford University Press.

Haas, Peter M., ed. 1992. "Knowledge, Power and International Policy Coordination." *International Organization* 46 (Special issue): 1–390.

Johnson, James D. 1991. "Rational Choice as a Reconstructive Theory." In *The Economic Approach to Politics*, edited by Kristen R. Monroe, 113–42. New York: HarperCollins.

Karns, Margaret, and Karen Mingst, eds. 1990. *The United States and Multilateral Institutions*. Boston: Unwin Hyman.

Kennedy, David. 1987. "The Move to Institutions." *Cardozo Law Review* 8:841–988.

Keohane, Robert O. 1984. *After Hegemony*. Princeton, NJ: Princeton University Press.

Keohane, Robert O., Andrew Moravcsik, and Anne-Marie Slaughter. 1997. "A Theory of Legalization." Draft paper presented at the Conference on Domestic Politics and International Law, June, Napa Valley, CA.

Kirgis, Frederic L. Jr. 1993. *International Organizations in Their Legal Setting*. 2d ed. St. Paul, MN: West.

Koremenos, Barbara, Charles Lipson, Brian Portnoy, and Duncan Snidal. 1997. "Rational International Institutions." Paper presented at the American Political Science Association Meetings, 28–31 August, Washington, DC.

Krasner, Stephen D., ed. 1983. *International Regimes*. Ithaca, NY: Cornell University Press.

Kratochwil, Friedrich. 1996. International Organization(s): Globalization and the Disappearance of "Publics." Unpublished manuscript.

Kratochwil, Friedrich, and John Gerard Ruggie. 1986. "The State of the Art on the Art of the State." *International Organization* 40:753–75.

Levy, Mark A. 1993. "European Acid Rain: The Power of Tote-Board Diplomacy." In *Institutions for the Earth: Sources of Effective International Environmental Protection*, edited by Peter M. Haas, Robert O. Keohane, and Marc A. Levy, 75–132. Cambridge, MA: MIT Press.

Lipson, Charles. 1985. *Standing Guard: Protecting Foreign Capital in the Nineteenth and Twentieth Centuries*. Berkeley: University of California Press.

Marreese, Michael. 1986. "CMEA: Effective but Cumbersome Political Economy." *International Organization* 40:287–327.

Martin, Lisa L. 1992. *Coercive Cooperation*. Princeton, NJ: Princeton University Press.

McNeely, Connie L. 1995. *Constructing the Nation-State: International Organization and Prescriptive Action*. Westport, CT: Greenwood.

Mearsheimer, John. 1995. "The False Promise of International Institutions." *International Security* 19:5–49.

Milgrom, Paul R., Douglass C. North, and Barry R. Weingast. 1990. "The Role of Institutions in the Revival of Trade: The Law Merchant, Private Judges, and the Champagne Fairs." *Economics and Politics* 2 (1):1–23.

Mitchell, Ronald. 1994. "Regime Design Matters: Intentional Oil Pollution and Treaty Compliance." *International Organization* 48:425–58.

Moravcsik, Andrew. 1991. "Negotiating the Single European Act: National Interests and Conventional Statecraft in the European Community." *International Organization* 45:19–56.

Morgenthau, H. 1967. *Politics Among Nations*. 4th ed. New York: Knopf.

Morrow, James D. 1994. "The Forms of International Cooperation." *International Organization* 48:387–424.

Ness, Gary D., and Steven R. Brechin. 1988. "IOs as Organizations." *International Organization* 42:245–74.

Olson, Mancur, and Richard Zeckhauser. 1966. "An Economic Theory of Alliances." *Review of Economics and Statistics* 48:266–79.

Oye, Kenneth A., ed. 1986. *Cooperation Under Anarchy*. Princeton, NJ: Princeton University Press.

Rochester, J. Martin. 1986. "The Rise and Fall of International Organization as a Field of Study." *International Organization* 40:777–813.

Russett, Bruce, John R. Oneal, and David R. Davis. 1998. "The Third Leg of the Kantian Tripod for Peace: International Organizations and Militarized Disputes." *International Organization* 42:1950–85.

Sanger, David E. 1995. "Big Powers Plan a World Economic Bailout Fund." *The New York Times*, 8 June, D 1.

Sanford, Jonathon. 1988. "The World Bank and Poverty: The Plight of the World's Impoverished Is Still a Major Concern of the International Agency." *American Journal of Economics and Sociology* 47:257–765.

Schermers, Henry, and Niels Blokker. 1995. *International Institutional Law: Unity Within Diversity*. 3d rev. ed. Cambridge, MA: Kluwer Law International.

Scott, W. Richard. 1992. *Organizations: Rational, Natural and Open Systems*. 3d ed. Englewood Cliffs, NJ: Prentice Hall.

Shihata, Ibrahim F. I., ed. 1991. *The World Bank in a Changing World*. Vol. 1. Norwell, MA: Kluwer Academic Publishers.

———. 1995. *The World Bank in a Changing World*. Vol. 2. Cambridge, MA: Kluwer Law International.

Slater, Jerome. 1969. "The Limits of Legitimation in International Organizations: The Organization of American States and the Dominican Crisis." *International Organization* 23:48–72.

Snidal, Duncan. 1985a. "Coordination Versus Prisoners' Dilemma: Implications for International Cooperation and Regimes." *American Political Science Review* 79:923–42.

———. 1985b. "The Game Theory of International Politics." *World Politics* 39:25–57.

———. 1996. "Political Economy and International Institutions." *International Review of Law and Economics* 16:121–37.

Sohn, Louis. 1950. *Cases and Other Materials on World Law*. Brooklyn, NY: Foundation.

———. 1967. *Cases on United Nations Law*. 2d rev. ed. Brooklyn, NY: Foundation.

Stein, Arthur. 1983. "Coordination and Collaboration: Regimes in an Anarchic World." In *International Regimes*, edited by Stephen D. Krasner, 115–40. Ithaca, NY: Cornell University Press.

Strange, Susan. 1983. "Cave! Hic Dragones: A Critique of Regime Analysis." In *International Regimes,* edited by Stephen D. Krasner, 337–54. Ithaca, NY: Cornell University Press.

Trachtman, Joel P. 1996. The Theory of the Firm and the Theory of International Economic Organization: Toward Comparative Institutional Analysis. Unpublished manuscript.

"Vienna Convention for the Protection of the Ozone Layer." 1985. *International Legal Materials* 26:1529–40.

Weber, Steven. 1994. "The European Bank for Reconstruction and Development." *International Organization* 48 (1):1–39.

Wendt, Alex. 1992. "Anarchy Is What States Make of It: The Social Construction of Power Politics." *International Organization* 46:391–425.

———. 1995. "Constructing International Politics." *International Security* 20:71–81.

Williamson, Oliver. 1995. *The Economic Institutions of Capitalism.* New York: Free Press.

———. *The Mechanisms of Government.* Oxford, UK: Oxford University Press.

Yarbrough, Beth V., and Robert M. Yarbrough. 1992. *Cooperation and Governance in International Trade.* Princeton, NJ: Princeton University Press.

Young, Oran R. 1994. *International Governance.* Ithaca, NY: Cornell University Press.

PART 2
Decisionmaking
Paul F. Diehl and Brian Frederking

THE COMMON PUBLIC PERCEPTION OF DECISIONMAKING IN international organizations is a narrow one. Many see the decision process confined to formal, roll-call votes on symbolic resolutions by member states in large legislative sessions; the various United Nations General Assembly resolutions are familiar examples that seem to confirm this perception. In this section, we hope to dispel this stereotype and give the reader a more sophisticated view of the activities and processes of international organizations.

One area of study is the role of leaders in international organizations. In Chapter 4, Ian Johnstone argues that the power of the UN Secretary-General derives from a mixture of legal standing and personal attributes. The dynamic leadership of Dag Hammarskjöld was a critical factor in the peacekeeping missions carried out by the United Nations during the late 1950s and early 1960s. The patterns of influence as well as the limitations on the ability to affect decisions in the case of the UN Secretary-General are mirrored in many ways in the experiences of the leaders of other organizations. Over time, the "executive heads" of international organizations have become increasingly influential. The UN Secretary-General is perhaps the visible representative of an organization, but it is the bureaucracy that s/he directs that often has the greatest impact in a wide variety of activities including the delivery of humanitarian assistance.

Although formal voting is not the only aspect of decisionmaking in international organizations, it is often an important component. Many international organizations adhere to the "one state, one vote" standard.

This results in a situation whereby microstates such as Tuvalu have the same theoretical voting strength as the People's Republic of China. In other organizations, such as the International Monetary Fund and World Bank, votes are weighted according to criteria such as economic wealth or level of budgetary contribution. At various times, the United States and other Western states have demanded a greater voice in the decision-making of the United Nations General Assembly based on the dispro-portionate amount of the organization's budget contributed by these states. The General Assembly bases its voting allocation on the concept of sovereign equality, the effect of which is that each state receives one vote.

Mirroring the Western demands for voting reform in the UN General Assembly has been the call from many states for changing the com-position and voting rules of the UN Security Council. Germany, Japan, and other states have clamored for permanent seats on the Security Council based on their strong global economies and financial support of UN activities. Third-world countries have sought to expand the number of seats on the Security Council to give themselves a greater say in a body no longer stalemated by the Cold War. Various other proposals would weaken or share the veto power held by the five permanent mem-bers. A driving force behind all of these proposals is the importance of legitimacy and the perceived fairness of decisionmaking processes. In Chapter 5, Ian Hurd explores the debates regarding a proposed expan-sion of the UN Security Council and the widespread argument that the Council's legitimacy is undermined unless it reforms itself to account for recent changes in world politics. He concludes that all arguments for Security Council reform involve a trade-off between increasing the Council's legitimacy and other values such as efficiency, effectiveness, or power. Even with some desirable effects from Security Council reform, any alteration would require an amendment of the UN Charter (only once before has the United Nations altered the composition of the Security Council, increasing the membership to fifteen), something that must be approved by the five permanent members (whose veto could kill any amendments), exactly the states whose power would be dimin-ished by certain kinds of changes.

An important factor in any organization's ability to implement deci-sions is the resources available to it, the most basic of which are finan-cial. With detailed taxing systems, backed by coercive power, govern-ments are able to secure necessary funds to perform their functions. International organizations, however, primarily rely on members' assessments and voluntary contributions, each of which is subject to political manipulation, "free-riding," and enforcement problems. In the concluding chapter in this section, Paul Diehl and Elijah PharaohKhan analyze the options for paying for the increased number and scope of peacekeeping operations. Although they focus on peacekeeping expenses, many of the suggestions for financing apply equally well to the UN general budget and international organizations more broadly.

4

The Role of the UN Secretary-General: The Power of Persuasion Based on Law

Ian Johnstone

IN AN ADDRESS TO THE UN GENERAL ASSEMBLY ON 12 SEP-
tember 2002, delivered fifteen minutes before President Bush's statement on Iraq, the secretary-general (SG) made it clear that he believed
new military action against Iraq should occur only on the basis of a new
Security Council (SC) resolution. Without stating explicitly that such
authorization was necessary, he suggested that respect for international
law and the "unique legitimacy provided by the UN" required it. He
added, however, that should Iraq continue to defy its obligations, the SC
"must face its responsibilities," implying that it must be prepared to
threaten or authorize the use of force.[1]

A year earlier, in August 2001, the SC adopted a little noticed resolution on conflict prevention, which invites the SG to refer "cases of serious violations of international law" to the SC.[2] The request would seem
to fly in the face of a decision taken in 1945 not to empower the SG to
bring to the attention of the SC violations of the legal instrument that
bears most directly on its work—the UN Charter itself.[3] While the SG
was expected and encouraged to perform independent political functions,
the UN's founders did not anoint him guardian of the charter. And yet,
with little fanfare, Resolution 1366 seems to call upon him to play precisely that role with respect to the charter and much charter-based law.

These two events—the SG's intervention in the debate over military action in Iraq and the invitation in Resolution 1366—highlight an
important and poorly understood dimension of the role of the SG. In

Reprinted from *Global Governance* 9, no. 4 (2003): 441–458. © 2003 Lynne Rienner
Publishers. Reprinted by permission of the publisher.

addition to being chief administrative officer of the UN and the world's top diplomat, he is an influential participant in the legal discourse that infuses much of global politics. Despite the defeat of the proposed amendment to Article 99, this is a role the SG has played (and could not help but play) since the earliest days of the UN. He is a key member of an interpretive community associated with the implementation and elaboration of charter-based law. With little formal authority and no material power, the SG's influence depends largely on his persuasive powers.[4] That influence, moreover, is wielded within an institutional and normative context that he helps shape. By examining the SG's role as a legal actor, this article aims to shed light on the sources of those persuasive powers. I argue that the political and legal roles of the SG are intertwined, and that his political influence is reinforced by his ability to draw upon values and principles embodied in the UN Charter.

I begin by reviewing the legal basis of the SG's authority and evolving conceptions of that authority under successive secretaries-general. I then offer a brief account of international law as a process of justificatory discourse, the terms of which are set and constrained by an interpretive community associated with a particular field of practice. As a participant in the practice of peace and security, the SG contributes to the interpretation, hardening, and progressive elaboration of charter-based law in that field. In the third section, I examine how various SGs have intervened in legal discourse and argue that the voice of the office carries considerable weight. The article concludes by summarizing the sources of the secretary-general's persuasive powers, laying stress on what may be called the normative authority of the office.

The Secretary-General as Legal Actor

The legal basis for the secretary-general's role lies in Articles 7 and 97 through 101 of the UN Charter. Article 97 names him chief administrative officer of the organization; Article 98 stipulates that he shall perform functions entrusted to him by the deliberative organs of the UN. More interesting from a constitutional point of view is the independent political role derived from Article 99, which reads: "the Secretary-General may bring to the attention of the Security Council any matter which in his opinion may threaten the maintenance of international peace and security."[5] The discretion embodied in the notion that he may (not must) bring any matter (not only disputes) which in his opinion may threaten peace requires the SG to exercise independent political judgment.[6] The Preparatory Commission of the UN also stated that the SG "more than anyone else, will stand for the UN as a whole. In the eyes of the world, he must embody the principles and ideals of the Charter to which this Organization gives effect."[7] The legal foundation for this expansive vision of the office is Article 7, which designates the Secretariat a principal organ of the UN. The SG is not equal to the other organs in every respect (Article 98 specifies that he takes instruction from the deliberative bodies), but at a minimum Article 7 implies that he has equal responsibility to uphold the aims and purposes of the charter.[8]

More important than the words of the charter is the manner in which those words have been interpreted. From Trygve Lie on, every SG has asserted the independence of the office, some more vigorously than others. Lie himself helped establish the SG's right to offer unsolicited opinions to the SC (later embodied in the Provisional Rules of Procedure)[9] and the right to engage in fact-finding in order to determine whether a matter should be brought to the attention of the Council under Article 99. Dag Hammarskjöld observed in a famous speech that Article 99 carries with it a broad discretion "to engage in informal diplomatic activity in regard to matters which may threaten international peace and security," thereby asserting the legal basis for his good offices role.[10] He invented the so-called Peking Formula by distancing himself from a condemnatory resolution adopted by the General Assembly (GA) in order to help secure release of a U.S. aircrew captured by China during the Korean War.[11] After augmenting the UN Observer Group in Lebanon, Hammarskjöld said to the SC in a strikingly self-conscious statement of the evolutionary process of charter interpretation, "were you to disapprove, I would of course accept the consequences of your judgment."[12] U Thant and Kurt Waldheim were less outspoken about the role of the SG, although the former in particular was known for effective quiet diplomacy, most successfully in Bahrain, a technique he later called an alternative to the "specific—and much more dramatic—invocation of Article 99."[13] Javier Pérez de Cuéllar, while cautioning against moral hubris, described the SG as "guardian of the principles of the Charter,"[14] and said about the trip he took to Iraq just before the SC-authorized bombing campaign in January 1991, "it is my moral duty as SG of the UN to do everything I can in order to avoid war."[15] Perhaps in a (failed) bid at reelection, Boutros Boutros-Ghali concluded a piece on global leadership at the end of the Cold War in *Foreign Affairs* as follows:

If one word above all is to characterize the role of the Secretary-General, it is independence. The holder of this office must never be seen as acting out of fear of, or in an attempt to curry favor with, one state or group of states . . . Article 100 [no staff member of the UN should take instructions from any government] is Psalm 100 to the Secretary-General.[16]

Kofi Annan amplified the words of his predecessors in reflecting on his visit to Iraq in February 1998, where he signed a Memorandum of Understanding (MOU) with Saddam Hussein, allowing the return of the weapons inspectors. He made it clear in dealings with permanent members of the SC that he believed he had the "constitutional right" to travel to Baghdad without a formal SC mandate.[17] He later said he had not wanted precise terms of reference from the SC, just its support for the trip and the parameters of what would constitute an acceptable settlement.[18] By putting some distance between himself and the SC in a modern version of the Peking Formula, the SG could avoid the fate of Pérez de Cuéllar, who Saddam Hussein perceived as a mere "letter carrier,"[19] while leaving the SC room to dissociate itself from any agreement he might reach. And in an undisguised response to the criticisms of his trip to Iraq after Saddam Hussein abrogated the MOU, Kofi Annan described the SG as "an instrument of the larger interest, beyond national rivalries and regional concerts," adding that "the end of the Cold War transformed the moral promise of the role of the Secretary-General. It allowed him to place the UN at the service of the universal values of the Charter, without constraints of ideology or particular interests . . . Impartiality [in the exercise of the SG's functions] does not—and must not—mean neutrality in the face of evil. It means strict and unbiased adherence to the principles of the Charter."[20]

Two points in particular are worth noting about the above comments. First, they represent implicit or explicit interpretations of the UN Charter by the SGs on their own powers. It was decided at the 1945 San Francisco conference that each organ of the UN should interpret those aspects of the charter that fall within its competence, limited only by the rather cryptic observation that "if an interpretation made by any organ of the Organization . . . is not generally acceptable it will be without binding force."[21] Interpretations of Article 99 by successive SGs illustrate what this elusive passage means: they are not treated as authoritative simply because the SGs assert them but only following debate among member states and a period of accepted practice. These were not unilateral assertions of authority or abstract exercises in UN reform, but rather instances of innovation that arose, were discussed, and ultimately were accepted in the context of particular disputes being dealt with in the UN. In the manner of the evolution of customary law, these creative interpretations of the SG's role became entrenched as accepted law of the UN Charter.

Second, the notion that the SG must be guided by the principles of the charter highlights the complex legal role he must play. Some of those principles conflict (for example, territorial integrity and self-determination) and there is often controversy about how they should be applied in a particular context. To assume the mantle of "guardian of the Charter" could be seen as the sort of hubris Pérez de Cuéllar warned against. A more modest approach might be for the SG to seek guidance from the deliberative bodies, not from charter principles as he interprets them. Is that an answer? The GA and SC play interpretive roles themselves, both explicitly by adopting resolutions that purport to interpret the charter (such as the SC's resolution defining HIV/AIDS as a threat to international peace and security) and implicitly through practice (such as various SC-authorized interventions for humanitarian purposes). But the GA is composed of 191 states and its interpretations of the charter are often as imprecise as the charter itself. While the SC is a more cohesive body in the post–Cold War era, its mandates are often contradictory, as a glance at the more than 150 resolutions and Presidential Statements on the former Yugoslavia between 1991 and 1995 reveals. To suggest that the SG should follow the directives and pronouncements of the intergovernmental bodies simply shifts the interpretive task to another level. He must interpret those directives in light of their objectives, and in accordance with evolving conceptions of charter principles.

Interpretation as an Enterprise-specific Activity

If the role of the SG necessarily involves an element of interpretation, then it is important to understand the nature of the interpretative task. Here, I rely on a concept of law as a process of justificatory discourse within interpretive communities.[22] All interpretation takes place within an enterprise and only makes sense in terms of the purposes, practices, and conventions of argument of that enterprise. Meaning, according to this conception, is a product of neither the text alone (pure objectivity) nor the reader alone (pure subjectivity), but rather the interpretive community in which both text and reader are situated. In international legal practice, some disputes are settled in courts or by quasi-judicial bodies, but many are not. Most interpreters of legal texts have an interest in the outcome and are politically or institutionally predisposed to interpretations that favor their government or state. Yet legal interpretation is not entirely unconstrained and the meaning of legal texts is not radically indeterminate. Rational discourse about competing interpretations is possible as long as there is an understanding, largely tacit, of the general purpose of the enterprise in which the text is encountered.[23] Interpretive practices are a function of the setting, within which certain assumptions and categories of understanding are taken for granted. Disputes over meaning are resolvable through "the conventions of description, argument, judgment, and persuasion as they operate in this or that particular field of profession or discipline or community."[24] As a participant in the enterprise, the interpreter deviates from its conventions at his or her peril. Since most interpretations of international law are not deemed authoritative simply by virtue of the office-holder who puts them forward, the goal is to be persuasive. Arguments that stray too far from the accepted parameters of discourse for the discipline will persuade no one and therefore are not worth making.

Why government officials and other international actors feel the need to be legally persuasive—to justify and explain their actions on the basis of law—is the subject of an extensive body of literature.[25] One can point to both interest-based reasons (the instrumental benefits of reciprocal compliance with the law and the stability provided by a law-based international system) and more normative, constructivist reasons (the sense of obligation that comes with membership in the international community, which becomes institutionalized at the domestic level in both bureaucratic and political processes). Moreover, it is not possible to draw a sharp distinction between interests and norms: the former are often defined in terms of the latter, and the latter can become placeholders for the former. As Andrew Hurrell puts it, once states see themselves as having a long-term interest in participating in an international legal system, "then the idea of obligation and the normativity of the rules can be given concrete form and can acquire a degree of distance from the immediate interests or preferences of states."[26] Either way, government officials rarely say about an action "we know it is illegal, but we are doing it anyway"; instead they offer an interpretation of the law that is consistent with the action.

Does that mean that any interpretation is as good as any other? In a decentralized legal system, who distinguishes good legal claims from bad? The interpretive community does. It sets the parameters of discourse in a field of practice, in effect serving as judge and jury. The SG, though he has no formal authority as interpreter of international law, is an influential participant in that discourse. He is a key member of the interpretive community associated with the UN, and he operates in a highly developed institutional and legal setting. The charter and charter-based law provide the normative framework within which questions of peace and security are debated. This framework, moreover, is constantly evolving. In recent years, for example, traditional notions of national security (the security of the state) have given way to broader conceptions of human security (the security of the individual). Indeed the unusual invitation to the SG to refer violations of human rights and humanitarian law to the SC may be seen as the latest manifestation of this evolving normative climate. An implication is that greater international concordance on the values embodied in the UN Charter gives the SG a more solid foundation for asserting and assessing legal claims. In interpreting the law and identifying violations, he is able to point to more precise conceptions than the general terms of the charter itself.

Interventions in the Legal Discourse by Successive Secretaries-General

SG interventions in international legal discourse on peace and security matters have taken various forms. Some are interpretations of the charter itself while others interpret charter-based law. Some are explicit legal findings, others are implicit interpretations in the form of operational decisions. Even silence on a contested point may sometimes have legal significance. In this section, I begin by highlighting several examples in which legal positions taken by previous SGs had an important political impact on SC deliberations; I then turn to a closer examination of the role Kofi Annan plays.

Reports on peace operations are critical contributions that SGs make to the work of the SC and few have been more influential than Dag Hammarskjöld's first report on the 1960 Congo crisis. In it he asserted that the breakdown of the Congo's institutions "represented a threat to peace and security," the threshold for Chapter VII action.[27] The SC only determined such a threat nine months later, at which point 11,000 UN troops were already on the ground. Thus by the time the SC invoked Article 39 of the charter, the threshold jurisdictional question had already been decided.[28] It would be an overstatement to say the SC was driven to this position by the SG, but there is no question that his early intervention affected the way the crisis was handled in the SC and had a longer-term impact on how Article 39 has been interpreted. Similarly, U Thant's involvement in the 1963 Yemeni civil war had an important impact on how Article 2(7) has been interpreted. On his own initiative, he sent a team of observers to prevent infiltration along the border. This implicit finding that the matter was not purely internal (and therefore beyond the UN's competence) was later approved by the SC.[29] Kurt Waldheim invoked his Article 99 powers in connection with the Iranian occupation of the U.S. Embassy and hostage-taking in Tehran. Not only did the SG call the situation a threat to international peace and security before the SC had done so (it later "followed the Secretary-General's assessment" in a resolution), he also branded Iran's acts as violations of international treaties.[30]

One of Pérez de Cuéllar's greatest innovations was the incorporation of human rights concerns into peacekeeping. His response to the request for a verification mechanism to oversee the Central America Esquipula II Agreement has been called "a singular contribution" to peacekeeping doctrine for operations that involve insurrectional groups and irregular forces.[31] Forefronting human rights in the El Salvador operation reinforced the notion that the promotion and protection of human rights is properly within the SC's competence by demonstrating that peace and justice could be compatible. Not since the troubled Congo operation of the early 1960s had the SC been so involved in matters typically viewed as the exclusive domain of domestic jurisdiction. It led to a spurt of new peacekeeping tasks—human rights and election monitoring, the reform of security and justice institutions, assistance in providing law and order—that go to the very heart of governance. That such external involvement was requested by the governments concerned and authorized by the SC—often at the urging of the SG—marks as dramatic a shift in perceptions of sovereignty as the more coercive humanitarian interventions under Chapter VII of the charter.

An unusually direct intervention in legal discourse was Pérez de Cuéllar's interpretation of SC Resolution 688 of April 1991. That resolution called the consequences of Iraq's repression of its Kurd and Shi'ite populations a threat to international peace and security, but did not explicitly cite Chapter VII of the UN Charter. Nevertheless, France, the United Kingdom, and the United States claimed authority for Operation Provide Comfort and the no-fly zones in northern and southern Iraq on the basis of it.[32] When asked by a journalist how he interpreted Resolution 688, the SG said it was not "put in the framework of Chapter VII" and therefore a UN military and police presence could not be deployed in northern Iraq without a new resolution or the consent of the Iraqi government.[33] For the most part, Boutros-Ghali refrained from joining that debate, but when airstrikes were launched on Iraq in January 1993, he stated that the action was lawful on the basis of Resolutions 678 (the initial authorization to use force to drive Iraq out of Kuwait) and 687 (setting out the terms of the cease-fire).[34] He pointedly avoided any mention of Resolution 688, one of the legal bases stated by the United States, even though the strikes were against missiles and infrastructure in the no-fly zone. Under the circumstances, Boutros-Ghali's forthright (and controversial) interpretation of Resolutions 678 and 687, and his silence on 688, were significant interventions in a hotly contested SC debate that exploded in the recent imbroglio over the U.S.-led intervention in Iraq.

Kofi Annan's most important legal interventions have been in two areas: the exercise of his good offices and his statements on human rights. An interesting example of the first is his trip to Nigeria in July 1998. Not long after Nigeria's ruler General Sani Abacha died, his successor (General Abdulsalami Abubakar) invited the SG to Abuja in order to help bring Nigeria out of its international isolation. The SG accepted in part because he thought Abubakar (unlike Abacha) was sincere about the transition to democracy, and felt that he, as SG, could facilitate that transition by signalling the international community's expectations of and willingness to engage the new government. As the SG departed Nigeria, he spoke of the importance of a speedy "return to democracy." Not long after, Abubakar announced a transition program and elections were held and power was handed over to President Olesegun Obasanjo in May 1999. Later, the SG stated that his visit had advanced "not only Nigeria's prospects, but also the aims of the Charter." The promotion of democracy is not one of the explicit goals of the charter, but a growing body of scholarly and official opinion sees it as flowing from the human rights and self-determination provisions subsequently elaborated in treaties, GA declarations, election-monitoring practices, and peacebuilding and good governance programs of UN entities and regional organizations.[35] In that context, the SG's mission to Nigeria could be seen as a step in the larger international legal project of securing an entitlement, if not right, to democratic governance.

Kofi Annan's good offices surrounding the Israeli withdrawal from Southern Lebanon in April 2000 also had important legal consequences.

Over a period of several months, the SG was directly involved in facilitating that withdrawal and ensuring it met the requirements of SC Resolutions 425 and 426. He insisted on official written notification by Israel to alleviate suspicion that the pull-out would not be complete, he set out the terms of what full compliance would entail, he had his field representatives and cartographers draw a "blue line" beyond which Israel had to withdraw, and he certified the withdrawal once it took place.[36] All of this represented the SG's determination of what SC Resolution 425 required from both a legal and policy perspective, and it effectively set the parameters of debate and deliberations within the SC.

In what may well go down as the hallmark of his secretary-generalship, Annan has spoken often on human rights. A recent example concerns the U.S. stance on the International Criminal Court (ICC). When the United States threatened to veto the extension of the Bosnia mission unless the SC exempted U.S. peacekeepers from jurisdiction of the ICC, the SG sent a letter to U.S. Secretary of State Colin Powell objecting that the U.S. demand would undermine both the cause of international criminal justice and the institution of peacekeeping.[37] The resolution ultimately adopted (Resolution 1422) provided a one-year deferral rather than blanket exemption for nationals of nonparties to the ICC. Even more influential were his actions on East Timor. At the height of the violence that followed the vote on independence in August 1999, the SG called on Indonesia to accept an intervention force, adding that those responsible must be called to account for "what could amount to . . . crimes against humanity." Human Rights Watch was so impressed, it labeled the SG's statement the "Annan Doctrine."[38]

Annan's most lasting contributions to discourse about the connection between peace and human rights are likely to be those made in the context of the Kosovo crisis. In June 1998, the SG characterized events in Kosovo as reminiscent of the "ghastly scenario" that took place in Bosnia,[39] and six months later told the North Atlantic Council that "the bloody wars of the last decade have left us no illusions about . . . the need to use force, when all other means have failed." These and other statements were relied on by NATO Secretary-General Solana[40] and British secretary of state for defense George Robinson (Solana's successor), who said later that they provided "the moral imperative" from which "flowed the legal justification" for the air war.[41]

Throughout the period of the NATO bombing campaign, the SG strove to ensure two elements remained in the discourse: the imperative to act in the face of massive human rights violations, and the fundamental role of the SC as the preeminent body responsible for international peace and security. On the day the bombing started, the SG issued the following carefully crafted statement:

> It is indeed tragic that diplomacy has failed, but there are times when the use of force may be legitimate in the pursuit of peace. . . . But as Secretary-General I have many times pointed out, not just in relation to Kosovo, that under the Charter the Security Council has primary responsibility for maintaining international peace and security—and this is explicitly acknowledged in the North Atlantic Treaty. Therefore the Council should be involved in any decision to resort to force.

He spoke in similar terms at the Human Rights Commission on 7 April and again on 18 May in a speech on intervention at the Centennial of the Hague Peace Conference.[42]

Both sides of the equation—the need to confront human rights violations and the authority of the SC—were noted and used by governments in their deliberations within and outside the SC.[43]

The SG also contributed to the more general discourse on humanitarian intervention at the start of the 1999 GA session where, reflecting on the SC's inaction in Rwanda and its lack of unity over Kosovo, he stated "the core challenge to the Security Council and the UN as a whole in the next century is to forge unity behind the principle that massive and systematic violations of human rights—wherever they take place—cannot be allowed to stand."[44] His purpose was to launch a debate on the issue of humanitarian intervention (he often drew an analogy to the "talking stick"), a debate that was joined initially through reactions in the GA itself and then later outside UN circles. Two blue-ribbon panels were established, the Independent International Commission on Kosovo and the International Commission on Intervention and State Sovereignty.[45] The latter was in direct response to what the co-chairmen called "the Secretary-General's challenge." Both commissions brought together respected figures from around the world, connected to officialdom but independent. They are in a sense institutionalized expressions of the interpretive community in that the members were chosen precisely because they are recognized experts and distinguished figures whose views on these matters deserve a hearing.

Finally, in the aftermath of September 11, 2001, the SG has made a number of legally significant statements. In a *New York Times* op-ed he offered a multipronged message that highlighted the UN's solidarity with the U.S. fight against terrorism, while stressing the importance of building a broad international coalition for whatever action is taken, in order to ensure global legitimacy while not creating new divisions between and within societies.[46] The president of the SC stated after informal consultations with the SC that the SG's piece "reflects exactly the general mood and the general will not only of the SC but certainly of the full membership."[47] When the U.S. military strikes in Afghanistan began, the SG recalled the SC's reaffirmation of the right of self-defense in respect to the September 11 attacks and observed that "the states concerned have set their current military action in Afghanistan in that context."[48] This comes close to an endorsement of the U.S. position that the strikes in Afghanistan were justified under Article 51 of the charter. It soon became apparent that this position also reflected the mood of the international community, as the responses of governments and organizations around the world illustrate.[49] The SG's statement to the GA on 12 September 2002, was the first of a number of interventions he made in the complex legal questions surrounding the events of September 11 and subsequent military action in Afghanistan and Iraq.

The Sources of the Secretary-General's Persuasive Powers

As these episodes illustrate, the SG's influence within the interpretive community depends not on material power but on the authority he is able to command. Authority as a source of power or influence is connected to legitimacy.[50] The SG's persuasiveness—his ability to get others to defer to his judgment—depends in part on the formal authority of the office and in part on the normative acceptability of positions he takes. Thus his political influence is closely tied to his legal role. The SG does not have a constitutional mandate to resolve interpretive disputes in the SC, but there is nothing in the charter that prohibits him from venturing a legal opinion. All SGs have done so cautiously, reflecting a keen sense of the limits of the role and a concern about squandering the legitimacy—and leverage—the office provides. Members of the SC, particularly the most powerful, do not typically want the SG to weigh in on interpretive disputes among them. Legal positions taken by SGs are in no way determinative, but they do lend political comfort to those on whose side the SG comes down and can complicate the efforts of those he goes against. Within the interpretive community that surrounds the SC, the opinion of the SG carries weight. Ironically, the reluctance of SGs to use their leverage is tangible evidence of the power of interpretive communities.

In a profile in the *New York Times Magazine,* James Traub was struck by Kofi Annan's "slightly mysterious powers of persuasion."[51] These powers are rendered less mysterious if one considers the self-conscious and unusually keen sense he has of the normative role of the UN, a point highlighted in his Millennium Report.[52] As the executive head of the UN, the SG is in a unique position to use the norms embodied in the charter as an instrument. Indeed SGs have seen themselves as spokespersons for the values of the charter and have assumed that their political functions must be conducted in accordance with charter principles. As Pérez de Cuéllar put it: "The aim of traditional diplomacy was often limited to a stable balance of power: whether the balance conformed to justice was a lesser concern. But peace as envisaged by the UN Charter is a just peace . . . The SG should have no part in any diplomatic deal or undertaking which ignores the principles of the Charter or relevant pronouncement of the competent organs of the UN."[53]

If the influence of the SG is built in part on his normative authority, how more precisely is that authority exercised? Three sources of leverage can be identified, all of which illustrate the nexus between the SG's political and legal roles. The first is "diplomacy backed by force." The SG himself is in no position to threaten the use of force, but the SC can. The 1998 MOU with Iraq was, by the SG's own admission, due in part to the U.S./UK threat of airstrikes. Upon his return, he publicly described President Clinton and Prime Minister Blair as "perfect peacemakers" because they had threatened force in order to achieve peace, a theme he echoed later when NATO began its bombing campaign over Kosovo. He felt justified in uttering these unusual (for an SG) words because they reflected a widespread mood in the international community. Even Russia, the closest thing Iraq had to an ally in the SC at the time, made it clear that Iraq's noncompliance with Resolution 687 could trigger the use of force, and that the SG's trip was a last chance.[54] The relative international consensus about the need to respond to Iraq's intransigence strengthened the SG's hand. He could fulfill what he saw as his diplomatic duty in traveling to Baghdad, confident that the threat of force backing his efforts carried the legitimacy of a relatively unified SC in demanding Iraqi compliance.

Second, the SG can use his authority to mobilize shame. Public condemnation stings more when it comes from the SG than an interested party, government, or nongovernmental organization (NGO).

Similarly, private threats to expose intransigence are a source of leverage in peacemaking efforts. The SG used this in his dealings with President Bacharuddin Jusuf Habibie over East Timor and then acted on it publicly in his statement of 10 September condemning Indonesia's inability to control the militias. The SG's legitimacy as broker of the agreement that led to the vote on independence, and the strength of his normative case, brought unique pressure to bear on Indonesian authorities. His coming in "as a friend" (in Habibie's words) complemented the material threats leveled by the United States and others; it is likely that one kind of leverage would not have succeeded without the other.

Relating to both of the above points is the credibility that comes with being an insider to high-level consultations on international crises (often by telephone). The SG, Hammarskjöld once said, is the "trustee of the secrets of all the nations."[55] Walter Lippman called him a "father confessor to member governments . . . the man in whom they confide, and who knows, therefore, from continued, private privileged information, the real position in an international controversy."[56] Government leaders confide not to confess their sins but to build or relieve pressure for a certain course of action. The SG becomes a channel of communication, a conveyor of signals, that he can present as the sentiment of those with the will and ability to act ("your friends are not going to be able to help you if you don't bend; your enemies are looking for an excuse to hurt you"). These are warnings, not threats: the SG does not threaten to cause X, but rather says X is likely to happen unless his interlocutor does (or refrains from doing) Y.[57] It is a tool Annan wielded in both East Timor and Nigeria. He was credible because his interlocutors knew that he knew how those with material power were likely to act. And the warnings were heeded in part because they were not of some arbitrary or self-serving action, but of a coordinated position based on an emerging international consensus about the right and wrong of a situation (the extreme violence in East Timor and the years of dictatorship in Nigeria). Coming from the SG of the United Nations, a message like that carries weight.

Conclusion

Most scholars who write on the SG consider the political context to be the ultimate determinant of his influence, and some note the irony that the early post–Cold War era may have constricted the independent political role of the office because the SC, no longer paralyzed, is less inclined to "let Dag do it."[58] Viewing the SG as a legal actor provides a more nuanced picture. The operational activities of the UN have expanded dramatically in the field of peace and security. The increased number and complexity of peace operations since 1989, combined with vague mandates and considerable delegated authority, require the SG to exercise broad discretion in interpreting and implementing SC resolutions, as well as the UN Charter and associated law. These operational decisions and activities, by giving content to inchoate norms, have contributed to an evolving climate—a climate that provides the SG a more solid foundation for intervening in legal debates. Changes in the normative climate, meanwhile, have been matched by changes in the political dynamics at the UN. The relative "power shift" from central governments to transgovernmental networks, NGOs, the business community, and other sources of global influence means that the UN's constituency has broadened.[59] These new actors are increasingly important participants and partners in UN deliberations and activities. The interpretive community associated with UN law is now much larger than the handful of diplomats seated at the table and their political masters at home. The political figures must appeal to networks of interested officials, experts, and citizens who, among other things, sit in judgment of legal claims. These networks both constrain and empower the SG. They constrain by setting the terms of discourse within which he—and all other international actors—must operate; they empower by creating new channels of influence, enabling the SG to project the values and norms that emerge from the UN-centered process of global governance.

Notes

1. Address by Secretary-General Kofi Annan to the General Assembly, SG/SM/8378, GA/10045 (12 September 2002).

2. S/RES/1366 (30 August 2001), para. 10.

3. A proposal to include that power in Article 99 of the charter was defeated by a vote of 16–13. United Nations Conference on International Organization VII, p. 163. Cited in Bruno Simma, ed., *The Charter of the United Nations: A Commentary* (Oxford: Oxford University Press, 1995), p. 1046.

4. As Kofi Annan recently said, "in the end, the only means I have is reason and persuasion. I cannot call on an air force or an army." Quoted in William Shawcross, *Deliver Us From Evil: Peacekeepers, Warlords and a World of Endless Conflict* (New York: Simon and Schuster, 2000), p. 278.

5. On the political content of Article 99, see Report of the Preparatory Commission of the UN (PC/20, 23 Dec. 1945), chap. VIII, sect. 2, para. 16. Scholarly comment goes back to Stephen Schwebel, *The Secretary-General of the UN: His Political Powers and Practice* (New York: Greenwood Press, 1952). More recent works include Thomas Boudreau, *Sheathing the Sword* (New York: Greenwood Press, 1991); B. Rivlin and L. Gordenker, eds., *The Challenging Role of the UN Secretary-General* (Westport, Connecticut: Praeger, 1993); Thomas Franck and George Nolte, "The Good Offices Function of the UN Secretary-General," in A. Roberts and B. Kingsbury, eds., *United Nations Divided World* (Oxford: Clarendon Press, 1993, 2d ed.); and Edward Newman, *The UN Secretary-General from the Cold War to the New Era* (New York: St. Marten's Press, 1998). See also the memoirs by or biographies about the various SGs themselves, including Trygve Lie, *In the Cause of Peace* (New York: MacMillan, 1954); Brian Urquhart, *Hammarskjöld* (London: Bodley Head, 1972); and Boutros Boutros-Ghali, *Unvanquished: A UN-US Saga* (New York: Random House, 1999).

6. Javier Pérez de Cuéllar, "The Role of the UN Secretary-General" in Roberts and Kingsbury, eds., *United Nations Divided World*, pp. 130–131.

7. Report of the Preparatory Commission of the UN.

8. Newman, *The UN Secretary-General from the Cold War to the New Era,* p. 19.

9. Schwebel, *The Secretary-General of the UN*, p. 94.

10. Dag Hammarskjöld, "Lecture at Oxford University," 30 May 1961, in W. Foote, ed., *The Servant of Peace: A Selection of Speeches and Statements of Dag Hammarskjöld* (London: Bodley Head, 1962), p. 335.

11. Boudreau, *Sheathing the Sword*, p. 42.

12. Security Council Official Records (SCOR), 13th year, 837th meeting, 22 July 1958, p. 4.

13. Quoted in Simma, *The Charter of the United Nations*, p. 1054. On the Bahrain initiative, see Brian Urquhart, *Ralph Bunche: An American Life* (New York: W. W. Norton & Co., 1993), p. 429.

14. Pérez de Cuéllar, "The Role of the UN Secretary-General," p. 126. See also the chapters by Alan James, Lawrence Finkelstein, and Innis Claude in Rivlin and Gordenker, eds., *The Challenging Role of the UN Secretary-General*, p. 5.

15. Quoted in *New York Times*, Vol. 10, January 1991, p. 1.

16. Boutros Boutros-Ghali, "Global Leadership After the Cold War," *Foreign Affairs* Vol. 75, No. 2 (1996): 98. As a matter of practice, senior secretariat posts tend to be allocated to particular countries, and nationals of the Permanent Five always have their share of high profile positions, but these individuals do not represent their countries and—especially in the post–Cold War era—most take very seriously the injunction not to take instructions from governments.

17. Quoted in William Shawcross, *Deliver Us From Evil*, p. 264. See also, James Traub, "Kofi Annan's Biggest Headache," *New York Times Magazine*, 5 April 1998.

18. Shawcross, *Deliver Us From Evil*, p. 263.

19. Franck and Nolte, "The Good Offices Function of the UN Secretary-General," p. 180.

20. Council on Foreign Relations speech, 1999. Significantly, this conception of impartiality was picked up by the Brahimi Panel in its Report on UN Peace Operations, A/55/305, S/2000/809 (21 Aug. 2000), para. 50.

21. United Nations Conference on International Organization, Report of Rapporteur of Committee IV/2, 1945. For a good review of the literature on the possibility of judicial review by the ICJ, see Jose Alvarez, "Judging the Security Council," *American Journal of International Law* Vol. 90, No. 1 (1996).

22. Ian Johnstone, "Security Council Deliberations: The Power of the Better Argument," *European Journal of International Law* Vol. 14, No. 3 (2003). On justificatory discourse, see Abram Chayes and Antonia Handler Chayes, *The New Sovereignty* (Cambridge: Harvard University Press, 1995); Thomas Franck, *Fairness in International Law and Institutions* (Oxford: Oxford University Press, 1995). The notion of interpretive communities comes from Stanley Fish, *Doing What Comes Naturally: Change, Rhetoric and the Practice of Theory in Literary and Legal Studies* (Durham, N.C.: Duke University Press, 1989).

23. Stanley Fish, Ronald Dworkin, and Cass Sunstein, despite their different legal theoretical approaches, all make the same point. See for example Fish, *Doing What Comes Naturally*, p. 116; Ronald Dworkin, *Law's Empire* (Cambridge: The Belknap Press of Harvard University Press, 1986), p. 52; Cass Sunstein, *The Partial Constitution* (Cambridge: Cambridge University Press, 1993), p. 113.

24. Fish, *Doing What Comes Naturally*, p. 116.

25. For an overview of the arguments, see Johnstone, "Security Council Deliberations." See also Oscar Schachter, *International Law in Theory and Practice* (Dordrecht, The Netherlands: Kluwer Academic Publishers, 1991); Harold Koh, "Why Do Nations Obey International Law?" *The Yale Law Journal* Vol. 106 (1997), p. 2599.

26. Andrew Hurrell, "International Society and the Study of Regimes," in Volker Rittberger, ed., *Regime Theory and International Relations* (Oxford: Clarendon Press, 1993).

27. UN Doc S/4389 (18 July 1960).

28. Franck and Nolte, "The Good Offices Function of the UN Secretary-General," p. 228.

29. Ibid., p. 177.

30. Simma, *The Charter of the United Nations*, p. 1055.

31. Olga Pellecier, "The United Nations in Central America," in Rivlin and Gordenker, eds., *The Challenging Role of the UN Secretary-General*, p. 185.

32. For U.S. and UK statements on their interpretation of Resolution 688, see Marc Weller, ed., *Iraq and Kuwait: The Hostilities and Their Aftermath* (Cambridge: Grotius Publications Ltd., 1993), pp. 714–720.

33. Remarks made by the SG on entering UN Headquarters, 10 May 1991. See also the remarks by legal counsel to the secretary-general, Carl August Fleischauer, at "The Year of International Law in Review," 86th Annual Meeting of the American Society of International Law (Buffalo: William S. Hein & Co.), 4 April 1992.

34. UN Department of Public Information Briefing, 14 January 1993, p. 2.

35. Boutros Boutros-Ghali, Agenda for Democratization, available online at www.library.yale.edu/un/un3d3.htm (posted December 1996). For a good

edited volume on this issue, see Gregory Fox and Brad Roth, eds., *Democratic Governance and International Law* (Cambridge: Cambridge University Press, 2000).

36. See UN Documents S/2000/322 (17 April 2000); S/2000/460 (22 May 2000); and S/2000/590 (16 June 2000).

37. Letter from the SG to Secretary of State Colin Powell, 3 July 2002.

38. *Human Rights Watch World Report* (New York: Human Rights Watch, 1999), p. 3.

39. "Secretary-General reflects on 'Intervention' in 35th Annual Ditchley Foundation Lecture," SG/SM/6613/Rev.1 (26 June 1998).

40. NATO Press Release [99] 11 (28 March 1999).

41. Speech by Secretary of State for Defence, The Rt. Honorable George Robertson, Royal United Services Institute, 29 June 1999, available online at http://news/press/news_press_notice.asp?newsItem_id=518 (accessed 14 July 2003).

42. Kofi Annan, "The Effectiveness of the International Rule of Law in Maintaining International Peace and Security," SG/SM/6997 (18 May 1999).

43. For example, the North Atlantic Council issued a statement on 24 April that "NATO's military action against the FRY supports the political aims of the international community, which were reaffirmed in recent statements by the UN Secretary-General." *NATO Review* (Summer 1999), p. D1.

44. SG/SM/136, GA/9596.

45. *Independent International Commission on Kosovo, The Kosovo Report: Conflict, International Response, Lessons Learned* (Oxford: Oxford University Press, 2000) and *Addendum to the Kosovo Report* (Oxford: Oxford University Press, 2001); *International Commission on Intervention and State Sovereignty, The Responsibility to Protect* (International Development Research Center, 2001).

46. *New York Times*, 21 Sept. 2001.

47. UN Newsservice, Press Statement on Terrorism by President of Security Council UN Doc. SC/7152 (21 Sept. 2001).

48. SG/SM/7985 (8 August 2001).

49. For a sample of the responses, see *New York Times*, 8–11 October 2001.

50. Ian Hurd, "Legitimacy and Authority in International Politics," *International Organization* Vol. 53, No. 2 (1999): 379–408; Michael Barnett and Martha Finnemore, "The Politics, Power and Pathologies of International Organizations," *International Organization* Vol. 53, No. 4 (1999), pp. 699–732.

51. Traub, "Kofi Annan's Biggest Headache."

52. "We the Peoples," Report of the Secretary-General to the Millennium Assembly of the UN, A/54/2000 (27 March 2000), paras. 9, 45 and pp. 320–325.

53. Pérez de Cuéllar, "The Role of the UN Secretary-General," p. 133. See also, Donald Puchala, "The Secretary-General and His Special Representatives," in Rivlin and Gordenker, eds., *The Challenging Role of the UN Secretary-General*, p. 89.

54. See the statement by Ambassador Lavrov quoted in *Shawcross, Deliver Us From Evil*, p. 266.

55. Quoted by Alan James, "The Secretary-General as an Independent Political Actor," in Rivlin and Gordenker, eds., *Deliver Us From Evil*, p. 28.

56. Quoted by Benjamin Rivlin, "The Changing International Political Climate and the Secretary-General," in Rivlin and Gordenker, eds., *The Challenging Role of the UN Secretary-General*, p. 4.

57. On threats and warnings, see Jon Elster, "The Strategic Uses of Argument," in Kenneth Arrow, Robert H. Mnookin, Lee Ross, Amos Tversky, and Robert Wilson, eds., *Barriers to Conflict Resolution* (New York: W. W. Norton & Co., 1995).

58. See for example, Innis Claude, "Reflections on the Role of the UN Secretary-General," in Rivlin and Gordenker, eds., *The Challenging Role of the UN Secretary-General*, pp. 253–254. Concerns about SC paralysis have reemerged in context of the recent Iraq crisis, but even if the SC were to return to its Cold War lethargy, an enhancement of the SG's role as a result is unlikely.

59. Jessica T. Matthews, "Power Shift," *Foreign Affairs* Vol. 76, No. 1 (1997); Ann-Marie Slaughter, "The Real New World Order," *Foreign Affairs* Vol. 76, No. 5 (1997); Martha Finnemore and Kathryn Sikkink, "International Norm Dynamics and Political Change," *International Organization* Vol. 52, No. 4 (1998); Wolfgang Reinicke, *Global Public Policy: Governing Without Government?* (Washington, D.C.: Brookings Institution, 1998).

5

Myths of Membership: The Politics of Legitimation in UN Security Council Reform

Ian Hurd

THE NEED TO EXPAND THE UN SECURITY COUNCIL IS USUALLY justified as necessary to update Council membership in light of changes in world politics. The mismatch between the existing membership and the increasingly diverse population of states is said to delegitimatize the Council. This rests on an implicit hypothesis about the source of institutional legitimacy. This article surveys reform proposals and finds five distinct claims about the connection between membership and legitimacy, each of which is either logically inconsistent or empirically implausible. If formal membership is indeed the key to institutional legitimacy, the causal link remains at best indeterminate, and we may have to look elsewhere for a theory of legitimation. We must also look for explanations for why the language of legitimation is so prevalent in the rhetoric of Council reform.

Among the competing proposals for reforming the UN Security Council, one theme is a near constant: that the Council's legitimacy is in peril unless the body can be reformed to account for recent changes in world politics. This consensus is driven by a number of developments: geopolitical changes (in the distribution of military and economic power), systemic changes after decolonization (which multiplied the number of UN members), and normative changes (in the value given to diversity, equity, and representation).

Reprinted from *Global Governance* 14, no. 2 (2008): 199–217. © 2008 Lynne Rienner Publishers. Reprinted by permission of the publisher.

Most arguments in favor of Council expansion identify the gap between Council membership and international realities as a threat specifically to the *legitimacy* of the Council. The gap is an objective fact, but the link to legitimacy is what gives it its political salience and has made it a controversial matter in world politics. This article investigates this link. Conventional wisdom holds that the Council's outdated membership causes delegitimation but the causal mechanics behind this delegitimation are rarely explained.

The process by which institutions become legitimized or delegitimized is a hotly contested matter among organizational sociologists, and yet in the Council reform debates the connection between legitimacy and membership has been treated as unproblematic, even self-evident. I set out below a number of potential causal mechanisms for delegitimation of the Council, which I derive from existing proposals for Council reform. Behind every proposal for Council reform is a different model for how legitimacy, effectiveness, and membership fit together. Comparing these models is important to understanding the stalemate in Council reform and the utility of legitimation claims in world politics.

This article compares the various claims made in Council reform proposals regarding the effects of membership change on the legitimacy of the Council. Its goal is to isolate the discrete elements that make up these claims and assess their logical consistency. All Council reform claims contain hypotheses about the effects of membership change on Council effectiveness. The first section defends my claim that the conventional wisdom is that the current membership structure constitutes a *legitimacy* crisis for the Council. The second section extracts five distinct empirical hypotheses about the relationship between membership and legitimacy as put forward in defense of Council expansion. It typologizes these claims according to their underlying theory of legitimacy. These are all, in principle, testable, though the difficulties inherent in measuring legitimacy or its effects mean that perhaps in practice the most we can do is look for logical consistency. The third section addresses the question, which among these claims are empirically plausible and logically sustainable? In conclusion, I speculate about the political interests that motivate these arguments and suggest implications about trade-offs, rhetorical entrapment, and legitimacy in international organizations.

My goal in this article is not to find empirical evidence by which we might test theories of legitimation. Rather, I seek to compare the logic of the legitimacy claims themselves, taking advantage of the fact that they are cast in terms of generalizable principles. As such, I necessarily leave aside several interesting questions. For one, I do not examine the connection between the effectiveness of the Council and its legitimacy. That these two are mutually implicated is obvious but the link between membership and legitimacy is conceptually prior to, and separate from, the connection between legitimacy and effectiveness. For another, I do not focus on the privileges of permanent over nonpermanent membership, including the veto. The role of the veto for new members is important in the debate on enlargement, but it is generally kept out of the framing of the legitimation problems of the Council. No states link a defense of the veto for new members to arguments about legitimacy. For that reason, and because the High-Level Panel, among others, have largely set it aside as well, the veto does not play a large role in my analysis.[1] In focusing on the internal logic of the claim that changing the Council's membership will affect its legitimacy, I seek first to understand the causal mechanisms implicit in such a claim and then to chart the implications that arise from those mechanisms.

Legitimacy, Inequality, and Council Reform

By far the most common malady identified at the Council is that the membership of the Council contains such inequalities that it threatens to delegitimize the body as a whole. The High-Level Panel said that "the effectiveness of the global collective security system . . . depends ultimately not only on the legality of decisions but on common perceptions of their legitimacy"[2] and that the anachronistic structure of membership rules "diminishes support for Security Council decisions."[3] Kofi Annan has expressed "the view, long held by the majority, that a change in the Council's composition is needed to make it more broadly representative of the international community as a whole, as well as of the geopolitical realities of today, and thereby more legitimate in the eyes of the world."[4] The Open-Ended Working Group (OEWG) reported in 1995 a pervasive view among delegations that "an increase in the permanent membership would strengthen the United Nations and increase its legitimacy through bringing the organization closer to present-day global realities."[5] Changing the formal membership, it is said, is a necessary step to increasing, or to halting the loss of, the legitimacy of the Council and of its resolutions.

These claims treat the Council's legitimacy as a precious resource that is important to its effectiveness. Being seen as legitimate is important to the Council because, it is said, it increases the likelihood that states will respect the decisions it makes.[6] A more legitimate Council might be better at encouraging states to implement economic sanctions, or to contribute resources to peace missions, or to accept a Council-mandated solution to a dispute. Without coercive resources or financial power of its own, the Council must rely on its legitimacy to increase state compliance with its decisions.[7]

Legitimacy is rarely defined by those who use it to justify Council reform. As I use it here, it refers to the belief by states that the Council has the right to make authoritative decisions in its area of legal competence.[8] The "right" in question is a normative one, rather than a legal one, and so states that hold this belief will feel a normative obligation to respect the decisions of the Council. The belief rests within individual states but has its most significant effects when it is shared by many states. Four elements of the definition should be underscored: first, this is a *belief* of states, and so it is necessarily subjective and psychological—outsiders might disagree with one's belief, but the behavioral effects depend only on what the actor thinks, not on the assessments of others; second, the belief is held by *states,* and so I presume the corporate agency of the state; third, the belief is about the *right* of the body to make decisions, and this puts the Council in a position of authority over states, distinct from questions about its capacity to act or its effectiveness when it acts; and, finally, the legal structures of the Charter set a limit on the areas over which this right extends. The existence of this belief has consequences for how world politics proceeds. Disagreements on the consequences are examined below, but a conventional view is that a legitimate organization will find itself with higher levels of compliance, lower costs to enforcement, and higher levels of respect among its audience. All of these should add to its power.

The connection between legitimacy and Council reform is a chain of four linked steps. First, it is said that the inequalities inherent in the structure of Council membership are a drag on the legitimacy of the Council. The different powers given to permanent and nonpermanent members keep it from achieving the maximum potential level of legitimacy that might in principle be available to an international organization. Second, this lack of legitimacy is then said to reduce the effectiveness of the Council as a whole. This step in the argument relies on a theory of the power of international organizations (IOs) that identifies legitimacy as a crucial element of their corporate existence.[9] Third, the argument suggests that changing the Council's membership, or changing its membership rules, would remedy the legitimation deficit and so, by the fourth step, the Council's increased legitimacy will lead to a consequent increase in its effectiveness. Together, these stages constitute a thoroughly consequentialist defense of the importance of legitimacy for the Council: legitimacy is to be valued in the Council because it produces an outcome (greater Council power) that is thought to be desirable.

These are four distinct causal claims, with distinct independent and dependent variables. Steps 1 and 3 make up a mirror-image pair, as do Steps 2 and 4. The four can be summarized as follows:

Step 1: inequality → loss of legitimacy
Step 2: loss of legitimacy → loss of power or effectiveness
Step 3: change in structure → increase in legitimacy
Step 4: increase in legitimacy → increase in effectiveness

This causal chain as applied to the Security Council is derived from a more general model of legitimation in sociological theory but deviates from it in crucial respects. Step 1 is based on a central tenet of modern sociology—that inequality in a society reduces its stability. Disparities between groups in wealth, power, or status are thought to generate social discontent and thus instability, and the modern tradition from Marx to Weber to Habermas presents legitimacy as a countervailing force that can buttress the unequal social order. In this tradition, inequality is not itself seen as a threat to legitimacy but rather as a threat to the stability of the regime; as James Olson and Carolyn Hafer say, "When a group or system distributes inequalities unequally among its members, those members (or most of them) must view the inequalities as justified if the system is to survive."[10] Legitimacy is a device to mitigate the threat. Legitimation is one source of reasons for individuals to accept the existing inequalities of society as appropriate (or natural, or defensible).[11] It does not *eliminate* the inequalities; rather it *justifies* them and reduces their political salience. In this light, legitimacy is always a conservative force that acts to defend favored values against revolution.

The absence of legitimacy is therefore a dangerous condition for a social order based on inequalities, and Step 2 of the chain specifies the dangers. Without legitimacy, a society must rely on other tools to maintain order, notably coercion and inducement. This is particularly problematic for the Security Council, which cannot reliably use coercion to exert compliance with its decisions, and it has no resources to use as inducements. A Council without legitimacy would therefore have few tools with which to win states' support and so would quickly lose power, influence, and effectiveness in world politics.

The sociological story about legitimacy says that legitimation is a cure for the instability that arises from social inequality. The Council reform story suggests that the inequalities of the Council are damaging to its legitimacy and thus to its power, and so reducing the inequalities is a step toward maximizing the Council's effective authority (Step 3). The difference is that the latter believes that it is possible, or desirable, to reduce the inequalities in the society. Nevertheless, the key assumptions behind the two approaches are the same: that inequality is a threat to the effectiveness of the institution and that enhancing its legitimacy leads to an increase in its effectiveness (Step 4).

[handwritten margin note: doesn't work in reverse?]

The practical dimension of the debate over the Council rests on Step 3. Competing theories of the link between Council structure and Council legitimacy produce very different proposals for Council reform. The policy debate is at present almost entirely over the question, What changes in the structure of the Council are most likely to lead to an increase in its legitimacy? The following sections address these arguments, first by specifying the competing answers to the question and then by assessing their empirical plausibility as accounts of legitimation. Resolving whether Step 3 is true or not is crucial to the institutional design of the Council and to the future of the UN more generally.

Council Structure and Legitimacy: Five Hypotheses

Ian Clark suggests that legitimacy is essential in resolving the question of who can rightfully be a member of the society. For him, one function of a consensus about legitimacy within society is that it provides a criterion for deciding "right membership."[12] In the debates on Council reform, however, the two concepts are usually put in the opposite order: manipulating the structure of the Council is believed to have effects on the level of legitimacy of the Council as perceived by the audience of nation-states. The views cited in the previous section all agree that the formal structure of the Council is an important factor in determining its legitimacy. In what ways might this be so?

The "empirical mechanics" by which changes in Council structure are hypothesized to affect Council legitimacy differ between different proposals. There are two main classes of claims for how this works, distinguished between the ideas that (1) *membership* produces legitimacy and (2) *deliberation* produces legitimacy. Variants of each are possible and they sometimes combine with each other, as we shall see, but a first cut into typologizing the claims must organize them according to whether they prioritize the legitimating effects of the practice of deliberation or of the formal structure of institutional membership. The two produce very different images of the work of the Council and therefore different policy prescriptions for improving it.

Membership

In 2005, the United States called for "a Security Council that looks like the world of 2005."[13] This could be operationalized in a number of ways, but the most logical is that the membership of the Council must be updated to reflect changes in the population of nation-states. The central element of these claims is a theory that the formal presence of certain states in the Council's membership will contribute to legitimizing the Council, and that conversely, maintaining the present structure contributes to delegitimation. The goal of "equitable geographic distribution" is enshrined already in the selection of nonpermanent members, and it is not challenged by any state; but differences in how the clause is understood produce different versions of the "membership" argument on reform.[14]

Three variants of the membership argument are in common circulation, each premised on different assumptions about *which* states' presence or absence affects the Council's legitimacy. First, many argue that legitimation may come from the degree to which the Council faithfully *represents* the composition of the population of states in the General Assembly.[15] A Council that poorly reflects the population of states would be illegitimate. For instance, the chairs of the OEWG have stated "that the effectiveness, credibility and legitimacy of the work of the Security Council depend on its representative character."[16] The ambassador of Germany has said that "the legitimacy of the Security Council is based on its representativeness."[17] Bruce Russett hints at it when he says that "if the Security Council adds Germany and Japan as permanent members without also adding some major less-developed countries it risks losing legitimacy in the eyes of the great majority of UN member states."[18] These arguments are sometimes explicitly connected to a broader theory of democracy, but this is not logically necessary;

whether an institution that is more representative is necessarily more democratic is a conceptually separate claim that should be evaluated on its own.

Second, legitimacy may come from having a Council that encompasses the *diversity* that exists in the General Assembly.[19] Distinct from representativeness, diversity might require over representing tiny minorities from the General Assembly in the interest of encompassing the full range of states and views into the Council. Reflecting diversity was one of the original motivations for the Council reform drive in the 1990s. If the goal is to have inside the Council as full a sample as possible of the views in the General Assembly, then we would be justified in adding states based on how different they are from the current Council members. We would strive to maximize the differences among Council members, and this could result in a very different composition of the Council than might come about if one pursued the goal of representativeness. A number of countries in the Non-Aligned Movement (NAM) have argued that global diversity should be reflected in the composition of the Council. Cuba, for instance, has held that the diversity within a regional group should be taken into account when deciding how many seats the region should hold, implying that the purpose of a regional group is to project the region's diversity into the Council. Singapore has asked whether adding more large countries to the Council as permanent members is really progress, arguing instead that small states must be included in the interest of diversity.

Both diversity and representativeness depend on a comparison with an appropriate referent population. Specifying this group is crucial and yet unavoidably political and controversial. The results will be different if we believe that the Council membership should faithfully represent the population of states in the General Assembly or the population of people in the world; striving to accommodate the diversity of world religions is different from accommodating the diversity of national economic capacities. These questions cannot be settled definitively outside the political process of negotiation. Most reform schemes based on membership agree that representativeness or diversity should be assessed compared to the regional distribution that exists in the General Assembly. This assumes that the relevant measure is *regional,* that states share their most important interests with others in their region rather than with those outside the region. Singapore, as cited above, suggests a different metric: small states have more in common with other small states than with large states, regardless of region.

Finally, legitimacy may be a product of having one's own country occupy a seat on the Council. Formal presence in a decision making body may lead a state to support its decisions more than it would if it had not been present. If the change is a product of the *legitimating* effect of the presence, then we could sustain the argument that adding new members to the Council could increase its legitimacy in their eyes and thus add to its effectiveness. This argument, with its obviously self-serving implications, is rarely made publicly by diplomats, but its logic underpins the argument that only with a seat in the Council will a state's population continue to support paying its UN dues.

For all three variants of the membership argument, the crucial element is a conviction that the formal structure of Council membership is the key source of legitimation or delegitimation. It is the formal, legal presence of certain states, or of certain kinds of states, that affects the institution's legitimacy. This structural view is in sharp contrast with the procedural view of the "deliberative" argument, discussed next.

Deliberation

Many Council reform proposals interpose the concept of deliberation between the formal membership of the Council and the legitimacy of its outputs. Deliberation, in this view, is the source of legitimacy for organizations and opening up the Council's membership is a means to increasing its deliberative qualities. This view sees the Council as primarily a deliberative chamber rather than an interest-aggregating body. [assumption]

The distinction between this approach and the membership approach above is clear when we trace the path for getting to legitimation: for the deliberative approach, participation in decision making legitimizes outcomes; for the membership view, formal presence in the decision making body legitimizes outcomes. If legitimacy is increased by deliberativeness, then changing the membership of the Council could lead to increased deliberation. Other strategies for increasing deliberation are contained in Cluster II issues in Council reform.

That deliberation might legitimize collective decisions is an important component of many theories of democracy. Amy Gutmann and Dennis Thompson argue that "deliberation contributes to the legitimacy of decisions made under scarcity . . . [because] the hard choices that democratic governments make in these circumstances should be more acceptable even to those who receive less than they deserve if everyone's claims have been considered on their merits."[20] James Fearon hypothesizes that "perhaps people feel that the decision process is fairer if they are allowed to have a discussion before voting, and this sense of procedural fairness then makes them more inclined to abide by or support the results."[21] This is confirmed by empirical surveys of Americans' attitudes toward legal and political institutions: Tom Tyler finds that "legitimacy is linked to judgments about the fairness of decision-making procedures. People are found to judge the legitimacy of institutions and authorities by focusing on the fairness of the procedures they utilize when making decisions. . . . [This] is demonstrated by their continued compliance with that decision over time, even in situations in which the incentives for complying . . . are weak or non-existent."[22] Deliberation is a key component of procedural fairness.

How does deliberation legitimize? Two mechanisms are possible: through change in the outcomes or through change in the deliberators. Diego Gambetta describes the former and John Dryzek the latter. Gambetta says that the "positive consequences of deliberation primarily concern the distribution of information" and its effect on the decision. He says, "If information and reasoning skills are, for whatever reason, unevenly distributed among deliberators, deliberation improves their allocation and the awareness of the relative merits of different means."[23] Fearon models deliberation as a strategy for lessening the problem of bounded rationality. To the extent that deliberation increases the amount of useful information available to decisionmakers, it should lead to better decisions.[24]

However, "better" decisions might not be the purpose of deliberation. Dryzek finds that "preferences can be transformed by deliberation" and sees the main value of deliberation to be the change it generates in participants themselves.[25] Independent of any effect it has on outcomes, deliberation might also have a "psychological effect," says Fearon, if "the opportunity to have one's say may make one more inclined to support the outcome of the discussion, even if one ends up opposing the collective choice."[26] If this is true, then deliberation might lead to higher rates of compliance regardless of whether it affects the substance of the decision.

Assessing the Five Hypotheses on Legitimacy in Council Reform

Taken together, the deliberative and membership arguments can be organized into five distinct hypotheses for how legitimacy is connected to Council membership. These are that a state will see the Council as more legitimate to the extent that:

H1: the membership of the Council is representative of the General Assembly membership.

H2: the membership of the Council is diverse.

H3: the state is a member of the Council.

H4: the state has an opportunity to participate in deliberations at the Council.

H5: the level of deliberation at the Council is high.

The first three hypotheses are centered on membership, the last two on deliberation. Other hypotheses about legitimation are possible where the independent variable might be changes to working methods or changes in the Council's outputs, but these only indirectly justify a formal change in membership. Article 23 of the Charter ensures that regional diversity is included in membership selection, and these hypotheses provide possible explanations for why that criterion is valued by states.

Hypotheses 1 and 2 are closely related. They differ on the value that they aim to see institutionalized in Council membership, but they share the same structure and the same weaknesses. Both rest on three premises that, if all are true, would make it possible to construct an enlargement scheme that successfully uses representativeness or diversity as a means to legitimize the Council. I trace through the case in terms of "representation" here, and then show that the "diversity" case is essentially the same.

The proposition that the Council's representation of the General Assembly controls its legitimacy rests on three assumptions. First, states must really believe that representation is an important institutional norm. If states are simply posturing in their statements about the importance of representation, then the hypothesis will fail. Assuming they are genuine, we could conclude that states do indeed have an internalized attachment to the value of representation and the international system should, as a result, favor institutions that are believed to be representative. Second, states must agree on what constitutes an appropriate metric for representation. As discussed, disagreement over the metric will lead to substantive differences in assessing the legitimation effects of any particular change in membership. The history of the debates over enlargement seems to show that there is a good deal of disagreement over which dimension of representation is most important, with the result that we may well face a trade-off between increasing the legitimacy of the Council to one audience and reducing it for another. The existence of such a trade-off would mean that the potential legitimating power of representation is small. Finally, the membership change must succeed in increasing representation along this metric. This depends on the particular countries chosen as new members. Not all enlargement schemes would increase representation, and some (such as adding Germany and Japan as permanent members) would create greater disparities of representation along many metrics.

The argument that legitimation is tied to diversity is analogous to that of representation, although the two values they put forward are different. H2 rests on versions of the same three assumptions as H1: that states really do value diversity in international organizations, that they possess a shared understanding of the appropriate metric for diversity, and that the specifics of the proposal do indeed increase diversity.

The degree of plausibility for both H1 and H2 turns out to be heavily dependent on a separate and prior question: Does the international community possess a reasonably consistent agreement on a metric for representation or for diversity? Only if this is true does it make sense to advance these values as a defense of enlargement. The debates over representation and over diversity would likely be more productive if they explicitly addressed the differences among states in their views of the correct metric.

There is less controversy in H3 because the issue of the metric does not arise. If H3 correctly describes the mechanics by which actors perceive legitimacy in institutions, its lesson for the Council is that its legitimacy will always remain limited to those few states that gain seats. Because it identifies legitimation as a product of having one's self-interest satisfied, this argument can justify the inclusion of individual states in the Council but cannot be generalized to all states. The legitimating effect does not extend beyond the particular state(s) added to formal membership. As a result, it is useful to the extent that we believe that the problem of delegitimation for the Council is limited to a few of the most important states but not beyond that. The United States, for instance, has said that its support for a Japanese permanent seat is a result of Japan's financial contribution to the UN. If the Japanese contribution is undermined by delegitimation that occurs due to not having a permanent seat, then adding it could be useful. Legitimacy in Japan's eyes could be served by adding it as a permanent member. But given that the maximum number of likely new members is around ten, the implication is that the legitimacy deficit of the Council cannot be improved for the rest of the world's states through membership changes. This would suggest that we could increase the legitimacy of the Council in the eyes of those ten countries but can do nothing, or only reduce it, for the rest of the UN population.

While membership is a scarce good, deliberation is in principle available to all. If we grant, for the sake of argument, that deliberation is the key to institutional legitimation, then we can inquire into how it might be manipulated for legitimation by expanding the Council. To assess both H4 and H5, we need to know the limits on Council deliberation at present.

The existing deliberative process at the Council includes some formal rights of participation for nonmembers. These represent an acknowledgment by the drafters of the Charter and of its rules of procedure, of the importance of deliberation to legitimizing outcomes. The Charter requires that the Council invite parties to a dispute to participate in its deliberations on the dispute (Article 32) and allows that the Council may invite any state whose interests it considers "specially affected" by the issue at hand (Article 31). In practice, the latter provision is used by nonmembers to request a seat in the deliberation. It is almost automatic that a nonmember state can add its voice to the *formal* deliberations of the Council when it wants to. Because the deliberative model is mainly concerned with the breadth of information flowing into the process rather than the formal status of the speakers, this goes some distance toward satisfying a purely deliberative model of legitimation in that it opens the channel for states to express their views in the Council without distinction between members of the Council and nonmembers.

There are limits on this access, however, and they are illuminating because they point to unresolved issues in the deliberative model. For instance, only states that are "party to a dispute" have a *right* to participate (Article 32); other nonmembers are invited at the discretion of the Council. Even if these invitations are routinely granted, the formal control of access rests with the Council's members. Also, nonmembers are allowed "voice" only. That is, they may express views and participate in the substantive discussions, but they may not vote. Their contribution is restricted to the currencies of argument and information. These limits create distinctions in status and formal decision making power among the participants in the deliberative process but do not affect their equality in the argumentative field. A purely deliberative model of legitimation should conclude that this does not matter, but one suspects that it does in practice. The opportunity to exercise voice through informal practices does not carry the same political status as does the chance to occupy a formal nonpermanent seat. The distinction needs to be accounted for by those who defend the deliberative approach in Council reform.

In this context, the only margin by which adding new formal members could increase the Council's deliberative quality is the same margin by which requests to participate (Article 31) are at present rejected by the Council. It is only the rejected states that stand to gain greater access to Council deliberation than they have at the moment. States that are accepted into the process under Article 31 already have the opportunity to contribute to the deliberation. Therefore, the potential increase in deliberation that could possibly come via adding new members must be quite small.

This conclusion may have to be amended based on changes in the Council's practice of informal consultations.[27] The issue depends on whether we see the many informal processes as extensions of Council deliberations or as circumventions of them. If Council members have greater access to these informal sessions than nonmembers have, then becoming a member might increase one's participation in the informal deliberative process outside of formal Council meetings. It is plausible that this might be true, though it probably depends on the state in question. Large states may already participate in informal consultations, even as nonmembers, and so giving them formal Council seats would not produce a net increase in deliberation. Small nonmember states are unlikely to be invited to informal sessions except in unusual circumstances—but even as formal members of the Council they might find themselves excluded from informal sessions too. The power of the informal process at present is precisely that it allows the dominant states on the Council to pick from among the members and nonmembers only those whose contribution to deliberation they feel is valuable to them. It allows the Council to ignore the distinction between member and nonmember and changes the patterns of deliberation. This has an ambiguous net effect on the quality and quantity of deliberation around the Council.

The fifth and final hypothesis is distinct from H4 in that it claims that it is the quality of deliberation in the organization that generates belief in its legitimacy by an actor, irrespective of whether that actor itself had the opportunity to contribute to the deliberation. Like H4, this argument is only as strong as the link between the deliberation that it sees as its goal and the expansion of formal membership that it suggests as its means. The identity of the deliberators is not important. What matters is that the Council be open to considering all morally relevant claims (and no irrelevant ones). Unless the limits of informal deliberation have already been reached, this argument looks hollow.

Assessing the Hypotheses

Does formal reform of membership contribute to legitimacy in any of the five hypotheses? The five are based on different empirical claims, but at least three general patterns emerge when one examines them as a group.

First, each claim ultimately rests on a trade-off, and each trade-off involves a political decision regarding one's priorities about the Council that cannot be resolved except by each state according to its own values and interests. Several of the hypotheses—H1, H2, and H3—set up a trade-off between increasing the Council's legitimacy for some states while necessarily reducing it for other states. We may not be able to predict which states will fall into each category, but we do know that the lack of consensus over metrics of representation and diversity means that privileging one interpretation over others will contribute to the delegitimation of an enlarged Council in the eyes of some states. This weakens H1 and H2. H3 can, at best, increase legitimacy in the eyes of the individual states that might be added to the Council while reducing it for those that are not. The deliberative models create a different kind of trade-off, one between increasing the range of voices and issues that can be raised in the Council (which is seen as the source of legitimation) and reducing the possibility of consensus in decisions. More interests on the table will necessarily mean that it will be harder to reach an agreement. Finally, all legitimation hypotheses involve a trade-off between increasing the Council's legitimacy and furthering other values, such as efficiency, effectiveness, or power. It is generally accepted that the size of the Council is negatively correlated to its effectiveness, and some countries raise this frequently as a cost of larger membership. A negative correlation here would mean that it was a fatal flaw for all legitimacy-through-enlargement arguments if, in fact, Council legitimacy was primarily a function of its substantive effectiveness rather than its membership.

Second, each hypothesis can be undermined by the possibility of "informal membership" in the Council. As the Council increases the opportunities for participation available to nonmembers, it steals the foundation from many of the reform arguments. The deliberative hypotheses, in particular, are weakened to the extent that Council rules of procedure, and Charter requirements, allow nonmembers of the Council to contribute to deliberation. The justification for adding new *formal* members is defeated if states' presence and participation can be solicited on a case-by-case basis. What remains is the potential legitimating power of the pure membership argument, where formal presence is thought by itself to have a legitimating effect (as in H1, H2, and H3). In the end, it is not clear that the formal structure of Council membership is the most important constraint on deliberation, or that adding new members would necessarily add to its deliberative quality.

Finally, the weakness of many of these arguments relative to empirical evidence makes it plausible to conclude that much of the "legitimacy talk" around which reform arguments are constructed is a false front, covering up the political interests of states. What aspirants to Council membership seem to be really seeking are the status and prestige that they believe go along with a seat. These real motives behind the rhetoric are not affected by the lack of evidence for the rhetorical claims. They are not without effect, however, given the nature of rhetorical power. Two new issues then come to the fore, each worthy of further research. First, the ubiquity with which reform arguments are defended by reference to the alleged "legitimacy deficit" of the Council suggests that the international community expects that proposals be couched in universal rather than particularistic values. Second, these generalizable claims may subject their speakers to the possibility of rhetorical entrapment, so that public statements about a principle of legitimation might be turned around by others in ways the speaker never intended but from which they can't escape.[28] International talk may be cheap, but it is never free.

Conclusion

My goal has been to assess the claim that adding members to the Security Council is a useful strategy to ensure the organization's legitimacy in the future. There are competing versions of this claim and I identified five distinct hypotheses about membership and legitimacy that are commonly presented in defense of changing the composition of the Council. Each is, in principle, testable by empirical methods, although in practice the evidence needed to confirm or falsify them is unobtainable. As a result, I presented assessments of the empirical and logical plausibility of each, drawn both from the past experience of the Council and from evidence on legitimation in other organizations. None of the five emerges with a strong defense. Each ultimately relies on prior assumptions that are themselves questionable—for instance, that states agree on a metric for measuring diversity or representation in the Council, or that states value the pure deliberative quality of the Council and not the status distinctions between members and nonmembers. Bardo Fassbender has suggested that "conflicting views of member states continue to block a solution" to Council reform.[29] The gaps in logic that undermine each of the five hypotheses may indicate that these "conflicting views" originate in incompatible notions about how legitimation works.

The hypotheses are not of a type that can be fully confirmed or disproved with evidence, but their evident weakness suggests that states may be largely insincere in their references to them. Assuming that what states really want is to gain a seat for themselves and to deny one to their rival, we should look at both *why* states find this to be an appealing goal and why talking in terms of legitimacy is seen as a useful strategy. While the hypotheses themselves may be weak, this article also shows the power that states see in using "legitimacy talk" to defend their interests. How this has come to be the case is itself an interesting question that combines the geopolitics of states competing over Council seats with the social construction of language resources.

Notes

1. Excellent analyses of the diplomatic history of the 1990s reform process are available in Mark W. Zacher, "The Conundrums of International Power Sharing: The Politics of Security Council Reform," in Richard M. Price and Mark W. Zacher, *The United Nations and Global Security* (New York: Palgrave Macmillan, 2004); Bardo Fassbender, *UN Security Council Reform and the Right of Veto: A Constitutional Perspective* (The Hague: Kluwer, 1998); Edward C. Luck, "Reforming the United Nations: Lessons from a History in Progress," AUNCS Occasional Paper No. 1, 2003.

2. United Nations, *A More Secure World: Our Shared Responsibility— Report of the Secretary-General's High-Level Panel on Threats, Challenges and Change,* A/59/565 (New York: United Nations, 2004), p. 57.

3. Ibid., p. 66.

4. Kofi Annan, "In Larger Freedom: Towards Development, Security and Human Rights for All," A/59/2005 (New York: United Nations, 2005).

5. United Nations, *Report of the GA Working Group on the Security Council for 1995,* A/AC.247/1 (New York: United Nations, 1995), www.global policy.org/security/reform/secwg2.htm.

6. See Michael Barnett, "Bringing in the New World Order: Liberalism, Legitimacy, and the United Nations," *World Politics* 49, no. 4 (July 1997): 526–551.

7. Ian Hurd, *After Anarchy: Legitimacy and Power in the UN Security Council* (Princeton: Princeton University Press, 2007); Ian Hurd, "Legitimacy, Power, and the Symbolic Life of the UN Security Council," *Global Governance* 8, no. 1 (2002): 35–51.

8. This definition accords with Ian Hurd, "Legitimacy and Authority in International Politics," *International Organization* 53, no. 2 (1999): 379–408. See also Ian Hurd, "Theories and Tests of International Authority," in Bruce Cronin and Ian Hurd, eds., *The UN Security Council and the Politics of International Authority* (Abingdon and New York: Routledge, 2008). For competing definitions, see Allen Buchanan, *Justice, Legitimacy, and Self-Determination: Moral Foundations of International Law* (Oxford: Oxford University Press, 2003); and Erik Voeten, "The Political Origins of the UN Security Council's Ability to Legitimize the Use of Force," *International Organization* 59, no. 3 (2005): 527–557.

9. Michael Barnett and Martha Finnemore, *Rules for the World: International Organizations in Global Politics* (Ithaca: Cornell University Press, 2005); and Hurd, *After Anarchy*.

10. James M. Olson and Carolyn L. Hafer, "Tolerance of Personal Deprivation," in John T. Jost and Brenda Major, eds., *The Psychology of Legitimacy: Emerging Perspectives on Ideology, Justice, and Intergroup Relations* (Cambridge: Cambridge University Press, 2001), p. 157.

11. Tom Tyler, "A Psychological Perspective on the Legitimacy of Institutions and Authorities," in Jost and Major, *The Psychology of Legitimacy*.

12. Ian Clark, *Legitimacy in International Society* (Oxford: Oxford University Press, 2005), pp. 26–28.

13. US Department of State, 20 June 2005, www.state.gov/r/pa/scp/2005/48332.htm (accessed 14 September 2005).

14. On nonpermanent members, see Article 23(1). Also see Ramesh Thakur, ed., *What Is Equitable Geographic Distribution in the 21st Century?* (Tokyo: United Nations University, 1999).

15. See, for instance, the Canadian position: "The membership of the Security Council should more clearly represent the international community of the 21st century," statement of the Ministry of Foreign Affairs, Canada, www.dfait-maeci.gc.ca/cip-pic/IPS/IPS-Diplomacy7-en.asp (accessed 13 September 2005).

16. United Nations, *Report of the GA Working Group on the Security Council for 1997*, A/51/47 (New York: United Nations, 1997), www.globalpolicy.org/security/reform/wk97-3.htm.

17. Ambassador Pleuger to General Assembly, 14 October 2003, archived at www.germany-un.org/archive/speeches/2003/sp_10_14_03.html.

18. Bruce Russett, "Ten Balances for Weighing UN Reform Proposals," in Bruce Russett, ed., *The Once and Future Security Council* (New York: St. Martin's Press, 1997), p. 20.

19. See Gordon, "Scenarios for Reforming the United Nations."

20. Amy Gutmann and Dennis Thompson, *Democracy and Disagreement: Why Moral Conflict Cannot Be Avoided in Politics, and What Should Be Done About It* (Cambridge: Harvard University Press, 1996), p. 41.

21. James D. Fearon, "Deliberation as Discussion," in Jon Elster, ed., *Deliberative Democracy* (Cambridge: Cambridge University Press, 1998), p. 57.

22. Tyler, "A Psychological Perspective," pp. 419–420.

23. Diego Gambetto, "'Claro!' An Essay on Discursive Machismo," in Elster, *Deliberative Democracy,* p. 22.

24. Fearon, "Deliberation as Discussion," p. 50.

25. John Dryzek, *Deliberative Democracy and Beyond: Liberals, Critics, Contestations* (Oxford: Oxford University Press, 2000), p. 1.

26. Fearon, "Deliberation as Discussion," p. 57.

27. Susan C. Hulton, "Council Working Methods and Procedure," in David M. Malone, ed., *The UN Security Council: From the Cold War to the 21st Century* (Boulder: Lynne Rienner, 2004); Luck, "Step One."

28. Thomas Risse, "'Let's Argue!' Communicative Action in World Politics," *International Organization* 54, no. 1 (2000): 1–40; Ian Hurd, "The Strategic Use of Liberal Internationalism: Libya and the UN Sanctions, 1992–2003," *International Organization* 59, no. 3 (2005): 495–526; Frank Schimmelfennig, *The EU, NATO, and the Integration of Europe: Rules and Rhetoric* (Cambridge: Cambridge University Press, 2003).

29. Bardo Fassbender, "Pressure for Security Council Reform," in Malone, *The UN Security Council,* p. 341.

6

Financing UN Peacekeeping:
A Review and Assessment
of Proposals

Paul F. Diehl and Elijah PharaohKhan

AMONG THE MANY ADJUSTMENTS THAT THE UNITED NATIONS has had to make in the so-called new world order is paying for the increased responsibilities it has assumed in the areas of international peace and security. . . . These changes have intersected with a long-standing problem of the United Nations, the unwillingness of states to meet their assessment obligations, to form perhaps the worst financial crisis in the organization's history. Many times . . . member states have withheld contributions to the UN or not paid them in a timely fashion, sometimes because of financial exigency, but more often for political reasons. . . . Some members did not pay their dues in order to extract reforms or concessions from the UN. More specifically, states may withhold funds for peacekeeping operations because they regard the mission as contrary to their national interests, they object to the institutional arrangements or control of the operation, or they take a principles stance that those responsible for the conflict should pay the costs (James, 1989). The United Nations in general is seriously in debt, but the focal point for much of the problem has been UN peacekeeping operations, which are responsible for almost 70 percent of the shortfall.

This essay reviews and assesses the various proposals offered to resolve the financing problems with UN peacekeeping operations. We have several goals. First, we hope to integrate and describe the plethora

Reprinted from *Policy Studies Review* 17, no. 1 (2000): 71–104. © 2000 Blackwell Publishers. Reprinted by permission of the publisher.

of funding ideas that exist, both historically and more recently in response to the UN financial crisis. Second, we wish to evaluate the viability of such plans, both from a financial standpoint as well as their ability to overcome political barriers that have inhibited the United Nations and its peacekeeping operations in the past. Third, we hope to draw conclusions about which schemes are best pursued and we do so based on our analysis of the alternatives rather than a political or ideological preference for any one, something characteristic of many prescriptive discussions of UN financing. Finally, many of the problems and proposals raised with respect to peacekeeping are closely related to UN and international organization financing in general, so many of the conclusions here are broadly applicable to those broader concerns.

Although there is a broad range of financing alternatives and some significant disagreement in the policy community over those alternatives, some consensus does exist on two points: the consequences of the financial crisis on UN peacekeeping are highly deleterious and both North and South states want a resolution of the problem (although for different reasons). Even though the success of peacekeeping missions during the Cold War was not severely compromised by financing problems (Diehl, 1994), the consequences seem much more severe over the past several decades. One risk is that financial constraints will limit the ability of the United Nations to staff and supply adequately the operations that it does authorize. For example, financial wrangling over the peacekeeping operation in Namibia led to a delay in the deployment of the mission and a suboptimal force size; in large part, the significant bloodshed in the first several weeks of the operation can be attributed to these factors (Diehl and Jurado, 1993.) In other operations, financial shortfalls have caused delays in buying necessary equipment and supplies, as well as paying soldiers and other personnel associated with the mission.

Perhaps even more importantly, the willingness and ability of UN members to authorize new peacekeeping missions will be influenced by the number and cost of extant missions. Thus as the cost of current operations becomes prohibitive in the eyes of the member states, they will be more reluctant to take on new missions that serve the interests of international peace and security. It might be plausibly argued that the failure of the UN operation in Somalia and its high costs were a significant influence on the organization's unwillingness to expand or reconfigure the observer mission in Rwanda at the same time. Although highly speculative, it is conceivable that some of the civil conflict and genocide might have been avoided with decisive UN action.

The leading industrialized states of the world, especially the United States, have been among the most vocal critics of the United Nations and its spending. Although many of these complaints stem from the alleged inefficiency of the UN bureaucracy, peacekeeping operations have also come under criticism for their length and attendant costs. Although the North-South split covers many issues, less developed states have also been critical of peacekeeping costs. Their major objection is that money spent on peacekeeping operations has lessened the availability of funds and programs for economic development. In each case, however, there is pressure for reform of UN peacekeeping financing.

Clearly, some view the solution as focused on reducing the demand for peacekeeping funds and this would involve authorizing fewer and shorter missions. Other proposals such as those developed by the "Group of 18" deal with promoting greater efficiency, often involving reductions in personnel and other budget-cutting suggestions. This is less applicable to peacekeeping operations, which are not usually over-staffed (indeed the opposite is generally true), and there is less room for belt tightening except perhaps for the use of technology as a substitute for peacekeeping soldiers in some roles (see Diehl, 1996). More likely the solution to financing peacekeeping operations lies on the supply side of the equation by either changing the source of funding for the operations and/or ensuring greater stability in their provision. Such proposals do not necessarily mean an increase or decrease in actual amounts spent on peacekeeping, but a good proposal is one that can be flexible enough to meet a variety of future scenarios with respect to an increase in the number of missions. As a beginning, we briefly outline the current system for funding UN peacekeeping operations with an eye to identifying the weaknesses of that approach and to provide a baseline for comparison with new proposals. We also discuss constraints that will limit any UN efforts at financial reform. We then move to an analy-sis of new proposals classifying them into one of three categories: (1) incremental changes, (2) international taxes, and (3) new programs. We note two important caveats. First, many of the proposals relate to financing the UN system as a whole whereas some are concentrated only on funding peacekeeping or other security operations. As our inter-est is in peacekeeping, we do not make a distinction in the analysis as the holistic approaches will certainly apply to peacekeeping operations and are generally divisible in that they could be used to fund only the peacekeeping element of the United Nations. Symmetrically, the cri-tiques we apply in the context of peacekeeping are also relevant in the broader context as well. Second, many proposals include more aspects of reforming the United Nations than just the financial element, such as regulating currency markets or altering the structure of UN peacekeeping operations. In those cases, we present such proposals, but concentrate on the financing elements contained within them. The viability and wisdom of such larger proposals are covered elsewhere and we prefer to narrow our focus to the financial element.

The Ad Hoc Current System of Financing

Unlike many governmental or organizational programs, the UN does not have one standard system for funding its peacekeeping operations. In part, this is because peacekeeping operations tend to be organized on an ad hoc basis according to the breaking events on the world scene. With some exceptions, the United Nations does not have the luxury of extensive advanced planning in putting together peacekeeping operations. Just before or once a peacekeeping operation is authorized, UN officials must scramble to organize the mission. Although some supplies are permanently stored and precedent facilitates the process, UN staff must solicit troop and other material contributions from member states. How those costs will be borne by the membership then tends to reflect the particular political context and operational needs of the mission. In contrast, were the United Nations to have a permanent peacekeeping force on standby for an emergency, costs and the systems to meet those costs would be more regularized.

Although peacekeeping missions are organized on an *ad hoc* basis, this should not imply that the method of financing is random or completely unique to the operation at hand. Despite some variation across missions, UN peacekeeping operations are financed through several different mechanisms. One way is to meet expenses out of the regular UN budget. This is characteristic of the funding pattern for several observation missions, including the United Nations Truce Supervision Organization (UNTSO). Nevertheless, this mechanism is problematic when a particular mission is very expensive (and observation missions are usually smaller and cheaper than traditional or second-generation peacekeeping operations) or when the organization must handle several operations at once. Having peacekeeping compete with other UN priorities complicates the ability of the organization to fulfill its multi-faceted mission, and is a poor solution all around in the face of severe budgetary pressures for the organization as a whole. Some indirect peacekeeping costs still remain under the rubric of the general budget, as political officers and the other members of the Secretariat assist peacekeeping missions in a variety of ways. Some early missions also had their costs borne by the disputants. This is a risky proposition in that the protagonists may be too poor to afford a peacekeeping mission or use their financial muscle to manipulate the conduct of the operation. Significantly, virtually no new proposals suggest reviving this practice.

With the development of more expansive operations than simple observer missions, the UN funded peacekeeping out of mission-specific special accounts; member states pay an assessment based on a formula similar to the one used for the regular budget, although this has varied over time, with all the money going to the peacekeeping operation. This has not always proven reliable as states that object to a given operation may decide to withhold funds from this special account while continuing to meet their financial obligations to the United Nations as a whole. The case of the United Nations Interim Force in Lebanon (UNIFIL) is illustrative. UNIFIL was originally funded out of a special account, but some states refused to pay their assessment for political reasons and the operation quickly encumbered a significant operating deficit. Less than two years after UNIFIL deployment, the UN General Assembly created a "Suspense Account for UNIFIL" to supplement the special account. It was to be financed by voluntary contributions from member states, international organizations, and private sources and was to be used solely for reimbursing states that contributed troops to UNIFIL. Other missions receive voluntary contributions including cash funds or contributions in kind (such as helicopters and other equipment). The clear problem with voluntary funds, however, is that they can be quickly withdrawn at the whim of the contributors. Some UN agencies in the social issue area are actually financed primarily or exclusively by voluntary contributions, as are some relief efforts, and these have traditionally been inadequately funded (well below needs). Furthermore, pledges of assistance have often far exceeded actual receipts. Thus, both special accounts and mechanisms to supplement special accounts have their flaws and neither has proved adequate for peacekeeping operations.

Many of the financial problems are short-term. The payment schedule for members' assessments does not necessarily conform to the timing of national budget allocations or the changing needs of the UN, and as a result there are temporary shortfalls. Also unexpected demands for new peacekeeping operations create short-term funding problems as the UN must scramble to gain authorization and assemble a peacekeeping force on short notice. More serious are the long-term funding problems for peacekeeping operations. Some of these are caused by the rise in the number of ongoing peacekeeping operations in the 1990s. Some member states are too poor or experience sudden financial difficulties that make them unable to meet assessment schedules or contribute voluntarily to peacekeeping operations. Most important is the unwillingness of states, either specifically for a given operation or generally for UN operations as a whole, to fund adequately peacekeeping operations. This leads to missing payment deadlines, a reluctance to authorize the necessary mandate if such authorization would result in higher expense, and an unwillingness to make voluntary payments to help support peacekeeping missions. The financial and political sources of UN financial problems are directly a consequence (although not a necessary one) of a reliance on members' contributions for funding.

The United Nations clearly needs a regularized method of financing its peacekeeping operations that ensures stability in funding, is insulated from politically motivated attempts to withhold funds, and is adequate to meet current and unanticipated peacekeeping needs (implying some flexibility). Yet before analyzing whether a series of proposals would be effective in addressing these problems, we briefly discuss the inherent constraints that limit UN reform efforts.

Constraints on UN Reform

An assessment of proposals to improve the financing of UN peacekeeping operations must take into account the context under which such reforms would occur. The general context that the UN operates is one in which the organization is subordinate to the interests of its members, most notably the powerful states among its membership. The limited autonomy of the UN may be a significant constraint on its ability to enact the proposals outlined below. First, legally, any major change in UN financing may require revisions to the UN Charter. Amendments to the UN Charter require two-thirds approval by member states, including all the permanent members of the Security Council (United Kingdom, France, Russia, China, and the United States). Effectively, the five permanent members have a veto over Charter reform. Given the domestic political opposition in the United States and its Congress, it might be presumed that few proposals would gain American approval. Those that would result in greater US contributions to the organization appear to have the greatest hurdles to acceptance. Depending on the US to provide leadership in the UN and spearhead financing reforms is unrealistic (Washburn, 1996); that the US would acquiesce in major changes to the organization is no more credible.

Second, and beyond considerations of major power interests, UN financing reforms must find a balance between preserving and eroding state sovereignty (Russett, 1997). Member states are likely to oppose measures that give too much autonomy to the United Nations. On the one hand, there is suspicion that the UN cannot manage its own financial affairs properly, and member states want to be able to exercise control over disbursements. On the other hand, doubts about UN management aside, most member states will resist greater UN autonomy for political reasons. States find it in their interests to withhold contributions to the UN in order to exercise influence within the organization. UN financial reforms that grant more autonomy to the organization eliminate or diminish that power, and one might expect that major contributors, especially the US, will block efforts that tip the balance too far in the direction of greater UN autonomy.

Third, the UN is inherently constrained by a classic "free-rider" problem (see Khanna, Sandier, and Shimizu, 1998). Many states will not contribute their share and withhold funds for a collective good (here international peace and security) with the expectation that those states with the greatest stakes in the situation will provide the necessary funding anyway. The lack of an effective enforcement to pressure or punish recalcitrants exacerbates the tendency (see discussion of Article 19 below). Thus, to the extent that UN financial reforms are accepted by the membership, we must recognize that there may be some slippage in implementation that leads to suboptimal effects.

With these broad constraints in mind, we move to a description, analysis, and assessment of the various financing reforms for UN peacekeeping.

Incremental Change Financing Proposals

The first set of proposals share the common feature of making only incremental changes to the existing ways of financing UN operations. Thus, none of these ideas represent dramatic overhauls of the size or source of UN funds, but rather are best viewed as attempts to fine-tune problematic elements of the current system.

Late Payment Charges

One suggestion for ensuring timely payments of UN assessment (much of UN debt is attributable to states failing to pay assessments) is the imposition of fees or penalties for late payments (Global Commission, 1995; Henderson, 1995; Boutros-Ghali, 1995; D'Orville and Najman, 1995; Ford Foundation, 1993; Mendez, 1997). The hope is that such a penalty will persuade balky contributors to pay their dues on time because there is significant cost-benefit incentive not to delay (under the current system, there may even be some economic incentives to not pay on time). The rationale is quite similar to those employed by financial institutions who apply penalties or interest to late payments on credit cards, loans, and the like. Were a significant number of states to pay late regardless, the UN would then at least have additional revenue to deal with the adverse consequences of being behind in its own payments. Clearly, however, the advantages of full compliance and enhanced revenue are mutually exclusive.

There are several reasons to doubt the viability of late payment proposals. In large part, this is because the proposals do not necessarily address the motivations that lie behind states' failure to pay. To the extent that states fall behind in their payments because of domestic economic or financial problems (characteristic of some poor countries), a penalty will not affect their ability to meet their obligations and only increase the burden of payment in the future. States that withhold funds because they object to the assessment scale (e.g., they believe that their own assessment is too high) or because they object to a given peacekeeping operation are unlikely to be persuaded by a late payment charge. Their objections are philosophical and are not made on the pure economic choice considerations that underlie the late payment proposal. Such proposals also do nothing to increase the funds necessary for current or expanded peacekeeping (the Security Council may authorize a sub-optimal sized force or withdraw it prematurely). Thus, late payment fees are far from a panacea to the financial shortfall in peacekeeping funds themselves, and may have only a marginal effect when combined with other proposals below.

Changing Payment Dates

Another set of proposals also focuses on the payment schedule of member states. The UN establishes assessments at the beginning of its fiscal year and requires members to pay their dues by 31 January of each year for the regular budget. A similar schedule is in effect for UN peacekeeping operations, although they do not necessarily arise or terminate on a regular schedule each year. Some states do not pay their assessments until after their own fiscal years have begun, often significantly later than the end of January deadline for the United Nations. The United States, for example, never makes any of its payments until the beginning of the American fiscal year in October and Japan, another large contributor, waits until about June of each year to pay its assessments (Saito, 1992; Laurenti, 1995). One proposal would be to change the due date for assessment from one to four quarterly installment dates (Childers, 1995; Ford Foundation, 1993).

As with instituting a late payment fee, this proposal does not address the political and economic motivations for why states don't meet their obligations. Four quarterly installments only increase the technical compliance that states will have in meeting assessments.

The proposal does not insure that the UN will receive more funds and it may even create some short-term financial problems in that states who formerly paid their dues all at once at the beginning of the year will, along with the so-called deadbeats, also stretch out their payments throughout the year. Thus, the new payment structure may actually cause more problems than the ones it solves. There is no compelling argument to suggest that the four quarterly payments will result in states paying more to the UN than doing so in one lump sum, be it late or not.

Modifying Article 19

Article 19 of the United Nations Charter stipulates that any UN member in arrears in the amount of two years' dues will lose its vote in the General Assembly. A suggested revision to that provision is to lower the debt amount that triggers the loss of voting privileges from two years to one year (D'Orville and Najman, 1995). The logic of this proposal is similar to that of the late payment penalty. It is hoped that the imposition of a sanction will induce member states to meet their obligations. Rather than a financial penalty, one imposed on political power and prestige is thought to have greater likelihood of success. Losing a vote in the United Nations (although rarely significant from a pivotal power perspective) may be viewed as more painful than merely having to ante-up more money. More likely, the symbolic cost of losing one's voting privileges may entail sufficient embarrassment to the state involved so that it will be reluctant to withhold funds.

Leaving aside the likelihood that Article 19 would be modified and enforced (issues addressed below), it is unclear whether this would necessarily be effective in resolving UN financial problems. Article 19 has the potential to address shortfalls arising from major contributors who withhold large amounts of funds, and indeed a good portion of UN debt is attributable to a relatively small number of countries. Yet the proposal will not address the situation of many countries being behind in their contributions, but short of the one year level designated in the new Article 19. Individually, these may be insignificant, but collectively the amount in arrears may complicate the ability of the United Nations to perform its peacekeeping duties or act as a disincentive to new operations. Indeed many states now make a minimum payment in order to avoid Article 19 sanctions. Increasing the penalty for late payments or withholding again assumes the adequacy of current funds to meet peacekeeping needs (a questionable assumption).

Perhaps more significant than not meeting all the needs of a good financing proposal, we contend that it is unlikely that a modification of Article 19 will be adopted or enforced. Modifying Article 19 would require an amendment to the UN Charter and therefore the approval of the Security Council. Historically, two of the largest UN debtors have been the United States and Russia (then Soviet Union). It is uncertain at best whether these two states would approve of a plan that would most likely be used against them. The two leading states have used their financial muscle to extract changes in the United Nations in the past and may not want to take any action which limits that exercise of power in the future. Other states may also want to retain the option of withholding funds without penalty as well.

Even were Article 19 provisions tightened, it is not clear whether the United Nations membership would choose to actually take away a debtor state's vote. Article 19 in its current form has been inadequate (Mills, 1989). In the early 1960s, the Soviet Union refused to pay some of its obligations (largely related to the Congo peacekeeping operation), but despite threats the UN membership did not invoke Article 19 and take away the Soviet vote. Largely, this reluctance was the product of the fear that the Soviets would then withdraw from the organization. The withdrawal of the Soviet Union from the UN would have crippled that organization. It was thought that it was better to tolerate Soviet debt rather than provoke a crisis that could shake the foundations of the organization. Since that showdown, Article 19 has been almost toothless and it is unlikely that minor changes in its provisions will change its enforcement potential. At least, it seems impotent vis-à-vis major state actors, precisely those whose contributions make a significant difference to the operation of the UN and exactly those who have been debtors in the past.

Changing the Assessment Schedule

Another set of proposals deals with altering the method used to calculate the assessments that stipulate how much each state will pay to the UN budget or a given UN peacekeeping operation (D'Orville and Najman, 1995; Cardenas et al., 1995; Childers, 1995; Laurenti, 1995; Mendez, 1997). The simplest idea is to use a three year rather than ten year average of GDP in setting the assessments, with the logic that the shorter period is a more recent and therefore more accurate indicator of ability to pay. Other proposals involve rearranging the assessment so that the largest burden does not fall on the most powerful states (Commission on Global Governance, 1995). The United States in particular, as well as its allies, pays a large share of the UN regular budget. These same countries pay even a larger share of the peacekeeping expenses (for example, the United States is assessed more than a fourth of peacekeeping costs). Providing a flatter distribution of assessments across countries would make UN peacekeeping less of a hostage to withholding by any one state (Stanley Foundation, 1986). Together with the three year GDP modification, such a system might also be perceived as fairer and thus large contributors might be more politically willing to honor financial commitments that they regard as legitimate.

It is not clear whether the General Assembly would approve fundamental assessment changes. Years of complaints by the United States have not yielded much change and those who would pay more may be reluctant to accept this new responsibility (at least without a quid pro quo such as some greater say in peacekeeping operations that would result from Security Council structural reform). It is also dubious whether these proposals address the key financial emergency or political reasons for withholding funds. The proposals also do nothing to raise peacekeeping funding from their inadequate status quo levels.

Increasing the Working Capital Fund

The Working Capital Fund (WCF) was established in the UN's original financial plan to cover regular budget and limited emergency expenditures. This fund was originally larger than the regular budget, but now is considerably less (over the years, the regular budget has expanded to reflect broader UN mandates and has been adjusted for inflation, whereas the WCF has only increased slightly). The UN taps funds from the WCF when member states are late paying their dues, and the fund is replenished when states finally pay their dues in full (Mills, 1989).

One proposal is to increase the WCF by $100 million, but that amount could be even higher according to the peacekeeping and other needs of the organization; each member state would be assessed a one-time charge to raise funds for the WCF (Boutros-Ghali, 1995; Childers, 1995; Ford Foundation, 1993). This "rainy day" fund would hopefully allow the organization to meet emergencies better and ease problems that accompany short-term budget shortfalls, especially for peacekeeping operations.

The problem with increasing the WCF is that states who are already reluctant to pay their regular dues on time may be equally hesitant to contribute to another fund (voluntary contributions to emergency fund accounts have been minimal, suggesting just such a reluctance); indeed they may be even more reluctant given that an additional contribution will be required. The WCF does insure some greater measure of stability in funding, but once again does not insulate the process from political manipulation and does not provide an increased source of revenue to meet peacekeeping needs. It also is better at addressing short-term financial problems than endemic ones. As with several other incremental changes, there are few disadvantages to such ideas, but their likely impact on peacekeeping's financial problems is not substantial.

Allowing the UN to Borrow Funds

A common method for businesses and government to raise funds, especially on a short-term basis, is to borrow money (Ratner, 1995; D'Orville and Najman, 1995; Boutros-Ghali, 1995). With respect to the United Nations, one proposal is to allow the organization to borrow funds from commercial institutions or other international lending agencies. A variation would accord Special Drawing Right (SDR) privileges to the UN similar to those enjoyed by state members of the International Monetary Fund. The borrowed funds would be used to make up for depleted funds until UN members paid their dues. Such an arrangement is not unprecedented for an international organization. The World Bank raises part of its capital by loans on the international capital markets.

The ability to borrow funds can be thought of as an alternative to increasing the Working Capital Fund, as both are designed to meet immediate needs occasioned by financial shortfalls. Yet there are a number of problems with this proposal, some similar to those of the

WCF, but many unique to this proposal. Borrowing funds would provide some stability to the financial base of peacekeeping operations, but only in the short term. Borrowed funds have to be paid back, and as such do not deal with the endemic problem of a shortage of funds.

More serious, the UN's ability to repay the funds is based on its members' willingness to pay dues; of course, the unwillingness to pay dues is the source of the problem to begin with, and international lenders may be reluctant to provide funds to what can only be regarded as a poor risk (Ford Foundation, 1993). Furthermore, short-term borrowing may have the effect of giving states more excuses not to pay their dues. In the absence of a perceived financial crisis, there may be less pressure and less need for recalcitrant states to pay up (Ford Foundation, 1993). Thus, paradoxically, allowing the UN to borrow funds may worsen its financial problems, not ameliorate them.

Allowing the UN to Sell Bonds

Another favorite mechanism of governments and corporations to raise funds has been the sale of bonds. Under another proposal, the UN would be given this authority (Henderson, 1995; Childers, 1995). Nevertheless, issuing bonds is merely another way to borrow money, as the principal and interest must be repaid, although bonds do open up a broader creditor market than traditional loans. Yet one would expect that the same drawbacks as noted above for loans would be applicable to the sale of UN bonds. Indeed, in 1961, the General Assembly gave the Secretary-General authority to sell up to $200 million in bonds in order to meet shortfalls in two peacekeeping operations. Yet these entailed long-term debt (over twenty-five years) and some members withheld some payments to the UN that they believed were going for the repayment of the bonds (Mills, 1989).

The Revolving Peace Fund

UN peacekeeping operations require funds before the UN can begin each mission and as we noted above there is often not substantial advance notice for such operations. Indeed, it may take several weeks for the UN to obtain the necessary emergency funds, leading to significant delay or complications for the operation as was the case in the early stages of the UN operation in Bosnia. The UN created a revolving peace fund for emergency peacekeeping operations with 40% of the $150 million dollars designated for start-up costs (Ford Foundation, 1993). Common to many analysts' suggestions for UN reform is increasing the amount of the revolving peace fund, perhaps up to $400 million dollars (Boutros-Ghali, 1995; Childers, 1995; Ford Foundation, 1993). In effect, an increase in the size of the fund will provide the UN with a greater cushion against unexpected costs and allow the organization to handle new crises as they arise with extant commitments limiting the timing and extent of the initial response.

Increasing the revolving peace fund does address one of the problems associated with peacekeeping, namely getting soldiers and materiel on the ground quickly in a crisis situation. Yet it does little to address longer-term UN financial problems beyond the start-up problem. There still remains the difficulty of financing the operations after their initial phases. The revolving peace fund has also not persuaded cost-conscious or politically motivated states to pay their obligations in full or to increase the number and scope of peacekeeping operations. Furthermore, the problems with the WCF cited above seem equally applicable to increasing the revolving peace fund.

An Assessment of Incremental Changes

Most of the incremental changes suggested for improving the financing of the United Nations peacekeeping operations (or the organization as a whole) address only one small aspect of a larger problem. In that sense, even if they were to work as planned, the impact of any one change would be slight. Collectively, they offer the prospect of a more efficient organization, one that is less subject to the worst short-term shocks of underfunding. Yet singularly or collectively they all fail to provide the necessary funds needed for current and expanded UN peacekeeping operations, and none are able to overcome the political and economic barriers that cripple the UN's ability to raise funds. Because they essentially rely on fine-tuning status quo mechanisms, they are still constrained by the weakest parts of the current funding system. The United Nations may need to move away from funding that essentially relies on the direct contributions of its members in order to solve those problems. Suggestions for financial reforms in the next two sections are consistent with this strategy.

International Taxes

A second category of proposals frees the United Nations and its peacekeeping operations from dependence on member's contributions, the primary source of the UN financial problems. Instead, the UN would raise revenue in a fashion common to most national or local governance structures: the imposition of taxes or duties on various international entities or activities. Most tax plans would not make United Nations financing completely autonomous of its members as those states would presumably determine the rates and applications of any international taxes as well as be responsible for the collection of those duties. Nevertheless, these various proposals represent a fundamental break with traditional methods of financing international organization activities of any variety (except for perhaps that related to seabed mining), and in particular peacekeeping operations. There are several variations on the idea of international taxes, differing primarily on the goods or services that might be the subject of international taxes.

Tobin Tax

One of the most prominent international tax suggestions has been proposed by the Nobel laureate economist James Tobin (Tobin, 1978). Although his proposal was broadly designed to fund a range of UN activities, it could easily be modified to apply only to peace and security operations. Tobin's proposal and any number of variations have received wide international attention (Felix, 1995; Henderson, 1995; Childers, 1995; Langmore, 1995; Bezanson and Mendez, 1995; Global Commission, 1995; Laurenti, 1995). Tobin's idea was to institute a small uniform tax on foreign exchange transactions. The specifics include (a) a tax applied at a uniform ad valorem rate by all key currency countries, (b) administered and collected by each government on all payments by residents within its jurisdiction that involved a spot currency exchange, (c) proceeds to be paid into a central fund controlled by the International Monetary Fund or World Bank, (d) small countries that formerly tied their currencies to a key currency would not be required to levy the tax on intra-area exchanges (Felix, 1995), and (e) subject to IMF consent, countries could form tax-free currency areas in which the tax would not apply.

A low tax rate would have a negligible economic impact on international financial flows, but still be able to raise large amounts of revenue for the United Nations given the tremendous size of international exchange transactions that occur regularly on the international market. For example, a less than 1% tax rate on the more than one trillion dollars traded daily on the international foreign exchange market would yield the UN more than enough revenue to fund its peacekeeping operations

(Miller, 1995). The tax might also contribute to decreased exchange rate speculation and have other positive international economic benefits beyond as a revenue source (see Felix, 1995, for a discussion). The Tobin tax has the benefit of raising significant amounts of revenue, and is flexible enough (rates could be lowered or raised to meet needs) to adjust quickly to various contingencies in peacekeeping. Furthermore, such a tax makes revenue generation less politicized and more automatic (note that sales taxes generate less opposition than income taxes in most societies), and private entities will presumably be the ultimate source of most of the money.

Although the Tobin tax has a number of attractive features, there are some potential drawbacks. First, the system relies heavily on the cooperation of state governments and there is the risk that some states may refuse to collect the taxes or turn over the revenue if they object to certain UN peacekeeping operations. Thus, the withholding risk from political unwillingness is not completely eliminated. Second, there is the possibility that black market transactions or tax havens will be created to circumvent the tax; rarely has an international agreement found signatories among all the states of the world and one might presume that there will be some holdouts. Third, and perhaps most important, it is not clear that states will be willing to relinquish the influence over the organization that is attendant to funding the organization by member contributions. States may wish to reserve the option of withholding funds and may be suspicious of any proposal that grants supranational authority out of their control to the UN. That reluctance may be heightened if they regard the Tobin tax as a first step toward granting the UN more autonomy.

International Commons Tax

An alternative form of taxation is the imposition of taxes or user fees in relation to the global commons (Cleveland, 1995; Kaul, 1995; Boutros-Ghali, 1995; Cassani, 1995; Bezanson and Mendez, 1995; Global Commission, 1995; Mendez, 1997). Global commons are defined as areas or resources that are the collective property of mankind and not under the sovereignty of any one state (e.g., most of the oceans or outer space). Among the various international commons tax proposals are those that include (a) sea routes, (b) exploration and work in the Antarctic, (c) airspace, (d) outer space including satellites, (e) environmental pollution, (f) international transfer of genetic resources, and (g) fishing rights.

The imposition of global commons taxes or user fees is not without precedent. The Seabed Authority under the Law of the Sea Treaty is funded by fees that are effectively taxes on mining and other activities in the global ocean commons. Such taxes are also consistent with the logic that global resources and areas are jointly owned by mankind, and their use and exploitation must not benefit only a few states, especially the most powerful ones. Similar logic is found in many national or local laws, which impose taxes or user fees to support collectively owned resources or property (e.g., national park and museum fees, and pollution taxes).

Most of the ideas for global commons taxes seem quite feasible. With the exception of the genetic resources and a few other items, use of global resources and property is usually well documented and thereby relatively easy to impose taxes. Indeed, many of the activities are already subject to national taxes (e.g., international airline flights) and therefore revenue-collecting mechanisms may already be in existence. Furthermore, the tax would be imposed most heavily on those who use or benefit the most from the global commons. This would not necessarily shift the major financing burden away from the industrialized states (indeed it would probably reinforce that burden), but it may be perceived as more equitable than current UN financing schemes which have been criticized by Western states as not directly benefiting their states. Although the global commons tax has many of the same benefits as the Tobin tax (e.g., flexibility) it also potentially suffers many of the same drawbacks, and one might not expect easy approval anytime in the near future (Cardenas et al., 1995).

Transnational Activities Tax

A variation of taxing usage of the global commons is imposing duties on transnational activities that usually do not involve common international property. Some examples of such activities include (a) international air travel (e.g., airport departure taxes), (b) air freight packages, (c) international telecommunications, (d) international postal services, (e) conventional arms sales, or (f) any of a number of categories of international trade (D'Orville and Najman, 1995; Henderson, 1995; Childers, 1995; Kaul, 1995; Cassani, 1995; Bezanson and Mendez, 1995; Global Commission, 1995; Laurenti, 1995). Taxing transnational activities rather than the global commons does not have the same normative legitimacy (here the world community is taxing private actions that do not directly impinge on the public good), but include a much broader pool of actions that might be revenue sources. One advantage then is that very low taxes could be applied to many activities with little economic impact on those activities, but in the aggregate produce a lot of potential revenue for UN peacekeeping operations.

The practicality of this approach largely depends on the target of the taxes. For items such as international air travel, the addition of a small surcharge is accomplished easily within the extant airline system and mirrors many national taxes and duties already applied to international and domestic tickets. Other tax applications are more complicated to apply on individual transactions. Applying international taxes on phone calls, faxes, and especially postal services may be somewhat impractical given the large number of transactions and the small percentage of tax attached to each transaction. In those instances, it may be better to tax the provider of those services directly based on projected or actual volume; the provider would then likely pass the cost along to the consumer systematically by some across the board increase on services. In either case, the additional cost is likely to be quite small.

The idea of taxing arms sales to fund peacekeeping efforts has an intuitive appeal. Conventional arms are the means of the destruction and loss of life in wars and it seems appropriate that some portion of arms sales profits should go toward addressing these deleterious effects (a similar logic attends cigarette or gambling taxes that are directed toward treatment programs for those addicted to such activities). Yet arms sales may be the most difficult enterprise to track accurately and there are already significant incentives to disguise such transactions. Arms sales are characterized by many covert transactions and sometimes through third parties; either of these might be difficult to track and assess duties. There also is the problem of how to treat direct transfers of weapons (are these sales and therefore subject to tax?) or more problematic how to deal with foreign aid that has a fungible effect of freeing up domestic resources that can then be used for indigenous military development. Despite its appeal, taxing arms sales is probably not advisable as a sole source of revenue.

Transnational activities taxes seem best applied to a wide range of activities so as to minimize dependence on the economic impact of any one source.

An Overview of International Taxes

International taxes have the strength of being able to raise a large amount of revenue rather easily. With respect to international peacekeeping, the costs of the operations are not large compared to the budgets of major corporations or national governments, or the value of various international transactions. Thus, one might expect that the tax rates would be very low and likely have little or no economic impact on the transactions themselves. Because corporations and other wealthy actors, rather than poor countries, are the ones who assume the financial burden, the system too is less subject to financial exigencies of its members. Furthermore, the tax rates could be modified to meet ebbs and flows in the demands for peacekeeping operations, making them more flexible than any of the incremental changes noted above.

The viability of the international tax schemes will depend heavily on the cooperation of the member states. Most obviously, they will be the entities responsible for collecting the revenues, and the risk of withholding those funds will still exist, although perhaps not as strongly as with direct contributions. More significant is whether governments will allow the United Nations to have a quasi-independent financial capacity. The proposal of Secretary-General Boutros-Ghali for an international tax received harsh criticism from political leaders in the United States. Many states view this limited taxing capacity as the first step on a "slippery slope" toward greater autonomy for the organization.

New Programs

A third category of proposals represents a dramatic break with past funding initiatives. Each of the proposals below involves creating new programs to raise money for the United Nations. They also are specifically geared toward UN activities in the area of peace and security, whereas several of the previous ideas addressed generic problems of funding in the organization.

United Nations Security Insurance Agency (UNSIA)

A particularly innovative idea for addressing UN funding as well as security needs is the creation of an insurance system for states (Kay and Henderson, 1995; Smith, 1995). The United Nations Security Insurance Agency (UNSIA) would be similar in design to insurance companies that write policies for home or auto insurance. The insurance policy would guarantee each country specific rights to UN services in the event of war or other incidents. Coverage might include the right to preventive military actions, defense, or a peacekeeping deployment for a state, although the policy would be tailored individually to each state. The proposal for a UNSIA seems to presume the presence of UN standing forces that are available on short notice to respond to emergencies, although one could easily envision a modified arrangement without this component but including a commitment for standby forces from member states. The major difference between UNSIA and conventional insurance is that recipients would be given military assistance instead of cashin the event of a calamity. Before a state would be issued a policy, there would have to be extensive investigation and analysis in order to ascertain the suitability of the state for coverage and to design the specifics of that coverage. It may be that some states will not "qualify" forcoverage if the state's background or history suggests a high propensity for conflict, much as bad drivers often have their auto insurance canceled. Those who do qualify for insurance will fund the program with their "premiums," and one presumes that there will be differential premiums based on the level of risk and the type of coverage for the state in question. Thus, like conventional insurance policies, the new system will be self-funding as it is assumed that not all policyholders (indeed the system is based on only a small fraction doing so) will need to collect insurance in any given year. Final approval of the policy would come from the UN Security Council.

Leaving aside the issue of having UN forces ready to meet the needs of the insured (a problem in its own right), there are several serious problems with this proposal. First, to exclude the most unstable states or those at highest risk may make sense in a traditional insurance (profit-maximization) context, but is counterproductive with respect to the UN's goal of ensuring international peace and security. High-risk states are exactly the ones that must be a priority of the United Nations. A system that is cost effective because it is rarely used makes no sense in dealing with peacekeeping. Despite the lack of similarity on this point, UNSIA does run into some traditional insurance problems. One is similar to the problem of the "uninsured motorist." A UN system is not assured that it will include all or even most states, leaving potentially large gaps in unstable parts of the world. Many states may choose not to spend resources for insurance and assume the risk themselves. Other states may not want to be publicly associated with the need to have such insurance; having such a plan may imply a failure of the government or an infringement on its sovereignty, issues that could undermine domestic political support for the regime. If those states request UN assistance anyway during a crisis, the organization is faced with an undesirable choice. If it responds with peacekeeping troops or other assistance (even if the recipient pays for them), it sets a precedent that will encourage all other states to free ride until they face a crisis, thereby undermining the whole UNSIA system. If the UN ignores those pleas, and it will be politically difficult to do so (imagine the UN ignoring calls for intervention to stop genocidal acts), then it fails in achieving one of its primary goals.

The United Nations may also be put in uncomfortable situations should it be deployed in some circumstances. Will this insurance program cover cases of internal instability? To exclude these situations would be to ignore the most likely sources of conflict in the post–Cold War world. On the other hand, intervention in support of the policyholder (the host state government) puts the UN in the position of taking sides in an internal conflict and perhaps propping up an authoritarian government. Intervention that favored challengers to the host government would never be approved in the original policy agreement. Even the hint of this possibility would seem to scare states away from this program.

Even the financing element of the program is potentially shaky. There does not seem to be much incentive for the wealthiest states to join; few of them have internal threats to their stability and all have the resources and the desire to handle any foreign policy crises themselves. Yet their financial and other contributions would seem to be essential to make the system viable. Thus, one might presume that some contributions from non-policyholders would be essential, as those most likely to require assistance are poorer states. Yet this exposes the UNSIA system to the same kind of political manipulation as the current system and adds the risk of free-riding from any state not directly at risk. It is also questionable about whether the system can withstand the shock of meeting many challenges to peace and security simultaneously, much as many insurance companies collapse under the weight of claims following a widespread natural disaster. Thus, this system may have limited flexibility to handle increases in peacekeeping activity (the alternative is to have almost constant, excess over-capacity, something that is expensive and unlikely to be supported by the UN membership). Thus, a UNSIA system does not meet the problems of political unwillingness, state financial difficulties, or over-demand that characterize the current UN system.

Single Peace Fund

A second proposed program is not so dramatic as the UNSIA, but is still designed to move UN peacekeeping operations away from the inefficient ad hoc methods of financing. The Single Peace Fund (SPF) would

have a separately funded and itemized budget, independent of the overall UN budget, specifically targeted for peacekeeping operations (Ford
Foundation, 1993). A variation of this is the Peace Endowment Fund to
handle short-term elements of peacekeeping financing (Boutros-Ghali,
1995). Establishing an annual operating budget is thought to have several advantages. First, it ensures that money for peacekeeping is available on short notice and relieves the UN staff of the obligations of
quickly soliciting funds for emergency operations. Second, it provides
the flexibility to have funds for unanticipated operations, not merely in
the short term but over the course of a year as well; it is presumed that
a peacekeeping budget would contain such a cushion to handle new
peacekeeping operations. Finally, maintaining a separate peacekeeping
budget may deter the UN from raiding peacekeeping funds in order to
pay for bills in other parts of the organization (there is some evidence
that the UN has chosen to fall behind on paying troop contributing
countries in favor of meeting other obligations). The net effect of a Single Peace Fund would be to insure better reaction time to crisis situations and perhaps better management as planning, training, communications, and other duties might be consolidated rather than scattered
across the UN bureaucracy as is currently the case.

There is little to quibble with about the improved efficiency of the
Single Peace Fund. Virtually any organization will run better with a set
budget that insures continuity and allows advance planning. Although
this new program has some advantages over the status quo, there
remains the problem that the source of funds still comes directly from
member state contributions. In a time when some countries, especially
the United States, are looking to decrease their contributions to the
United Nations, the addition of a permanent new budget item will not
be welcomed. Furthermore, there is no indication that states will behave
any differently in paying their assessments to the SPF than they do with
the regular UN budget or special accounts for peacekeeping operations.
Thus, one might anticipate a pattern of late payments and withholding
to also plague the Single Peace Fund. The concept of a separate budget
for peacekeeping is sound, but it may be necessary to find other ways
to fund it than member contributions.

Incorporating Peacekeeping in National Defense Budgets

A third new program would shift the funding of UN peacekeeping operations away from direct member contributions to an ad hoc peacekeep-

ing fund in the direction of funding operations out of national defense budgets (Ford Foundation, 1993; Childers, 1995; D'Orville and Najman, 1995). Member states would have a line item present in their defense budgets for peacekeeping operations or contribute a set percentage (10% has been suggested) of their defense budget to UN peacekeeping. States in the region of a peacekeeping operation might pay for all the costs associated with that operation, either by paying for a specific operation directly or contributing to a fund designed to pay for all peacekeeping operations in their geographic area.

The shift of payments from member contributions to national defense budgets appears to be more of a shell game than a dramatic shift in how peacekeeping operations are funded. The UN still is reliant on the willingness of states to provide funds. Political or economic decisions not to support peacekeeping operations now are manifested in the national defense budget policy process rather than in a United Nations forum. One might presume that other national interests will leave UN peacekeeping concerns in a less advantageous position than they might be in an international forum. Thus, the partnership proposal solves none of the adequacy and flexibility problems of the current system and may even exacerbate them.

Furthermore, the proposal to have states in the region fund peacekeeping operations has some potential serious drawbacks (see Diehl, 1994). First, some regions, such as Africa, may be too poor to adequately fund peacekeeping operations without external assistance, making the partnership proposal unrealistic. Second, it has been the hallmark of traditional UN peacekeeping missions not to have states in the same region or with a vested interest participate directly or prominently in its missions. To rely heavily on neighboring states for funding runs the risk that the peacekeeping mission could be blackmailed or manipulated by those states, and may undermine the credibility of the force as it seeks to maintain its neutrality and impartiality. One need look no further than Nigeria's central role in the ECOMOG peacekeeping operation in Liberia to see the risks involved.

Conclusion

Under its present configuration, the United Nations can only do what its members allow and this applies particularly to financing its peacekeeping operations (James, 1989). As long as it remains in the political interests of key member states to withhold funds, the United Nations will be inherently constrained in how many peacekeeping operations it conducts and the ways it conducts them. This leads one to be somewhat pessimistic that UN reform efforts will include significant changes in the way that the organization, and peacekeeping operations in particular, are funded. Nevertheless, the current system does not serve the organization well and some of the proposals for change have merit.

For the most part, incremental changes in the financing system (e.g., late payment fees, new methods of assessment calculation) would have a marginal effect on the UN financial crisis. As they are not necessarily mutually exclusive, collectively they may result in modest, at best, improvements in ensuring the adequacy of peacekeeping funds. They impose few direct costs or risks on the system, and therefore some experimentation with one or more of the ideas may have some merit. One would hope, however, that these incremental changes would not have the effect of deterring the organization and its members from exploring and implementing more radical proposals. Other changes, including new mechanisms for the UN to borrow funds (e.g., loans and bonds) address only short-term funding concerns and may exacerbate long-term problems. As with incremental changes, their costs and benefits are relatively minor under the best or worst scenarios.

The creation of new programs, such as the UNSIA, appears severely flawed in several ways. They do not seem to guarantee that the UN will be free of the same problems as the current system, and they tend to create new problems that may make the financial problems of the organization worse or jeopardize the mission of the UN in promoting international peace and security. It is also the case with the new programs that their likelihood of adoption remains relatively low.

The most attractive alternatives in many ways involve the imposition of new international taxes. Compared to the status quo and the other alternatives, international taxes (and several variations exist) could provide adequate revenue for peacekeeping operations and have the flexibility to meet unexpected demands in the security area. Unlike most other proposals, they remove the dependency of the UN on direct member contributions, the source of most of the financial difficulties. An added bonus is that international taxes might be expected to have a negligible economic impact on the international transactions and activities to which they are applied. The main stumbling block to their implementation (and the prognostication for their adoption is pessimistic—see Cardenas et al., 1995) is the unwillingness of states to allow the organization this power. Members remain reluctant to move the organization away from state contributions as much as they complain about those assessments. They are as yet unwilling to relinquish the influence that comes with directly providing or withholding (usually with impunity) funds to the UN. Until that changes, it may be reasonable to expect that UN peacekeeping, and the organization in general, will continue to experience financial shortfalls that bureaucratic reform, voluntary contributions, and private sources of funding will be unable to surmount fully.

References

Ayres, Ed, "Giving the UN Financial Muscle," *World Watch* 8 (1995): 7.

Bezanson, Keith and Ruben Mendez, "Alternative Funding: Looking Beyond the Nation-State," *Futures* 27, no. 2 (Mar. 1995): 223–9.

Boutros-Ghali, Boutros, *An Agenda for Peace.* 2nd ed. (New York: United Nations, 1995).

Cardenas, Emilio, R. Carlos Sersale di Cehsano, and Oscar Avalle, "Financing United Nations Operations: A Frustrating Nightmare," *Futures* 27, no. 2 (Mar. 1995): 145–59.

Cassani, Robert, "Financing Civil Society for a Global Responsibility," *Futures* 27, no. 2 (Mar. 1995): 215–21.

Charter of the Global Commission to Fund the United Nations, *Futures* 27, no. 2 (Mar. 1995): 258–60.

Childers, Erskine, "Financing the United Nations: Some Possible Solutions," *Futures* 27, no. 2 (Mar. 1995): 161–70.

Cleveland, Harlan, "The United Nations: Its Future Is Its Funding," *Futures* 27, no. 2 (Mar. 1995): 107–11.

Commission on Global Governance, *Our Global Neighborhood* (Oxford: Oxford University Press, 1995).

Diehl, Paul F., *International Peacekeeping,* revised ed. (Baltimore: Johns Hopkins University Press, 1994).

Diehl, Paul F., "The Political Implications of Using New Technologies in Peace Operations," Paper presented at the Technology for Peace Workshop, Chicago, 1996.

Diehl, Paul F. and Sonia Jurado, "United Nations Election Supervision in South Africa: Lessons from the Namibian Peacekeeping Experience," *Studies in Conflict and Terrorism* 16, no. 1 (1996): 61–74.

D'Orville, Hans and Dragoljub Najman, "A New System to Finance the United Nations," *Futures* 27, no. 2 (Mar. 1995): 171–9.

Felix, David, "The Tobin Tax Proposal: Background, Issues, and Prospects," *Futures* 27, no. 2 (Mar. 1995): 195–208.

Ford Foundation, *Financing an Effective United Nations, A Report of the Independent Advisory Group on UN Financing* (New York: Ford Foundation, 1993).

"Foundations Experts Outline Ways to Finance a More Effective UN," *UN Chronicle* 30 (June 1993): 73.

Griesgraber, Jo-Marie, "Rethinking Bretton Woods," *Futures* 27, no. 2 (Mar. 1995): 240–6.

Henderson, Hazel, "New Markets and New Commons: Opportunities in the Global Casino," *Futures* 27, no. 2 (Mar. 1995): 113–24.

James, Alan, "The Security Council: Paying for Peacekeeping," in David Forsythe, ed., *The United Nations in the World Political Economy* (New York: St. Martin's Press, 1989), pp. 13–35.

Kaul, Inge, "Beyond Financing: Giving the United Nations Power of the Purse," *Futures* 27, no. 2 (Mar. 1995): 181–8.

Kay, Alan F. and Hazel Henderson, "Financing UN Functions in the Post–Cold War Era: A Proposal for a United Nations Security Insurance Agency," *Futures* 27, no. 2 (Mar. 1995): 3–10.

Khanna, Jyoti, Todd Sandier, and Hirofumi Shimizu, "Sharing the Financial Burden for UN and NATO Peacekeeping, 1976–1996," *Journal of Conflict Resolution* 42, no. 2 (1998): 176–195.

Langmore, John, "Restructuring Economic and Financial Power: The Potential Role of a Foreign Exchange-Transaction Levy," *Futures* 27, no. 2 (Mar. 1995): 189–94.

Laurenti, Jeffrey, *National Taxpayers and International Organizations: Sharing the Burden of Financing the United Nations* (New York: United Nations Association of the United States of America, 1995).

Leurdijk, Dick A., *A UN Rapid Deployment Brigade: Strengthening the Capacity for Quick Response* (The Hague: Netherlands Institute of International Relations, 1995).

Mackinlay, John and Jarat Chopra, "Second Generation Multinational Operations," *Washington Quarterly* 15, no. 3 (Summer 1992): 113–34.

Mendez, Ruben P., "Paying for Peace and Development," *Foreign Policy* 100 (Fall 1995): 19–31.

Mendez, Ruben P., "Financing the United Nations and the International Public Sector: Problems and Reform," *Global Governance* 3 (1997): 283–310.

Miller, Morris, "Where Is Globalization Taking Us? Why We Need a New Bretton Woods," *Futures* 27, no. 2 (Mar. 1995): 125–44.

Mills, Susan R., *The Financing of United Nations Peacekeeping Operations: The Need for a Sound Financial Basis.* International Peace Academy Occasional Papers on Peacekeeping (New York: International Peace Academy, 1989).

"Paying for the Peacekeepers UNIFIL, UNAVEM, UNAMEIT: International Peacekeeping Needs to Be Better Run and More Soundly Financed," *The Economist* 322 (25 January 1992): 17–8.

"Piece-Rate for Peacekeepers: As United Nations Peacekeepers Fan Out Across the World, the Bills Come In," *The Economist* (25 January 1992): 38.

Ratner, Stephen, *The New UN Peacekeeping* (New York: St. Martin's Press, 1995).

Russett, Bruce, "Ten Balances for Weighing UN Reform Proposals," in Bruce Russett, ed., *The Once and Future Security Council* (New York: St. Martin's Press, 1997), pp. 13–28.

Saito, Naoki, *Financing of UN Peacekeeping Operations: U.S. and Japanese Responses* (Tokyo: International Institute for Global Peace, 1992).

Smith, Daniel, "The United Nations Security Insurance Agency (UNSIA) Proposal: A Preliminary Assessment," *Futures* 27, no. 2 (Mar. 1995): 209–13.
Stanley Foundation, *UN Budgetary and Financial Impasse* (Muscatine, IA: Stanley Foundation, 1986).
Tobin, James, "A Proposal for International Monetary Reform," *Eastern Economic Journal* 4, no. 3-4 (July-October, 1978): 153–9.
Washburn, John, "United Nations Relations with the United States: The UN Must Look Out for Itself," *Global Governance* 2, no. 1 (Jan.-Apr. 1996): 81–96.

PART 3

Peace and Security Affairs

Paul F. Diehl and Brian Frederking

THE REALIST VIEW OF INTERNATIONAL ORGANIZATIONS HAS
been most prevalent in the area of peace and security affairs. The inci-
dence of war around the world over the past sixty-plus years attests to
the mostly failed efforts of international organizations to prevent the
outbreak of war. With no international police force on the immediate
horizon, there is little prospect for global governance mechanisms that
can prevent large-scale violence. Furthermore, the collective security
provisions in Chapter VII of the UN Charter have never been fully
implemented (the Korean and Kuwaiti efforts were not truly international operations, conducted under international command with broadly
representative groups of contributing states).

Historically, there are several reasons for the relative ineffective-
ness of the United Nations and other regional organizations in preventing war. First, and most obvious, was the stalemate among the permanent members of the Security Council, with the split largely along
ideological lines. Cold War tensions and the great-power veto in the
Security Council often prevented the United Nations from launching
concerted actions when faced with threats to international peace and
security. The superpower rivalry was also manifested in proxy conflicts
around the world, making the ability of regional bodies to form consensus on actions difficult. Second, international organizations have been
hampered by a lack of political will on the part of the members to take
strong action, even when consensus exists. The financial and human
costs associated with security operations are considered too high by
many key states who believe they have few direct national interests

affected by conflicts far from their home base. Finally, international organizations usually become involved in disputes only after one or more of the disputants has threatened or actually used military force. At that stage, it becomes very difficult to resolve the dispute without further violence.

The end of the Cold War and the establishment of a so-called new world order gave many idealists great hope for the role of international organizations in the realm of peace and security affairs. The Security Council was no longer stalemated and greater consensus on taking strong action in conflicts such as the First Gulf War and Haiti (during the 1990s) emerged. Furthermore, many regional organizations, such as the European Union, sought to develop policies for dealing with conflicts in their own backyards. There was also increasing global attention to the concept of early warning, the notion that the international community should be able to detect nascent conflict before it reaches the militarized stage and thereby take action that actually prevents violence rather than just dealing with its aftermath.

Failures in Bosnia, Somalia, and Rwanda revealed that international organizations could not be expected to succeed in all the ventures they undertook, and the lack of political will and the presence of complex conflicts remained obstacles to the establishment of a true new world order. Even though the United Nations could reach decisions more easily on security matters than ever before, the strategies adopted were not uniformly more successful than in the Cold War era. Currently, international organizations are still struggling with the new global environment and searching for the right mix of organizational structures, procedures, and strategies to deal with the variety of security challenges that they now face. The three chapters in Part 3 consider these questions and seek to shed some light on how the international community might adapt to a world without a superpower rivalry, but one still threatened by international militarized conflict.

Early on, the United Nations adopted the peacekeeping strategy to deal with various conflicts around the world. Yet by the beginning of the 1980s, international peacekeeping efforts were largely moribund, and it was thought that this strategy for dealing with international conflict might be abandoned. Yet the peacekeeping strategy was renewed with vigor starting in 1989, with more than twice as many UN peacekeeping operations being deployed in the decade following than in the almost forty-five years of the Cold War period. Traditional peacekeeping operations are characterized by the deployment of a small number of neutral, lightly armed troops, with the consent of the host state, to act as an interposition or buffer force between protagonists, usually after a cease-fire, but prior to conflict resolution. Along with the expansion in the number of peacekeeping operations, however, has been a shift away from the traditional model and an expansion in the type and scope of duties for peacekeeping operations. In Chapter 6, Peter Wallensteen and Birger Heldt explore the debates about the relative effectiveness of UN and regional peacekeeping missions. They conclude that while the UN more often deals with the most difficult conflicts, it has the same success rate as regional organizations.

In Chapter 7, Alex Bellamy analyzes UN efforts to implement the emerging norm of the "responsibility to protect." This norm moves beyond the idea that states have the *right* to intervene in situations in which there are large-scale human rights abuses, but actually have an *obligation* to do so. This norm has generated criticism from some developing countries that it will be used to justify military intervention. The chapter highlights the tensions between emerging humanitarian norms, relations among the major powers on the Security Council, and state sovereignty.

Finally, in Chapter 8, Renee de Nevers explores the role of NATO in counter-terror operations. Because NATO is an alliance rather than a "tool" of the US, and given that the US and its allies have different understandings of the relative importance of terrorism and how to fight terrorism, NATO has struggled to develop a coherent and effective counter-terrorism approach. The organization has also struggled to redefine its purpose and activities as the traditional military threats of the Cold War have disappeared and new security threats, often "out of area" and involving non-state actors, have emerged.

7

International Peacekeeping: The UN Versus Regional Organizations

Peter Wallensteen and Birger Heldt

AN OLD THEME IN THE DEBATE ON INTERNATIONAL PEACE-
keeping concerns whether it should be carried out by the United
Nations, regional organizations (such as the OAS, OAU/AU,
ECOWAS, EU, OSCE, or NATO), or ad hoc coalitions of willing states.
Chapters VI and VII of the UN Charter have been used to authorize UN-
led operations, whereas Chapter VIII has given additional legitimacy to
non-UN operations. It may even be argued that the Charter (Article 52)
expresses that the UN should be the last resort, while regional organizations and neighboring states should be given priority, when it comes
to dealing with threats to international peace and security. Only when
such initiatives have failed may they be referred to the UN.

Building on data compiled by Birger Heldt at the Folke Bernadotte
Academy, Stockholm, Sweden, this chapter explores the empirical landscape of this old question. Covering 1948–2005, it compares peacekeeping in different organizational frameworks. Box 7.1 presents the
guiding definition for a peacekeeping operation. Focusing on patterns in
terms of number, location, and type of conflict, it identifies trends, similarities, as well as differences between peacekeeping operations carried
out by the UN and those conducted by regional organizations or ad hoc
coalitions of states. It also summarizes available evidence on success

Reprinted from *Peace and Conflict 2008,* by J. Joseph Hewitt, Jonathan Wilkenfeld, and
Ted Robert Gurr. © 2008 Paradigm Publishers. Reprinted by permission of Paradigm
Publishers and the Center for International Development and Conflict Management at
the University of Maryland.

Box 7.1   Defining Peacekeeping Operations

In this study, *a peacekeeping operation* is defined as a third-party
state intervention that:

- involves the deployment of military troops and/or military
  observers and/or civilian police in a target state;
- is, according to the mandate (as specified in multilateral
  agreements, peace accords, or resolutions of the UN or
  regional organizations), established for the purpose of sepa-
  rating conflict parties, monitoring ceasefires, maintaining
  buffer zones, and taking responsibility for the security situation (among other things) between formerly, potentially, or
  presently warring parties; and
- is neutral towards the conflict parties, but not necessarily
  impartial towards their behavior.

This definition has fewer implications for UN-led operations
than for many peace- and capacity-building missions. Such missions, for instance by the Organization for Security and Cooperation in Europe (OSCE), the European Union (EU), and the
UN, are excluded. In many of these cases, the personnel were either
civilian and/or had no operational duties but focused, for instance,
on training local police. The Kosovo Verification Mission and the
Sri Lanka Monitoring Mission are excluded, as only civilian personnel were deployed. The definition also excludes operations such
as the present, large multinational force in Iraq as well as ISAF
(International Security Assistance Force) in Afghanistan. In the former case it was not a neutral force interpositioned between two or
more identified warring parties, but an occupation force much like
Operation Uphold Democracy in Haiti 1994–1995; in the latter
case, the operation was not an interposition force but a force initially deployed to assist in maintaining security in Kabul.

rates and offers some conclusions on the significance of the organizational framework for international action.

The Arguments

The common positive arguments favoring the use of a global organization for peacekeeping is that it has a strong standing in international law, access to global resources (finances, troops, logistics), and competence. This means it can act in an even-handed manner vis-à-vis the conflicting parties and in conflicts around the world. There are equally compelling arguments against regional organizations that consequently favor the use of the global institution. For instance, it is often claimed that regional organizations are too closely tied to the developments in their vicinity, and that strong regional powers may use the organizations to their own advantage. Thus, a global organization offers capacity and an element of protection, particularly for weaker regional or local actors. Common positive arguments for regional organizations and ad hoc coalitions contend that they may have more local knowledge and are thus more capable of dealing with local conditions, have equipment adapted to local conditions, are quicker to reach decisions on deployment, and are closer to the scene and consequently can be deployed more quickly than the UN.

Although conflicting and possible to refute by historical examples, the various arguments are convincing. Therefore, it may not be surprising to find that during the past ten years the UN has attempted to increase the contribution of regional actors to peacekeeping, while at the same time trying to coordinate global and regional actors. This UN-led process is often said to have been initiated by the UN Secretary-General's report *An Agenda for Peace* (Boutros-Ghali 1992). Noting the dramatically increased demand on the UN for peacekeeping, the report urged a larger contribution by regional actors to peacekeeping. At the initiative of the UN, a series of high-level meetings between the UN and regional organizations were held in 1994, 1998, 2001, 2003, and 2005 (cf. Heldt and Wallensteen 2006). These meetings have touched upon how regional actors can make a larger contribution (including peacekeeping) to address threats to international peace and security, and how such efforts can be coordinated with UN efforts (Heldt and Wallensteen 2006).

However, prudence has been urged, in that the choice between UN or non-UN efforts should be made on a case-by-case basis rather than having non-UN operations as the first choice. This note of caution has been based on the observation that regions with crises and conflicts are often characterized by insufficient capacity to carry out peacekeeping. In essence, regions (such as Africa) with the greatest demand for peacekeeping are said to have the least peacekeeping capacity. This in turn implies that regions (such as Europe) with the lowest demand for peacekeeping, also have the largest capacity. This has led to concerns that a larger regional responsibility for peacekeeping will deplete the UN's pool of well-trained and well-equipped peacekeeping resources. A fear is that troop-contributing countries will use their resources for regional operations to the detriment of the most conflict-prone regions. Yet, if the regions with the lowest demand for peacekeeping also have the largest capacity, then these regions will not experience a large demand for peacekeeping in their own backyards. This suggests that, in the end, these regions' peacekeeping capacity may still be placed at the disposal of the UN.

Global Patterns

Because the arguments concerning both UN and regional organizations are compelling, it is not unexpected to find that the number of peacekeeping operations is virtually identical for the two types of organizational frameworks. There were 13 ongoing non-UN operations as of December 2005, at a time when the UN was carrying out 15 operations. This striking numerical similarity applies also when looking at all operations since 1948: from 1948 to 2005 non-UN actors initiated 67 operations, while for the UN the corresponding number is 59. The patterns are very similar also in terms of historical trends as found in Figure 7.1. During the Cold War the number of missions was small, whether within or outside the UN. Dag Hammarskjöld, the UN Secretary-General at the time, argued against activities outside the UN framework, claiming that the UN was the foremost body for international peace and security and could not be bypassed (Urquhart 1994).

Data for the period up to the end of the Cold War, around 1990, do not show dramatic shifts in absolute numbers, which are low. The number of UN operations started to increase in 1988, while the growth in operations carried out by other actors began in 1992. This increase occurs not just as the Cold War ends, but also coincides with an increase in wars and armed conflicts in the first part of the 1990s—when more

Figure 7.1   Number of Peacekeeping Operations, 1948–2005

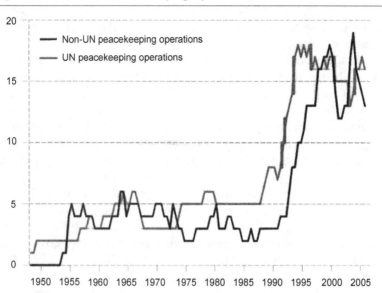

than 50 annual armed conflicts were recorded globally by the Uppsala Conflict Data Program. Another observation is that the number of both types of operations is comparable after the mid-1990s, just after the UN explicitly started to encourage more regional peacekeeping efforts. The trends appear to indicate that the UN may have inspired or induced other actors, notably regional organizations, to take on peacekeeping.

While we find more UN operations from the mid-1970s to the early 1990s, there are more ongoing non-UN operations during parts of the 1990s. That may be attributed to the developments of one particular region: Europe, and Europe's increased willingness and capacity to deal with threats to the region's peace and security. A large part of the non-UN operations in recent years consists of missions deployed by the EU, OSCE, and NATO. As such, Europe's ability and desire to deal with regional security is presently unsurpassed by any other region. Apparently, an interplay has been at work, where one body took over responsibility from another, and where many non-UN missions were either authorized, or recognized, by UN Security Council resolutions. Thus, regional initiatives cannot be regarded as challenges to UN authority. It appears that the leading actors are in agreement on the UN's unique standing in international law. To support this, we can observe that 28 of the non-UN operations were welcomed, authorized, endorsed, commended, or approved by Security Council resolutions. For one reason or another, the remaining operations never reached the Security Council's agenda.

While overall there have been fewer UN-led operations, there were more UN operations at almost every point in time. This pattern can best be explained by a longer average duration for UN operations and as such confirms that the UN has had a primacy in peacekeeping. There is no evidence in favor of a consistent pattern of regionalization of peacekeeping for the past ten years, as has often been claimed: only during a few brief periods have UN-led operations been in the minority. Burden-sharing may instead be a useful concept for describing this historical pattern, as it means that costs are shared regardless of their size and without concern for UN and regional peacekeeping abilities.

Whereas regional organizations can decide on their own and through their appropriate organs to welcome UN operations, UN member states are not in a legal position to decline UN action, when decisions are made under Chapter VII. However, since the end of the Cold War it has been rare for the choice of organizational framework to be stated in such a strong manner. Polemics have also given way to arguments of efficiency and capability. The discussion has moved to questions such as: Which organization is best equipped—politically, financially, militarily, culturally—to act in a particular crisis situation? Which ones are already strained by peacekeeping tasks? Where is there some free capacity?

There are differences with respect to the type of conflict in which the peacekeeping operation is placed. A significant dimension is the one of interstate and intrastate conflicts. It is worth exploring, as intrastate conflict customarily has been seen to be outside the scope of international organizations. For instance, global bodies have been regarded as more threatening to state sovereignty, partly as they appear to invite major power interests within a state's borders. Thus, interstate conflicts may get priority, particularly for a global organization.

For the whole period there were 17 UN-led operations in interstate conflicts and 18 non-UN operations. Interestingly, none of the latter was authorized or recognized by the UN Security Council. As is evident from Figure 7.2, most of the regional peacekeeping operations between states took place in 1973 or earlier. Examples are the Arab League observer mission in Yemen 1972, the cease-fire commission for the Algeria-Morocco conflict 1963–1964, and the commissions launched during dif-

Figure 7.2   Peacekeeping Operations, Interstate Conflict, 1948–2005

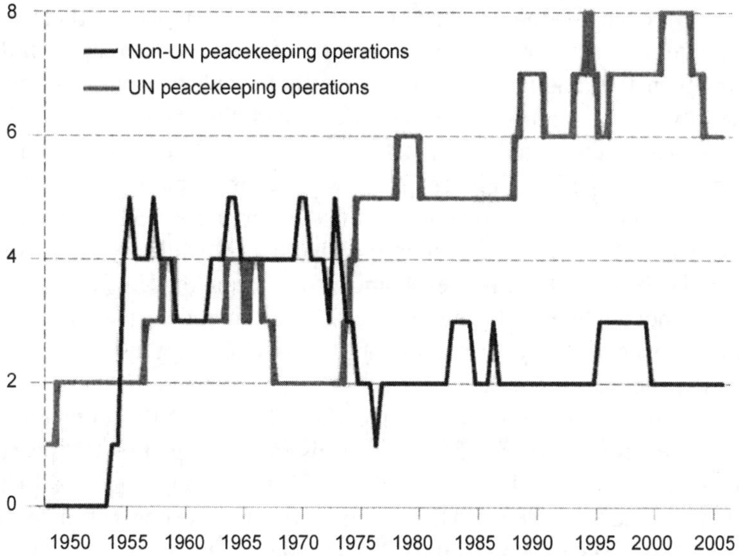

ferent phases of the conflicts in Indochina. Since the end of the Cold War, interstate conflicts have most often seen UN missions. In other words, the Cold War period saw an element of regionalism, but that often masked action under major power tutelage. By the end of 2005, the UN led six operations in interstate conflicts, other actors only two. Given that the number of interstate wars and armed conflicts is low in comparison to intrastate conflicts, interstate peacekeeping constitutes a large proportion of all operations. The UN as well as regional organizations is more likely to be used in interstate conflicts than in other conflicts.

A final observation is that there is virtually no relationship between the number of operations carried out by non-UN actors and those conducted by the UN in interstate conflicts. Whereas UN operations have a primacy, the UN does not inspire a trend in, or set a path for, the management of interstate conflicts. This observation leads us to an interesting insight: whatever factors motivate/allow the UN to intervene, they are not the same as those which motivate regional actors to intervene. From this it follows that we cannot understand why regional actors deploy peacekeepers in interstate conflicts by using the same models that can be used for understanding UN motivations.

For the whole period the UN deployed 43 operations in intrastate conflicts, while non-UN actors deployed 50 (of which, as mentioned, 28 were approved by the UN Security Council). As most conflicts are intrastate, this is the record that would be expected, or perhaps a little lower than the amount of intrastate conflict would warrant. Furthermore, the resort to non-UN led operations, with the endorsement of the UN, supports the argument that this is a matter of complementarity rather than competition. Figure 7.3 shows that for the period 1996–2005 there were more non-UN operations, but this was at a time when the UN itself was aiming at strengthening regional bodies while trying to control and coordinate their peacekeeping efforts. From the UN perspective this was not a matter of losing its preeminence but rather making it possible to concentrate on particularly urgent or demanding tasks and sharing the peacekeeping tasks.

It is important to note that for the 1989–2005 period and in particular for the period 2000–2005, Africa received a large part of UN peacekeeping resources. By December 2004, Africa had 75 percent of all UN operations and 80 percent of UN operations in intrastate conflicts in terms of all UN peacekeeping personnel. The past decade has been one of a UN

Figure 7.3   Peacekeeping Operations, Intrastate Conflict, 1948–2005

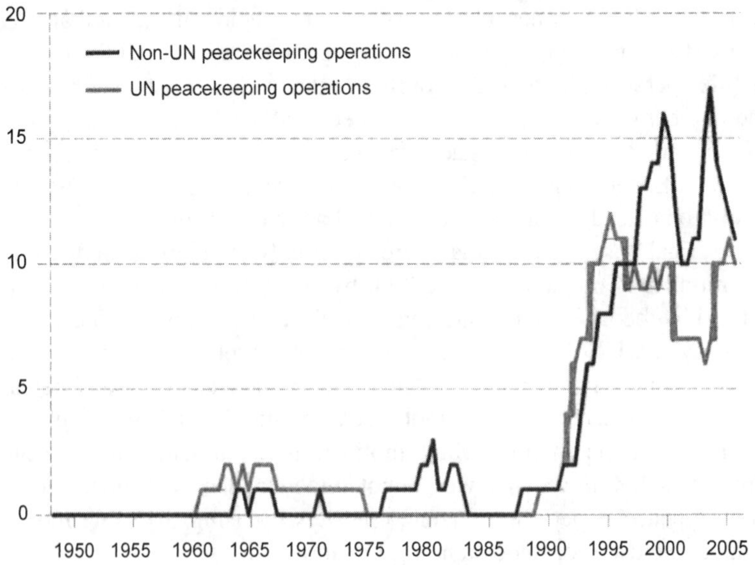

focus on—not a neglect of—Africa. This observation serves to refute arguments and concerns that a larger regional responsibility for peace-keeping will deplete the UN pool of well-trained and well-equipped peacekeeping resources, to the detriment of the most conflict-prone regions. The pattern has in fact been the opposite one. It is also important to recall that by late 2004 some 45 percent of the UN peacekeepers in Africa came from African countries. In a sense, although under the UN flag and with UN financing, Africa is carrying out its own peacekeeping.

Regional Patterns

Table 7.1 shows the total number of peacekeeping operations from 1948 to 2005 by region, conflict type, and organization. The most conspicu-ous pattern is that in the Americas the UN has been entrusted to address intrastate conflicts, and regional actors have dealt with interstate con-flicts, while in the Middle East the UN has dealt only with interstate conflicts, and regional actors have addressed both types of conflict. Interestingly, the three regions of Africa, Europe, and Asia differ from the other two by displaying a similar pattern for both types of conflicts. The markedly different patterns for the Americas and the Middle East beg an explanation. A closer look at the Middle East suggests that all the non-UN intrastate operations concerned the same conflict and location. Three of the operations were deployed in Lebanon, and the fourth one

Table 7.1   Peacekeeping Operations, by Region and Conflict Type (1948–2005)

	UN-led Operations		Non-UN-led Operations	
	Interstate Conflict	Intrastate Conflict	Interstate Conflict	Intrastate Conflict
Africa	3	19	3	21
Asia	3	6	6	9
Americas	0	9	5	2
Europe	2	9	0	14
Middle East	9	0	4	4

Source: Heldt and Wallensteen (2006) for the period 1948–2004, and data collected by Heldt for 2005.
Note: The UN operation in Cyprus (UNFICYP) is counted twice, as it was an intrastate peacekeeping operation until 1974, after which it became an interstate operation. The UN operation in Lebanon (MNF I) is counted twice, as it was an intrastate as well as an interstate peacekeeping operation.

in Jordan. The conflicts were also interconnected. It may therefore not be surprising that one actor, in this case the Arab League, having initiated peacekeeping, ends up handling all subsequent peace operations.

The same pattern applies to interstate operations in the Americas. Four out of five operations took place in Central America, often involving Honduras. Moreover, El Salvador and Nicaragua were involved in two conflicts each, and two of the conflicts were between the same parties. Again, the conflicts in Central America demonstrated an interconnectedness, similar to the one in the Middle East, and may offer an explanation for the pattern: having initiated peacekeeping, the same actor tends to end up handling subsequent peace operations in interconnected conflicts. Also, Europe exhibits a comparable pattern of clustering, in that eight UN operations concern conflicts of the Balkans. Such clustering of peace operations can be found in other regions. For instance, of the nine UN operations in the Americas, five dealt with Haiti. The global pattern of peacekeeping is thus characterized by inertia. It suggests that the initial decisions are important, as they set the stage for which organization will be involved in the long run.

It is important to note that 13 of the non-UN operations were carried out by actors from outside the region of conflict. Such out-of-area operations were rather common in Asia, evenly distributed in the Middle East and Africa, while rare in the Americas. Hence, two-thirds of the non-UN operations in Asia, and half of the operations in the Middle East, were neither carried out by the region itself, nor by the UN. Such out-of-area operations appear to be a thing of the past: during the past 20 years only four such operations were launched.

Asia deserves some more attention, as it is unique in several aspects. First, almost half of the non-UN operations were such "out-of-area" operations. All of the operations in interstate conflicts were carried out by such actors. This includes the operation between the two Koreas—in place for more than 50 years—and the five operations established during the Vietnam War. The remaining intrastate operations consist almost entirely of those deployed in Papua New Guinea and the Solomon Islands that consisted of just a couple of small (with the exception of Australia) troop-contributing countries, and were of limited size. None of the pivotal East Asian countries contributed to these operations, while a few (Malaysia, the Philippines, Republic of Korea, and Thailand) contributed to the INTERFET operation in East Timor. This provides for a unique intervention pattern of (1) nonintervention by regional actors, and (2) ad hoc coalitions of the willing rather than regional intergovernmental organizations (IGOs).

As noted by many scholars, North East Asia is among the few regions that lack regional structures for conflict management and prevention (e.g., Swanström 2005). This means that there is no institutionalized preparedness in Asia for peacekeeping in the region. In addition, some of the conflicts are located inside pivotal member states, making peacekeeping difficult to establish. There are also a number of unresolved interstate issues that reinforce mutual distrust: the Korean peninsula is still formally in a state of war, the Taiwan issue has varied in intensity and experienced serious crises over the years, the border conflict between India and Pakistan has caused several wars, and there are many sea border disputes in North East Asia. There is also a conflict legacy from the first part of the 1900s, carrying memories of injustices that influence interstate cooperation. The absence of Asian intraregional peacekeeping, or even the absence of security-oriented IGOs, should not come as a surprise.

Impact

This brings us to the issue of the impact of peacekeeping on war and whether there is a significant difference between the different types of organizations. The issue of "success" is not easy to settle. In general, there is a detrimental confusion in the field over whether success should refer to performance (e.g., mandate fulfillment) or impact (e.g., conflict control, war avoidance, or even transitions to democracy), whether it should involve positive or negative peace, proper time frames, etc. The mandates for the operations vary, and even the time perspectives: should there be peace in terms of no war when the peacekeepers leave or should they stay for decades? What about the other goals, such as humanitarian aid, the building of democracy, state reconstruction? Many of these mandates require fairly long-term perspectives and a sharper differentiation among types of missions.

Here we will settle for a minimal definition: short-term impact in terms of absence of war during deployment. That means that we ask whether the peace operation achieves what its name suggests: maintaining the peace while the operation is in place. After all, this is the fundamental responsibility and goal of peacekeeping, and is at the heart of peacekeeping operations regardless of whether the mandate is broad and borders on nation-building. Peacekeeping may contribute to peace also after its departure by leaving a legacy behind, but then a host of other factors are also likely to affect the conditions of a society or a relationship between states.

A question that carries important policy implications for the ongoing debate on whether the UN or regional actors should be entrusted with peacekeeping concerns success rates. A series of studies (e.g., Doyle and Sambanis 2000, 2006; Fortna 2003a, 2003b, 2004) has demonstrated that peacekeeping does extend the duration of post-conflict peace, and even increases the probability of transitions to post-civil war democracy. Yet, these studies have not yet dealt with the question of the relative degree of success for UN and non-UN missions. Neither have they had access to the most recent data on non-UN missions. The focus on post-conflict situations also means that many operations deployed either in advance of—and during—conflicts are excluded. If we want to evaluate comparative success rates, it may be preferable to include all peacekeeping operations in the analysis.

An alternative research design could thus examine the question, "Under what conditions are peacekeeping operations successful?" Some operations were successful, while others were not, and this variation across cases requires an explanation. The design would thus try to account for variation in success across peacekeeping operations by examining whether type of mission makes any difference. As such it answers one important question—"Under what conditions are peacekeeping operations successful?"—but at the same time cannot answer another important question—"Is there a relationship between peacekeeping operations and the duration of peace?" With this implication in mind we will now pursue the research question with the help of the alternative research design.

It is often claimed that peacekeeping operations should be deployed where there is a peace to keep. This presupposes an agreement between warring parties. For the peacekeepers it would also be an "easier" task, and for the home public of the troop contributors this is reassuring: These states are not risking the lives of their citizens. In reality, and as illustrated in Table 7.2, peacekeeping operations in intrastate conflicts often find themselves deployed where there is no peace to keep, either because peace has not yet been established, or because peace has bro-

Table 7.2   Operation Overlap (% of months) with Ongoing Conflict (1948–2004)

Conflict Type	UN	Non-UN
Intrastate conflict	20.5	21.4
Interstate conflict	1.3	0.65

Source: Heldt and Wallensteen (2006).

ken down during the course of the operation. There is a marked difference between the types of conflict, but not between the types of organizational frameworks: intrastate conflicts are clearly more risky, and interstate conflicts less risky, regardless of organizational framework.

In fact there is a clear pattern: peacekeeping in interstate conflicts is seldom deployed until after the parties have stopped violence; in intrastate conflicts peace operations are often launched without similar strong guarantees. Twenty percent of the time in intrastate conflicts the peace operations find themselves in situations where there is no peace to keep. One can also see this the other way around; 80 percent of the operations actually find a peace to keep, either because of their own activities or because the parties have managed to contain the violence themselves. From the point of view of the civilian population, peace only four out of five days is not likely to be satisfactory. For a war-weary world it may still sound better than continuous fighting and gives some prospect for a better future. In the medical field, treatments that are able to cure 80 percent of a very serious disease are probably hailed as very successful. Yet, over time, a 20 percent failure rate generates a large number of casualties.

The conclusion that UN and regional operations are overall and substantially equally successful during deployment appears to suggest that the two types are substitutable. However, the figures do not take into account the degree of difficulty faced by these peacekeepers. These success rates may therefore reflect either the effectiveness of different types of operations, or different degrees of difficulties. Implicit in such an argument is the plausible assumption that not all cases are equally war prone. For instance, it is sometimes claimed that the most difficult cases are referred to the UN, and if this is correct, then the equal success rates would speak in favor of the UN. Indeed, Haas (1987) reports that during the 40-year period 1945–1984, the UN was not only more likely to attempt to manage interstate disputes, but was also—with the exception of the five-year period 1971–1975—more likely to be entrusted to manage the more serious ones.

A similar picture is at hand for peacekeeping, as UN-led operations are less likely to be deployed to prevent armed conflict, and consequently more likely to be deployed during and after wars. Of the 42 UN intrastate operations, only 10 were deployed where civil war had not recently taken place. The corresponding figure for the 50 non-UN-led operations is 18. Thus, UN operations were almost twice as likely to be sent to more difficult situations. For UN-led operations in interstate conflicts, the numbers are 6 out of 17, compared to 13 out of 18, suggesting a similar ratio. Regional actors are obviously more likely to deploy conflict prevention operations than the UN. One interpretation is that regional actors initially try to manage conflicts, and if they fail the conflicts are referred to the UN Security Council, just as indicated by the UN Charter. By the time a conflict reaches the UN agenda, it is more likely to have developed into war. There is a selection effect at play here: difficult cases will ultimately reach the UN agenda and end up being managed by UN peacekeepers.

Whatever interpretation, the data show that the UN tends to be entrusted with more of the difficult cases, but still is not less successful. This suggests that UN operations are in fact more likely to succeed than those carried out by other organizations. This is, however, only a rough way of treating a subject that requires more study and where more refined measurements can be developed to estimate the difficulty or severity of the challenge a peace operation faces. Moreover, as new forms of peacekeeping are developing—either involving a combination of different organizations (e.g., UN+AU); or different organizations replacing each other; or with mandates involving long-term peacebuilding—the task is increasingly complex.

The only large-scale comparative empirical study so far that has attempted to control for degree of mission difficulty finds no robust evidence of a difference in success rates (with regard to absence of war) that applies without restrictions throughout time (1948–2000) and across space (all regions of the world). This means that knowing whether an operation is led by the UN or by a regional organization or ad hoc coalitions does not assist in predicting its success. While some regions, for reasons of military resources and capabilities are in a better position than others to take on peacekeeping tasks, non-UN-led operations have overall not been less successful than UN operations. Nevertheless, if peacekeeping operations are primarily confidence-building measures where physical presence rather than war fighting is essential, then issues of military resources and capabilities, or even command and control, are not of major importance.

The policy implication of these admittedly first-cut findings is that if the goal is to stop violence, then UN efforts to address international peace and security can continue to coexist with non-UN-led efforts, just as has been the case for 50 years. The UN Charter has got it right in that sense. Meanwhile, it is not possible to infer that the two types of missions are entirely substitutable. Rather, there might be a historical pattern with a selection process: the choice between UN and non-UN operations has been made on a case-by-case basis focusing on suitability and probability of success, at least in the narrow terms here defined. Meanwhile, and to complicate the picture, we have also observed a pattern where the organization that is used in the first instance, often is used also in later phases of the same conflict or in conflicts in the immediate neighborhood. This may be a choice of convenience rather than one based on close evaluation of what is most appropriate as a situation becomes more complex. Another observation is that non-UN operations are more likely than UN ones to be preventive operations. This indicates that it is not just suitability and probability of success that matters, but also inertia as well as ability to intervene at an early stage.

This raises the question of how a global division of labor should be designed. There are at least three possibilities: (1) the UN takes on some missions, regional organizations (and informal coalitions) take on other missions, both basically doing the same type of peacekeeping, but in different situations; (2) UN-led and other operations coexist within one conflict and divide the tasks among themselves within that particular setting; and (3) the UN takes on some types of missions (e.g., multidimensional operations) whereas regional actors focus on others (such as traditional peacekeeping). Let us elaborate on these three possibilities.

The first form is the one that has been in existence for more than 50 years, and it appears overall to have worked, as the data presented here demonstrate. The second option has been practiced only on a few occasions. However, there is no broad empirical evidence to settle the question of how this division of labor could be designed, or even whether it should be generally promoted. From experiences in development cooperation it has been observed that coordination problems are likely to arise, and local actors may play different organizations against each other. We have, however, observed a pattern of one organization being replaced by another, sometimes referred to as "re-hatting," in that regional peacekeepers are placed at the UN's disposal and change their national hat to a blue helmet, or vice versa. If different organizations develop special skills this might in fact become an effective strategy.

The third option follows from this argument and has in fact been at hand ever since the UN initiated multidimensional peacekeeping in 1989. Regional actors have almost exclusively carried out traditional short-term operations in intrastate conflicts, while the UN has more often been engaged in long-term multidimensional operations. Access to training, capacity for more complex missions, and financial resources may suffice to explain such difference. However, the desirability of this task-specific division of labor should be thoroughly assessed in future research.

Conclusion

The question asked initially in this essay was whether there is a contradiction or even competition between global and regional peacekeeping activities. The conclusion is that there has not been. Furthermore, there is a pattern of burden-sharing and a functional division of labor. Over the period, both types of missions have increased in numbers and significance, but regional initiatives and coalitions of states have almost exclusively carried out traditional peacekeeping missions even in intrastate conflicts, whereas the UN has become a provider of multidimensional operations with extensive mandates. Regional missions have often been deployed in early phases of conflict, what may amount to preventive actions. This means they may have an advantage in being able to act earlier than the UN, and at a point in time when resource demands are less restraining. UN missions, however, may more often be used at later stages of a conflict, when the difficulties are larger and the resource requirements higher. Considering the UN's larger pool of peacekeepers as well as financial resources, such a division of labor appears to be reasonable. Even so, the success rates do not differ between the organizational frameworks.

Regional organizations may have a stronger will, capacity, and interest in preventing conflicts in their own neighborhood from becoming serious, and this may account for the preventive nature of their peacekeeping efforts. The UN certainly can support such activities, but its decision-making may make it more likely for use in complex peacekeeping and post-conflict peacebuilding. Developing specific skills within different organizations geared to different elements in the typical conflict cycle would possibly constitute a way in which global resources for peacekeeping can be utilized in an optimal way, as far as preventing the onset, escalation, and/or diffusion of direct violence.

References

Boutros-Ghali, Boutros. 1992. *An agenda for peace*, United Nations, New York.
Doyle, Michael & Sambanis, Nicholas. 2000. "International peacebuilding: A theoretical and quantitative analysis," *American Political Science Review*, vol. 94, pp. 779–802.
Doyle, Michael & Sambanis, Nicholas. 2006. *Making war and building peace: United Nations peace operations*. Princeton University Press, Princeton.

Fortna, Virginia Page. 2003a. "Inside and out: Peacekeeping and the duration of peace after civil and interstate wars," *International Studies Review*, vol. 5, no. 4, pp. 97–114.

Fortna, Virginia Page. 2003b. "Scraps of paper? Agreements and the durability of peace," *International Organization* 48, pp. 337–372.

Fortna, Virginia Page. 2004. "Does peacekeeping keep peace? International intervention and the duration of peace after civil war," *International Studies Quarterly*, vol. 48, pp. 269–292.

Haas, Ernst. 1987. "The collective management of international conflict, 1945–1984." Pp. 7–70 in *The United Nations and the maintenance of international peace and security*. Dordrecht: Martinus Nijhoff Publishers.

Heldt, Birger, and Peter Wallensteen. 2006. *Peacekeeping operations: Global patterns of intervention and success, 1948–2004*, 2nd ed. Sandoverken, Sweden: Folke Bernadotte Academy Press.

Swanstron, Nicholas, ed. 2005. *Conflict management and conflict prevention in North Asia*. Uppsala: Uppsala University, Silk Road Studies Program.

Urquhart, Brian. 1994. *Hammarskjold*. New York: Norton.

8

The Responsibility to Protect and the Problem of Military Intervention

Alex J. Bellamy

FROM INAUSPICIOUS BEGINNINGS, THE "RESPONSIBILITY TO protect" (R2P) has come a long way in a relatively short space of time. The principle was endorsed by the United Nations General Assembly in 2005 and unanimously reaffirmed by the Security Council in 2006 (Resolution 1674).[1] Ban Ki-moon has identified the challenge of translating R2P "from words into deeds" as one of the cornerstones of his Secretary-Generalship.[2] The principle has also become part of the working language of international engagement with grave humanitarian crises: the head of the Human Rights Council's mission to Darfur, Jodie Williams, used it to evaluate the government of Sudan's performance, finding that it had "manifestly failed" in its responsibility to protect its citizens;[3] the Security Council referred to the principle in mandating the UN–African Union (AU) hybrid mission for Darfur (UNAMID) (Resolution 1706, 2006); and both Kofi Annan and Ban Ki-moon used R2P in relation to their diplomatic efforts to resolve the post-election conflict in Kenya.

Yet evidence of international disquiet with R2P abounds. The Williams Report was denounced by Arab and Asian members of the Human Rights Council, and it took six months to persuade the Security Council to reaffirm a principle to which its members had given their assent in 2005. Several governments have argued that they did not in fact endorse the principle in 2005 and have committed themselves only to further deliberation. . . .

These problems originate from a common source: confusion about the relationship between R2P and nonconsensual military intervention.

Reprinted from *International Affairs* 84, no. 4 (2008): 615–639. © 2008 Blackwell Publishers. Reprinted by permission of the publisher.

On the one hand, there is a common belief among governments (especially members of the Non-Aligned Movement) that R2P is simply a more sophisticated way of conceptualizing and hence legitimizing humanitarian intervention.[4] These concerns have been expressed by governments for as long as the concept has been around but have been fuelled by events.[5] For instance, since 2005 it has been widely suggested that R2P "legalizes" or "legitimizes" nonconsensual intervention potentially without the sanction of the UN Security Council.[6] Stephen Stedman, a senior adviser to Kofi Annan on UN reform, argued that Annan's agenda had included "a new norm, the responsibility to protect, to legalize humanitarian intervention" and then claimed that the 2005 World Summit had succeeded in establishing "a new norm to legalize humanitarian intervention."[7] Governments have themselves tried to use R2P to win support for coercive interference since 2005. The most obvious recent example was the French attempt to use R2P to persuade the Security Council to authorize the forcible distribution of humanitarian assistance in the wake of Cyclone Nargis in May 2008. This prompted discussion about the potential for humanitarian intervention in Myanmar/Burma and attracted criticism from China, Indonesia, Vietnam and South Africa.

Given all of this, it is not hard to see why many governments continue to suspect that R2P is simply a "Trojan horse" for the legitimization of unilateral intervention. On the other hand, some supporters of R2P argue that the principle that emerged from the 2005 World Summit was inadequate because it did not provide clear guidance about the circumstances in which coercive military intervention might be justified or about the appropriate decision-making process in situations where the Security Council is deadlocked. They argue that the set of criteria proposed by the International Commission on Intervention and State Sovereignty (ICISS) in 2001 to guide international decision-making in times of major humanitarian emergencies was an important casualty of pre-summit diplomacy in 2005 and should be put back on the international agenda.

Achieving a deeper consensus on R2P and making progress towards the Secretary-General's goal of translating it from "words into deeds" is unlikely while confusion remains about what the principle's implications are for military intervention. Sceptics will continue to see R2P as a "Trojan horse" for unilateral intervention and supporters will focus on finessing and applying criteria to guide intervention. The principal aim of this article, therefore, is to clarify what R2P says about military intervention and what it can contribute in practice. To do this, I proceed in three stages. The first seeks to clarify the meaning of R2P. . . . I then set out what world leaders signed up to in 2005–2006 and what this means for military intervention. The second section focuses on criteria for decision-making and argues that R2P should be dissociated from the criteria put forward by the ICISS. Although they undoubtedly constituted an innovative proposal, there is little likelihood of international consensus on criteria, and its proponents overstate their practical and political utility. The final part of the essay explores what R2P can contribute to the practice of military intervention. R2P is well placed to make at least three important contributions, I argue. First, it can help minimize the problem of "moral hazard" identified by Alan Kuperman.[8] Second, it can reduce the temptation for policy-makers to focus exclusively on military responses to grave humanitarian problems.[9] Finally, by establishing a political commitment to protection it creates a mandate for progress in thinking about the capacities and doctrines needed to increase the effectiveness of protective forces once deployed.

R2P and Military Intervention

The ICISS report *Responsibility to Protect* was primarily concerned with reconceptualizing humanitarian intervention in the wake of the Kosovo crisis and the Secretary-General's challenge to the 1999 General Assembly to resolve the tension between sovereignty and fundamental human rights.[10] The commission had its genesis in early 2000, when Canadian foreign affairs officials Don Hubert, Heidi Hulan and Jill Sinclair began advocating an "International Commission on Humanitarian Intervention" in response to events in Kosovo and Annan's challenge. Canada's foreign minister, Lloyd Axworthy, persuaded Annan to endorse the commission, though its title was revised to omit the controversial "humanitarian intervention" label.[11] Nonetheless, the alternative adopted—"Intervention and State Sovereignty"—indicated the body's main aim: to reconcile the occasional need for armed intervention to protect vulnerable populations with the principles of state sovereignty.

The commission's recommendations are well known. They were premised on the notion that when states are unwilling or unable to protect their citizens from grave harm, the principle of non-interference "yields to the responsibility to protect." The report aimed to escape the irresolvable logic of "sovereignty versus human rights" by focusing not on what interveners are entitled to do ("a right of intervention") but on what is necessary to protect people in dire need and the responsibilities of various actors to afford such protection. These responsibilities were about much more than just armed intervention. In addition to a "responsibility to react" to massive human suffering, international society also had responsibilities to use non-violent tools to prevent such suffering from happening, and, where it did happen, to rebuild polities and societies afterwards. Indeed, the commission argued that prevention was the most important aspect of R2P.[12]

Despite stressing the critical importance of prevention, the commission's main focus was on intervention. It dedicated only 9 of its 85 pages to prevention, and only 16 to the responsibilities to prevent and rebuild, whereas 32 pages were devoted to intervention. The commission's discussion of intervention centered on two questions: In what circumstances is intervention legitimate? And what institutions are entitled to authorize intervention? In relation to the first question, the commission proposed just cause thresholds ("large scale loss of life" and "large scale ethnic cleansing") and precautionary principles ("right intention," "last resort," "proportional means" and "reasonable prospects"), arguing that if states committed themselves to these principles, it would be easier to build consensus on how to respond to humanitarian emergencies. In addition, it would be harder for states like China and Russia to oppose genuine humanitarian intervention because they would have committed themselves to a responsibility to protect in cases of large-scale loss of life and ethnic cleansing (just cause thresholds). On the other hand, it would be harder for states to abuse humanitarian justifications because it would be very difficult to satisfy all the criteria in non-genuine cases. In relation to the question of authority, the commission argued that the Security Council had the primary responsibility to act when a host state was unwilling or unable to protect its citizens.

To improve the Council's decision-making, the commission suggested that the permanent members (P5) agree to refrain from casting their veto in threshold-crossing situations where no vital national interests were at stake and where a majority of the Council supported collective action. If the Council nevertheless failed to act in the face of threshold-crossing crises where the precautionary principles indicated that intervention was appropriate, concerned states could approach the General Assembly and, failing that, relevant regional organizations. Thus the commission outlined a hierarchy of responsibility, starting with the host state and rising through the Security Council to the General Assembly, regional organizations and coalitions of the willing to, finally, individual states.

The ICISS succeeded in reframing the humanitarian intervention debate by stressing the primary responsibility that states had towards their own citizens, situating nonconsensual intervention within a wider continuum of measures including prevention, rebuilding and non-forcible means of reaction, and identifying a range of practices other than armed intervention that could contribute to the prevention and mitigation of genocide and mass atrocities. However, the commission's own regional round tables, as well as post-report consultations with NGOs and governments organized by the Canadian government and civil society organizations, all highlighted widespread hostility to "humanitarian intervention"—and a broad consensus against the idea of a so-called "right of intervention"—especially where that right was associated with unilateralism.[13] But this deep-seated skepticism towards intervention did not necessarily translate into a rejection of the underlying purpose of R2P—the prevention of genocide and mass atrocities, and the protection of vulnerable populations. The adoption of language focusing on the rights of endangered populations rather than the rights of interveners helped illuminate a broad constituency of states and civil society actors prepared to acknowledge that sovereignty entailed responsibilities and that international engagement might be legitimate in certain circumstances.

However, the commission's focus on nonconsensual intervention and apparent openness to intervention not authorized by the Security Council meant that R2P was unlikely to command consensus among world leaders without some important revisions. It is not surprising, therefore, that the R2P principle that emerged from the 2005 World Summit was different in many respects from the doctrine espoused by the ICISS, even if the name and the central idea remained the same. The key to understanding what R2P has to say about military intervention lies in recognizing that R2P as an international principle is *different* from the concept proposed by the ICISS and from the doctrine espoused by Deng and Cohen,[14] even though it draws on both.

International Consensus on R2P

When governments, regional organizations and the UN talk about R2P they mean not the concept put forward by the ICISS but the principle endorsed by world leaders at the 2005 World Summit and reaffirmed by the Security Council in 2006. That principle was informed by the commission's work, by Deng and Cohen's work on IDPs,[15] and by the UN's work on the protection of civilians (including the Security Council's interest in this theme, which predates the ICISS), but is different from all of them in important respects. The principle can be boiled down to four basic commitments. First, all states acknowledge that they have a responsibility to protect their citizens from genocide, war crimes, crimes against humanity and ethnic cleansing. Second, they agree to provide assistance to help other states to build the capacity they need to discharge this responsibility. Third, in situations where the host state is "manifestly failing" in its responsibility, they agree to use all peaceful means to protect vulnerable populations. Fourth, should those measures fail or be deemed inappropriate, the Security Council stands ready to use all necessary means, including nonconsensual force.

What are the principal differences between the concept as espoused by the ICISS and the principle as agreed by world leaders? In the latter form, R2P no longer proposed criteria to guide decision-making about when to intervene; there is no code of conduct for the use of the veto; and there is no opening for coercive measures not authorized by the Security Council. The threshold on when R2P is transferred from the host state to international society was raised from the point at which the host state proved itself "unable and unwilling" to protect its own citizens to that at which the state was "manifestly failing" in its responsibility to do so. Finally, the idea that R2P implied responsibilities—even obligations—on the part of international society and especially the Security Council was all but removed, with the Council committed only to "standing ready" to act when necessary. Of course, prudence dictates a "case-by-case" approach; but the insertion of words to that effect was a deliberate attempt to water down the Security Council's responsibility to protect.[16]

We should not, however, succumb to the view that the R2P principle that emerged from the 2005 World Summit was too weak or insubstantial to contribute to the practice of nonconsensual intervention for humanitarian purposes. First, the World Summit clarified the principle's scope. R2P applies to genocide, war crimes, crimes against humanity and ethnic cleansing, all of which have fairly precise legal meanings grounded in the Genocide Convention, the Rome Statute of the International Criminal Court, and the practice of the international criminal tribunals for former Yugoslavia and Rwanda. This is a much clearer formulation than that offered by the ICISS. Second, the World Summit has clarified relevant roles and responsibilities. All states have a primary responsibility towards their own citizens. All other states have a responsibility to assist their peers in fulfilling this primary responsibility. Should a state manifestly fail in its responsibility, the Security Council in partnership with relevant regional organizations has a responsibility to use whatever means it determines necessary and appropriate. Finally, there is no such thing as an "R2P event or crisis," in that there is no moment at which something becomes relevant to R2P. To suggest that such a thing exists is to revert to the old language of intervener's rights. A state's responsibility to its citizens does not appear and then evaporate; nor does the world's responsibility to assist and support that state, or the Security Council's responsibility to take all necessary means when appropriate. In other words, it is not the nature of the responsibility that changes, but the most appropriate means of preventing genocide, war crimes, crimes against humanity and ethnic cleansing, and of protecting vulnerable populations in any given situation.

R2P on Military Intervention

As Edward Luck has argued, it is important not to confuse what we would like the R2P principle to be with *what it actually is*.[17] R2P sets out responsibilities that states have to their own citizens (the primary responsibility to protect), responsibilities that all states have as members of the international community (responsibilities to help build capacity and use peaceful means to prevent and protect) and responsibilities that certain institutions have (the Security Council's responsibility to use all appropriate means when necessary, in partnership with relevant international organizations). Contrary to much contemporary writing on the subject, R2P does *not* set out criteria for the use of force, offer pathways for intervention not authorized by the Security Council, amend the way the Council does business, apply more widely than to the four specific crimes listed in the extract reproduced above or promise intervention in every case.

My task in the remainder of this article is twofold. In the next section I seek to show that the rejection of criteria was politically inevitable and practically inconsequential. Then, in the final section, I will set out three ways in which R2P can make an important contribution to the prevention of genocide, war crimes, crimes against humanity and ethnic cleansing and the protection of vulnerable populations.

The Limits of Criteria

The ICISS criteria (just cause thresholds and precautionary principles) to guide decisions about military intervention were intended to fulfill three primary functions. First, in an attempt to avoid any future cases like that of Rwanda, where the world stood aside as 800,000 people were butchered in genocidal violence, the just cause thresholds were intended to create expectations about the circumstances in which the international community—primarily the UN Security Council—should become engaged in major humanitarian catastrophes, consider intervening with force and constrain permanent members from casting pernicious vetoes for selfish reasons.[18] Second, responding to a need to avoid future situations like that of Kosovo, where the Security Council was blocked by veto, the criteria provided a pathway for legitimizing intervention not authorized by the Security Council.[19] Finally, Ramesh Thakur, one of the most prominent commissioners, argued that criteria should be viewed as constraining governments' ability to "abuse" R2P and limiting the scope of potential Security Council interventionism.[20] According to Thakur, the criteria would both "make it more difficult for coalitions of the willing to appropriate the language of humanitarianism for geopolitical and unilateral interventions" and make the Security Council's deliberations more transparent.[21] Consensus on criteria, he insisted, would make it more, not less, difficult for states to claim a humanitarian mantle for armed intervention.[22]

Before we assess the extent to which the criteria would be able to fulfill these functions, it is important to begin by stressing how little political support they received. Most of the P5 were skeptical about them from the outset. At the Security Council's annual retreat in May 2002 the United States rejected them outright on the grounds that permanent members should not constrain their right to cast their veto whenever they saw fit. Russia and China expressed concern that the criteria could be used to bypass the Security Council. Although the British government had earlier presented its own version of criteria to guide decision-making and circumvent a Security Council veto, along with France it worried that agreement on criteria would not necessarily deliver the political will and consensus required for effective responses to humanitarian crises. Negative attitudes towards criteria were only hardened by the US-led invasion of Iraq in 2003. Fearing that criteria might be used to justify the invasion, a forum of social democratic governments rejected a British proposal to endorse the idea. In the post-invasion context, the Canadian government recognized that a full-scale effort to persuade the General Assembly to endorse criteria could "backfire terribly," destroying potential consensus on R2P.[23] To be fair, there was some international support for a limited role for criteria. The proposal was endorsed by the UN's High Level Panel, convened by Kofi Annan, and in Annan's personal blueprint for reform.[24] Significantly, however, Annan separated the commitment to R2P from the proposed criteria, placing the former in a section on the rule of law and leaving the latter in a section on the use of force. He did this to reinforce the view that R2P was not only about the use of force and to protect R2P from the almost inevitable rejection of criteria.[25] The AU's "Ezulwini Consensus" on UN reform endorsed the High Level Panel's criteria for guiding the Security Council but, at the insistence of South Africa, observed that these guidelines "should not undermine the responsibility of the international community to protect."[26]

It was clear from the outset of the negotiations preceding the 2005 World Summit that there would be no consensus on criteria. Whereas several African states endorsed the view that criteria were essential to making the Security Council's decisions more transparent, accountable (to the wider membership) and hence legitimate, the United States, China and Russia opposed them—though for very different reasons: the United States because it believed that criteria would limit its freedom of action, the others because they feared that criteria might be used to circumvent the Council. Many other influential states, most notably India, shared this latter view; although it was publicly expressed by only a few states, Canada's regional consultations had revealed that it was a significant underlying concern in many parts of the world, especially Asia. In consequence, the recommendation for criteria was watered down into a commitment to continue discussing criteria, in order to keep the Americans, Chinese, Russians and Indians on board.[27] Ultimately, however, the diplomats charged with selling R2P to the world recognized that criteria would be a "bridge too far" for the Americans and the proposal was never seriously put on the table.[28]

From this brief overview it is clear that it was always unlikely that members of the General Assembly or Security Council would be persuaded to adopt criteria, and that there was a real danger that persisting with the linkage of criteria to R2P would have prevented the endorsement of R2P in 2005 and its reaffirmation the following year.[29] Moreover, a diplomatic effort to persuade states to adopt criteria in the future would require the investment of a significant amount of political capital with little chance of success and a heightened likelihood that such advocacy would create a backlash resulting in a retreat from the principle endorsed in 2005.[30] Finally, it is not at all clear that the R2P principle itself would be strengthened by the addition of criteria. In what remains of this section, I will examine the three putative functions of criteria.

The first function of criteria—creating expectations—is most easily dispensed with, because although the 2005 World Summit did not endorse criteria, it did identify the crimes from which governments had a responsibility to protect populations and the circumstances in which that responsibility ought to be taken up by international society. The summit, it will be recalled, insisted that states have a responsibility to protect their populations from genocide, war crimes, crimes against humanity and ethnic cleansing, and that this responsibility should be taken up by the Security Council in cases where a government was "manifestly failing" to provide such protection. There is broad agreement that the Security Council should be engaged in such circumstances. For example, the Chinese government's 2005 position paper on UN reform agreed that "massive humanitarian" crises were "the legitimate concern of the international community."[31]

It is important to recognize, however, that agreement on thresholds does not guarantee agreement on whether the thresholds have been breached or on what is the most appropriate response in actual cases. It has also been evident in practice: in relation to Kosovo, the disagreement between NATO and Russia boiled down to judgments about whether the conflict there was sufficiently grave to warrant armed intervention;[32] more recently, in relation to Darfur, governments more or less agreed on the gravity of the threat but disagreed about the most appropriate course of action and the responsibility of the Sudanese government.[33] Indeed, even advocates of R2P disagreed on whether the just cause thresholds and precautionary principles justified armed intervention in this case.[34] On the other hand, agreement has been reached in less high-profile cases, such as those of the Democratic Republic of Congo (DRC) and Burundi, without the need for thresholds.[35]

Nor is there much evidence to suggest that the thresholds could constrain the use of the veto. It has been suggested, for example, that Russia and China might have been "compelled" into abstaining on a vote authorizing intervention in Darfur had such a resolution been tabled in the Council and backed by the argument that intervention would be the only means of relieving the humanitarian catastrophe.[36] But China's actual performance in the Council suggests that it would be more than willing to use its veto in such cases. In relation to Darfur, China threatened vetoes on measures far less intrusive than nonconsensual military intervention, such as comprehensive targeted sanctions and no-fly zones.[37] Given that China's position on Darfur enjoyed the support of a significant chunk of the Non-Aligned Movement, the League of Arab States and the Organization of the Islamic Conference, it is not clear where the pressure to abstain in such a vote would have come from.

What, then, of the second function of criteria—to provide a way of legitimizing armed intervention without Security Council authorization? We should note at the outset that this has been the most oft-cited function of criteria since they were first mooted in the 1970s.[38] Interest in criteria was reignited by the Security Council's failure to reach a consensus over Kosovo. In the wake of the storm over Kosovo, Tony Blair called for five tests to guide decisions on intervention and the Foreign Office circulated a draft paper on the subject among the P5.[39] Blair's view that criteria would provide guidelines for when regional organizations and coalitions of the willing might legitimately intervene without the sanction of the Security Council was endorsed by the Independent International Commission on Kosovo (IICK). Working towards its finding that the intervention in Kosovo was "illegal but legitimate," the IICK lent support to the idea of using criteria as thresholds for determining whether or not to use force to alleviate humanitarian emergencies. It recognized that while the UN Charter's restrictions on the use of force contributed to international peace and security by prohibiting aggressive war, there might be circumstances—as in Kosovo—where intervention was needed as a last resort but was not likely to be authorized by the Security Council because of a threatened veto. Criteria, the commission reasoned, might create pathways for states to intervene legitimately in the most extreme emergencies without Council authorization.[40]

There was never much likelihood that the UN membership would endorse guidelines providing a pathway to intervention not authorized by the Council. Moreover, it is not altogether clear what such a pathway would contribute. After all, states already have moral arguments for armed intervention in the worst cases. For example, the US used moral rather than legal language to justify its participation in Operation Allied Force, arguing simply that the moral imperative to protect people—in this case, the Albanian population of Kosovo—from ethnic cleansing overrode the legal ban on the use of force.[41] Critics did not argue in response that massive ethnic cleansing did not, in some circumstances, provide grounds for intervention. Instead, as mentioned earlier, they quibbled over the gravity of the threat, the prudence of intervention and the appropriate source of authority for it.[42] It is difficult to see how criteria would help in a case like this. Interveners would argue that the criteria were satisfied and that their actions were thus legitimate; critics would argue that they were not. In the end, international society is left with borderline judgments about the legitimacy of armed intervention and individual states are left making up their own minds on the basis of their perception of the facts of the case and the relative importance of sovereignty, non-intervention, the protection of human rights and prudential calculations.[43] International law relating to the use of force and crimes such as genocide already provides a common language for this debate. It is not clear what criteria would contribute in addition.

This brings us to the third putative function of criteria: restricting abuse. This concern has become somewhat redundant in the wake of the World Summit's adoption of R2P. The danger of abuse is raised whenever there is a pathway to legitimate intervention that circumvents a deadlocked Security Council. Paragraph 139 of the outcome document clearly declares that it is for the Security Council to determine whether enforcement measures are necessary in the event of states manifestly failing to protect their citizens. Consequently, the constraining function of criteria would apply only to Security Council decision-making, and the Council already contains mechanisms for guarding against abuse— not least the requirement for a majority vote and the veto.[44] The closest historical case we have of Council-sanctioned "abuse" was its endorsement of the French Operation Turquoise at the end of the Rwandan genocide. The French intervention was widely regarded as "abusive" because France's primary aim was not humanitarian and the intervention could have done more to save lives.[45] The problem in that case was not that France intervened, but that it did not do enough to protect Rwandans. Given that this is the best case we have of Council "abuse," it seems safe to conclude that the Council's own operating procedures are sufficient guard against potential future "abuse."

The argument that criteria are to be valued because they make it harder to put forward humanitarian justifications for intervention is plausible only in either of two circumstances: first, if criteria are connected to a pathway for legitimizing intervention not authorized by the Security Council—and, by specifying that coercive measures must be authorized by the Security Council, R2P clearly does not offer such a pathway; second, if we believe that the Security Council has become *too* proactive and requires limitation—an argument not often aired by either academics or governments, and with good reason.

It is difficult to see, therefore, what the just cause thresholds and precautionary principles would add to R2P or contribute to decision-making about armed intervention. As it stands, R2P clearly identifies its scope, its thresholds (genocide, war crimes, crimes against humanity and ethnic cleansing) and the international bodies responsible for discharging the responsibility. Although R2P thresholds are unlikely to generate political will by themselves in relation to particular cases, the endorsement of R2P by the General Assembly and Security Council demonstrates a broad consensus that international society should be engaged in protecting populations from grave harm. Beyond this basic admission of responsibility, criteria are unlikely to foster consensus on how to act, deter the use of vetoes, provide anything other than a self-serving pathway to the legitimization of intervention not authorized by the Security Council, or—although they may be able to constrain interventions not authorized by the Council—add anything to the Council's mechanisms for preventing "abuse."

If this analysis is correct, then advocates of R2P should not invest political capital in persuading governments to endorse criteria. Endorsement in the medium term is in any case highly unlikely; but my argument here is that even if the campaign were successful, criteria would not actually improve decision-making about the use of force. Rather than trying to amend R2P by the addition of criteria, therefore, advocates should instead focus on operationalizing the principle as it is. In the final part of this article, I will identify three practical ways in which R2P can make a positive contribution to the problem of military intervention.

R2P's Contribution to the Problem of Military Intervention

This section identifies three important contributions that R2P can make to the problem of military intervention. First, by replacing old debates about "humanitarian intervention" with a broad continuum of measures aimed first and foremost at preventing genocide and mass atrocities and, if those fail, protecting vulnerable populations, R2P can contribute to reducing the "moral hazards" associated with intervention. Second, by incorporating political and diplomatic strategies along-side legal, economic and military options, R2P points towards holistic strategies of engagement that can overcome the temptation to visualize complex problems in exclusively military terms.[46] Third, by turning attention to the protection of civilians from genocide and mass atrocities, R2P provides a stimulus for new thinking about the practicalities of protection. If translated "from words into deeds," these three contributions could deliver better protection to vulnerable populations.

Moral Hazards

In the 2000 Millennium Report, Kofi Annan noted concerns that humanitarian intervention "might encourage secessionist movements deliberately to provoke governments into committing gross violations of human rights in order to trigger external interventions that would aid their cause."[47] This problem has been described by Alan Kuperman as a "moral hazard." It refers to the phenomenon whereby the provision of protection against risk encourages or enables risk-taking behavior. In this context, the promise of international intervention encourages groups to use violence in order to provoke reprisals and attract international support for their cause.[48] For example, Kuperman argues that talk of military intervention in Kosovo in 1998 emboldened the Kosovo Liberation Army, encouraging it to use violence to provoke Serbian reprisals and take an uncompromising political position to secure NATO intervention. The reality is often more tragic: in most circumstances, having inadvertently encouraged violent rebellion by promises of intervention, international society does not deliver on its promise, leaving civilian populations more vulnerable to attack.[49] While there is certainly room to quibble about the explanatory power of this moral hazard, and more research is needed, Kuperman has performed an important service in deepening our understanding of the problem identified by Annan in 2000.[50]

Kuperman proposes four sensible policy measures to reduce the threat of moral hazard. First, there should be no foreign intervention unless a government's actions are "grossly disproportionate." Second, external actors should "expend substantial resources" to persuade states to address the legitimate grievances of non-violent movements. Third, there should be no intervention to force regime change or "surrender of sovereignty" without robust military deployments to protect civilians against violent backlashes. Fourth, humanitarian relief should be delivered in ways that minimize benefits to the rebels.[51] Bearing in mind the fact that the promise of protection is often not backed up with the actual provision of protection, we might add a fifth proposal: that governments should only promise to do that which they are actually prepared to deliver on. While Kuperman describes his position as a "deviation" from R2P, his proposals actually help highlight an important contribution that the principle can make.

First of all, in relation to the threshold for intervention, rather than promising intervention in many cases, R2P is reserved for only those cases involving genocide, crimes against humanity, war crimes and ethnic cleansing. Indeed, R2P sets the bar substantially higher than the Security Council, which has proven willing to authorize peace operations under Chapter VII in cases that do not cross the R2P thresholds.[52] According to the Rome Statute of the International Criminal Court, to count as a crime against humanity a particular crime must be committed on a "widespread or systematic" basis *and* there must be evidence that links the perpetrators' acts to a state or organizational policy.[53] While Kuperman's threshold of "grossly disproportionate" action is not as clearly defined as R2P's "crimes against humanity," it is hard to see how crimes against humanity could be described as anything but grossly disproportionate. Governments are given considerable leeway to use force against rebels before triggering R2P. As such, rather than encouraging rebels, R2P provides precisely the sort of disincentives to rebel action that Kuperman is seeking.

Kuperman's other proposals are similarly consistent with R2P. The second calls for governments to encourage their peers to address the legitimate grievances of nonviolent groups. This is precisely what is called for by R2P. Recall that in paragraph 138 of the World Summit outcome document, member states pledged to "encourage and help States to exercise this responsibility [to protect]." This is a short phrase with heavy import that implies a policy agenda focusing on encouraging (i.e., with incentives) and helping states to build the capacities they need to prevent genocide and mass atrocities.[54] Chief among those capacities would be the capacity to identify and resolve genuine political grievances. Kuperman's third proposal calls for a commitment to the protection of civilians, which is a core aspect of the operationalization of R2P and will be discussed at length below.

My main point here is that, far from encouraging rebellions and leaving endangered populations high and dry, R2P properly understood and translated into practice would act as a damper on moral hazards which have the potential to increase the risks to which civilian populations are exposed.

Overcoming the Military Focus

All too often, military intervention is the first port of call in inter-national debates about how to respond to massive humanitarian emergencies, irrespective of the viability or utility of the military option. At least one commentator lays the blame for this squarely at the door of R2P.[55] Referring to the international response to the crisis in Darfur, Alex de Waal argued that R2P contributed to a naïve obsession with the deployment of military forces without much serious thinking about what international forces would actually do once deployed or how, exactly, they would contribute to building stable peace in the troubled Sudanese province.[56] This line of thinking created "wildly inflated" expectations of what UN troops would do—including disarming the Janjaweed and providing protection to both displaced populations and those returning home.[57] According to de Waal, "many activists and some political leaders simply assumed that an international force could succeed in the Herculean task of providing physical protection to Darfurian civilians in the middle of continuing hostilities."[58] In the crucial period between 2004 and 2006 international actors focused on four issues relating to the deployment of peacekeepers (Who would command them? How many would be deployed? What would their mandate be? Who would pay?) and ignored much more important questions about the strategic purpose of the operation. This R2P-inspired focus on military peacekeepers drew attention away from the political process, which—de Waal argued—was a necessary precursor for the deployment of military forces. . . .

The problem . . . seems to be that there is something inherently militaristic about R2P that diverts attention away from nonmilitary solutions. On closer inspection, however, this is a problem produced by serious misunderstandings about what R2P says (and does not say) and about its potential to harness a wide range of measures—military and nonmilitary—to the prevention of genocide and mass atrocities and the protection of populations from them. As noted earlier, the use of military intervention is only one of four key commitments associated with R2P as conceived by the World Summit. The other three—especially the commitments to encourage and help states to fulfill their responsibility, and to use a range of non-coercive measures to prevent and protect vulnerable populations—have not attracted the attention they deserve and remain under-conceptualized. Indeed, as the UN Secretary-General's special adviser commented, we have not yet begun to scratch the surface of the immense policy agenda associated with these two commitments.[59]

A comprehensive global policy agenda based on the mandate handed down by the General Assembly in 2005 would include (but not be limited to) measures to improve the capacity of the UN and regional organizations to provide better early warning of genocide and mass atrocities and better briefings for the UN's decision-makers; measures to help states build the necessary capacity to prevent these crimes; measures to improve international capacity to dispatch teams of peace negotiators with adequate international support; measures to enhance human rights reporting and capacity-building through the UN's Human Rights Council; measures to improve the deterrence capability of the International Criminal Court; a more systematic approach to implementing Kofi Annan's action plan for the prevention of genocide; the use of peacekeepers as preventers of, as well as reactors to, genocide and mass atrocities; and a comprehensive system for implementing and monitoring targeted sanctions.[60] All of this, in addition to the other measures described in this article, is necessary if R2P is to be properly operationalized. If it were operationalized in this way, it is not difficult to see how it would actually militate against the tendency to focus exclusively on the use of military force, and instead place the use of force within a broader spectrum of measures that can be used to prevent genocide and mass atrocities and to protect vulnerable populations.

Operationalizing Protection

The third contribution made by R2P is to foreground the need for practical thinking about how international peacekeepers should go about protecting civilians. Although questions about legality, legitimacy and political will are important, the ultimate test in the direst of situations is whether international engagement succeeds in protecting vulnerable populations. Questions about the way a peace operation is organized, configured, tasked and equipped are just as important as broader political and legal questions when it comes to protecting vulnerable populations. It should be recalled that the UN's Independent Inquiry on the Genocide in Rwanda maintained that "a force numbering 2,500 [UNAMIR's strength at the time of the genocide] should have been able to stop or at least limit massacres of the kind which began in Rwanda" at the start of the genocide.[61] Despite this, the question of how best to protect civilians from genocide and mass atrocities has received comparatively little attention.

Indeed, there is still no military doctrine that provides guidance on how peacekeepers should go about protecting vulnerable citizens. By fore-grounding the protection of potential victims, R2P provides an important impetus for developing doctrine in this area and translating lessons learned into action.

The development of R2P as an international principle has been accompanied by a transformation of the place of civilian protection in peace operations and, as noted earlier, the Security Council invoked R2P in relation to the UN–AU hybrid mission for Darfur (Resolution 1706). Traditionally, it was thought that peacekeepers should remain impartial and neutral and not be proactive in the protection of civilians. Although peacekeeping operations sometimes contained human rights components, only very infrequently was the protection of civilians con-sidered a core part of the peacekeeper's mandate.[62] The Security Coun-cil has begun to take heed of R2P in its mandating of peace operations in two ways. Today's peace operations tend to be larger and therefore better able to protect civilians than their predecessors. The UN's mis-sions in the DRC, Sudan and Darfur are all mandated to comprise in excess of 20,000 peacekeepers. Furthermore, a combination of better coordination between the Security Council and troop-contributing nations, the UN's standby forces arrangements, and closer cooperation between the UN and regional organizations has seen a progressive decline in the gap between the number of troops mandated by the Secu-rity Council and the number actually deployed—the slow deployment of UNAMID notwithstanding.[63] Despite progress in this area, it still takes 18 months on average to deploy a peace operation fully, with sig-nificant negative consequences for endangered civilians.[64] Moreover, the Security Council has begun to create mandates for the protection of civilians more frequently, and has gradually relaxed the early restric-tions it imposed on such mandates.[65] . . .

Thanks in large part to the Security Council's interest in civilian protection (into which its affirmation of R2P was incorporated) and the pioneering work of researchers such as Victoria Holt and Tobias Berk-man, we have a relatively comprehensive understanding of what the protection of civilians by peacekeepers entails in practice, though there remains little by way of doctrinal guidance.[66] In short, it entails "coer-cive protection"—the positioning of military forces between the civil-ian population and those who threaten them.[67] This may involve mili-tary measures to defeat and eliminate armed groups that threaten civilians. Since 2002, for instance, the UN's standing rules of engage-ment for peace operations have authorized the use of force "to defend any civilian person who is in need of protection."[68] Sometimes, coercive protection may involve measures short of force, such as erecting military barriers around civilian populations and the gradual removal of threats through negotiated (and sometimes coerced) disarmament.[69] In the absence of military doctrine, however, we lack a clear understanding of how these tasks should be accomplished. The final version of the UN's capstone doctrine for peace operations (rebadged "principles and guidelines" for political reasons) limited itself to simply observing that "most . . . peacekeeping operations are now mandated by the Security Council to protect civilians under imminent threat" and noting that this task requires "coordination with the UN's civilian agencies and NGOs."[70] This raises difficult questions about the relative importance of civilian protection and other important principles of peacekeeping such as consent, impartiality and minimum force.[71] Draft UN training modules reportedly insist that these other principles do not justify inactivity in the face of atrocities, but do not provide guidance on how these concerns should be reconciled.[72] For more detailed guidance we have to make do with learning lessons from current and past missions—at least for the time being. . . .

UN peacekeepers have therefore begun to operationalize R2P in a way that incorporates the protection of civilians into their core business. To date, while the Security Council hands down mandates for the protection of civilians with greater regularity and fewer restrictions, operationalization has largely relied on improvisation in the field. . . . Despite the evident limitations of this approach, the focus on civilian protection has contributed to a marked decline in the overall number of civilians killed in sub-Saharan African wars since 2003.[73] R2P can make an important contribution to the further development of civilian protection by providing the core rationale for such operations, marshalling the political will necessary to establish peace operations and equip them with civilian protection mandates, and emphasizing the need for long-term and multidimensional approaches to civilian protection which incorporate the prevention of genocide, war crimes, crimes against humanity and ethnic cleansing, and the rebuilding of states and societies in the wake of such suffering.

Conclusion

The first step along the road of translating R2P from words into deeds is a proper understanding of what the principle does and does not say about the use of nonconsensual military force for humanitarian purposes. As agreed by world leaders in 2005, R2P does not countenance nonconsensual military force without the authorization of the Security Council and does not set out criteria for the use of force beyond the four threshold crimes and the idea that the Council should assume responsibility in cases where the host state is "manifestly failing" to protect. Many advocates of R2P lament the loss of key elements of the recommendations put forward by the ICISS, and it is appropriate and legitimate to call for amendments to the R2P principle in the future to accommodate some of these recommendations. But it is important to distinguish the R2P principle from ideas, concepts and recommendations put forth by the ICISS, various governments and individuals such as Francis Deng. Continuing confusion about what R2P has to say about military intervention helps neither the principle itself nor those charged with making difficult decisions about how best to prevent genocide and mass atrocities and protect potential victims.

It is also important not to overstate the capacity of those "lost recommendations"—especially the proposed criteria to guide decisions about the use of force—to resolve policy dilemmas or forge consensus in actual cases. Criteria enjoyed little international support, would not generate additional political will, would in all likelihood not constrain the use of the veto (if past practice is a good guide) and would not provide an avenue for legitimately bypassing the Security Council. For these reasons, although it is legitimate to press UN member states to adopt criteria, the energies of R2P advocates would be better spent elsewhere. Not least, they should focus on identifying and operationalizing those aspects of R2P that could make an important difference to the way international society conceptualizes and practices military intervention: mitigating moral hazards, building multifaceted engagement strategies that reduced the tendency to focus exclusively on military solutions and developing the doctrine and capacity needed to enable peacekeepers to protect civilians better once deployed. Focusing on these aspects would help deliver on Ban Ki-moon's promise to translate R2P "from words into deeds" and lay the foundations for a deepening consensus on the new principle.

Notes

1. On the impact of the war in Iraq, see Gareth Evans, "When Is It Right to Fight?" *Survival* 46, no. 3 (2004): 59–82; Alex J. Bellamy, "A Responsibil-

ity to Protect or a Trojan Horse? The Crisis in Darfur and Humanitarian Intervention After Iraq," *Ethics and International Affairs* 19, no. 2 (2005): 31–54.

2. Ban Ki-moon, "Annual Address to the General Assembly," 25 Sept. 2007, SG/SM/11182.

3. The Williams Report, *Report of the High-Level Mission on the Situation of Human Rights in Darfur Pursuant to Human Rights Council Decision S-4/101*, A/HRC/4/80, 7 March 2007, paras. 19–20.

4. Jennifer M. Welsh, "Conclusion: Humanitarian Intervention After 11 September," in Jennifer M. Welsh, ed., *Humanitarian Intervention and International Relations* (Oxford: Oxford University Press, 2004), pp. 176–88.

5. See the reports on "Regional Roundtables and National Consultations," in Thomas G. Weiss and Don Hubert, *The Responsibility to Protect: Research, Bibliography, Background (supplementary volume)* (Ottawa: International Development Research Centre, 2001), pp. 349–98.

6. Alicia L. Bannon, "The Responsibility to Protect: The UN World Summit and the Question of Unilateralism," *Yale Law Journal* 115, no. 5 (2006): 1156–65.

7. Stephen John Stedman, "UN Transformation in an Era of Soft Balancing," *International Affairs* 83, no. 5 (Sept. 2007): 933, 938.

8. Alan J. Kuperman, "The Moral Hazard of Humanitarian Intervention: Lessons from the Balkans," *International Studies Quarterly* 52, no. 1 (2008): 49–80.

9. Alex de Waal, "Darfur and the Failure of the Responsibility to Protect," *International Affairs* 83, no. 6 (Nov. 2007): 1039–54.

10. International Commission on Intervention and State Sovereignty, *The Responsibility to Protect* (Ottawa: International Development Research Centre, 2001), p. 9; Kofi Annan, "Annual Report of the Secretary-General to the General Assembly," 20 Sept. 1999.

11. Lloyd Axworthy, "Human Rights and Humanitarian Intervention," address, Washington, DC, 16 June 2000; Lloyd Axworthy, *Navigating a New World: Canada's Global Future* (Toronto: Knopf, 2003), p. 191.

12. ICISS, *Responsibility to Protect,* p. xi.

13. See World Federalist Movement and International Policy Group, *Civil Society Perspectives on the Responsibility to Protect*, final report, 30 April 2003.

14. Roberta Cohen and Francis M. Deng, *Masses in Flight: The Global Crisis of Internal Displacement* (Washington, DC: Brookings Institution, 1998), p. 275.

15. Cohen and Deng, *Masses in Flight.*

16. Alex J. Bellamy, *Responsibility to Protect: The Global Effort to End Mass Atrocities* (Cambridge: Polity, forthcoming 2009), ch. 3.

17. See Edward C. Luck, "The Responsible Sovereign and the Responsibility to Protect," *Annual Review of United Nations Affairs 2006/2007* (New York: Oxford University Press, 2008), vol. 1, pp. xxxiii–xliv.

18. Nicholas J. Wheeler, "Legitimating Humanitarian Intervention: Principles and Procedures," *Melbourne Journal of International Law* 2, no. 2 (2001): 566.

19. Independent International Commission on Kosovo, *Kosovo Report: Conflict, International Response, Lessons Learned* (Oxford: Oxford University Press, 2000), opening summary.

20. Ramesh Thakur, *The United Nations, Peace and Security: From Collective Security to the Responsibility to Protect* (Cambridge: Cambridge University Press, 2007), p. 260.

21. Ramesh Thakur, "A Shared Responsibility for a More Secure World," *Global Governance* 11, no. 3 (2005): 284.

22. Ramesh Thakur, "Iraq and the Responsibility to Protect," *Behind the Headlines* 62, no.1 (2004): 1–16.

23. "Civil Society Meeting on the Responsibility to Protect," final report, Ottawa, 8 April 2003, p. 9.

24. UN High Level Panel on Threats, Challenges and Change, *A More Secure World: Our Shared Responsibility*, A/59/565, 2 Dec. 2004, para. 203.

25. William R. Pace and Nicole Deller, "Preventing Future Genocides: An International Responsibility to Protect," *World Order* 36, no. 4 (2005): 25.

26. African Union Executive Council, "The Common African Position on the Proposed Reform of the United Nations," ext/EX.CL/2(VII), Addis Ababa, 7–8 March 2005, sec. B (i).

27. Pace and Deller, "Preventing Future Genocides," p. 28.

28. Memo from Allan Rock to the author, 12 Nov. 2007.

29. Richard M. Price, ed., *Moral Limits and Possibility in World Politics* (Cambridge: Cambridge University Press, 2008).

30. On the post-2005 "revolt against R2P" see Bellamy, "Responsibility to Protect."

31. "Position Paper of the People's Republic of China on the United Nations Reforms," 8 June 2005.

32. See Simon Chesterman, *Just War or Just Peace? Humanitarian Intervention and International Law* (Oxford: Oxford University Press, 2001), pp. 221.

33. Alex J. Bellamy, "A Responsibility to Protect or a Trojan Horse?"

34. Gareth Evans' International Crisis Group argued not. See International Crisis Group, "Getting the UN into Darfur," Africa Briefing 43, 12 October 2006, pp. 15-17. Others, such as Eric Reeves and Samantha Power, disagree with this perspective.

35. Susan C. Breau, "The Impact of Responsibility to Protect on Peacekeeping," *Journal of Conflict and Security Law* 11, no. 3 (2007): 450–52; Victoria K. Holt and Tobias C. Berkman, *The Impossible Mandate? Military Preparedness, the Responsibility to Protect and Modern Peace Operations* (Washington, DC: Henry L. Stimson Center, 2006), pp. 201–224.

36. Nicholas J. Wheeler and Justin Morris, "Justifying the Iraq War as a Humanitarian Intervention: The Cure Is Worse Than the Disease," in Ramesh Thakur and Waheguru Pal Singh Sidhu, eds., *The Iraq Crisis and World Order* (Tokyo: UN University Press, 2006), p. 460.

37. Bellamy, "A Responsibility to Protect or a Trojan Horse?"; Paul D. Williams and Alex J. Bellamy, "The Responsibility to Protect and the Crisis in Darfur," *Security Dialogue* 36, no. 1 (2005): 27–47.

38. See, e.g., Richard B. Lillich, ed., *Humanitarian Intervention and the United Nations* (Charlottesville, VA: University Press of Virginia, 1973).

39. Tony Blair, "Doctrine of the International Community," speech to the Economic Club of Chicago, Hilton Hotel, Chicago, 22 April 1999. See John

Kampfner, *Blair's Wars* (London: Free Press, 2003), pp. 50–53; Wheeler, "Legitimating Humanitarian Intervention," p. 564 and n. 51.

40. IICK, *Kosovo Report*, opening summary.

41. Nicholas J. Wheeler, *Saving Strangers: Humanitarian Intervention in International Society* (Oxford: Oxford University Press, 2000), p. 279; Michael Byers, *War Law: International Law and Armed Conflict* (London: Atlantic Books, 2005), p. 101.

42. For the full range of views on Kosovo, see Albrecht Schnabel and Ramesh Thakur, eds., *Kosovo and the Challenge of Humanitarian Intervention: Selective Indignation, Collective Action and International Citizenship* (Tokyo: UN University Press, 2000).

43. For a discussion of borderline legitimacy judgements in relation to intervention, see Ian Clark, *Legitimacy in International Society* (Oxford: Oxford University Press, 2005), pp. 199–205.

44. Thakur, *The United Nations, Peace and Security,* p. 60.

45. Wheeler, *Saving Strangers*, pp. 208–41.

46. A problem identified by de Waal in "Darfur and the Failure of the Responsibility to Protect."

47. Kofi Annan, *"We the Peoples": The Role of the United Nations in the Twenty-First Century*, A/54/2000, 27 March 2000, para. 216.

48. Kuperman, "The Moral Hazard."

49. See Roberto Belloni, "The Tragedy of Darfur and the Limits of the 'Responsibility to Protect,'" *Ethnopolitics* 5, no. 4 (2004): 327-46.

50. A call issued by Ramesh Thakur and Thomas G. Weiss, "R2P: From Idea to Norm—and Action?" *Global Responsibility to Protect* 1, no.1 (forthcoming 2009).

51. Kuperman, "The Moral Hazard," p. 73.

52. For instance, MINUSTAH and UNOCI in Haiti and Côte d'Ivoire respectively. See Thomas Weiss, "The Sunset of Humanitarian Intervention? The Responsibility to Protect in a Unipolar Era," *Security Dialogue* 35, no. 2 (2004): 135–53; Michael Byers, "High Ground Lost on UN's Responsibility to Protect," *Winnipeg Free Press*, 18 Sept. 2005, p. B3.

53. See Asia–Pacific Centre for the Responsibility to Protect, "Burma Briefing: Cyclone Nargis and the Responsibility to Protect," 17 May 2008, p. 7.

54. Luck, "The Responsible Sovereign." Gareth Evans argues that the sorts of capacities needed are those that well-functioning states use as a matter of habit. See Gareth Evans, *Cooperating for Peace: The Global Agenda for the 1990s and Beyond* (St. Leonards, NSW: Allen & Unwin, 1993).

55. De Waal, "Darfur and the Failure of the Responsibility to Protect."

56. The principal example pointed to by de Waal was a report by the International Crisis Group: ICG, *To Save Darfur*, ICG report 105, 17 March 2006.

57. De Waal, "Darfur and the Failure of the Responsibility to Protect," p. 1043.

58. De Waal, "Darfur and the Failure of the Responsibility to Protect," p. 1044.

59. Luck, "The Responsible Sovereign."

60. These and other measures are discussed in detail in Bellamy, *Responsibility to Protect.*

61. Independent Commission, *Report of the Independent Inquiry into the Actions of the United Nations During the 1994 Genocide in Rwanda*, 12 Dec. 1999, p. 2.

62. See K. Månsson, "Integration of Human Rights in Peace Operations: Is There an Ideal Model?," *International Peace-keeping* 13, no. 4 (2006): 547–63.

63. Briefing by Jean-Marie Guéhenno, Under-Secretary General for Peacekeeping Affairs to the UN Security Council.

64. Citizens for Global Solutions, "United Nations Emergency Peace Service: One Step Towards Effective Genocide Prevention" (New York: 2008), p. 68.

65. On the links between this mandating practice and R2P, see Breau, "The Impact of Responsibility to Protect on Peacekeeping," esp. pp. 450–52.

66. See Victoria K. Holt, *The Responsibility to Protect: Considering the Operational Capacity for Civilian Protection* (Washington, DC: Henry L. Stimson Center, 2005); Holt and Berkman, *The Impossible Mandate?*

67. Thomas G. Weiss, "The Humanitarian Impulse," in David M. Malone, ed., *The UN Security Council: From the Cold War to the 21st Century* (Boulder, CO: Lynne Rienner, 2004), p. 48.

68. D. S. Blocq, "The Fog of UN Peacekeeping: Ethical Issues Regarding the Use of Force to Protect Civilians in UN Operations," *Journal of Military Ethics* 5, no. 3 (2006): 205.

69. Holt and Berkman, *The Impossible Mandate?*, p. 52.

70. UN Department of Peacekeeping Operations, *United Nations Peacekeeping Operations: Principles and Guidelines*, 18 Jan. 2008, para. 42.

71. The so-called holy trinity. See Alex J. Bellamy, Paul D. Williams and Stuart Griffin, *Understanding Peacekeeping* (Cambridge: Polity, 2004).

72. Holt and Berkman, *The Impossible Mandate?*, p. 190.

73. Human Security Report Project, *Human Security Brief 2007*, pp. 22–30.

9

NATO's International Security Role in the Terrorist Era

Renee de Nevers

THE NORTH ATLANTIC TREATY ORGANIZATION'S ENGAGEMENT in missions ranging from Bosnia to Darfur suggests that the alliance has overcome the doubts about its future that arose after the Cold War. The war on terror that followed al-Qaida's attacks on the United States on September 11, 2001, would appear further to reinforce NATO's significance. While unilateral actions by the United States and U.S. cooperation with loose coalitions in Afghanistan and Iraq have garnered the bulk of international attention, experts agree that multilateral cooperation is essential in fighting terrorism. Moreover, several of NATO's activities, such as its missions in Afghanistan and the Mediterranean, are closely linked to the war on terror, with other NATO missions also contributing to this fight. These activities have led NATO's secretary-general, Jaap de Hoop Scheffer, to declare that "more than ever, NATO is in demand, and NATO is delivering."[1]

This apparent vibrancy, however, may not accurately reflect NATO's true condition. Although its missions have expanded dramatically since the end of the Cold War and alliance members agree on the threat posed by terrorism, NATO's actual role in the multifaceted struggle against terrorists is minor. This could have long-term implications for alliance unity.

This article investigates how the United States has worked with NATO in prosecuting the war on terror. The U.S. government conceives of this struggle broadly, with counterinsurgency and efforts to constrain the spread of weapons of mass destruction (WMD) as essential elements.

Reprinted from *International Security* 31, no. 4 (2007): 34–66. © 2007 MIT Press. Reprinted by permission of the publisher.

NATO is the United States' premier alliance, and most of Washington's closest allies are members. But how does NATO contribute to this war on terror? To be sure, NATO is not simply a "tool" of U.S. policy. The war on terror is a U.S. creation, however, and NATO has been forced to adjust to this fact. The United States perceives terrorism as the key national security threat it will face in the coming years. Just as the United States is working to transform its strategies in response to this threat, we would expect it to evaluate key alliances and security relationships with this measure.

I argue that NATO is playing a largely supportive role in U.S. efforts to combat terrorism. The focus of both the European "fight against terrorism" and the U.S. "war on terror" lies elsewhere, leaving NATO's contribution to efforts to quell terrorism somewhat tangential. NATO is conducting a defensive mission in the Mediterranean in response to the terrorist threat, and it has adopted strategies ranging from new technology development to consequence management to prevent or mitigate terrorist attacks. In Afghanistan the alliance has assumed a frontline role in seeking to deny terrorist groups a foothold there, making this NATO's first de facto combat operation ever. But many of the essential elements of the fight against terrorism, such as intelligence sharing, occur outside NATO. Afghanistan aside, NATO members participate in offensive efforts to respond to terrorism outside NATO through bilateral activities or loose coalitions of the willing. There are three main reasons for NATO's limited role: shifts in alignments and threat perceptions caused by systemic changes, NATO's limited military capabilities, and the nature of the fight against terror.

The United States needs allies in its fight against terrorism, but does it need the alliance?[2] To be sure, the United States values NATO, and indeed has been the driving force behind efforts to expand the alliance by incorporating new members. In addition, NATO has become more than simply a military alliance. Glenn Snyder defines "alliances" as "formal associations of states for the use (or nonuse) of military force, in specified circumstances, against states outside their own membership."[3] NATO is far more than this. It is commonly described as a political-military alliance that combines the key political function of guiding members' foreign and security policy and providing a forum for alliance consultation with the operational function of ensuring that members can train and develop the capabilities to cooperate militarily.[4] This dual role helps to explain why NATO has endured.[5] The key issues are whether its members continue to agree on its value and what its core tasks should be, as well as the threat that it confronts. Moreover, if NATO's members do not seek to address their core security threats within the alliance, the alliance's military value to its members is likely to be questioned.

In the next section, . . . I assess NATO's contribution to the U.S. fight against terrorism. The following section examines factors that help to explain why NATO's contribution to the U.S. war on terror has been relatively limited. I look at three elements: systemic changes and their consequences for NATO, alliance capabilities, and the nature of the fight against terrorism. Finally, I discuss the implications of NATO's elusive role in combating terrorism for U.S. policy and for the alliance. . . .

NATO's Role in the U.S. War on Terror

In this section I assess NATO's contribution to the U.S. war on terror in the following categories: (1) prevention and defense, (2) denial, (3) counterterrorism, and (4) consequence management—all of which are essential to confronting terrorism. These categories incorporate both elements of the U.S. strategy and NATO's political and military efforts to fight terrorism. For each category, I evaluate how NATO's efforts correspond to U.S. goals, as well as to the nature of the terrorist threat.

Prevention and Defense Against Terrorist Attacks

Efforts to prevent and defend against terrorist actions fall into two main areas: intelligence sharing and surveillance to detect preparations for an attack. NATO has engaged in both activities, primarily through Operation Active Endeavor (OAE). It is also exploring new technologies to detect and defend against terrorist attacks, a third preventive activity.

Operation Active Endeavor. OAE is NATO's only article 5 operation, and it was the first substantive military action the alliance took after the September 11 attacks to address the terrorist threat.[6] This activity corresponds both to Washington's goal of preventing terrorist attacks and to NATO's antiterrorism strategy. After deploying in the eastern Mediterranean in October 2001 as a deterrent and surveillance measure in support of the U.S. intervention in Afghanistan, OAE evolved into a broader counterterrorism initiative. It expanded to cover the entire Mediterranean in 2003; and during the U.S. invasion of Iraq, it escorted ships through the Strait of Gibraltar (at the United States' request) to alleviate concerns that terrorists might target such ships. OAE has focused on monitoring shipping and the safety of ports and narrow sea-lanes. A second goal, particularly since 2003, has been to expand participation by non-NATO states, both by countries that are formal NATO partners and by countries participating in NATO's Mediterranean Dialogue, a consultative forum intended to improve cooperation with countries in the Mediterranean area.[7]

OAE has devoted much attention to expanding its intelligence-sharing activities, including efforts to develop a network for tracking merchant shipping throughout the Mediterranean, and improving means to share this intelligence with relevant governments. This should help to address not only terrorist concerns but also alliance efforts to prevent drug smuggling and the spread of weapons of mass destruction.[8]

OAE has clear military objectives, and NATO has developed valuable experience in maritime surveillance and interdiction through this mission. At the same time, the mission has had both strategic and political aims. NATO has sought to include Russia in OAE, for example, to gain Moscow's agreement to extend the operation's activities into the Black Sea. Expansion into the Black Sea has not happened, due to objections from both Russia and Turkey to allowing NATO operations there, but Russia participated in OAE patrols in the Mediterranean in 2006.[9] Efforts to include more Mediterranean countries are designed to improve cooperation and, if possible, to share the burden for sustaining the operation with a greater number of countries. This is in keeping with NATO's ongoing efforts to explore expanded partnerships with countries around the globe.[10]

The United States values OAE because it facilitates intelligence sharing and because it is an alliance-wide activity. Still, NATO's efforts do not always go as far as the United States would like. OAE's guidelines allow it to board only ships whose masters and flag states are willing to comply with the boarding, in keeping with international law. In contrast, the United States is willing to act alone if there is confusion about whether ships will comply.[11] This has led to instances in which the United States has boarded ships unilaterally, although based on suspicions raised by OAE's monitoring activities.

OAE is NATO's most prominent defense activity, but the alliance has also undertaken numerous surveillance and patrolling missions to defend against possible terrorist attacks. NATO AWACS aircraft conducted surveillance at more than thirty events ranging from NATO's Istanbul summit in 2004 to the 2006 World Cup in Germany. NATO also deployed its new Multinational Chemical, Biological, Radiological, Nuclear (CBRN) task force to the 2004 Athens Olympics.

Intelligence. Intelligence is widely viewed as the most important tool in preventing terrorist attacks, and the United States shares intelligence regarding terrorist activities with a broad range of countries.[12] NATO's intelligence contribution to U.S. efforts against terrorism is limited, however, for four reasons. First, most of the military intelligence NATO relies on, which is shared through the NATO Special Committee, is provided by the United States to the alliance. The Multinational Battlefield Information and Exploitation System, for example, is a "near-real-time all-source system" through which the United States feeds information to NATO commands.[13]

Second, the United States and its European allies have diverging views about the role of military intelligence. From the U.S. perspective, military intelligence is an increasingly important component on the battlefield. The Department of Defense emphasizes that military intelligence is no longer just a staff function, but rather a war-fighting function that soldiers on the battlefield will be actively engaged in at all times. In addition, as part of its broader interest in network-centric warfare, the Defense Department is pushing to establish a fully "networked battle space," with the goal of "information dominance" in any conflict.[14] NATO's European members do not place the same degree of emphasis on real-time military intelligence.

Third, the capabilities gap that has presented a chronic problem for NATO is increasing in the intelligence area, which suggests growing problems for interoperability. Already in the 1990s, the U.S. military had to maintain "legacy" communications systems to enable it to operate with other NATO members, and allied forces depended heavily on U.S. communications and intelligence during the 1999 Kosovo bombing campaign.[15] One reason the United States rejected some European offers of military assistance in its intervention in Afghanistan in 2001 was the difficulties presented by different levels of technological sophistication. The United States spends far more on research and development than its allies; the Defense Department's budget request for research and development for FY 2007 is $57.9 billion. In contrast, the entire defense budget for the United Kingdom, NATO's next largest spender, was $50.2 billion in FY 2006.[16] The United States also has a more robust domestic high-technology industry than does any of its European allies.

To be sure, alliance members agree on the need for improvements in intelligence capabilities and interoperability. NATO adopted an initiative on developing new capabilities, particularly in areas such as intelligence and surveillance, in November 2002. In addition, some alliance members are working to improve their information warfare capabilities.[17] That better intelligence capabilities continue to be problematic is evident in repeated references to the need for improved intelligence sharing both among national agencies and internationally.[18]

The problem, however, is deeper than merely the need for better intelligence capabilities; NATO's members have developed diverging operational concepts because their military capabilities differ. Differences in their views on the role of information in war fighting are one example of this divergence. The United States approaches the use of force differently than do most European militaries, which means that cooperation on the battlefield could be increasingly difficult.[19] Although joint exercises may highlight these differences, they do not necessarily resolve them.

Fourth, the most vital terrorist-related intelligence information generated in Europe is outside NATO's scope, because it comes from police and domestic intelligence agencies. The bulk of intelligence sharing within Europe, and between the United States and European states, occurs bilaterally or among select groups of states, not in NATO. U.S. intelligence cooperation is closest with the United Kingdom, and its cooperation with members of the UK-USA network is far more intensive than is its intelligence sharing with other NATO countries.[20] The major European mechanism for sharing domestic intelligence is the Berne Group, a club of European intelligence organizations to which the United States does not belong. Three factors hinder greater cooperation in nonmilitary intelligence sharing: the problem of ensuring protection of sources when information is dispersed, differences between the United States and many European allies over appropriate domestic privacy standards, and disagreements over legal constraints on intelligence collection.[21] The turmoil caused by reports of secret CIA detention centers in Europe, and Italy's indictment of several CIA officers for operating illegally on Italian soil when they kidnapped a terrorist suspect, illustrate the differences in views regarding the acquisition and use of intelligence.[22]

Technology development. NATO's effort to develop counterterrorism technologies represents the alliance's third defensive activity. The

Defense against Terrorism (DAT) program was established by the alliance's Conference of National Armaments Directors after the 2004 Istanbul summit. Its goal is to develop technologies to help prevent terrorist attacks ranging from the use of improvised explosive devices to rocket attacks against aircraft. Different NATO countries have taken the lead on each of the ten project initiatives.[23]

This effort has strong U.S. support. As part of the alliance's defense investment program, the DAT program reflects Washington's interest in persuading U.S. allies to devote more resources to their military capabilities, and it corresponds to the increasingly high-technology approach to warfare adopted by the U.S. military. Some new defensive technologies, such as mechanisms to detect improvised explosive devices, are currently being developed, but it is too soon to determine whether the program will improve the alliance's ability to prevent terrorist attacks. Notably, the United States is using the defense investment program to promote allied transformation goals. NATO's new transformation command, Allied Command Transformation, established after the alliance revised its military command structure in 2002, is based in Norfolk, Virginia, near the U.S. Atlantic Fleet's headquarters; and the defense investment program is led by an American, Marshall Billingslea, who worked in the Pentagon on counterterrorism and special operations before moving to NATO. U.S. efforts to use this co-location to promote NATO's transformation have led to some resentment within the alliance that the United States is "feeding" its views through the new headquarters and the defense investment program.[24] NATO's contribution to ongoing efforts to prevent terrorist attacks is thus important, but it may not be central to U.S. policy. While OAE's surveillance activities contribute to tracking potential terrorist movements, the intelligence developed through OAE may be more directly relevant to law enforcement than to military missions.

To be sure, U.S. officials agree that many NATO members have strong intelligence capabilities, and they can provide valuable intelligence that the United States does not possess. But the most important elements of intelligence gathering in Europe take place outside NATO and are conducted by domestic intelligence organizations. This intelligence is more likely to be shared bilaterally, rather than through NATO. Bilateral intelligence sharing among key allies continued despite severe strains in political relations in the months prior to the U.S. invasion of Iraq, as revelations about German intelligence cooperation with the United States to designate military targets and civilian locations just prior to the invasion made clear.[25] Five European states with substantial terrorism concerns developed their own forum for intelligence cooperation in March 2005. In 2006 the alliance established a new intelligence "fusion center" to ensure that needed intelligence can be distributed to troops in the field. It also created the Terrorist Threat Intelligence Unit to provide a forum for joint analysis of nonclassified information. But these are better means to share and interpret information.[26] NATO as such does not generate raw intelligence useful to preventing terrorism. Finally, NATO's effort to develop new defense technologies to protect against terrorist attacks reinforces the U.S. goal of promoting allied defense transformation. Whether the program will contribute to NATO or U.S. defense remains to be seen.

Denial: WMD, Sanctuary, and State Control

Denying terrorists certain weapons and the benefits of state support, ranging from use of a state's territory to outright control over its government, is a central feature of the U.S. strategy against terrorism. Denial is less evident in NATO's strategy; the goal of disrupting terrorist activities comes closest to the U.S. concept. NATO's contribution to this effort varies considerably; it is marginally involved in efforts to deny terrorists WMD, but it plays a significant role in efforts to deny terrorists state support.

Denying access to WMD. Preventing the spread of WMD is a core NATO goal, though preventing terrorist acquisition of these weapons is not. Moreover, NATO's contribution to international efforts to confront the problem of WMD proliferation is complicated by two central questions. First, should denial efforts be primarily multilateral or bilateral? If multilateral, what is NATO's "value added" in seeking to address proliferation problems? Some NATO members have been involved in cooperative threat reduction efforts in Russia and other former Soviet republics. These nonproliferation efforts have been conducted bilaterally or by small groups of states, however, rather than as multilateral NATO initiatives. The United Kingdom, for example, is working with Russia on projects ranging from dismantling nuclear submarines to developing sustainable employment for scientists and engineers formerly employed in Soviet WMD programs. Canada, France, and Germany have engaged in efforts to develop plutonium disposition methods.[27] And several core NATO countries—France, Germany, and the

United Kingdom—have sought to induce Iran to end its nuclear enrichment program since 2004. The group seeking to deal with Iran is generally referred to as the EU-3, and the broader proposals by these countries and the United States, China, and Russia were presented to Iran in June 2006 by Javier Solana, the European Union's foreign policy chief—not a NATO representative.[28] The only alliance-wide efforts to address WMD proliferation have sought to encourage political dialogue through forums such as the NATO-Russia Council, established in 2002, and consultations with other NATO partner states such as Ukraine.

Second, what means are appropriate for preventing terrorists from acquiring WMD? Although alliance members generally agreed that Iraq did possess WMD capabilities,[29] this question was at the heart of the bitter 2002–03 debate over invading Iraq. The differences were over the response, and core NATO allies disagreed with the United States about whether preemption was an appropriate counter to Iraqi efforts to develop WMD. This is not a new debate, but it was sharpened by the fight over Iraq policy.[30]

U.S. policy favors preemption against the potential spread of WMD, as stated in the 2006 *NSS*. This reflects Washington's concern that rogue states and terrorists will acquire WMD for use in terrorist attacks. Given alliance differences over means, it is not surprising that NATO does not figure centrally in U.S. counterproliferation activities. Moreover, to the degree that it relies on multilateral efforts to prevent WMD proliferation, the Bush administration has stated its preference for more flexible partnerships, such as the Proliferation Security Initiative.[31] From the U.S. perspective, the PSI has two main advantages: it is a coalition of the willing, involving only those states that share the PSI's goals, and it is results oriented, emphasizing action rather than legislation or rule making.[32] Although many NATO members participate in the PSI, this is not an alliance activity.

The United States demonstrated its preference for informal coalitions to deny WMD to terrorists by agreeing with Russia on July 15, 2006, to establish the Global Initiative to Combat Nuclear Terrorism. Like the PSI, this informal agreement is open to states that share the United States' concern about nuclear terrorism. There is no plan to establish a treaty or institution to formalize this program; its legal authority is based on the International Convention on the Suppression of Acts of Nuclear Terrorism, signed in 2005, as well as on United Nations Security Council resolutions 1373 and 1540, which proscribe terrorist financing and the spread of WMD-related materials.[33] The initiative seeks to set new standards for securing nuclear materials, engaging in law enforcement, and prosecuting terrorist suspects and their supporters. In this, it resembles the requirements of earlier UN resolutions regarding terrorist financing and law enforcement. Several NATO members are likely to participate in this initiative, which had its first meeting in October 2006, but it is not a NATO activity.

Although many of NATO's European members share the United States' concern about the proliferation of WMD and their acquisition by terrorists, this has not translated into cooperation through NATO to actively confront this security problem. Instead, individual states have worked bilaterally or through alliance consultations to address WMD proliferation. The alliance has done better, however, with regard to denying terrorists sanctuary.

Denying state support or sanctuary. NATO has contributed substantially to the U.S. goals of denying support or sanctuary from rogue states to terrorist groups and ensuring that such groups do not gain control over states. NATO's mission in Afghanistan, the International Security Assistance Force (ISAF), has assumed control over international military forces throughout the country. NATO forces are also involved in ongoing efforts to train Iraqi security forces.

The U.S. intervention in Afghanistan that began in October 2001 caused some tension within the alliance. While several NATO states offered to contribute troops to this mission, and NATO declared that the September 11 attacks constituted an article 5 attack against all alliance members, the United States did not seek NATO's participation in the invasion. This reflected President Bush's desire to avoid having allies dictate how the war would be fought, as well as the preference among some in the Pentagon to avoid the headaches of having to gain allied consensus on strategy similar to those that had developed during NATO's bombing campaign against Serbia in 1999.[34] Equally important was the question of whether NATO allies could contribute the specialized capabilities needed for the campaign the United States was planning.[35] Nonetheless, a few NATO countries took part in the initial attack against Afghanistan—including Denmark, France, Germany, Turkey, and the United Kingdom—and NATO AWACS aircraft patrolled U.S. airspace in the fall of 2001, "backfilling" to ensure that U.S. territory was defended while freeing U.S. forces for the invasion.[36]

ISAF was initially established with UN Security Council authorization under British command in October 2001, after the United States overthrew Afghanistan's Taliban government. NATO assumed control of ISAF in August 2003.[37] Initially ISAF's mission was limited to patrolling Kabul, but since 2004, ISAF has undertaken a four-stage expansion of its mission into the northern and western provinces of Afghanistan, and later to the south and east. It has also deployed several provincial reconstruction teams, which are based on a model developed by the U.S. military that combines security and reconstruction functions in an effort to help stabilize the countryside.[38] ISAF assumed responsibility for security throughout Afghanistan in October 2006. At that point, it was NATO's largest operation, involving about 31,000 troops, including roughly 12,000 U.S. troops under ISAF command.

ISAF represents a valuable contribution to the U.S. goal of denying terrorists sanctuary or allies, given al-Qaida's close ties with the previous Taliban regime and ongoing efforts to pursue al-Qaida members in the border region between Afghanistan and Pakistan. All twenty-six NATO members participate in ISAF, as do ten non-NATO partner countries.

At the same time, ISAF has suffered from three significant problems. First, since 2003 the alliance has been unable to secure sufficient troop commitments to meet the target force size. When NATO took control of the southern and eastern regions of Afghanistan in August 2006, its 31,000-strong force represented about 85 percent of the troops and equipment that NATO commanders had requested for the mission. Since July 2006, NATO troops have confronted far more intense fighting than expected.[39] The alliance appealed for more troops in September 2006, but only one member country, Poland, offered to send additional troops.[40] At the November 2006 summit meeting in Riga, Latvia, new pledges from member states raised the troop and equipment totals to 90 percent of requirements.[41] ISAF's commander at that time, Lt. Gen. David Richards, said that it can manage with the current troop strength, but additional troops would allow it to conduct major operations more rapidly and with less risk to NATO soldiers.[42]

Second, many troops in Afghanistan operate under "national caveats," whereby governments place limits on what military activities their troops are allowed to do or where they are allowed to go in carrying out their missions. These caveats are problematic for two reasons: they hurt operational effectiveness; and alliance members do not share risks equally, which can cause friction.[43] Germany's troops can be deployed only near Kabul, for example, and in 2006 Poland resisted sending additional troops to southern Afghanistan, where they are needed the most. Only six NATO members operate without caveats.

The problem is not unique to ISAF; national caveats caused headaches during NATO's peacekeeping mission in Bosnia as well, and they have long been a problem in UN peacekeeping missions.[44] Recognition of the operational problems such caveats pose has led to a marked decline in their use, but they have made both multinational cooperation and operations in general more difficult in Afghanistan.[45] Caveats tend to creep back in, moreover, as is evident in repeated efforts to eliminate them. NATO leaders agreed to reduce caveats at the 2006 Riga summit, for example, with the result that 26,000 troops of the increased force of 32,000 had broader freedom to act.[46]

Third, the Afghan leadership fears that the United States will abandon it, and it is unsure what NATO's authority over both the security and counterterrorism mission will mean in the long run. Concern has also been raised about whether NATO has the political will and capabilities to fight a sustained counterinsurgency campaign.[47] Since NATO forces assumed responsibility for security in southern Afghanistan, the frequency and intensity of Taliban attacks have increased.[48] This renewed fighting forced the United States to reverse plans to reduce its military commitment in Afghanistan and led the British to expand their troop contribution to ISAF.[49] The United States decided in January 2007 to extend the tours of 3,200 troops in Afghanistan, and further troop increases were under consideration.[50] Notably, U.S. forces, ISAF's largest contingent, will continue to conduct the bulk of counterterrorism activities aimed at al-Qaida. The U.S. military also retains 11,000 troops outside ISAF's command to sustain a separate counterinsurgency function in addition to peacekeeping.[51]

NATO has played a far smaller role in Iraq. Whereas the Bush administration sought to frame the March 2003 invasion as part of the war on terror, the alliance remained deeply split and did not formally participate in the invasion. The NATO Council never discussed Iraq, an indication of the depth of discord within the alliance. NATO did offer some support for the U.S.-led operation, however. It contributed to Turkey's defense against possible Iraqi retaliation during the invasion, and it agreed to the Polish government's request for allied support when Poland took over leadership of one sector of the stabilization force in Iraq in May 2003.[52] Fifteen NATO states have contributed forces to the coalition since 2003.[53] And although Germany did not participate in the coalition and strongly opposed the U.S. invasion, it deployed hundreds of chemical and biological weapons–detection troops in Kuwait and Turkey to aid coalition forces in the event of a WMD attack.[54]

In 2004, at U.S. urging, NATO agreed to play a central role in training Iraqi security forces. NATO's training effort has several elements: mentoring of Iraqi military officers by NATO personnel; creation of an officer training facility in Iraq; and training of Iraqi officers in NATO facilities. NATO's target is to train 1,000 officers inside Iraq annually and 500 outside the state; by September 2006, NATO had trained 650 Iraqi officers in European facilities and roughly 2,000 officers overall.[55] NATO has also donated military equipment to Iraq's security forces. This equipment comes primarily from former Warsaw Pact countries that have become NATO members, and it is compatible with Iraq's Soviet-supplied military hardware.

NATO's training mission has faced significant difficulties, however. First, the need to gain consensus on all decisions hamstrung efforts to get the mission up and running and greatly slowed the process; residual bitterness over the U.S. decision to invade Iraq contributed to this problem. Some members objected to the precedent set by taking on the training mission, which also slowed decisionmaking.[56] Second, as in Afghanistan, some troop contributions have operated under national caveats, which has hindered commanders' efforts to coordinate NATO's activities. Third, funding for the mission has been a serious problem. Countries contributing troops are expected to cover their own costs. NATO set up a "trust fund" to pay for the establishment of a defense university in Iraq, but contributions to the fund have thus far been insufficient. As a result, although the Iraqi government has stressed its preference for in-country training to help gain popular trust and support for the new security forces, more officers have been trained outside Iraq.[57]

Offensive Measures: Counterterrorism

NATO's offensive role in fighting terrorism is limited. Although its Military Concept for Defense Against Terrorism stresses that NATO must be prepared to take on offensive missions if required, the alliance has operated primarily in support of member state efforts to conduct offensive counterterrorist operations. NATO officials point out that this is appropriate given that the alliance's task is to defend its members and support them in the event of attacks, rather than to take the lead in offensive operations.[58]

The only example of NATO assuming a combat role is found in Afghanistan, where ISAF took control over security operations throughout the country in October 2006. Although the security problems on the ground in Afghanistan range from crime and drug trafficking to counter-terrorism, ISAF's rules of engagement do not explicitly cover missions other than peacekeeping; ISAF does not have a formal counterterrorist mission.[59] ISAF's limited mandate is due in large measure to member states' nervousness about the prospect of taking on counterterrorism or counterinsurgency responsibilities, as well as concern that acknowledging the potential combat elements of the mission would make it even harder to obtain sufficient troop commitments to ISAF.

NATO's mission in Afghanistan shifted from a primary focus on reconstruction and stability to counterinsurgency when it took responsibility for security in the southern region of the country at the end of July 2006, and it adopted more robust rules of engagement.[60] Since then, British, Canadian, and Dutch forces on the ground have been engaged in counterinsurgency operations. Commanders dropped their earlier vagueness about their activities in Afghanistan and now acknowledge the war-fighting nature of the mission. Lieutenant General Richards of ISAF stated in August 2006 that NATO's goal was "to strike ruthlessly" at Taliban fighters seeking to undermine the Afghan government.[61] Similarly, in parliamentary debates over extending Canada's deployment to Afghanistan in May 2006, members openly acknowledged the combat nature of the mission.[62]

NATO's mission in Afghanistan is of crucial importance to the alliance. NATO troops are engaged in their most militarily challenging mission since the alliance was formed in 1949. NATO leaders regarded the mission as a success at the end of 2006; the alliance has shown the ability to fight and to maintain support for the mission. But continued success is not guaranteed. Both NATO and U.S. commanders expressed growing concern in late 2006 that without significant advances in reconstruction and development in Afghanistan, the military effort would ultimately fail. As Lieutenant General Richards noted, "Fighting for its own sake in a counterinsurgency will get us nowhere over time."[63] The military commanders argued that the international community had failed to convince the Afghan people that international involvement would make their lives better in terms of either security or living standards. If it did not do so soon, the resurgent Taliban would win their support, or at least acquiescence.[64]

There are also worrisome hints, however, that some NATO members may be unwilling to sustain their commitments to ISAF. Not only has the alliance had difficulty convincing members to send more troops to Afghanistan, but some governments were starting to pull out troops at the end of 2006. The French government decided to withdraw 200 special forces troops from the southern region of Afghanistan in December 2006, for example, although some 1,100 French troops would remain near Kabul.[65] The Italian government has faced pressure to set a deadline for withdrawal of its 1,800 troops in ISAF.[66] The ambivalence toward ISAF is partly explained by the fact that even governments that acknowledged the dangers confronting their troops were surprised by the strength of the insurgency in Afghanistan; in other participating states, the failure to prepare their publics for the true nature of the mission damaged support for ISAF. Finally, the Afghan mission suffers from the European public's residual resentment about Iraq, with which it is often associated.[67]

Consequence Management

The U.S. strategy for confronting terrorism gives priority to preventing attacks. In contrast, NATO's Military Concept emphasizes consequence management and has two main goals: to respond to an attack once it occurs, and to minimize the effects of an attack that has taken place. At the 2002 Prague summit, the alliance adopted a Civil Emergency Planning Action Plan to improve its ability to respond to attacks involving WMD, and it has developed a range of capabilities to respond to such attacks, including the multinational CBRN Defense Battalion, a deployable analytical laboratory, an event response team, a chemical and biological defense stockpile, and a disease surveillance system.[68] The alliance has also established a center of excellence to further explore defenses against WMD.

NATO has also expanded its disaster relief plans to enhance its terrorism response capabilities. The alliance has conducted several WMD-related exercises, and its Euro-Atlantic Disaster Response Center has assisted in responding to floods, forest fires, and snowfalls in states both within and outside the alliance, as well as to Hurricane Katrina in the United States. NATO also contributed to disaster relief operations after a major earthquake in Pakistan in October 2005. This was considered a significant step because it represented the first time the alliance had offered disaster assistance outside its own geographic area, which could set a precedent for such operations.

Some analysts have argued that NATO should expand its consequence management abilities because this is a logical role for the alliance, and it would encourage NATO members to do more to enhance their militaries' capabilities to respond and coordinate in the event of terrorist attacks or other disasters. There are two obstacles to expanding

NATO's role in this area. First, NATO can act only if its members request assistance. For example, NATO was not asked to aid Spain's response to the terrorist bombings in Madrid in 2004, nor did it respond to the 2005 London bombings.[69] Whether other states will turn to NATO in the future is likely to depend on the gravity of the attack and on NATO's ability to provide specialized capabilities such as CBRN. Second, European states disagree about whether this function should be carried out by NATO or by the European Union. Moreover, although the need for greater cooperation between NATO and the EU in areas such as emergency response is widely recognized, little progress has been made in this area.

Summary

This examination of NATO's participation in the U.S. war against terror yields three main insights. First, the chronic capabilities gap between the United States and its allies is growing, and increasingly may be limiting the alliance's operational cooperation. Second, the gap between what the United States and European states are willing to do militarily is also growing. This reflects their disparate capabilities and the differences in operational planning that follow from them. Third, the United States' commitment to working through the alliance is unclear. While NATO's chief military officer stresses the value of NATO's military mechanisms and political consultation, the U.S. government is often unwilling to rely on NATO in campaigns that relate directly to defending the United States. Not only do Pentagon leaders want to avoid the effort of working to build consensus within the alliance, but they see it as compromising the mission and the safety of U.S. forces. Moreover, some U.S. government officials note that the Bush administration sees NATO as unreliable, because of the difficulty in gaining troop commitments from member states in recent years. This has fostered the view expressed by one State Department official, who noted, "We 'ad hoc' our way through coalitions of the willing. That's the future."[70]

NATO's Limited Role in the U.S. War on Terror

Three factors help to explain why NATO's contribution to the U.S. war on terror has been relatively limited: shifting alignments and threat perceptions due to systemic changes, NATO's chronic and growing capabilities gap, and the war against terror itself.

Alignments and Threats After the Cold War

Two critical changes in the nature of the international system have influenced NATO's evolution since the collapse of the Soviet Union in 1991. First, the distribution of power in the international system is no longer bipolar. For all its tensions, the international system was relatively stable during the Cold War, with the two superpowers and their allies aligned in opposition. This made core alliance cohesion relatively easy to maintain. NATO's European members were unlikely to defect from the U.S.-led alliance, and the United States was unlikely to abandon Europe, though fears to the contrary emerged periodically. Although scholars continue to debate whether the current international system is unipolar, multipolar, or something else, today U.S. military power dwarfs that of other powers in the international system.

Second, a security community developed among the European powers, Japan, and the United States concurrently with the erosion and eventual collapse of Soviet power. As a result, the option of war between these powers has become virtually unthinkable. This is an equally momentous change in the international system, given that great power war has been a constant in history.[71]

NATO has defied realist predictions that it would not survive in the absence of the threat it was created to defend against: the Soviet Union. But the aforementioned systemic changes have led alliance members to perceive security threats differently. They have also renewed uncertainties about alliance stability and the U.S. commitment to NATO.

The crosscutting pressures created by changing and sometimes competing interests have made it more difficult to reach consensus on how to deal with security threats confronting NATO.[72] The disappearance of the Soviet threat made intra-alliance differences on issues including trade, the environment, and human rights more salient. NATO's European members also responded to concern about U.S. willingness to act through NATO, and Europe's inability to act collectively without the United States, by expanding efforts to build a viable European security identity that would make it possible for European states to operate independent of the United States.[73]

NATO has always been a political-military alliance, rather than a purely military union. It has had a long-standing goal of cementing its members' shared democratic ideology and values,[74] as evidenced by NATO's expansion in the 1990s.[75] In expanding eastward, NATO accomplished two objectives: it extended the European security community and it removed the potential threat of unstable countries along the borders of member states. This expansion, however, has led to further divergences in threat perception among alliance members. While some of NATO's new members continue to have territorial security concerns due to their proximity to Russia, some long-standing members feel less threatened by "traditional" security concerns. Moreover, European perceptions of the gravity of the terrorist threat vary widely. Some states perceive the threat to be limited, whereas others view it as significant. Notably, only five states—France, Germany, Italy, Spain, and the United Kingdom—had legislation dealing with terrorism before the September 11 attacks.

NATO's members also differ on the means to respond to threats confronting the alliance. This was most apparent in the bitter dispute over the 2003 U.S. invasion of Iraq. The dispute illustrated three points of disagreement. First, it reflected different understandings of the nature of the terrorist threat and how to combat it. Second, it exposed deep differences about the appropriate use of force, and in particular about the U.S. policy of preventive war. Whereas the United States insisted that the urgency of the threat posed by Saddam Hussein's supposed possession of WMD mandated immediate action, several European allies argued that Hussein was contained and could be deterred. Third, the dispute illustrated increasing European concern about U.S. unilateralism and the fear that NATO's European members might be "entrapped" by their alliance commitments to support a reckless military operation.[76] As a result, both France and Germany balked at supporting the United States.[77] Although the Bush administration sought to repair relations with key European allies and institutions after the 2004 presidential elections, the acrimony caused by this dispute has left a residue of ill will.

The shifting alignments and attitudes toward threats confronting NATO have reduced the United States' willingness to accept alliance constraints.[78] Moreover, the United States' strategic focus has changed, with greater attention being given to the Middle East, Central Asia, and East Asia. This is evident both in the changing base deployments in Europe and the State Department's decision to shift at least 100 diplomatic positions from Europe to other regions, including Africa, South Asia, East Asia, and the Middle East.[79] This move is a logical step and if anything overdue, given the end of the Cold War, but it is telling of shifts in U.S. policy priorities.

Differences in member states' views of the role of military force have probably contributed to U.S. frustration with alliance constraints. National caveats attached to military operations sometimes reflect limited capabilities, but they can also reveal different political goals. U.S. inability to count on allies for military cooperation in Iraq, Afghanistan, and elsewhere has produced great frustration within the Bush administration. This is evident in Secretary of Defense Donald Rumsfeld's comment, "It's kind of like having a basketball team and they practice and practice and practice for six months. When it comes to game time, one or two say, 'We're not going to play.' Well, that's fair enough. Everyone has a free choice. But you don't have a free choice if you've practiced for all those months."[80]

Alliance Capabilities

From the United States' perspective, the perennial frustration regarding NATO is the difficulty of convincing its European allies to increase defense spending and thus to improve capabilities. During the Cold War, NATO members agreed that defense spending should be roughly 3 percent of a state's gross domestic product; in 2006 the minimum spending level set by the alliance was 2 percent. Yet only six states other than the United States met this threshold.[81] Furthermore, how this money is spent causes concern in Washington. Many states continue to expend the bulk of their resources on manpower, rather than on transforming their forces in ways the United States hopes they will—and to which NATO has agreed. Some, such as Greece and Turkey, still have military forces focused at least in part on each other.

As NATO has taken on new tasks, differences in capabilities have hindered the alliance's operational cooperation. Moreover, willingness to address this gap appears limited; although many European states acknowledge the problem, defense spending and military transformation remain low domestic priorities in several states because they do not see major military threats to their security. Additionally, the large number of operations in which NATO is currently engaged means that many states do not have the manpower and resources to devote to transformation given current budgets. Notably, the United States has funded operations in both Iraq and Afghanistan through supplemental budget requests, rather than the annual defense budget. It has also financed some allied contributions, such as the Polish division in Iraq.[82]

U.S. officials would like to see NATO undertake a transformation similar to what the United States is adopting: that is, to develop expeditionary forces and what Defense Department officials call twenty-first century military capabilities. The alliance's adoption of transformation as one of its goals in 2003 represents a welcome step in this direction; indeed, NATO's reorganized command structure designates one of its two new commands the Allied Command Transformation.[83]

The United States and some other alliance members disagree over the kinds of capabilities NATO members should seek to acquire. The *QDR* affirms U.S. support for "efforts to create a NATO stabilization and reconstruction capability and a European constabulary force" that could build on the EU's existing constabulary forces. It suggests that allied states should aim to "[tailor] national military contributions to best employ the unique capabilities and characteristics of each ally, [to achieve] a unified effort greater than the sum of its parts."[84] This implies the development of "niche" capabilities. If the alliance moves in this direction, it could reinforce the perception that the United States, along with only a few alliance members such as the United Kingdom and France, has combat-ready troops able to conduct frontline operations, while NATO as a whole is relegated to post-conflict operations and "cleanup." The need for such post-conflict capabilities is increasingly apparent, notably in both Afghanistan and Iraq. Less clear, however, is whether NATO states are willing to codify this division of labor, and how this would affect alliance unity and decisionmaking.

Yet there is an element of hypocrisy in Washington's annoyance with its NATO allies, because the U.S.-backed expansion of the alliance contributed to the erosion of NATO's military capabilities. The United States was the strongest voice encouraging two rounds of NATO expansion to incorporate Central European states after the Cold War, in 1999 and 2004, and it supported the decision at the Riga summit to consider further enlargement of the alliance as early as 2008. When the second expansion decision was made in 2004, however, it was already apparent that the states that joined NATO in 1999 had failed to meet the goals set for transforming their militaries to accord with NATO standards; and they were not likely to achieve them soon. Moreover, none of the second-round applicants met NATO's military capability standards, and they were far behind the first-round states in their ability to transform their militaries.[85] Lessened alliance capabilities may have been unproblematic to the United States because it did not intend to incorporate alliance forces in its major operations.

The Nature of the War on Terror

The final factor explaining NATO's limited role in the war on terror is the very nature of that conflict. Although the Bush administration determined that this is a war, it is not one in which most "battles" are fought by military forces. Different means are required as well. Indeed, this is partly why Europeans tend to refer to the "fight," rather than "war," against terrorism. Combating international terrorism requires cooperation in a wide range of areas among different countries and international organizations. Key elements of the struggle include diplomatic efforts to maintain and strengthen international treaties and norms proscribing terrorism, as well as economic cooperation to find and eliminate sources of terrorist financing. In addition to military activities, security cooperation is needed to ensure that states can share intelligence regarding terrorists and that law enforcement agencies can work together across borders. U.S. efforts to combat terrorism in these areas involve extensive cooperation with European states, but this does not occur through NATO. Rather, it occurs either bilaterally or with the EU.

Additionally, the threats facing the United States and its European allies are different. The United States has chosen to combat terrorism as far from its shores as possible, through military actions in Afghanistan and Iraq; it also emphasizes the role of covert special-operations forces to conduct counterterrorist missions overseas.[86] In contrast, several European states face a domestic threat. Their large Muslim minorities create the potential for "homegrown" terrorists, particularly to the degree that these minorities have not been integrated into the broader society. Indeed, the July 2005 bombings in London were carried out primarily by British citizens. This gives European states a different set of priorities in fighting terrorism, because the threat they confront is local, not distant.[87]

Conclusion

NATO plays a largely supportive role in the war on terror. To the degree that NATO countries are engaged in key elements of U.S. efforts to combat terrorism, they do so on the basis of bilateral ties or loose coalitions— not through NATO. Operation Active Endeavor provides important support for U.S. military operations in the Middle East. It contributes to the prevention of and defense against terrorism; it is not, however, a combat operation. The contribution that NATO members make by providing intelligence in the struggle against terrorists occurs largely bilaterally, and it is generated primarily by law enforcement agencies, rather than by allied military intelligence capabilities. NATO's defense investment programs may help to create better defenses against terrorism, but it is too soon to tell how successful these will be.

Similarly, NATO does not have a direct role in denying terrorists access to WMD. NATO maintains political dialogues with countries at risk for the theft or sale of weapons or WMD-related products, and individual members participate in threat reduction activities. These are not designed to address the problem of terrorist acquisition, however. The alliance is split on the use of preemption as a means to prevent the spread of WMD to states that might let terrorists obtain weapons of mass destruction, and the United States prefers the PSI and the new Global Initiative to Combat Nuclear Terrorism to NATO as means to prevent the spread of WMD to terrorists.

NATO's ISAF mission in Afghanistan directly contributes to the U.S. goal of denying terrorists sanctuary there. ISAF troops are in essence conducting counterterrorism as well as counterinsurgency operations, and this is NATO's first combat mission since its creation. The lead role in counterterrorism in Afghanistan continues to be played by U.S. Special Forces, however, not NATO; and U.S. troops are the largest contingent in ISAF. NATO's role in Iraq is even more limited. Many member states have individually contributed troops to the U.S.-led coalition in Iraq, but the alliance's sole contribution to stabilizing the country has been the training of Iraqi military officers.

NATO has begun to develop consequence management capabilities to respond to terrorist attacks, particularly those with WMD. This could give the alliance a valuable support role. The nature of the terrorist threat confronting individual member states will likely determine whether they take advantage of NATO's support capability.

Three factors explain Washington's circumvention of the alliance in prosecuting the war on terror. First, two critical changes in the international system, U.S. hegemony and the emergence of a security community, particularly among European states, have led NATO's members both to differ among themselves on a broad range of global issues and to perceive security threats differently. They also differ on the appropriate means for responding to perceived threats, as was most evident in the dispute over the U.S. invasion of Iraq. These shifting alignments and attitudes have reduced U.S. willingness to accept alliance constraints.

Second, U.S. military capabilities are greater and more sophisticated than those of its allies, which makes it difficult for even close U.S. allies to coordinate with U.S. forces in frontline military activities. Some U.S. officers point out that one goal of NATO training exercises is to illuminate these differences, as a way to spur allies to improve their capabilities.[88] But NATO's expansion has eroded its military capabilities further. Combined with the increasing use of national caveats, which constrain what individual military forces can do in NATO operations, the alliance's ability to work with the United States in confronting immediate military threats appears limited, at best.

Third, the nature of the war on terror itself constrains NATO's contribution to U.S. strategy. Iraq and Afghanistan notwithstanding, terrorism is fought primarily by nonmilitary means, such as law enforcement and intelligence gathering. Moreover, NATO's members face different threats.

The United States is unlikely to abandon NATO, however. In spite of its rejection of alliance constraints on its own actions, NATO provides a crucial forum in which the United States can discuss foreign and security policy with its key allies to reach common understandings of shared problems. This is particularly vital to the United States as the EU's Common Foreign and Security Policy begins to coalesce and influence the policies of European states. Only in NATO does the United States have a voice in European security affairs. This helps explain U.S. support for expanding the alliance, and it has sought to make NATO the forum for discussion of a broad range of security problems affecting Europe and North America.

Moreover, Washington recognizes that combating international terrorism requires extensive cooperation, both bilateral and multilateral. This is best built on a shared understanding of the problem states confront, and NATO can play an important role in generating common views regarding terrorism. So long as the United States views NATO as a valuable forum in which it can convince its European allies that they share the same goals and that they confront the same threat in the war on terror, it will continue to value the alliance. If threat perceptions within the alliance diverge further, however, this could make it harder to reach agreement on common policies. Notably, European states appear to have differing views of the threats they face; this is not simply a transatlantic divide.

U.S. policy increasingly acknowledges the importance of nonmilitary measures such as public diplomacy and the "war of ideas" in combating terrorism.[89] Increasing recognition that the terrorist threat is evolving means that U.S. approaches are likely to move toward greater concurrence with European policies on terrorism, which stress intelligence, law enforcement, and quiet engagement with the Muslim world. This would ease some of the frictions in Washington's relations with its European allies. It would not, however, lead to a greater role for NATO in confronting terrorism. Rather, it could accelerate the tendency to utilize mechanisms outside the alliance framework to address this urgent threat.

NATO's military value as a partner to the United States in the war against terrorism also remains in question. Should the United States confront terrorists militarily in the future, it will likely do so with special operations forces working either alone or with host-government troops. A few alliance members may participate in such operations, but the alliance itself will not. Further, the bulk of the struggle against terrorism requires substantial nonmilitary means. NATO may have a useful diplomatic role to play, both among its members and with regard to key states such as Russia. But many of the critical tasks in this fight are outside the military domain, leaving NATO with little role.

In 2003 NATO Supreme Cmdr. James Jones noted that if the attempt at defense transformation fails, the alliance may lose its military value.[90] Others point to NATO's ISAF mission as the essential test for its survival. Its success or failure in Afghanistan will be a critical indicator of the alliance's ability to address the type of security threats that will emerge in contested regions around the globe. Success would confirm NATO's unity and capability to act "out of area," but a defeat would undermine NATO's claim to a broader global mission. The alliance would continue to provide for the defense of Europe, and the alliance members' shared values may be sufficient to sustain NATO as an organization, assuming its political consultation and dialogue functions continue to thrive. But such a defeat would raise serious questions about NATO's contribution to its members' core security concerns, if these are seen as out of area. If NATO's major member states do not seek to address their most urgent threats within the alliance framework, its military value could atrophy.

Notes

1. Jaap de Hoop Scheffer, "Speech at the 42nd Munich Conference on Security Policy," Munich, Germany, February 4, 2006, http://www.security conference.de/.

2. At the end of the Cold War, realist scholars predicted the alliance's demise, and during the 1990s, realist and institutionalist scholars sought to explain NATO's longevity. For realist approaches, see John J. Mearsheimer, "Back to the Future: Instability in Europe after the Cold War," *International Security* 15, no. 1 (Summer 1990): 5–56; and Kenneth N. Waltz, "The Emerg-

ing Structure of International Politics," *International Security* 18, no. 2 (Fall 1993): 44–79. For realist discussions of NATO's continued utility, see Charles L. Glaser, "Why NATO Is Still Best: Future Security Arrangements for Europe," *International Security* 18, no. 1 (Summer 1993): 5–50; and Robert J. Art, "Why Western Europe Needs the United States and NATO," *Political Science Quarterly* 111, no. 1 (Spring 1996): 1–39. For institutionalist approaches, see John S. Duffield, "NATO's Functions after the Cold War," *Political Science Quarterly* 109, no. 5 (Winter 1994–95): 763–787; Robert B. McCalla, "NATO's Persistence after the Cold War," *International Organization* 50, no. 3 (Summer 1996): 445–475; and Celeste A. Wallander, "Institutional Assets and Adaptability: NATO after the Cold War," *International Organization* 54, no. 4 (Autumn 2000): 705–735.

3. Glenn H. Snyder, *Alliance Politics* (Ithaca, N.Y.: Cornell University Press, 1997), p. 4.

4. Celeste A. Wallander and Robert O. Keohane propose that NATO has become a security management institution rather than an alliance. See Wallander and Keohane, "Risk, Threat, and Security Institutions," in Helga Haftendorn, Keohane, and Wallander, eds., *Imperfect Unions: Security Institutions over Time and Space* (Oxford: Oxford University Press, 1999), pp. 21–47.

5. Relatively little theoretical research has examined NATO's current situation. Some recent exceptions include evaluations of the alliance's effort to adjust to shifting power relations, and of soft balancing as an alternative to traditional balance of power behavior. See Galia Press-Barnathan, "Managing the Hegemon: NATO under Unipolarity," *Security Studies* 15, no. 2 (April–June 2006): 271–309; Seyom Brown, *Multilateral Constraints on the Use of Force: A Reassessment* (Carlisle, Pa.: Strategic Studies Institute, U.S. Army War College, 2006); Robert A. Pape, "Soft Balancing against the United States," *International Security* 30, no. 1 (Summer 2005): 7–45; T.V. Paul, "Soft Balancing in the Age of U.S. Primacy," *International Security* 30, no. 1 (Summer 2005): 46–71; and Stephen G. Brooks and William C. Wohlforth, "Hard Times for Soft Balancing," *International Security* 30, no. 1 (Summer 2005): 72–108. For discussions of alliance persistence and maintenance, see Stephen M. Walt, "Why Alliances Endure or Collapse," *Survival* 39, no. 1 (Spring 1997): 156–179; Patricia A. Weitsman, "Intimate Enemies: The Politics of Peacetime Alliances," *Security Studies* 7, no. 1 (Autumn 1997): 156–192; and Barry Buzan and Ole Waever, *Regions and Powers: The Structure of International Security* (Cambridge: Cambridge University Press, 2003).

6. General James L. Jones, "NATO: From Common Defense to Common Security," Senate Committee on Foreign Relations, 109th Cong., 2d sess., February 7, 2006, http://foreign.senate.gov/ hearings/2006/hrg060207a.html.

7. NATO, "NATO Elevates Mediterranean Dialogue to a Genuine Partnership, Launches Istanbul Cooperation Initiative," NATO Update, 29 June 2004, http://www.nato.int/docu/update/2004/ 06-june/e0629d.htm.

8. Robert Cesaretti, "Combating Terrorism in the Mediterranean," *NATO Review* no. 3 (Autumn 2005), http://www.nato.int/docu/review/2005/issue3/english/art4.html.

9. Russia was unwilling to agree to this move unless it gained a greater decisionmaking role over the activity, which NATO was not willing to accept.

Vladimir Socor, "Russians Not Joining NATO Operation Active Endeavor," *Eurasia Daily Monitor* 1, no. 136 (November 30, 2004); Jones, "NATO: From Common Defense to Common Security"; and Igor Torbakov, "Turkey Sides with Moscow against Washington on Black Sea Force," *Eurasia Daily Monitor* 3, no. 43 (March 3, 2006), http://www.jamestown.org/.

10. NATO, "NATO Looks to Global Partnerships," NATO Update, April 27, 2006, http://www.nato.int/docu/update/2006/04-april/e0427c.htm.

11. NATO, "Briefing: Response to Terrorism," Online Library, March 2005, http://www.nato.int/docu/brie*ng/rtt/html_en/rtt01.html. p. 5.

12. Derek S. Reveron, "Old Allies, New Friends: Intelligence-Sharing in the War on Terror," *Orbis* 50, no. 3 (Summer 2006): 453–468.

13. Richard J. Aldrich, "Transatlantic Intelligence and Security Cooperation," *International Affairs* 80, no. 4 (July 2004): 731–753.

14. William G. Boykin, "Intelligence Support to Allied and Coalition Operations: Strategic Environment for Coalition Warfare," Sixteenth Annual NDIA SO/LIC Symposium, Washington, D.C., February 2–4, 2005, http://www.dtic.mil/ndia/2005solic/2005solic.html. On network-centric warfare, see Nancy J. Wesensten, Gregory Belenky, and Thomas J. Balkin, "Cognitive Readiness in Network-Centric Operations," *Parameters* 35, no. 1 (Spring 2005): 94–105; and Paul Murdock, "Principles of War on the Network-Centric Battlefield: Mass and Economy of Force," *Parameters* 32, no. 1 (Spring 2002): 86–95.

15. David S. Yost, "The NATO Capabilities Gap and the European Union," *Survival* 42, no. 4 (December 2000): 97–128.

16. NATO Europe spends about $12 billion a year on research and development. See Stephen J. Flanagan, "Sustaining U.S.-European Global Security Cooperation," *Strategic Forum,* no. 217 (September 2005): 1–6; Steven M. Kosiak, *Analysis of the FY 2007 Defense Budget Request* (Washington, D.C.: Center for Strategic and Budgetary Assessments, April 25, 2006); and International Institute for Strategic Studies, *The Military Balance, 2005–2006* (London: IISS, 2005), p. 107.

17. Aldrich, "Transatlantic Intelligence and Security Cooperation," pp. 745–748.

18. NATO, "Lessons Learned from Recent Terrorist Attacks: Building National Capabilities and Institutions," Chairman's Report, 6 October, 2005, http://www.nato.int/docu/conf/2005/050727/index.html.

19. I thank Terry Terriff for pointing this out.

20. UK-USA was established in 1947. Denmark, Norway, Turkey, and West Germany later joined the network. Reveron, "Old Allies, New Friends," p. 460.

21. Aldrich, "Transatlantic Intelligence and Security Cooperation," pp. 738–740.

22. Dana Priest, "CIA Holds Terror Suspects in Secret Prisons: Debate Is Growing within Agency about Legality and Morality of Overseas System Set Up after 9/11," *Washington Post,* 2 November 2005; and Craig Whitlock, "Prosecutors: Italian Agency Helped CIA Seize Cleric," *Washington Post,* 6 July 2006.

23. NATO, "Defense against Terrorism Program: Countering Terrorism with Technology," Topics, 14 November 2005, http://www.nato.int/issues/dat/index.html.

24. NATO official, interviewed by author, Brussels, Belgium, June 2006.

25. Bob Drogin, "German Spies Aided U.S. Attempt to Kill Hussein in Aerial Attack," *Los Angeles Times,* 12 January 2006.

26. NATO, Allied Command Operations, Supreme Headquarters Allied Powers Europe, "Launch of the Intelligence Fusion Center in Support of NATO," 17 January 2006, http://www.nato.int/shape/news/2006/01/060117a.htm.

27. Tony Blair, *The Global Partnership Annual Report, 2005* (London: Department of Trade and Industry, 2005), http://www.dti.gov.uk/files/file 14426.pdf; Robin Niblett, ed., *Test of Will, Tests of Efficacy: Initiative for a Renewed Transatlantic Partnership, 2005 Report* (Washington, D.C.: Center for Strategic and International Studies, 2005), pp. 25–31; and Matthew Bunn and Anthony Wier, *Securing the Bomb, 2006* (Cambridge, Mass., and Washington, D.C.: Project on Managing the Atom, Harvard University, and Nuclear Threat Initiative, July 2006).

28. Breffni O'Rourke, "Iran: Solana Delivers EU Offer on Nuclear Program," Radio Free Europe/ Radio Liberty Newsline, 6 June 2006, http://www.rferf.org/featuresarticle/2006/06/9ee3bf6e-955d-4ccd-a1b7-a6f7db90afae.html.

29. The French government supplied the CIA with contrary information from one of Saddam Hussein's cabinet ministers, who was a French spy. According to a former CIA official, however, "He said there were no weapons of mass destruction . . . so we didn't believe him." Drogin, "German Spies Aided U.S. Attempt to Kill Hussein in Aerial Attack."

30. On the ongoing debate over preemption, see Gareth Evans, "When Is It Right to Fight?" *Survival* 46, no. 3 (September 2004): 59–82; and Peter Dombrowski and Rodger A. Payne, "The Emerging Consensus for Preventive War," *Survival* 48, no. 2 (June 2006): 115–36.

31. Chaim Brown and Christopher F. Chyba, "Proliferation Rings: New Challenges to the Nuclear Nonproliferation Regime," *International Security* 29, no. 2 (Fall 2004): 5–49; and Stephen G. Rademaker, "Proliferation Security Initiative: An Early Assessment," hearing before House Committee on International Relations, 109th Cong., 1st sess. (Washington, D.C.: U.S. Government Printing Office, 9 June 2005), http://www.internationalrelations.house.gov/archives/109/21699.pdf.

32. George W. Bush, *The National Security Strategy of the United States of America* (Washington, D.C.: White House, September 2002), http://www.whitehouse.gov/nsc/nss.pdf. p. 46.

33. "Global Initiative to Combat Nuclear Terrorism: Joint Fact Sheet," 31 July 2006, http://en.g8russia.ru/docs/7.html. For the International Convention on the Suppression of Acts of Nuclear Terrorism, see http://www.un.org/sc/ctc/law.shtml.

34. Bob Woodward, *Bush at War* (New York: Simon and Schuster, 2002), p. 81; Terry Terriff, "Fear and Loathing in NATO: The Atlantic Alliance after the Crisis over Iraq," *Perspectives on European Politics and Society* 5, no. 3

(2004): 424; and Tomas Valasek, "NATO's New Roles: A Vision from Inside the Alliance" (Washington, D.C.: CDI Terrorism Project, Center for Defense Information, 19 October 2001), http://www.cdi.org/terrorism/nato-pr.cfm.

35. Indeed, initial operations in Afghanistan were conducted by the CIA, which was able to act more rapidly than the Pentagon. See Ron Suskind, *The One Percent Doctrine: Deep Inside America's Pursuit of Its Enemies since 9/11* (New York: Simon and Schuster, 2006), pp. 18–21; Ivo H. Daalder and James M. Lindsay, *America Unbound: The Bush Revolution in Foreign Policy* (Washington, D.C.: Brookings, 2003), pp. 101–102; and Peter van Ham, "Growing Pains," *NATO Review,* no. 3 (Autumn 2005), http://www.nato.int/docu/review/2005/issue3/english/analysis_pr.html.

36. "Backfilling" is one of NATO's support goals in its strategy for confronting terrorism.

37. On NATO's role, see "NATO in Afghanistan," last updated 18 December 2006, http://www.nato.int/issues/afghanistan/index.html.

38. While initially designated "provisional," these teams are now called Provincial Reconstruction Teams. Robert Borders, "Provincial Reconstruction Teams in Afghanistan: A Model for Post-conflict Reconstruction and Development," *Journal of Development and Social Transformation* 1 (November 2004): 5–12; and CARE, "NGO Concerns Regarding Deployment of U.S. Military Provisional Reconstruction Teams," ACBAR (Agency Coordinating Body for Afghan Relief) Policy Brief, 15 January 2003, http://www.care.org/newsroom/specialreports/afghanistan/a_policypositions.asp.

39. François Heisbourg points out that NATO is trying to stabilize Afghanistan as the Soviet Union sought to do earlier, but the Soviet Union failed, with three times as many troops. "International Perspectives on the Use of Force and Legitimacy," transcript (Washington, D.C.: Brookings, 11 October 2006), p. 32, http://www.brook.edu/comm/events/20061011.pdf.

40. Molly Moore and John Ward Anderson, "NATO Faces Growing Hurdle as Call for Troops Falls Short," *Washington Post,* 18 September 2006.

41. NATO, "NATO Boosts Efforts in Afghanistan," last updated 8 December 2006, http://www.nato.int/docu/comm/2006/0611-riga/index.htm.

42. U.S. Department of Defense, "DoD News Briefing with General Richards from Afghanistan," news transcript, 17 October 2006, http://www.defenselink.mil/transcripts/transcript.aspx?Transcript1D?3757. As part of its normal rotation, Richards was replaced as ISAF commander by U.S. Gen. Dan McNeill on February 4, 2007. Carlotta Gall, "America Takes over Command of NATO Force as Its Mission Grows," *New York Times,* February 5, 2007.

43. Some of the national caveats, for example, are imposed for technical reasons, such as aircraft that are not properly equipped to conduct nighttime operations. Philip H. Gordon, "Back Up NATO's Afghanistan Force," *International Herald Tribune,* 8 January 2006.

44. I thank Chantal de Jonge Oudraat for pointing this out.

45. James L. Jones, "Prague to Istanbul: Ambition versus Reality," presentation at "Global Security: A Broader Concept for the 21st Century," Twenty-first International Workshop on Global Security, Berlin, Germany, May 7–10, 2004, pp. 27–30; and John D. Banusiewicz, "'National Caveats' among Key Topics at NATO Meeting," American Forces Press Service, Department of Defense, 9 Feb-

ruary 2005, http://www.defenselink.mil/news/Feb2005/n02092005_2005020911.html.

46. NATO, "NATO Boosts Efforts in Afghanistan."

47. Kristin Archick and Paul Gallis, *NATO and the European Union,* CRS Report for Congress (Washington, D.C.: Library of Congress, 6 April 2004), Order Code RL 32342; and Seth Jones, "Averting Failure in Afghanistan," *Survival* 48, no. 1 (Spring 2006): 111–128.

48. This was apparently intended to test the will of NATO's member states to sustain their commitment. U.S. Department of Defense, "DoD News Briefing with General Richards from Afghanistan."

49. Eric Schmitt, "Springtime for Killing in Afghanistan," *New York Times,* 28 May 2006; and "Britain to Send More Troops to Afghanistan," Agence France-Presse, 10 July 2006.

50. Gall, "America Takes Over Command of NATO Force."

51. Amin Tarzi, "Afghanistan: NATO Expansion Demands Common Approach," Radio Free Europe/Radio Liberty, 6 October 2006, http://www.rferl.org/featuresarticle/2006/10/18ba3c2d-cd22-4963-af8d-52ac0963832b.html.

52. Agreement to aid Turkey was reached in spite of French resistance by taking the decision to NATO's military committee, of which France is not a part. On Poland's request, see NATO, "NATO Council Makes Decision on Polish Request," NATO Update, 22 May 2003, http://www.nato.int/docu/update/2003/05-may/e0521b.htm. On NATO debates over aid to Turkey, see NATO, "Consultations on Measures to Protect Turkey," NATO Update, 6 March 2003, http://www.nato.int/docu/update/2003/02-february/e0210a.htm.

53. Some of these troop contributions are quite small. Participating states include Bulgaria, the Czech Republic, Denmark, Estonia, Hungary, Italy, Latvia, Lithuania, the Netherlands, Norway, Poland, Romania, Slovakia, Spain, and the United Kingdom.

54. Daalder and Lindsay, *America Unbound,* p. 190.

55. Rick Lynch and Phillip D. Janzen, "NATO Training Mission Iraq: Looking to the Future," *Joint Force Quarterly* 40 (1st Quarter 2006): 33; IISS, *The Military Balance, 2005–2006,* p. 45; and NATO, "Iraq Gets National Defense College," 3 September 2006, NATO Update, http://www.nato.int/docu/update/2006/09-september/e0903a.htm.

56. NATO officials, interviewed by author, Brussels, Belgium, 8 June 2006.

57. Lynch and Janzen, "NATO Training Mission Iraq," pp. 32–34. The funding problem is not unique to this mission; the NATO Response Force has been referred to as a "reverse lottery" because troop-contributing nations must bear all the costs. De Hoop Scheffer, "Speech at the 42nd Munich Conference on Security Policy"; and Jones, "NATO: From Common Defense to Common Security."

58. Indeed, some members, notably France, continue to insist that NATO's military role should be limited to article 5 operations. NATO officials, interviewed by author.

59. Ali A. Jalali, "The Future of Afghanistan," *Parameters* 36, no. 1 (Spring 2006): 4–19.

60. "Oral Statement of General James L. Jones, United States Marine Corps, Supreme Allied Commander, Europe, before the Senate Foreign Relations Committee," 109th Cong., 2d sess., 21 September 2006.

61. Richard Norton-Taylor, "British General Takes Command and Promises Ruthless Strikes on Taliban," *Guardian* (London), 1 August 2006. British forces had killed at least 700 combatants in ongoing battles with Taliban forces in southern Afghanistan by August 2006. It is notoriously difficult, however, to determine the number of Taliban casualties. According to one estimate, 4,000 people died in fighting in 2006, many of whom were believed to be rebels. See "France to Withdraw Special Forces from Afghanistan," Agence France-Presse, 17 December 2006, http://www.france24.com/france24Public/en/news/france/20061217-Afghanistan.html; Thomas Harding, "Paras Claim 700 Taliban Lives," *Telegraph,* 29 July 2006; and "Taleban Death Toll 'Inaccurate,'" *BBC News,* 10 December 2006, http://news.bbc.co.uk/2/hi/south_asia/6166577.stm.

62. Quoted in Stephen Harper, "Canada's Commitment in Afghanistan," 39th Parl., 1st sess., May 17, 2006, http://www.parl.gc.ca/39/1/parlbus/chambus/house/debates/025_2006-05-17/HAN025-E.htm#OOB-1543354.

63. U.S. Department of Defense, "DoD News Briefing with General Richards from Afghanistan."

64. Ibid.; and "Oral Statement of General James L. Jones." On the fragility of the situation in Afghanistan, see also Barnett R. Rubin, "Still Ours to Lose: Afghanistan on the Brink," prepared testimony for the House and Senate Committees on Foreign Relations (Washington, D.C.: Council on Foreign Relations, September 21, 2006).

65. "France to Pull Troops Fighting against Taliban in Afghanistan," *New York Times,* 18 December 2006. In both the Netherlands and Canada, parliaments raised serious questions about sending troops to Afghanistan; both Dutch and Canadian troops are actively engaged in fighting insurgent forces there. "Canada Committed to Afghan Mission, Harper Tells Troops," *CBC News,* 13 March 2006, http://www.cbc.ca/world/story/2006/03/13/harper_afghanistan060313.html; and "More Dutch Troops for Afghanistan," *BBC News,* 3 February 2006, http://news.bbc.co.uk/2/hi/europe/4673026.stm.

66. Helene Cooper, "NATO Allies Wary of Sending More Troops to Afghanistan," *New York Times,* 27 January 2007.

67. Moore and Anderson, "NATO Faces Growing Hurdles as Call for Troops Falls Short."

68. Dagmar de Mora-Figueroa, "NATO's Response to Terrorism," *NATO Review* no. 3 (Autumn 2005), http://www.nato.int/docu/review/2005/issue3/english/art1.html; Eric R. Terzuolo, "Combating WMD Proliferation," *NATO Review* no. 3 (Autumn 2005), http://www.nato.int/docu/review/2005/issue3/english/art3.html; and "Boosting NATO's CBRN Capabilities," *NATO Review* no. 3 (Autumn 2005), http://www.nato.int/docu/review/2005/issue3/english/features1.html.

69. Jean-Yves Haine, "Military Matters: ESDP Transformed?" *NATO Review* no. 2 (Summer 2005), http://www.nato.int/docu/review/2005/issue2/english/military_pr.html; and NATO, "Press Conference by NATO Secretary-

General on the Extraordinary Meeting of the North Atlantic Council," Online Library, 8 July 2005, http://www.nato.int/docu/speech/2005/s050708a.htm.

70. Guy Dinmore, "U.S. Sees Coalitions of the Willing as Best Ally," *Financial Times,* 4 January 2006.

71. Robert Jervis, *American Foreign Policy in a New Era* (New York: Routledge, 2005), pp. 11–36. See also Karl W. Deutsch, Sidney A. Burrell, and Robert A. Kann, *Political Community and the North Atlantic Area: International Organization in the Light of Historical Experience* (New York: Greenwood, 1969), pp. 5–8; and Buzan and Waever, *Regions and Powers,* pp. 343–376.

72. Brown, *Multilateral Constraints on the Use of Force,* pp. 19–21.

73. Press-Barnathan, "Managing the Hegemon," pp. 290–301.

74. Thomas Risse-Kappen, "Collective Identity in a Democratic Community: The Case of NATO," in Peter J. Katzenstein, ed., *The Culture of National Security: Norms and Identity in World Politics* (New York: Columbia University Press, 1996), pp. 357–399.

75. On NATO expansion, see James M. Goldgeier, *Not Whether but When: The U.S. Decision to Enlarge NATO* (Washington, D.C.: Brookings, 1999); David S. Yost, *NATO Transformed: The Alliance's New Roles in International Security* (Washington, D.C.: United States Institute of Peace Press, 1998); and Jonathan Eyal, "NATO's Enlargement: Anatomy of a Decision," *International Affairs* 73, no. 4 (October 1997): 695–719. For a contrary view, see Dan Reiter, "Why NATO Enlargement Does Not Spread Democracy," *International Security* 25, no. 4 (Spring 2001): 41–67.

76. Press-Barnathan, "Managing the Hegemon," pp. 301–303.

77. Brown, *Multilateral Constraints on the Use of Force,* p. 19.

78. To be sure, frictions over U.S. unilateralism are not new to the alliance. Similar tensions were evident during President Bill Clinton's administration, which rejected several attempts to establish international institutions that it believed might undermine U.S. national security, such as the 1997 Ottawa Convention, which banned antipersonnel land mines, and the International Criminal Court.

79. U.S. Department of State, Office of the Spokesman, "Transformational Diplomacy," 18 January 2006, http://www.state.gov/r/pa/prs/ps/2006/59339.htm.

80. Quoted in Banusiewicz, "'National Caveats' among Key Topics at NATO Meeting."

81. Donald H. Rumsfeld, "Speech at the 42nd Munich Conference on Security Policy," 4 February 2006, http://www.securityconference.de.

82. Office of the Press Secretary, "Fact Sheet: Request for Additional FY 2004 Funding for the War on Terror," September 8, 2003, http://www.white house.gov/news/releases/2003/09/20030908-1.html.

83. "Briefing on NATO Military Structure," August 2005, http://www.nato .int/docu/briefing/nms/nms-e.pdf; and NATO, Allied Command Operations, Supreme Headquarters Allied Powers Europe, "New NATO Command Structure," 4 May 2004, www.nato.int/shape/issues/ncs/ncs_index.htm.

84. Donald H. Rumsfeld, *Quadrennial Defense Review Report* (Washington, D.C.: Department of Defense, February 6, 2006), p. vii, http://www

.defenselink.mil/qdr/report/Report20060203.pdf. p. 88. On constabulary forces for NATO, see David T. Armitage Jr. and Anne M. Moisan, "Constabulary Forces and Postconflict Transition: The Euro-Atlantic Dimension," *Strategic Forum* no. 218 (November 2005): 1–7; and Hans Binnendijk and Richard L. Kugler, "Needed—A NATO Stabilization and Reconstruction Force," *Defense Horizons* no. 45 (September 2004): 1–8.

85. On this point, see in particular Wade Jacoby, "Is the New Europe a Good Substitute for the Old One?" *International Studies Review* 8, no. 1 (March 2006): 178–197; and Zoltan Barany, "NATO's Post–Cold War Metamorphosis: From Sixteen to Twenty-six and Counting," *International Studies Review* 8, no. 1 (March 2006): 165–178.

86. Rumsfeld, *Quadrennial Defense Review,* pp. 23–24; and Jonathan Stevenson, "Demilitarizing the 'War on Terror,'" *Survival* 48, no. 2 (Summer 2006): 37–54.

87. Jeremy Shapiro and Daniel L. Byman, "Bridging the Transatlantic Counterterrorism Gap," *Washington Quarterly* 29, no. 4 (Autumn 2006): 33–50.

88. U.S. official, interview by author.

89. Bush, *National Security Strategy* (2006), p. 9.

90. Jim Garamone, "Jones Discusses Changing Troop 'Footprint' in Europe," American Forces Press Service, 10 October 2003.

PART 4

Economic Issues

Brian Frederking and Paul F. Diehl

INTERNATIONAL ORGANIZATIONS HAVE GREATLY INFLUENCED the maintenance of global economic stability since World War II. The current international economic system is built around the pillars of the World Trade Organization (WTO), the International Monetary Fund, and the World Bank. These institutions are largely controlled by Western states, either through formal voting procedures or sheer economic power. Developing countries argue that the current system is at best not designed to meet their needs and at worst designed to perpetuate the dominance of the Western states. The debates between developed countries of the North and the developing countries of the South dominate the agendas of international economic organizations. The WTO, of course, has received considerable attention since its inception, hailed as an important vehicle for promoting open markets and vilified by protestors for hurting the interests of the world's poor.

The WTO is a significant innovation among international organizations because it can enforce its rules through a binding dispute resolution process. When countries join the WTO, they agree to settle all disputes through this process and comply with the outcome of the WTO rulings. In Chapters 10 and 11, Keisuke Iida and John Jackson analyze the WTO dispute settlement mechanism. Iida traces the changes that occurred when the General Agreement on Tariffs and Trade was institutionalized into the WTO and then evaluates the effectiveness of the WTO dispute settlement mechanism. Jackson spells out the logic behind the necessity for the dispute resolution process and illustrates that logic with multiple examples. Both authors conclude that compliance with the WTO rulings is generally high.

The international monetary system is another significant issue area in which international organization is crucial to maintaining economic stability. While the International Monetary Fund no longer oversees a fixed exchange-rate system, global arrangements among the G-8 countries or G-20 countries are often necessary to minimize the chances of financial crises or wildly fluctuating currency values. In Chapter 12, Benjamin Cohen outlines the challenges of governance in this issue area because states see autonomy over their own currency values as an indispensable element of state power. Cohen analyzes the three most important recent developments in the international monetary system: the introduction of the Euro, the wide gaps in the balance of payments between China and the United States, and the globalization of financial markets.

10

Is WTO Dispute Settlement Effective?

Keisuke Iida

THE WORLD TRADE ORGANIZATION (WTO) HAS BECOME ONE of the most controversial international institutions, as evidenced by the massive protests in Seattle in November 1999.[1] Curiously, both the defendants and the critics of the WTO seem to believe that it is a highly effective institution, but that should not be assumed. Rather, that assumption has to be examined and demonstrated objectively and systematically. This article makes a first step in that direction.

The WTO has two major functions: legislative and judicial. The legislative function refers to the role of the WTO as a forum in which to reach trade agreements. The judicial function is performed by the dispute settlement system, one of the new major features of the current multilateral trade system. The political features and underpinnings of these two functions, although somewhat similar, are distinct enough to warrant separate analyses. Furthermore, due to the long stalemate in multilateral negotiations until the breakthrough at the Doha ministerial conference in November 2001, the legislative function of the WTO has been in low gear, and the real action has been taken by the judicial arm. Therefore, in this article, I focus only on dispute settlement, or the judicial arm of the WTO.

Effectiveness

Recent regime analyses have concentrated on the question of effectiveness. This trend is particularly notable in environmental studies, presum-

Reprinted from *Global Governance* 10, no. 2 (2004): 207–225. © 2004 Lynne Rienner Publishers. Reprinted by permission of the publisher.

ably because the idea of "effectiveness" moves our attention away from formalism and directs it to substance. For instance, questions about an international environmental regime's effectiveness are not directed to the formal language of a treaty, but rather to whether or not it does anything useful for the environment. Oran Young and Marc Levy distinguish between several different types of effectiveness: problem solving, legal, economic, normative, and political.[2] Effectiveness in problem solving is the most intuitive: whether or not a regime solves the problem that the regime is supposed to combat or to help solve. Although this is clearly one of the most important concerns, Young and Levy argue that this definition sometimes poses several difficulties. Legal effectiveness focuses on compliance: whether or not contracting parties behave according to the rules specified in the regime. While measurement is easier with regard to this dimension, it may trap us into a purely formal analysis. Economic effectiveness adds an economic-cost dimension to the problem-solving approach mentioned above. Normative effectiveness refers to whether or not a regime achieves values, such as fairness and participation. Finally, political effectiveness refers to the effectiveness of a regime in altering the behavior of actors in favor of better management of environmental problems. According to this yardstick, a regime could be "politically" effective without full compliance, presumably a difficult goal to achieve in international politics.

While this classification suffers from some operational ambiguities, it is useful in generating a multifaceted approach to the analysis of international regimes. Some of the questions I pose later in this article could be classified accordingly. For example, the questions of the effectiveness of the WTO in facilitating dispute resolution and preventing unilateralism are problem-solving approaches. The analysis of its effectiveness in assuring a level playing field and reconciling trade and nontrade concerns is a normative approach, and the discussion of the legislative-judicial balance in dispute settlement is "political."

A major concern in the literature has been to search for clues to establish causal connections between regimes and their effectiveness with regard to some of these dimensions. However, an equally important research question is "What makes international regimes effective?"—if effectiveness can be measured and can be traced back to the regimes. The answers to this question have been few and far between.

One of the most promising answers is that "regime design matters." In a path-breaking work on oil pollution, Ronald Mitchell showed that the way a maritime oil pollution regime was designed affected the effectiveness of the regime in a crucial manner.[3] In particular, he showed that a regulatory change in the direction of greater visibility of an individual ship's actions prevented pollution. This gives an insight into international regulation and human behavior in environmental issues, but it remains to be seen if it is generalizable to other issue areas. Since the dispute settlement mechanism of the multilateral trade system has undergone a substantial change in regime design, as I describe shortly, it provides us with a quasi-experiment in examining its impact on effectiveness.

Institutional Framework

Before proceeding to the evaluation of the effectiveness of WTO dispute settlement, I need to discuss some of the changes in the institutional procedures that were made from the previous GATT to the new WTO regime. There have been four major changes from GATT to the WTO in terms of dispute settlement, and these changes affect the desiderata for firms and governments involved in trade disputes. First, the most decisive change from GATT to the WTO is the introduction of "negative consensus": the rulings of the panel (first instance) and the Appellate Body (AB) are adopted automatically unless there is a consensus within the Dispute Settlement Body, an intergovernmental organ, to overturn them. This essentially means that if the case is appealed, the AB has the final say. Given the assumption that the AB renders rulings independent of government pressure and that it is neutral in not favoring particular governments,[4] firms and governments will weigh the "merits" and "precedents" of the case and decide whether they should file a case on which they have grievances. This means that the cases with greater merits and clear precedents of winning are more likely to be filed at the WTO. On the other hand, the defending party is not oblivious to this fact. Even the most risk-taking governments and firms would concede if the chance of losing were nearly 100 percent. Shifting resources to market competition may bring higher profits (or smaller losses) than persisting with a futile litigation. Therefore, the cases brought to the WTO have high merits but do not have a 100 percent chance of winning; there is at least some residual uncertainty about how the rulings will go.

Another accompanying change to this "automaticity" is the greater likelihood of facing retaliation when the defending party refuses to comply with a guilty verdict. In GATT days, the losing side could easily block the panel report or a request for retaliation (retaliation happened only once at GATT). Now neither a "guilty" finding nor a request for retaliation is easily blocked. Hence, the defending party, once it has received a violation finding, has to resign itself to the likelihood of retaliation authorized by the WTO. However, the likelihood of retaliation is not 100 percent either. The complaining party has to weigh various factors when it decides to retaliate, not the least of which is the cost to its own industry. This is where a "realist" concern may creep in, even in this nonrealist setting. A large economy with a large import market—for example, the United States—that is important to the defending party can wield more influence by threatening retaliation than a small economy with vulnerable industries dependent on imports.

The second major change from GATT to the WTO is the speeding up of the process. While GATT cases could drag on forever, there is a strict timetable for proceedings at the WTO. Firms involved in disputes have welcomed this change. The more quickly their cases are resolved, the more quickly the benefits of winning are reaped. Therefore, firms on the offensive side have greater incentive to file disputes at the WTO. Conversely, firms on the defending side have greater incentive to concede. In GATT days, they could rely on delaying tactics, but at the WTO, delaying tactics are less effective, although still used.

The third change that the WTO brought is the addition of the appellate process. Although the AB is not likely to overturn the panel rulings completely, partial modifications are common. Given this fact, the government on the defending side (with a loss at the panel stage) is likely to appeal, hoping for a more lenient ruling from the AB. Equally, the complainant government is likely to appeal if the panel report is unfavorable or does not give enough relief. Moreover, appeals are good for reputational concerns of the government: it can show to its constituency that it has fought a good fight. Therefore, the appeal process is used quite often. Of the seventy-eight panel rulings issued from 1995 to October 2003, fifty-three cases (68 percent) have been appealed.

A fourth major change from GATT to the WTO is the participation of nongovernment organizations (NGOs). While the WTO is an intergovernmental dispute resolution mechanism, denying standing to nonstate actors, it has made its processes more transparent and accessible. For instance, the Appellate Body allowed NGOs to attach their briefs to the U.S. government's submission to the WTO in the shrimp-turtle case.[5] This has already changed the character of the WTO process. More and more nontrade issues are involved in the disputes. This poses

an interesting question: Is the WTO more influenced by trade considerations than nontrade considerations?

Finally, apart from the institutional changes in dispute settlement,
the Uruguay Round, which led to the creation of the WTO, produced a
number of important changes in substantive rules. It is beyond the scope
of this article to examine all the ramifications of these changes—not to
mention the changes likely to be made during the Doha Round. However, worthy of mention is the addition of new issues, such as agriculture, services, trade-related investment measures, and intellectual property rights. To date, about a third of the disputes have concerned these
"new" issues.[6] The expansion in the jurisdiction of the multilateral trade
system is likely to have considerable impact on the effectiveness of the
dispute settlement procedure as well.

Is the WTO Dispute Settlement System
Effective in Settling Disputes?

In the rest of this article, I examine the effectiveness of the WTO dispute settlement system in five areas: actually solving disputes, fending
off unilateralism, assuring a level playing field, reconciling trade and
nontrade concerns, and balancing legislative and judicial functions.

First, does the WTO dispute system do what it is intended to do—
that is, facilitate dispute resolution? Let me give an overview of the
numbers of disputes. As of October 2003, more than 300 complaints
have been filed at the WTO. This caseload is comparable to that of
GATT over the forty years of its history. However, this number is somewhat misleading. Several countries often complain about the same trade
measure of a particular country. The WTO treats each of these complaints as distinct, but as long as the substance of the complaints is the
same and provided that the same panel handles them, I have treated
them as one complaint.[7] According to this method of counting, 248 distinct complaints have been filed.

What is the overall track record of dispute resolution? This question,
while simple, is not so easy to answer. It depends on the analyst's judgment as to what counts as a "satisfactory" outcome. I have tried to rely on
the parties' assessment as much as possible. There are two main categories
of satisfactory outcome: (1) the parties have implemented the WTO rulings, and (2) the parties have settled the dispute between themselves, with
or without WTO adjudication. While the first type is relatively easy to

track, the second category is not. Therefore, I have relied on the parties'
notification to the WTO as to whether or not they have reached a mutually agreed solution. A third "possibly satisfactory" category is one in
which the WTO found no wrongdoing on the part of the defendants, and
hence no action was required. This could be considered a "successful"
dispute outcome, at least from a legal point of view. All of these cases
are classified as "resolved" in Figure 10.1. There are two classes of
pending cases. One is the class of cases that are still going through the
adjudication procedures or have gone through adjudication and are in
the implementation stage. The WTO allows a "reasonable period of
time" for implementation, which ranges from several months to a maximum of fifteen months. A number of cases are at this stage. This class
is named "ongoing" in Figure 10.1. The second class of pending cases
(denoted as "pending" in Figure 10.1) comprises those cases on which
consultations have been held without reaching concrete agreement. It is
possible that some of these cases have actually been settled, but the parties have not notified the WTO of that fact, thereby making the interpretation of this class of cases difficult. Finally, there are a few cases for
which the final result is not known.

Figure 10.1   Outcomes of WTO Disputes, 1995–2003

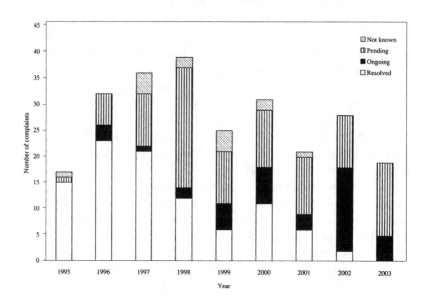

Figure 10.1 shows the classification of disputes according to these criteria.[8] The complaints are divided according to the year in which they were initially filed. This shows that during the first two to three years of dispute settlement, the WTO had a good track record, but from 1998 on, the number of possibly unsatisfactory outcomes increased. This may be partly due to the fact that not enough time has elapsed since the inception of disputes. This can be seen in the number of "ongoing" cases since 1998. However, a majority of unresolved cases are so-called pending consultations cases, as seen in Figure 10.1. For this class of cases, especially those on which consultations were held in 1998 or 1999, it is hard to argue that the parties have not had enough time. I suspect that for a large proportion of cases in this category, the complainants have all but abandoned the complaint, for one reason or another, but have not made this fact public. Based on this analysis, we could tentatively conclude that in the first few years of dispute settlement, the WTO performed well, whereas since 1998, it has not been working as smoothly.

A comparison with the track record of GATT may be useful. Robert Hudec has assembled the most comprehensive data on GATT disputes, and of 207 cases that were filed at GATT from 1948 to 1989 (data for the cases from 1990 through 1994 are missing), there were 88 rulings, of which 20 were no-violation findings and 68 were violation findings. Since no action was required for the 20 no-violation cases, they would be included in our "success" category. Of the 68 violation rulings, 45 led to fully satisfactory outcomes and 15 led to partly satisfactory outcomes. Of 64 cases that were settled or conceded without GATT rulings, 37 led to fully satisfactory outcomes and 25 reached partly satisfactory outcomes. Therefore, by the most conservative measure, the overall success rate of the GATT dispute system was 102 of 207 cases, or 49 percent. Hudec reports a different figure, using only the cases with known results (139 cases). According to his calculation (excluding those with nonviolation findings), the success rate is 60 percent.[9] That said, a decade-by-decade breakdown shows some fluctuations, with success rates lower in the 1950s and 1960s.

Therefore, the performance of the first few years of the WTO dispute settlement is comparable to, or above, the success rate of the GATT system, but the rate has been below that of GATT since 1998. It has to be admitted that the number and nature of disputes filed are different and that no totally comparable analysis can be made. Nevertheless, it should be emphasized that the conventional wisdom that the WTO is extremely "effective" in resolving disputes (in particular, relative to GATT) should be questioned.[10]

One possible explanation for the decline in the effectiveness of the WTO dispute system since 1998 is the complication of U.S.–European Union relations. The WTO ruled on two of the most difficult cases in 1997—bananas and beef hormones—and on finding the European Union's compliance insufficient in the banana dispute and nonexistent in the beef dispute, the United States resorted to sanctions in 1999 in both cases. This soured U.S.–European Union relations considerably. The subsequent case brought by the European Union against the United States over foreign sales corporations,[11] for example, is widely reputed to have been a retaliatory suit. In addition, according to negotiators in Geneva, political bargaining is often suspended during the panel and AB proceedings, with haggling restarting only after all the legal procedures are exhausted. This is not an efficient use of time, since it causes substantial delays.

A related question with regard to this dimension of effectiveness is whether or not the WTO has restrained the outbreak of trade wars. The answer depends on how one defines trade wars and what would have happened without the WTO. As already mentioned, so far the United States has resorted to sanctions in two disputes against the European Union—bananas and hormones. In the former, Ecuador also joined the retaliation, and in the latter, Canada joined. If one includes these cases as trade wars, the WTO has certainly not stopped trade wars. In each case, however, the WTO appointed an arbitrator to determine the size of countermeasures. This has had a restraining effect on the parties' behavior.[12]

Is WTO Dispute Settlement Effective in Fending Off Unilateralism?

Another purpose for which the WTO dispute settlement system was constructed was to fend off unilateralism. There is more than one way to resolve trade disputes. In the 1980s, the United States in particular turned increasingly to unilateral measures authorized under Section 301 of the U.S. Trade Act of 1974. Hudec has described how the United States increasingly defied GATT rulings, using its power to block adoption of panel rulings.

While the U.S. government wanted a stronger dispute settlement system during the Uruguay Round negotiations, the Europeans and Japanese wanted the annulment of Section 301 in exchange. Therefore, an important question is whether or not this has happened. Has the WTO disarmed Section 301?

The most important factor in this regard is the perception of the firms. If they feel that they can more effectively achieve their purposes of market opening abroad through Section 301 rather than through the WTO, they will continue to file complaints. On the other hand, if they find that the WTO is more likely to resolve their disputes in their favor, if the U.S. government is more reluctant to receive their complaints under Section 301, or if they find that the WTO disputes are cheaper than using Section 301, they will increasingly route their complaints through their governments to the WTO. One of the desiderata for the firms is the propensity of their government to resort to the WTO rather than to unilateral measures.

In this regard, it seems that there has been a learning process for the United States. One of the first disputes fought at the WTO was the auto talks between the United States and Japan. The United States was frustrated with Japanese recalcitrance in the negotiations and threatened to impose retaliatory duties on luxury cars from Japan. In turn, Japan filed a complaint regarding this unilateral measure at the WTO. At the last minute in this game of "chicken," the United States blinked and decided not to retaliate unilaterally.

A similar process was repeated in a film dispute, when Kodak initially filed a complaint against Japan under Section 301. However, during the investigation the U.S. trade representative (USTR) decided to route this dispute through the WTO, fearing that Japan would repeat its tactic during the auto talks and would file a WTO complaint against any retaliation under Section 301.[13] Because of this learning process, the USTR started routing most Section 301 cases through the WTO, causing Section 301 to become moribund as a unilateral measure. Of the twenty-seven Section 301 cases that were initiated between January 1995 and August 2002, seventeen cases were adjudicated at the WTO and the rest settled bilaterally without WTO intervention.[14] More important, since the Kodak case, the United States has not resorted to retaliation under Section 301 without first going through the WTO.

Another sign that the WTO has tamed U.S. unilateralism is the fact that most of the recent invocations of Section 301 have been self-initiated cases in connection with WTO proceedings. A USTR official says that the industry is learning this fact and refrains from filing Section 301 cases.[15] Indeed, after the Kodak case (filed in May 1995), the private sector filed only six Section 301 petitions (up to August 2002). All the others have been self-initiated by the USTR. In contrast, the private sector filed 98 petitions (70 initiated, 28 rejected or withdrawn) during the GATT period (1975–1994), or about five cases per year on average.

In summary, the U.S. government has learned that any Section 301 retaliation will be a target of countersuit at the WTO and has decided to route most of the Section 301 cases through the WTO. In addition, U.S. industry has learned that the U.S. government will bring their Section 301 cases to the WTO and hence has changed its strategy.[16]

Is WTO Dispute Settlement Effective in Assuring a Level Playing Field?

Suppose that a firm in a developing country has a legitimate grievance about the trade practices of a large developed country. Will it ask its government to pursue a dispute at the WTO? Several negative considerations dictate otherwise. First of all, WTO disputes are not cheap.[17] A small firm or the government of a developing country may find it unaffordable. Therefore, it will simply keep silent. This would leave many such cases invisible to third parties, including myself. In these situations, the best that could be done would be to negotiate these problems bilaterally. However, as long as the government (and firm) on the other side knows that the complainant cannot afford to file a WTO dispute, there is less incentive to concede.

These considerations lead to the following hypotheses: poor developing countries will be underrepresented in the WTO dispute settlement system (as plaintiffs), and the legitimate grievances they may have will not come to the WTO. None of the above considerations suggests that poor countries are immune from disputes as defendants. Although developing countries receive special treatment in the GATT/WTO system (their obligations are less stringent and their implementation has a grace period of five years or more), many of them have been targeted by developed countries in WTO disputes. Hudec had noted the underrepresentation of developing countries in the previous GATT dispute system: "Developing countries accounted for 44 of 229 complaints (19 percent) and 29 of 223 appearances as defendant (13 percent)."[18]

However, there has been some improvement in the underrepresentation of developing countries at the WTO. Until 2000, developing countries were reluctant to file disputes at the WTO. From 1995 through

1999, developing countries filed (either alone or jointly) only forty-one complaints (or 27 percent of 149 disputes). Since 2000, however, they have been more aggressive. As many as 51 percent of disputes in 2000 and 71 percent of disputes filed in 2001 came from developing countries. In addition, developing countries are just as frequently targeted: ninety-one complaints (37 percent) were filed against developing countries.

The only notable exception to underrepresentation is Africa.[19] While Africa currently includes thirty-three WTO members (nearly a quarter of the membership), only Egypt (twice) and South Africa (twice) have appeared in WTO disputes, and both appeared only as defendants. None has filed a complaint. In other words, Africa is not even a target of disputes.

Reputational considerations work somewhat against hauling developing countries before the WTO. For instance, Canada and Brazil have been locking horns over subsidies on regional aircraft (or commuter airplanes), which are mainly sold in U.S. markets. Canada obtained WTO authorization for retaliation but did not retaliate. An official from Canada admitted that the authorization was highly embarrassing: it would not be good for Canada's image to impose sanctions on a "poor" country like Brazil.[20]

Cost considerations and the lack of legal expertise[21] have so far inhibited developing countries from fully taking advantage of the WTO dispute settlement system. As a consequence, they are still handicapped as plaintiffs at the WTO, but their trade practices are increasingly complained about at the WTO. Although reputational considerations should work against developed countries suing developing countries, these considerations have not been strong enough to stop those countries from doing so.

The developing countries have begun to address this problem. At the Seattle meeting in 1999, some developing country members of the WTO agreed to establish the Advisory Center on WTO Law to help themselves and others utilize the WTO dispute system more effectively. The center was inaugurated in Geneva in October 2001,[22] but it remains to be seen how this will affect the course of future litigation at the WTO.

Another possible concern for developing countries is whether the WTO panels and the AB are truly impartial. As described below, there have been a few controversies over the decisions that the AB has made. It is beyond the scope of this article to evaluate the legal merits of WTO rulings, which have to be left to legal scholars. Statistically, it is hard to determine whether WTO rulings are biased in favor of, or against, developing countries, partly because once the disputes reach the ruling stages, it is very rare for the WTO to find no violations. The probability that the WTO will make violation findings is slightly higher when the defendant is a developing country, but the chances that the WTO will find violations are also higher when the complainants include developing countries.[23]

Is WTO Dispute Settlement Effective in Reconciling Trade Concerns with Nontrade Concerns?

As many NGOs fear, there are several reasons why we might expect the WTO to give greater weight to trade concerns than nontrade concerns if there is a need for a balance to be struck between them. First, when WTO agreements are negotiated, firms and industries speak the loudest, and they are the most likely to be heard. Although firms and industries are hardly monolithic, they are unified in the sense that they give priority to economic concerns. Other considerations, such as environmental concerns, consumer safety concerns, human rights, and cultural and other values will not figure prominently in their demands and pressures on the government officials and diplomats who negotiate trade agreements. Second, firms are a key force behind the WTO dispute process, and therefore most of the cases are likely to reflect significant trade concerns. Finally, the incentive for retaliation may also be influenced by corporate concerns, as already alluded to in this article. All these considerations seem to suggest that the WTO dispute process will not be very favorable to environmentalists, cultural purists, human rights advocates, and other noncorporate actors.

This being said, the WTO has already opened the door to these NGOs, albeit modestly. NGOs have also had a significant impact on some government policies. Thus, either directly or indirectly, they may be able to influence the course of events. Unfortunately, there have not been enough cases involving nontrade concerns on the WTO docket to make definitive judgments. Some high-profile cases give mixed answers to this question.

There have been two major WTO dispute decisions that have incensed environmentalists: the reformulated gasoline case and the shrimp-turtle case. In the former, the Environmental Protection Agency's decision to impose differential treatment on foreign unreformulated gasoline was ruled to be in violation of the principle of national treatment (equal treatment of domestic and foreign goods once foreign goods have entered the country). The second, higher-profile case of shrimp imports concerned a U.S. measure to prohibit imports of shrimp from countries that did not mandate the use of turtle excluder devices. Four shrimp-exporting countries from Asia sued the United States at the WTO and won a ruling in their favor. Although the panel report categorically reprimanded the United States for taking a unilateral measure to pursue the environmental protection goal of protecting turtles, the AB toned down the criticism of the U.S. policy by upholding the principle of environmental protection while still disapproving the specific measure that the United States took. The most controversial issue was the AB decision that the term "exhaustible resources" in Article XX included living resources such as turtles, allegedly contrary to the original intent of the drafters. This "evolutionary" ("read in light of contemporary concerns") interpretation was heavily criticized by developing counties.

The asbestos case is another interesting case, pitting Canada, an exporter of asbestos, against France, which banned the importation of asbestos for public health reasons. In a rare decision, accepting the general exception of GATT Article XX(b), the panel and the AB upheld the French ban.[24] This shows that as long as there is firm scientific evidence in support of the trade-restrictive measure in question, the WTO supports those nontrade concerns.

Finally, confrontation has been averted in a very controversial case concerning Brazil's drug policy. To fight increasing levels of human immunodeficiency virus (HIV) infection, the Brazilian government is promoting local manufacturing of generic acquired immunodeficiency (AIDS) drugs. In order to comply with the WTO law, Brazil had to pass a new patent law to protect new drug patents. However, by using the local manufacturing requirement in the new law (to deny patents unless the firms promised to manufacture locally), the Brazilian government threatened to manufacture generic copies of two new drugs produced by two foreign companies—America's Merck and Switzerland's Roche Holding—unless they started making them in Brazil or importing them at a lower cost.[25] The United States brought this patent case against Brazil to the WTO in 2000, and the WTO established a panel to adjudicate it. However, to avoid unnecessary controversy, the United States dropped the case in June 2001.[26]

The UN and the WTO quickly became aware of this problem as politically explosive. In the summer of 2000, the UN Sub-Commission on the Promotion and Protection of Human Rights called on the secretary-general and the high commissioner for human rights to analyze the impact that the WTO's Agreement on Trade-Related Aspects of Intellectual Property Rights (TRIPS) had on human rights. In its August 17 resolution, the subcommission said, "There are apparent conflicts between the intellectual property rights regime embodied in the TRIPS Agreement on the one hand, and international human rights law on the other."[27] Human rights activists argued that provisions of the TRIPS agreement obligating countries to patent pharmaceuticals restricted access to drugs in poorer countries. The WTO also held a special meeting of the Council on Intellectual Property Rights to discuss this issue in June 2001, well timed to coincide with the UN Special Session on AIDS. Finally, the Doha ministerial meeting issued a special ministerial declaration on TRIPS and public health, affirming the broad-ranging rights of states to break intellectual property rights in the name of protecting public health. After a year-long negotiation, a final agreement was reached in August 2003. This example underscores the fact that important "political" decisions need to be made through multilateral negotiations—or through the legislative function of the WTO—and not through dispute settlement.

In sum, the WTO dispute settlement system is capable of reconciling trade (or commercial) interests with nontrade concerns, but in a limited way. In the view of many environmentalists, consumer advocates, and others, the hurdles for accepting trade-restrictive measures as legitimate are too high. For instance, the precautionary principle, which is becoming established in international environmental law, is yet to be firmly embedded in WTO law.[28] There is certainly room for improvement in this regard, but reform has to be implemented by legislative bodies, such as the General Council and/or the Committee on Trade and Environment, not by dispute settlement.

Is WTO Dispute Settlement Too Effective (Powerful)?

The last consideration in the previous section leads to the question of the balance between legislation and adjudication. Even in a domestic system with separation of powers, there is some overlap between the legislative branch and the judicial branch. Since a court is required to settle urgent disputes at times, it is obliged to "fill the gap" when legislation is not sufficiently clear on some points in question. In that instance, the court performs a quasi-legislative function. However, if a court goes too far in encroaching on the legislative (that is, political) territory, there is bound to be a backlash, with a criticism that unelected judges do not have the right to write legislation. A similar problem happens at the WTO. Since the dispute settlement system has been highly automatic in making decisions lately, there is sufficient ground for concern. Suppose that the AB makes a substantial legal error or a new interpretation of some WTO agreements that was not intended or foreseen by negotiators. Due to the automaticity of adoption, the ruling is most likely to be adopted and implemented. Although judicial activists would welcome such an outcome, most governments are increasingly wary of this danger.

While the most controversial decision has been the procedural ruling regarding amicus briefs, which led to turmoil at the Dispute Settlement Body,[29] some have criticized the AB for trespassing on legislative ground in interpreting substantive rules as well. For instance, in an article published by the Third Trade Network, Chakravarthi Raghavan argued that panels and the AB have gone to the extent of adjudicating between two conflicting provisions of the agreements, citing the example of the Indonesia auto case.[30] To avoid this kind of problem, he suggested that the General Council, the legislative organ of the WTO, give guidelines to the panels and the AB regarding the interpretation of the agreements.[31] Frieder Roessler, former director of the GATT Legal Division and currently executive director of the Advisory Center on WTO Law, was reported to have drawn attention to the trend that the panels/AB are transgressing into areas that should rightly be the jurisdiction of various other organs of the WTO.[32]

A similar concern arose in the U.S. Congress; and in the Trade Promotion Authority legislation, Congress instructed the executive branch to look into the issue. In a subsequent report to Congress, the Department of Commerce agreed that "panels and the Appellate Body must ground their analyses firmly in the agreement text and accept reasonable permissible interpretations of the WTO Agreements by the Members."[33] Perhaps taking a cue from the U.S. concern, the AB is beginning to place more emphasis on textual analysis than before. The change was most dramatically symbolized by the AB's overturning of the panel ruling in the German steel case in late 2002.[34] However, room for legal maneuver for panels and the AB is limited, and here again a fundamental "political" resolution awaits decisions by the Ministerial Conference or other "legislative" bodies.

Conclusion

The central message of this article is that "effectiveness" is not one-dimensional, as many seem to believe. The WTO is no exception; its effectiveness needs to be measured with regard to several dimensions. To summarize the main findings, the WTO dispute settlement system has been most effective in "disarming" Section 301. Since the debacle of the auto talks in 1995, the United States has rarely resorted to Section 301 unilaterally, as it often had in the 1980s. American industries have been filing fewer and fewer cases under Section 301. Even with this most spectacular success, however, the WTO has not been completely effective: the panel that was asked directly to rule on the WTO consistency of Section 301 did not outlaw the statute, given the recent U.S. practice.[35]

The most obvious criterion of effectiveness—whether the WTO actually resolves disputes—is much harder to assess. However, on a relatively simple operationalization of this dimension—whether or not disputes have reached mutually agreeable solutions or implementation of WTO rulings—the scorecard is good only in the first few years of the system. Since 1998, the stockpile of pending cases has been increasing.

The WTO is less effective when measured with regard to the more demanding dimensions, such as creating a level playing field and balancing trade and nontrade concerns. Developing countries are more active in the system than before, but some countries are still completely excluded. The scorecard on balancing disparate interests is very low as well, as indicated by various criticisms leveled at the WTO by NGOs. Finally, the most curious criticism of the WTO is that it is too effective, at least in one sense: going beyond its mandate. Some suggest that the WTO is stepping out of bounds—in essence, making new rules—while the rulemaking bodies such as the General Council and the Ministerial Conference are still hampered by the consensus rule. Unless some kind of political decision is made, this problem is bound to grow in the future, despite the WTO's recent exercise of self-restraint. Legalism does not exist in a political vacuum. If legalism goes too far, other dimensions of effectiveness may suffer as a result.

Notes

1. Lori Wallach and Michelle Sforza, *The WTO: Five Years of Reasons to Resist Corporate Globalization* (New York: Seven Stories Press, 1999); Lori Wallach and Michelle Sforza, *Whose Trade Organization? Corporate Globalization and the Erosion of Democracy* (Washington, D.C.: Public Citizen, 1999). For a description of the Seattle protests, see Janet Thomas, *The Battle in Seattle: The Story Behind and Beyond the WTO Demonstrations* (Golden, Colo.: Fulcrum, 2000).

2. Oran R. Young and Marc A. Levy, "The Effectiveness of International Environmental Regimes," in Oran R. Young, ed., *The Effectiveness of International Environmental Regimes: Causal Connections and Behavioral Mechanisms* (Cambridge: MIT Press, 1999), pp. 4–5.

3. Ronald B. Mitchell, "International Oil Pollution of the Oceans," in Peter M. Haas, Robert O. Keohane, and Marc A. Levy, eds., *Institutions for the Earth: Sources of Effective International Environmental Protection* (Cambridge: MIT Press, 1993), pp. 183–247; Ronald B. Mitchell, "Regime Design Matters: Intentional Oil Pollution and Treaty Compliance," *International Organization* 48, no. 3 (Summer 1994): 425–458; Ronald B. Mitchell, Moira L. McConnell, Alexi Roginko, and Ann Barrett, "International Vessel-Source Oil Pollution," in Young, ed., *The Effectiveness of International Environmental Regimes*, pp. 33–90.

4. Geoffrey Garrett and James McCall Smith doubt this proposition, however. See Geoffrey Garrett and James McCall Smith, "The Politics of WTO Dispute Settlement," paper presented at the annual meeting of the American Political Science Association, Atlanta, 1999.

5. WTO, WT/DS58/R (15 May 1998), par. 91.

6. Of the 248 disputes that are examined in this article, 48 cases concerned agriculture, 20 intellectual property rights, 5 investment, and 5 services.

7. However, the same panel may deliberate on similar complaints separately. In that case, they are counted as distinct. For instance, the European Union and Japan complained separately about the 1916 Antidumping Act of the United States, and the panel proceedings were separate (the European Union panel moved before the Japan panel), although the Appellate Body proceedings were merged. However, I have counted all the complaints about the U.S. steel safeguard measure in 2002 as one dispute, because it is most likely that a single panel will handle all the complaints.

8. The data in Figure 10.1 are taken from WTO, Update of WTO Dispute Settlement Cases, WT/DS/OV/16 (17 October 2003).

9. Robert E. Hudec, *Enforcing International Trade Law* (Austin, Tex.: Butterworth Legal Publishers, 1993), Table 11.13, p. 293.

10. Busch and Reinhardt have reached the same conclusion independently. See their "Transatlantic Trade Conflicts."

11. WT/DS108/1 (28 November 1997).

12. There is a tension between enforcement and restraints on escalation, however. It may be argued that for the sake of ensuring compliance, the degree of retaliation should be greater than the amount of injury to the complainant, but that may aggravate the conflict.

13. Kodak actually tried to pursue a three-track approach: the WTO, the 1960 GATT CP Decision (regarding private restrictive practices), and Section 301 (for the remainder of the issues). The latter two approaches were eventually dropped.

14. Office of the United States Trade Representative, "Section 301 Table of Cases," available online at http://www.ustr.gov/html/act301.htm (accessed 2 December 2003).

15. Interview with author, 22 March 2001.

16. For a similar view, see Matthew Shaefer, "Section 301 and the World Trade Organization: A Largely Peaceful Coexistence to Date," *Journal of International Economic Law* 1, no. 1 (March 1998): 156–160.

17. For instance, Powell, Goldstein, Frazer & Murphy of Atlanta, Georgia, one of the first American law firms to open a WTO practice in Geneva, quotes U.S.$250,000 per dispute. "WTO Is New Mecca for Lawyers," *Gazetta Mercantil Online*, 21 June 2000.

18. Hudec, *Enforcing International Trade Law*, p. 295.

19. A regional breakdown of parties shows that Latin America is dominant, followed by Asia, among developing countries. Up to October 2003, Latin American countries had filed 61 disputes while Asian developing countries filed 41 disputes. On the defending side, Latin America was a target of complaints in 56 disputes while Asian developing countries were targeted in 25 disputes.

20. Interview with author, 13 September 2000.

21. Another factor may be a fear of aid being withdrawn, but this has not been confirmed.

22. See http://www.acwl.ch/ (accessed 5 December 2003). The center provided legal assistance to developing countries in six WTO disputes in its first year of operation. Also see "Legal Centre for Poor Nations to Be Launched," *Financial Times*, 1 December 1999, p. 12; Kim Van der Borght, "The Advisory Center on WTO Law: Advancing Fairness and Equality," *Journal of International Economic Law* 2, no. 4 (December 1999): 723–728.

23. As of the 78 rulings issued up to October, the panels and/or the AB found some WTO inconsistencies in 68 cases (87 percent). When the defendant was a developing country, the rate was 92 percent (24 out of 26 cases). When the complainants included developing countries, the rate was also 92 percent (25 out of 27 cases).

24. DS135/R (18 September 2000), DS135/AB/R (12 March 2001).

25. Miriam Jordan, "Brazil May Flout Trade Laws to Keep AIDS Drugs Free for Patients," *Wall Street Journal*, 12 February 2001, p. B1; Stephen Buckley, "U.S., Brazil Clash over AIDS Drugs," *Washington Post*, 6 February 2001, p. A1.

26. Helen Cooper, "U.S. Drops WTO Claim Against Brazilian Patent Law," *Wall Street Journal*, 26 June 2001, p. B7. This WTO case is extremely similar to a civil case litigated in South Africa, but the pharmaceutical companies had to abandon the latter case because of the bad publicity it generated.

27. "UN Calls for Analysis of Human Rights Impacts of TRIPS," *Inside US Trade*, 25 August 2000.

28. However, there is a minor provision in the Sanitary and Phytosanitary (SPS) agreement (Article 5.7) of the WTO that incorporates this principle.

29. See Claude E. Barfield, *Free Trade, Sovereignty, Democracy: The Future of the World Trade Organization* (Washington, D.C.: AEI Press, 2001), pp. 50–53; James McCall Smith, "Manufacturing Legitimacy: Judicial Politics in the WTO," paper presented at the annual meeting of the American Political Science Association, Boston, 29 August–1 September 2002, pp. 17–21.

30. Chakravarthi Raghavan, *The World Trade Organization and Its Dispute Settlement System: Tilting the Balance Against the South* (Penang, Malaysia: Third World Network, 2000), pp. 15–16.

31. Ibid., p. 28.

32. "WTO's Defective Dispute Settlement Process," *The Hindu*, 6 July 2000; Frieder Roessler, "The Institutional Balance Between the Judicial and the Political Organs of the WTO," paper presented at the conference "Efficiency, Equity, and Legitimacy: The Multilateral Trading System at the Millennium," J. F. Kennedy School of Government, Harvard University, 1–2 June 2000.

33. Department of Commerce, "Executive Branch Strategy Regarding WTO Dispute Settlement Panels and the Appellate Body," 30 December 2002, p. 8. See http://www.ita.doc.gov/ReporttoCongress.pdf (accessed 5 December 2003).

34. WT/DS213/AB/R (28 November 2002).

35. WT/DS152/R (22 December 1999).

11

The Case of the
World Trade Organization

John H. Jackson

THE WORLD TRADE ORGANIZATION (WTO) IS REMARKABLE FOR
a number of reasons, among them the degree of rule orientation in what
is often described as the most powerful international juridical institution
in the world today. This makes it an important, perhaps the most important, case-study regarding the relationship between power and rules in
the context of current international relations.

In this chapter I will draw on a number of my works on the WTO
and its predecessor, the GATT, to illustrate some important propositions
regarding rules and power.[1] I shall focus on certain aspects of the
WTO's history and activity, including the surprising "bottom-up" evolution of the dispute settlement process in the GATT and WTO; the way
in which political and diplomatic leaders improvised and filled in the
gaps of international institutions when the original idea for an "International Trade Organization" failed; the remarkably elaborate development of the WTO dispute settlement jurisprudence; and the constant
tension between the role of nation-state power and the allocation of
some of that power to international institutions apparently necessitated
by the huge impact of "globalization" and interdependency in world
affairs (especially economic affairs) today.

This article will first explore the policy context and underpinnings
of the WTO institutions (especially its dispute settlement system). It
will then briefly outline the history of the WTO with emphasis on that
system. Next it will turn to some particular issues developed in the
WTO dispute settlement jurisprudence which demonstrate the tensions

Reprinted from *International Affairs* 84, no. 3 (2008): 437–454. © 2008 Blackwell Publishers. Reprinted by permission of the publisher.

between nation-state power and international cooperative institutions. The final part offers some reflections on this story, although only a small part of the total story can be developed in the space available here.

The Policy Context:
Why Have a Dispute Settlement System?

Underlying the world trading system and its goals is the concept of the market. The years since 1990 have witnessed a swing away from socialist planning concepts and a renewed enthusiasm for the idea of the market. There is broader recognition of the value of markets in increasing the welfare of the world's population. But several Nobel Prize–winning economists—Joseph E. Stiglitz (2001), Douglass C. North (1993) and Ronald H. Coase (1991)—have emphasized that the market will not work unless there is an institutional framework supporting it.[2] An institutional structure implies the existence of rules that must be complied with, and that in turn implies a dispute settlement system of some kind. A rule-oriented dispute settlement system brings the modicum of predictability and stability that are essential for the market to function properly. It is recognized, for example, that entrepreneurs are often willing to accept a lower rate of return on their investments in exchange for a lowered risk. A lowered risk premium means greater efficiency. Accordingly, those two words—predictability and stability—are used in the WTO Dispute Settlement Understanding (DSU) treaty text. However, there are other perspectives on market organization and structure, perspectives that value goals other than reducing the risk premium: protection of the environment, promotion of human rights, reduction of poverty not only at home but abroad, and so on. Thus, inevitably, some balancing of these different goals is necessary. At the nation-state level, this balancing occurs constantly. Those in the legal profession recognize this need for balancing, which, especially in Europe, is often called "proportionality."

The WTO has evolved as an organization against the background of these various goals, ultimately growing out of the last trade round of the GATT (1986–94). Clearly, then, governments see the advantages to be gained from this institution, although equally clearly there are some problems associated with it. Specifically, there is broad agreement (expressed by, among others, the WTO Consultative Board, in a report issued in January 2005)[3] that the WTO dispute settlement system is probably the most powerful and most significant international tribunal system in existence today. With compulsory jurisdiction, and an automatic obligation to perform or comply with the result of the system, this is indeed a powerful institution. Further, the scope of the dispute settlement system is vast: every dispute involving the agreements covered by the WTO is supposed to be brought, in accordance with obligations under international treaty law, to this WTO system.

Besides the goals of predictability and stability mentioned above, the system also aims for prompt settlement and satisfactory settlement. Thus a tension among its goals that requires a process of balancing immediately becomes apparent: prompt settlement is not always compatible with the highest quality in respect of predictability and stability. The story is further complicated by the fact that there exist at least twelve different goals for international dispute settlement systems, and thus the choice of which goals such a system should promote is itself very complex.[4]

It is worth briefly examining the architecture of the dispute settlement system before going into more detail. At the first level there are ad hoc panels (each usually consisting of three persons), which was also the practice under the GATT. The First Level Panel report is automatically adopted under a procedure called "reverse consensus."[5] What is new under the WTO, and unique to it, is the appeals process. This involves an Appellate Body, consisting of seven persons who sit in divisions of three at a time, designed and selected so that no potential appellant will know which three members will hear its appeal. The selection of each group of three is a secret process, partly random, and partly conducted according to a distribution of the workload, with a very quick turnaround time. The dispute settlement statistics so far are impressive. In the 13 years to January 2008, 369 complaints were filed. Fewer than half of these actually went on to a panel; in other words, there is a lot of settlement going on, and this can be viewed as a strength of the system. There have been 115 adopted First Level Panel reports and 84 adopted Appellate Body reports. The number of panel reports appealed has been declining as a percentage of cases. Of the "big" players, the United States and the EU are involved in nearly half the cases, as either complainant or respondent. But developing countries are also major participants in this process, and are involved in almost 80 percent of the cases, either as complainants or as respondents.

One of the core concepts of the WTO (and other international dispute settlement procedures) is the concept of "rule orientation" compared to "power orientation." The following paragraphs elaborate on this comparison.[6]

One can roughly divide the various techniques for the peaceful settlement of international disputes into two types: settlement by negotiation and agreement with reference (explicitly or implicitly) to the relative power status of the parties; or settlement by negotiation or decision with reference to norms or rules to which both parties have previously agreed.

For example, countries A and B have a trade dispute regarding B's treatment of imports of widgets from A. The first technique mentioned would involve a negotiation between A and B in which the more powerful of the two would have the advantage. Foreign aid, military maneuvers or retaliatory import restrictions on other key goods would figure in the negotiation. Implicit or explicit threats (for example, to impose quantitative restrictions on some other product) would be a prominent part of the technique employed. Thus a small country would hesitate to challenge a large one on which its trade depended. Domestic political influences would probably play a significant part in the approach of the respective negotiators in this system, particularly as regards the negotiator for the more powerful party.

The second technique mentioned—reference to agreed rules— would see the negotiators arguing about the application of one or more rules (for example, was B obliged under a treaty to allow free entry of A's goods in question?). During the process of negotiating a settlement it would be necessary for the parties to understand that an unsettled dispute would ultimately be resolved by impartial judgments based on the rules, so that the negotiators would be negotiating with reference to their respective predictions as to the outcome of those judgments, and not with reference to potential retaliation or the exercise of power by one or more parties to the dispute.

In both techniques negotiation to a settlement is the dominant mechanism for resolving disputes; but the key difference lies in the perception of the participants as to what are the "bargaining chips." In so far as agreed rules for governing the economic relations between the parties exist, a system which predicates negotiation on the implementation of those rules would seem preferable for a number of reasons. The mere existence of the rules, however, is not enough. When the issue is the application or interpretation of those rules (rather than the formulation of new rules), it is necessary for the parties to believe that when their negotiations reach an impasse the settlement mechanisms which take over for the parties will be designed to apply or interpret the rules fairly. If no such system exists, then the parties are left essentially to rely upon their prospective "power positions," tempered (it is hoped) by the good will and good faith of the more powerful party (cognizant of its long-range interests).

All diplomacy, and indeed all government, involves a mixture of these techniques. To a large degree, the history of civilization may be described as a gradual evolution from a power-oriented approach, in the state of nature, towards a rule-oriented approach. However, the extreme in either case is never reached. In modern Western democracies as we know them, a prominent role continues to be played by power—particularly political power, as wielded by the electorate, but also to a lesser degree economic power, such as that of trade unions or large corporations. However, these states have passed far along the scale towards a rule-oriented approach, and generally have an elaborate legal system, involving court procedures and a monopoly of force, through a police and a military, to ensure the rules will be followed. The distance travelled by the US government in this direction is demonstrated by the resignation of a recent president; the evolutionary hypothesis of a transition from power to rule is supported by the history of England over the past thousand years; and more recently, when one looks at the development of the EU, one is struck by the evolution towards a system that is remarkably elaborate in its rule structure, effectuated through a court of justice, albeit without a monopoly of force.

Moving on to consider international economic policy, we find that the same dichotomy between power-oriented diplomacy and rule-oriented diplomacy can be seen. In international affairs, a strong argument can be made that to a certain extent a similar evolution towards a rule-oriented system must occur, even though it has not yet progressed very far. The initiatives taken during and after the Second World War to develop international institutions are part of this evolution. As in most evolutions, there have been setbacks, and mistakes have been made. Nevertheless, a particularly strong argument exists for pursuing gradually and consistently the progress of international economic affairs towards a rule-oriented approach. Apart from the advantages that accrue generally to international affairs from such an approach—less reliance on raw power, and less temptation to exercise it or flex one's muscles, both of which can get out of hand; a fairer break for the smaller countries, or at least a perception of greater fairness; the development of agreed procedures to achieve the necessary compromises—in economic affairs there are additional reasons.

Illustrations from the Jurisprudence

The WTO case reports, both at the panel level and at the appellate level, are extraordinarily detailed and analytical. This author is not aware of any other so large a body of international tribunal jurisprudence (over

60,000 pages) which probes so elaborately and carefully the recurring problems of the tension between "sovereign" national states and international institutions with regard to the overwhelming problem of how to allocate decision-making competence between those entities. Clearly the concept of sovereignty itself needs to be rethought, and this thinking leads inevitably to questions about international law itself—its source, its legitimacy and its functionality in today's world of rapid change and world interdependence. These issues are probed in much greater detail by the present author in other works.[7]

Having briefly but, it is hoped, adequately laid the groundwork and context for our subject, I turn now to the complex jurisprudential issues that arise in the WTO dispute settlement system. Space constraints confine the examination to the "tip of the iceberg" of several issues, some of which are so complex that entire books have been written about them. Those chosen for discussion here, out of the many that could be selected, are as follows: first, the relationship between the WTO system and international law, or the international law context; second, the concept of deference, sometimes called standard of review; third, the reference to, or use of, precedent; fourth, the different techniques of interpretation; and finally, the issue of compliance. All of the cases discussed below are Appellate Body cases, with the exception of the Section 301 case.[8] This jurisprudence is very detailed, complex, and many would argue of very high quality, compared with national legal systems as well as other international systems. This good reputation and high quality do not mean, however, that mistakes have not been made.

International Law Context

The very first case in the dispute settlement system was brought against the United States by Venezuela and Brazil, which argued that US regulations on the importation of gasoline were discriminatory when compared with regulations on its own gasoline.[9] The regulation in question was designed to improve the environment through stipulations relating to the chemical composition of gasoline. The case held against the United States, the United States appealed, and the appeal held against the United States. However, on appeal the United States was granted a point it wanted, which was a different form of the logic; this resulted in a different ruling, and so the United States claimed victory. But the other side also claimed victory, for the United States was required to change its regulation, and it did so. Thus the outcome was, essentially, the perfect diplomatic resolution.

A critical point in this case was that the Appellate Body began by saying that the WTO is clearly part of international law, and not a separate, independent regime, as some political scientists had said of the GATT a decade or two earlier. And, although by the later years of the GATT it was clear that it was not an independent regime, this WTO ruling clinched that issue. The Appellate Body logically turned to the customary international law of interpreting treaties, a phrase that is actually mentioned in the DSU.[10] It was suggested that even though the Vienna Convention on the Law of Treaties (VCLT) is not specifically named in the treaty text, the VCLT best answers this question of how to interpret treaties under customary international law. The Appellate Body's view of the VCLT is challengeable, and this author has some hesitations as to whether that treaty is actually the best guide for treaty interpretation, particularly in the context of the WTO dispute settlement system; but the US–Gasoline case was clearly a pivotal point for situating that system in customary international law.

At the end of this first Appellate Body report is a very interesting comment on deference to nation-state actions in the following words:

> It is of some importance that the Appellate Body point out what this does not mean. It does not mean, or imply, that the ability of any WTO Member to take measures to control air pollution or, more generally, to protect the environment, is at issue. That would be to ignore the fact that Article XX of the General Agreement contains provisions designed to permit important state interests—including the protection of human health, as well as the conservation of exhaustible natural resources—to find expression. WTO Members have a large measure of autonomy to determine their own policies on the environment (including its relationship with trade), their environmental objectives and the environmental legislation they enact and implement. So far as concerns the WTO, that autonomy is circumscribed only by the need to respect the requirements of the General Agreement and the other covered agreements.

Another case, very soon after US–Gasoline, was Japan–Alcoholic Beverages, also a discrimination case.[11] In the case brought by the United States and EU, Japan was alleged to be discriminating against imported alcoholic beverages. In reality, at base this was a case of imported vodka versus domestic shochu (a Japanese clear liquid alcohol beverage). The ruling was that Japan was discriminating, and that these two products were "like products." Thus the phrase being interpreted was "like products." That simple little phrase is enormously complex. The author of one book describes dozens of ways to interpret it, based on different kinds of assumptions—some economic assumptions, others deriving from a particular bias towards either the producer or the consumer.[12] This gives rise to the question of who are the actual intended beneficiaries of this system that is part of international law. Are they the sovereign nation members of the WTO? They clearly are among the intended beneficiaries, but they are not the only ones.

This line of questioning leads us to the US–301 Case, brought by the EU and eight other countries to challenge the United States on its so-called Section 301 statute, which allows it to take retaliatory measures against other countries in some circumstances. The First Level Panel ruled (there was no appeal) that the US statute, as such, was inconsistent with the requirements of the WTO. In other words, even if no measure had been taken under it, because the statute allowed a measure which, if taken, could have constituted a violation, the statute itself was in violation of WTO law. The panel went on to say that the United States had assured panel members that, and had given them written representations to the effect that, the US executive branch has the authority to interpret the 301 statute, and will never interpret it to violate the WTO rule. Thus, the panel declared that because the US interpretation, as represented to the panel, in effect trumps what the statute actually says, the United States is not in contravention of its WTO obligations. But the United States was warned that it would be "watched" on this matter.

The 301 case has sometimes been called a "diplomatic masterpiece and a jurisprudential disaster." Regardless of which way you choose to view its outcome, the point here is that the market participants, and not just governments, are beneficiaries of the WTO dispute settlement system. The language of the US–301 case stresses that when decisions are made account must be taken of a whole group of people who are not at the table; who are, in a sense, third-party beneficiaries.

There are some other international law concerns embedded in this broader analysis that are worth mentioning. One of these is the concept of good faith. Good faith is problematic because it is such an open and general concept in international law that there is a substantial amount of hesitation about using and relying on it. The fear is that, without a strict guideline on its meaning, judges can "pour into that bottle" a lot of personal predilections.

Another problem is the very elaborate remedy system set up in the DSU, involving what some people loosely call retaliation. The more precise word is compensation, by which is meant not a "cheque in the post" but, rather, compensatory measures.[13]

Deference and Standard of Review

The second jurisprudential issue to be discussed here is deference, or standard of review. A crucial question throughout the operation of an international organization is the amount of deference that should be accorded to the sovereign nation-state. The EC–Hormones case, brought by the United States and Canada against the European Communities, was one of the first WTO cases to dig into the standard of review issue.[14] But the outcome of the case did not provide very much guidance for future reference. The hormones in question make it less costly to produce beef. The US tended to use hormones in beef production, while Europe had not and had taken the step of banning all hormones. The ruling held that the EC had not done an adequate risk assessment (that is, had not adequately assessed the risks of the use of artificial hormones for the production of beef), and therefore that its policy was not consistent with the Sanitary and Phytosanitary Texts of the WTO.[15] The First Level Panel and Appellate Body grappled with the standard of review question—of how much deference should be given to the nation-state—because, of course, there is a certain amount of ambiguity in the treaty language. (This kind of ambiguity is unavoidable, incidentally, as it is nearly impossible to negotiate a treaty text with one hundred nations without leaving some gaps and ambiguities.) The Appellate Body said that complete deference is not owed, but neither is the standard de novo. There is a large grey area between complete deference and de novo review, and it remains unsettled as to where on the spectrum analysis should begin.

Precedent

The third issue is how much weight should be given to precedent in the WTO dispute settlement system. Some have argued that the system approaches one of stare decisis, similar to the very strong precedent system known (almost exclusively) in "common law" countries. It is quite clear that the WTO dispute settlement system does not operate by stare decisis, but rather by the principle that an opinion has no binding force except between the parties to that litigation in that particular case. This is the more common international law approach found, for instance, in the World Court statute.

Although there is some ambiguity, the DSU itself, with its explicit goals of stability and predictability, suggests that a degree of continuity is required. In addition, the WTO Charter ("Charter" is an informal term) contains a clause saying that GATT decisions should serve as guidance to WTO decisions, but are not to be automatically implemented as a matter of treaty law.[16] The word "guidance" is very important in that context. Furthermore, article IX of the WTO Charter allows the members, by a three-quarters majority of the entire membership, to make a definitive interpretation, which would indeed be binding. But because it rarely happens that representatives of three-quarters of the WTO membership are together in a room (and an even more remote prospect is that they could get their respective governments to agree on such a thing), a binding interpretation is not likely to arise.

Another way to tackle this question of precedent is to examine the VCLT language of "subsequent practice in the application of the treaty."[17] One could argue on this basis that WTO decisions are practice under the WTO agreement. But in the Japan–Alcoholic Beverages case, the Appellate Body said that one case does not constitute practice; that there must be something more than one case, although they did not elaborate on what that "something more" must be.[18]

Also instructive in this context is the US–Steel Safeguards case.[19] This case involved an escape clause safeguards question about the steel industry and was enormously complex. Approximately 80 law firms were involved in this case, which was brought by the EC, Brazil, China, Japan and five other countries, and it hit on a lot of "hot button issues." The First Level Panel Report was almost 1,000 pages long because there were 13 different practices that had to be evaluated against five different standards. Almost all of the 5,800 footnotes were references to prior cases of the WTO Appellate Body. Thus it is simply not credible to argue that there is no precedent effect in the WTO dispute settlement system. The critical question is rather: How much weight is given to precedent? The Appellate Body ruled against the United States in the US–Steel Safeguards case, and the US president withdrew the contested measures; but he also said that the withdrawal had nothing to do with the WTO decision, and was done solely in the interests of US domestic constituents. David Sanger of the *New York Times*, however, wrote that this case was the *Marbury v. Madison* of the WTO,[20] referring to the fundamental case in US constitutional law establishing the power of the judiciary over the other branches of government through "judicial review."

Thus one may imagine a ladder of precedent effects, with stare decisis at the top and a lot of weaker precedent effects further down—

some so far down that, in some administrative decision-making (such as is prevalent in some regulatory agencies within the US government), there exists no sense of precedent whatsoever. But this author thinks that the WTO is not very far below the stare decisis top rung of the precedent ladder.

Interpretation

Interpretation is obviously related to the precedent issue, but it is a vast topic, needing separate treatment. There are literally dozens of different kinds of interpretative techniques. The VCLT goes through a series of about ten or twelve (depending on how you count) techniques in articles 31 and 32, but there are a myriad of other possible techniques not mentioned therein. This raises the question of whether the VCLT is really appropriate in the WTO context. (It has not been accepted by large numbers of WTO members.)

The Appellate Body began with a very strong textual bias, a very stark textualism, relying on the dictionary. But a problem exists because textualism itself is not a "settled science." There are several dictionaries, and when the same word is looked up in three different dictionaries, you will sometimes find three different definitions. One could, indeed, question what textualism itself is. Nevertheless, the dispute settlement system strives very hard to follow the WTO treaty text, which has led to some decisions that have surprised the negotiators of that text. The negotiators have claimed that the interpretation handed down was not the result they had intended, invariably receiving the answer: "but that's what the treaty language says." Thus the question is raised whether more attention should be given to the negotiators' intent. The VCLT seems to downplay the importance of preparatory work, and there are good reasons for this (for instance, the lack of a satisfactory record).

Finally under the heading of interpretation, it is worth mentioning one very important case, namely the Shrimp–Turtle case.[21] The Shrimp–Turtle case brings to bear a lot of interesting concepts, and in the view of the present author is, even given the many new cases that are quite interesting, the single most significant and important case of the jurisprudence of the WTO. More specifically, paragraph 121 of the Appellate Body's report is perhaps the single most important paragraph of that case. Here the Appellate Body says that it may be the case that unilateral measures are inherently those that must be permitted under the exceptions of article XX of the GATT. Article XX sets out a series of bases for exception, including moral reasons and conservation of natural exhaustible resources (the basis of both the US–Gasoline case and the Shrimp–Turtle case). The Shrimp–Turtle case involved a US law that prohibited the importation of shrimp that had been gathered in a process that killed an endangered species of turtle. US environmentalists had pushed for this law, and got it through. The problem was that it did not accord with the normal rules of trade, and so, prima facie, that law was a violation by the United States of its WTO obligations, and was so held by the Appellate Body. But the United States claimed that the exception in article XX for the conservation of natural resources applied in this case, and the Appellate Body agreed. Since an exception was cited, the measure in dispute then had to be measured against a series of criteria, prohibiting discriminatory measures and unjustifiable measures, in the so-called "chapeau," or preface, to article XX.

In evaluating whether those chapeau criteria were fulfilled, the Appellate Body looked to a variety of different sources, including documents and practices outside the trade discipline. The Appellate Body said, with respect to evaluating the words "natural resources," that their interpretation had to be evolutionary, because they believed that the phrase could now apply to living species, not just to water, minerals and the like. They went on to say that they were looking at such documents as the Convention on International Trade in Endangered Species and other environmental measures, and at the preamble of the WTO, which is certainly appropriate, and which calls for a sustainable development policy. In looking at these various sources, the Appellate Body said that they were interpreting the preamble or chapeau to article XX, which contains wording about arbitrary or unjustifiable discrimination, and were bringing to bear this language from outside sources. This constituted the first instance of jurisprudence in all of GATT and WTO history thus far to deal with policies other than trade policies. The First Level Panel had looked only within the trade discipline, and the Appellate Body said that was wrong, instead calling for a balancing of different policies. That decision created a firestorm of criticism. Critics claimed that it was not up to the international organization to do this balancing, that the sovereign nation must do it. This author does not believe that conception is sustainable in light of the globalization landscape described above.

The Shrimp–Turtle decision clearly manifested a measure of deference towards nation-state "sovereign" authority, with the Appellate

Body starkly overruling a more "internationalist" panel report. This case demonstrates the effort of the Appellate Body to maneuver delicately between competing notions of allocating power. The balancing approach clearly prevailed in this case.

Compliance

Compliance with WTO decisions has generally been quite good. The remedies for non-compliance are outlined in the DSU. Some observers question whether remedies such as compensatory measures, if freely chosen, do away with the obligation to perform by the losing party in the long run. This author's view is that there persists an obligation in international law to perform the result of a case in which a country is held not to be consistent with its obligations under the WTO, even though, for an interim period, it may be willing to tolerate retaliatory measures or undertake compensatory measures.[22]

There are many implications of this system for domestic law, because at least in some systems, such as that in the United States, and possibly also in the UK (although this may depend on decisions and developments in the EU legal system), the result of a case in the dispute settlement system is not ipso facto part of the domestic law. There is a time lag, so to speak, between the decision and the required act of transformation to embed that decision in domestic law. Thus there is a potential difficulty in getting compliance from, for example, the United States, because of the necessity to persuade Congress to act.

Furthermore, some cynical countries (including the United States) have decided in many instances to go ahead with whatever action they intended, and take the consequences in the dispute settlement process. This attitude arises largely because it takes three years to get through the dispute settlement process, and thus countries have a three-year "free pass." If higher duties can be amassed during those three years, and if there are also monopoly rents involved, the state can garner rewards adding up to millions, if not (in the steel industry, for instance) billions of dollars. There is no provision for retrospective remedies, or even for provisional remedies. This creates a compliance incentive problem. Furthermore, asking the winning country to impose so-called "retaliatory measures" amounts to asking it to shoot itself in the foot, because the measures inflict an economic harm on the imposing country, and often affect third parties that usually have nothing to do with the case—in effect, innocent bystanders. These problems show clearly how the views of sovereign nations constrain the authority of the WTO.

Notes

1. John Jackson, *World trade and the law of GATT* (Indianapolis: Bobbs-Merrill, 1969); John H. Jackson, *The world trading system: Law and policy of international economic relations*, 2nd ed. (Cambridge, MA: MIT Press, 2002); John H. Jackson, "Sovereignty—modern: A new approach to an outdated concept," *American Journal of International Law* 97, 2002, pp. 782–802; John H. Jackson, *Sovereignty, the WTO and the changing fundamentals of international law* (New York: Cambridge University Press, 2006); John H. Jackson, "The World Trade Organization after ten years: The role of the WTO in a globalized world," *Current Legal Problems*, Volume 59, 2006, pp. 427–46; Jane Holder and Colm O'Cinneide, eds., *Current Legal Problems*, Volume 59, 2006 (Oxford: Oxford University Press, 2007); John H. Jackson, William J. Davey and Alan O. Sykes, *Legal problems of international economic relations: Cases, materials and text on the national and international regulation of transnational economic relations*, 4th ed. (St. Paul, MN: West Group, 2002); M. Bronckers and R. Quick, eds., *New directions in international economic law: Essays in honor of John H. Jackson* (Boston: Kluwer Law International, 2000).

2. See Ronald H. Coase, *The firm, the market and the law* (Chicago: University of Chicago Press, 1988), ch. 5; Douglas C. North, *Institutions, institutional change and economic performance* (Cambridge: Cambridge University Press, 1990); Joseph E. Stiglitz, *Globalization and its discontents* (New York: Norton, 2002), p. 219.

3. Peter Sutherland (chairman), Jagdish Bhagwati, Kwesi Botchwey, Niall W. A. Fitzgerald, Koichi Hamada, John Jackson, Celso Lafer and Thierry de Montbrial, *The future of the WTO: Addressing institutional challenges in the new millennium*, report by the Consultative Board to the Director-General Supachai Panitchpakdi (Geneva: WTO, 2005), http://www.wto.org/english/thewto_e/10anniv_e/future_wto_e.pdf, accessed 14 Jan. 2008.

4. For more explanation of this point, see John H. Jackson, *Sovereignty, the WTO and the changing fundamentals of international law* (New York: Cambridge University Press, 2006), sec. 5. 3.

5. "Reverse consensus" means that the matter is adopted unless there is consensus against adoption. Since such consensus against adoption is defeatable by any member, the disputing member who "won" can prevent a blocking vote. See Jackson, *Sovereignty*, sec. 5. 4.

6. Text is drawn from Jackson, *The world trading system*, pp. 109–11.

7. See Jackson, *Sovereignty*; Jackson, "Sovereignty—modern."

8. US—sections 301–310 of the Trade Act of 1974, WTO doc. WT/DS152/R, adopted 27 Jan. 2000.

9. US—standards for reformulated and conventional gasoline, WTO doc. WT/DS2/AB/R, adopted 22 April 1996.

10. "Understanding on rules and procedures governing the settlement of disputes," article 3. 2, Marrakesh Agreement Establishing the World Trade Organization, 15 April 1994, annex 2, in *World Trade Organization, the legal texts: The results of the Uruguay Round of multilateral trade negotiations* 354 (1999).

11. Japan—customs duties, taxes and labelling practices on imported wines and alcoholic beverages, GATT L/6216, 34S/83, adopted 10 Nov. 1987.

12. Won-Mog Choi, *"Like products" in international trade law: Towards a consistent GATT/WTO jurisprudence* (Oxford: Oxford University Press, 2003).

13. See Jackson et al., *Legal problems*, ch. 7.

14. EC measures concerning meat and meat products (hormones), WTO docs. WT/DS26 and 48/AB/R, adopted 13 Feb. 1998.

15. "Agreement on Sanitary and Phytosanitary Measures," in *World Trade Organization, the legal texts*, p. 59.

16. World Trade Organization, article xvi, par. 1.

17. The Vienna Convention on the Law of Treaties, 1155 UNTS 331, opened for signature 23 May 1969, entered into force on 27 Jan. 1970, repr. in *ILM* 8: 679 (1969), article 31. 3(b).

18. Japan—taxes on alcoholic beverages, WTO doc. WT/DS8, 10 and 11/AB/R, adopted 1 Nov. 1996, e.g., pp. 7, 13–16.

19. United States—definitive safeguard measures on imports of certain steel products, WTO docs. WT/DS248/R and WT/DS248/AB/R, adopted 10 Dec. 2003.

20. David E. Sanger, "A blink from the Bush administration," *New York Times*, 5 Dec. 2003, p. 28.

21. United States—import prohibition of certain shrimp and shrimp products, WTO doc. WT/DS58/AB/R, adopted 6 Nov. 1998.

22. See John H. Jackson, "Editorial comment: International law status of WTO DS reports: Obligation to comply or option to 'buy-out'?" *American Journal of International Law* 98, Jan. 2004, p. 109.

12

The International Monetary System: Diffusion and Ambiguity

Benjamin J. Cohen

AMPLE EVIDENCE EXISTS TO SUGGEST THAT THE DISTRIBUTION of power in international monetary affairs is changing. But where does monetary power now reside, and what are the implications for governance of the international monetary system? On these questions, uncertainty reigns. The aim of this article is to shed some new light on the dynamics of power and rule-setting in global finance today.

I will begin with a brief discussion of the meaning of power in international monetary relations, distinguishing between two critical dimensions of monetary power: autonomy and influence. The evolution of international monetary power in recent decades will then be examined. Major developments have dramatically shifted the distribution of power in the system. Many have noted that power is now more widely diffused, both among states and between states and societal actors. Finance is no longer dominated by a few national governments at the apex of the global order. Less frequently remarked is the fact that the diffusion of power has been mainly in the dimension of autonomy, rather than influence—a point of critical importance. While more actors have gained a degree of insulation from outside pressures, few as yet are able to exercise greater authority to shape events or outcomes. Leadership in the system thus has been dispersed rather than relocated—a pattern of change in the geopolitics of finance that might be called leaderless diffusion.

A pattern of leaderless diffusion generates greater ambiguity in prevailing governance structures. Rule-setting in monetary relations

Reprinted from *International Affairs* 84, no. 3 (2008): 455–470. © 2008 Blackwell Publishers. Reprinted with permission from the publisher.

increasingly relies not on negotiations among a few powerful states but rather on the evolution of custom and usage among growing numbers of autonomous agents—regular patterns of behavior that develop from longstanding practice. Impacts on governance structures can be seen at two levels: the individual state and the global system. At the state level, the dispersion of power compels governments to rethink their commitment to national monetary sovereignty. At the systemic level, it compounds the difficulties of bargaining on monetary issues. Formal rules are increasingly being superseded by informal norms that emerge, like common law, not from legislation or statutes but from everyday conduct and social convention.

Monetary Power

For the purposes of this article, the international monetary system may be understood to encompass all the main features of monetary relations across national frontiers—the processes and institutions of financial intermediation (mobilization of savings and allocation of credit) as well as the creation and management of money itself. As Susan Strange once wrote: "The financial structure really has two inseparable aspects. It comprises not just the structures of the political economy through which credit is created but also the monetary system or systems which determine the relative values of the different moneys in which credit is denominated."[1] Both aspects are influenced by the distribution of power among actors.

And what do we mean by power in monetary relations? To summarize briefly an argument that I have developed at greater length elsewhere,[2] I suggest that international monetary power may be understood to comprise two critical dimensions, autonomy and influence. The more familiar of the two is the dimension of influence, defined as the ability to shape events or outcomes. In operational terms, this dimension naturally equates with a capacity to control the behavior of actors—"letting others have your way," as diplomacy has jokingly been defined. An actor, in this sense, is powerful to the extent that it can effectively pressure or coerce others; in short, to the extent that it can exercise leverage or managerial authority. As a dimension of power, influence is the essential sine qua non of systemic leadership.

The second dimension, autonomy, corresponds to the dictionary definition of power as a capacity for action. An actor is also powerful to the extent that it is able to exercise operational independence: to act

THE INTERNATIONAL MONETARY SYSTEM   257

freely, insulated from outside pressure. In this sense, power does not mean influencing others; rather, it means not allowing others to influence you—others letting you have your way.

The distinction between the two dimensions of power is critical. Both are based in social relationships and can be observed in behavioral terms; the two are also unavoidably interrelated. But they are not of equal importance. Logically, power begins with autonomy. Influence is best thought of as functionally derivative—inconceivable in practical terms without a relatively high degree of operational independence first being attained and sustained. First and foremost, actors must be free to pursue their goals without outside constraint. Only then will an actor be in a position, in addition, to exercise authority elsewhere. Autonomy may not be sufficient to ensure a degree of influence, but it is manifestly necessary. It is possible to think of autonomy without influence; it is impossible to think of influence without autonomy.

For state actors in the monetary system, the key to autonomy lies in the uncertain distribution of the burden of adjustment to external imbalances. National economies are inescapably linked through the balance of payments—the flows of money generated by international trade and investment. One country's surplus is another country's deficit. The risk of unsustainable disequilibrium represents a persistent threat to policy independence. Excessive imbalances generate mutual pressures to adjust, which can be costly in both economic and political terms. Deficit economies may be forced to curtail domestic spending or devalue their currencies, at the expense of growth and jobs; surplus economies may experience unwanted inflation or an upward push on their exchange rates, which can threaten international competitiveness. No government likes being compelled to compromise key policy goals for the sake of restoring external balance. All, if given a choice, would prefer to see others make the necessary sacrifices. For states, therefore, the foundation of monetary power is the capacity to avoid the burden of adjustment required by a payments imbalance.

The capacity to avoid the burden of adjustment is fundamentally dual in nature, subdividing into what I have characterized as the two "hands" of monetary power.[3] These are the power to delay and the power to deflect, each corresponding to a different kind of adjustment burden. One burden is the continuing cost of adjustment, defined as the cost of the new payments equilibrium prevailing after all change has occurred. The power to delay is the capacity to avoid the continuing cost of adjustment by postponing the process of adjustment. The other burden is the transitional cost of adjustment, defined as the cost of the change itself. Where the process of adjustment cannot be put off, the power to deflect represents the capacity to avoid the transitional cost of adjustment by diverting as much as possible of that cost to others. The power to delay is largely a function of a country's international liquidity position relative to others, comprising both owned reserves and borrowing capacity. A particular advantage is enjoyed in this respect by the issuers of currencies that are widely used by others as reserve assets, since these can finance deficits simply by printing more of their own money. The power to deflect, by contrast, has its source in more fundamental structural variables that determine an economy's relative degree of openness and adaptability.

For societal actors in the monetary system, the key to autonomy lies in the uncertain relationship between relevant market domains and legal jurisdictions. In an increasingly globalized world, the reach of financial markets is persistently growing. Yet political authority remains rooted in individual states, each in principle sovereign within its own territorial frontiers. Hence a disjuncture prevails between market domains and legal jurisdictions that create ample room for opportunistic behavior by enterprises or private individuals. The very policy independence that is so prized by governments tends to create differences in market constraints and incentives that may well be exploited to advantage. For societal actors, the foundation of monetary power is the ability to navigate successfully in these interstices between political regimes.

Autonomy, in turn, is the key to influence. Because monetary relations are inherently reciprocal, a potential for leverage is automatically created whenever operational independence is attained. The question is: Will that potential be actualized? Two modes are possible in the exercise of monetary influence: passive and active. Autonomy translates into influence in the accepted sense of the term—a dimension of power aiming to shape the actions of others—only when the capacity for control is deliberately activated.

The requirement of actualization is often overlooked. The potential for leverage that derives automatically from autonomy—the passive mode of influence—is another way of describing what economists call externalities. At best, it represents a contingent aspect of power, exerted without design and with impacts that tend to be dispersed and undirected. Only when the potential for leverage is put to use with self-conscious intent do we approach the more common understanding of influence: the active mode, involving sharper focus in terms of who is targeted and to what end. Unlike the passive mode, the active mode implies a "purposeful act." Both modes begin with monetary autonomy as a basic and necessary condition, and in both cases other actors may feel compelled to comply. But in the passive mode externalities are incidental and unpremeditated, whereas in the active mode pressure is applied directly and deliberately. The active mode, in effect, politicizes relationships, aiming to translate passive influence into practical control through the instrumental use of power. From a political economy point of view, as we shall see, the difference between the two modes is critical.

Diffusion

For both states and societal actors, the distribution of monetary power has shifted dramatically in recent decades. Not long ago the global system was dominated by a small handful of national governments, led by the United States. Most countries felt they had little choice but to play by rules laid down by America and, to a lesser extent, its partners in the Group of Seven (G7); markets operated within strict limits established and maintained by states. Today, by contrast, power has become more widely diffused, both among governments and between governments and market agents. The diffusion of power, however, has been mainly in the dimension of autonomy, rather than influence—a pattern of leaderless diffusion in financial geopolitics. The days of concentrated power in a largely state-centric system are now over.

Three major developments share principal responsibility for this change: (1) the creation of the euro; (2) the widening of global payments imbalances; and (3) the globalization of financial markets. Each of these developments has effectively added to the population of actors with a significant degree of autonomy in monetary affairs.

The Euro

The creation of the euro in 1999 was always expected to have a major impact on the geo-politics of finance. Even without the participation of Britain and some other EU members, Europe's economic and monetary union (EMU) was destined to become one of the largest economic units in the world, rivaling even the United States in terms of output and share of foreign trade. A shift in the balance of power across the Atlantic thus seemed inevitable. Europe's new money, building on the widespread popularity of Germany's old Deutschmark, would pose a serious threat to the predominance of America's greenback as an international currency. The euro area—Euroland, as some call it—was bound to become a leading player on the monetary stage. Robert Mundell, a Nobel laureate in economics, voiced a widely held view when he expressed his conviction that EMU would "challenge the status of the dollar and alter the power configuration of the system."[4]

To a significant degree, those early expectations have been realized. A decade on, Europe's monetary power has clearly been enhanced. The euro has smoothly taken over the Deutschmark's place as the second most widely used currency in the world. Euroland itself has grown from eleven members to 15, with as many as a dozen or more countries set to join in future years. Some measure of power has indeed shifted across the Atlantic.

Europe's gains, however, have been mainly in the dimension of autonomy, rather than influence. Currency union has manifestly reduced the area's vulnerability to foreign exchange shocks. With a single joint money replacing a plethora of national currencies, participants no longer have to fear the risk of exchange rate disturbances inside Europe and, in combination, are now are better insulated against turmoil elsewhere. For a continent long plagued by currency instability, that is no small accomplishment. Moreover, with the widespread acceptability of the euro, EMU countries now enjoy a much improved international liquidity position. Deficits that previously required foreign currency may now be financed with Europe's own money, thus enhancing the group's power to delay. Operational independence plainly is greater now than it was before.

So far, though, Europe has conspicuously failed to convert its enhanced autonomy into a greater capacity for control in monetary affairs.[5] Contrary to the predictions of many, the euro has yet to establish itself as a truly global currency, and this has deprived participants of an instrument that might have been used to help shape behaviour or outcomes. Nor has membership in EMU yet enabled European governments to play a more assertive role in world monetary forums such as the IMF or G7. Though freer now to pursue internal objectives without external constraint, Euroland has yet to actualize the potential for overt leverage that monetary union has created.

The euro's weaknesses as an international currency are by now familiar. The new money did start with many of the attributes necessary for competitive success, including a large economic base, unquestioned political stability and an enviably low rate of inflation, all backed by a joint monetary authority, the European Central Bank (ECB), fully committed to preserving confidence in the currency's value. But, as I have argued previously,[6] the euro is also hampered by several critical deficiencies, all structural in character, that dim its attractiveness as a rival to the greenback. These include limited cost-effectiveness, a serious anti-growth bias and, most importantly, ambiguities at the heart of the monetary union's governance structure. Not surprisingly, therefore, experience to date has been underwhelming. Only in the EU's immediate neighborhood, where trade and financial ties are especially close, has the euro come to enjoy any special advantages as the natural heir to the Deutschmark. That is EMU's natural habitat—"the euro's turf," as economist Charles Wyplosz calls it.[7] Elsewhere, Europe's money remains at a distinct disadvantage in trying to overcome the incumbency advantages of the already well-established dollar.

Equally obvious by now are Euroland's weaknesses as a political actor. Joined together in EMU, one would have thought, European states would surely have more bargaining power than if each acted on its own. Europe's voice would be amplified on a broad range of macroeconomic issues, from policy coordination to crisis management. Yet here too experience to date has been underwhelming. In practice, membership of EMU has not enabled EU governments to play a more influential role in the IMF or other global forums, mainly because no one knows who, precisely, speaks for the group. Since no single body is formally designated to represent EMU in international discussions, the euro area's ability to project power on monetary matters is inherently constrained. Fred Bergsten, a euro enthusiast, laments that EMU "still speaks with a multiplicity, even a cacophony, of voices . . . Hence it dissipates much of the potential for realizing a key international role."[8]

Overall, therefore, the power configuration of the system has been altered far less than Mundell or others anticipated. The Europeans clearly are now better placed to resist external pressures. Their collective autonomy has been enhanced. But Europe is still a long way from exercising the kind of leverage that monetary union might have been expected to give it. Influence has not been effectively actualized. Monetary power, on balance, has been dispersed rather than relocated from one side of the Atlantic to the other.

Global Imbalances

A second major development in recent years has been the emergence of unprecedented global imbalances—most particularly, a wide gap in the balance of payments of the United States, matched by counterpart surpluses elsewhere, particularly in East Asia and among energy-exporting nations. (Notably missing is Euroland, which has maintained a rough balance in its external accounts.) In 2006 America's deficit swelled past $850 billion, equivalent to some 6.5 percent of US GDP. Although it is now shrinking a bit, the shortfall continues to add to an already record level of foreign debt. Net of assets abroad, US liabilities reached $2.6 trillion at the end of 2006, equal to roughly a fifth of GDP. Correspondingly, reserve holdings of dollars in surplus countries have soared, having risen to above $3 trillion by 2006. For many, imbalances on this scale seem certain to alter the balance of monetary power between the United States and the larger surplus countries. The only question is: How much?

In terms of the autonomy dimension of power, the impact is obvious. With their vastly improved international liquidity positions, countries in surplus are now much better placed to postpone the process of adjustment when they wish: their power to delay is clearly enhanced. A decade ago, when financial crisis hit East Asia, governments in the region—under intense pressure from the United States and the IMF—felt they had little choice but to initiate radical economic reforms, backed by tight monetary and fiscal policies. Resentful of being forced to pay such a high transitional cost of adjustment, they were determined to insulate themselves as much as possible against similar pressures in the future. The result today is a greatly heightened capacity for operational independence.

The most notable example of this phenomenon is China, whose currency reserves are now above $1.4 trillion and continue to grow by as much as $20 billion each month. China has been the target of a determined campaign by the United States and others to allow a significant revaluation of its currency, the yuan (also known as the renminbi). Beijing, however, has stood firm, resisting all pleas. Since a well-publicized switch from a dollar peg to a basket peg in mid-2005, the yuan has appreciated in small steps by little more than 15 percent—far short of what most observers think is needed to make a real dent in China's trade surplus. Plainly, the world's largest stockpile of reserves gives China more room for maneuver than it might otherwise enjoy.

But does enhanced autonomy translate into greater influence? Certainly there is an increase of influence in the passive mode. Simply by exercising their power to delay, surplus countries have placed more pressure on the United States to do something—or, at least, to think about doing something—about its deficits. But are we witnessing an increase of influence in the active, purposive mode? There the outlook is more ambiguous.

Indirectly, influence might be increased through the operations of the newly fashionable sovereign wealth funds that many surplus countries have created to generate increased earnings on a portion of their reserves. Already there are more than 30 such funds controlling assets in excess of $2.5 trillion, a figure that could grow to as much as $15 trillion over the next decade. In principle, it is possible to imagine that at least some of these funds might be deployed strategically to gain a degree of leverage in recipient states. Investments might be carefully aimed towards institutions that are known to have privileged access to the corridors of governmental power—institutions like Citibank and Merrill Lynch in the United States, which in the midst of the recent credit crunch together attracted more than $20 billion from wealth funds in Asia and the Middle East. In practice, however, potential target states are not without means to monitor or limit politically risky investments within their borders. The balance of power has by no means tipped as much as might appear.

Alternatively, influence might be increased directly through the use of newly acquired reserve stockpiles to threaten manipulation of the value or stability of a key currency such as the dollar. There is nothing complicated about the option. Indeed, as Jonathan Kirshner reminds us, "currency manipulation is the simplest instrument of monetary power and . . . can be used with varying degrees of intensity, ranging from mild signaling to the destabilization of national regimes."[9] Yet the results could be devastating for the issuer of a key currency, such as the United States. If any nation is in a position to use its newly acquired influence in this manner, it is China. At any time, Beijing could undermine America's money by dumping greenbacks on the world's currency exchanges or even simply by declining to add dollars to China's reserves in the future. Such threats would take little effort on China's part and could be carefully calibrated for maximum effect. The advantages for China are enormous.

But there are also disadvantages, as the Chinese themselves well understand. Beijing's dollar hoard could hardly be sold all at once. Hence any depreciation of the greenback would impose costs on China as well, in the form of capital losses on its remaining holdings. China's dollar reserves today are equal to about one-third of the country's GDP. For every 10 percent depreciation of the greenback, therefore, China would lose something in excess of 3 percent of GDP—no small amount. In addition, dollar depreciation would greatly erode the competitiveness of the exports that are so vital to China's economic growth. In reality, currency manipulation is a two-edged sword that could end up doing China far more harm than good—a kind of "nuclear option," to be used only in extremis.

Here too, then, it is not at all clear that the balance of monetary power has tipped as much in favor of China and other surplus countries as might appear to be the case. Indeed, now that dollar holdings have grown so large, it actually makes more sense for China and others to support rather than threaten the greenback, whether they like it or not, in order to avert a doomsday scenario. Some see this as nothing more than enlightened self-interest. Others see it as more akin to the notorious balance of terror that existed between the nuclear powers during the Cold War—a "balance of financial terror," as former US Treasury Secretary Lawrence Summers has described it.[10] Neither side wants to risk a MAD (mutually assured destruction) outcome.

In short, global imbalances too have caused a shift in the balance of monetary power—but, as in the case of EMU, mainly in the dimension of autonomy. Reserve accumulations have not clearly amplified the influence, whether direct or indirect, of the large surplus countries. Here too, power has been largely dispersed rather than relocated.

Financial Globalization

Finally, there is the change in the international monetary environment that has been wrought by the globalization of financial markets. The story is familiar. Where once most financial markets were firmly controlled at the national level and insulated from one another, today across much of the globe barriers to the movement of money have been greatly reduced or effectively eliminated, resulting in a scale of financial flows unequalled since the glory days of the nineteenth-century gold standard. One consequence, observers agree, is a distinct shift in the balance of power between states and societal actors. By promoting capital mobility, financial globalization enhances the authority of market agents at the expense of sovereign governments.

Key to the shift is the wider range of options made available to privileged elements of the private sector with the integration of financial markets: a marked increase of autonomy for those societal actors in a position to take advantage of the opportunities now afforded them. In effect, financial globalization means more freedom for selected individuals and enterprises—more room for maneuver in response to actual or potential decisions of governments. Higher taxes or regulation may be evaded by moving investment funds offshore; tighter monetary policies may be circumvented by accessing external sources of finance. Ultimately, it means a fading of the strict dividing lines between separate national moneys, as weaker domestic currencies are traded in for more attractive foreign moneys like the dollar or euro—a phenomenon to which I have previously referred as the new geography of money.[11] No longer, in many places, are societal actors restricted to a single currency, their own domestic money, as they go about their business. Now they have a choice in what amounts to a growing competition among currencies. The functional domain of each money no longer corresponds precisely to the formal jurisdiction of its issuing authority. Currencies have become increasingly deterritorialized, their circulation determined not by law or politics but by the preferences of market agents.

Mirroring the increased autonomy of societal actors is a loss of some measure of operational independence by states. Financial globalization has forced governments into a trade-off between exchange rate stability and autonomy in monetary policy. Some still prioritize the external value of their currency, resigning themselves to a loss of control over domestic monetary aggregates and interest rates. Many others have moved towards some form of inflation targeting, substituting this for exchange rate targeting as a monetary rule. Either way, state authority is compromised. The essence of the challenge has been captured by David Andrews in what he calls the capital mobility hypothesis: "The degree of international capital mobility systematically constrains state behavior by rewarding some actions and punishing others . . . Consequently, the nature of the choice set available to states . . . becomes more constricted."[12] Governments are compelled to tailor their policies, at least in part, to what is needed to avoid provoking massive or sudden financial movements. Market agents gain leverage in relation to public officials.

Here again, though, we must note that the influence gained is largely passive rather than active. Few knowledgeable observers of the decentralized decision processes of the marketplace would argue that the pressures now exerted on governments are somehow designed with conscious political intent. An informal kind of veto over state behavior has emerged. But it is a power that is exercised incidentally, through market processes, rather than directly in pursuit of a formal policy agenda. State autonomy is threatened, but not from a design that is purposive or hostile. Here too the pattern is essentially one of a leaderless diffusion of power.

Ambiguity

All these developments are having a profound impact on governance structures in the monetary system. The greater the population of actors with a significant degree of autonomy in monetary affairs, the harder it is to reach any sort of consensus on critical questions. By definition, autonomous agents can more easily resist pressures to conform. Hence a greater degree of ambiguity is introduced into the way the system is run. Increasingly, structures of governance are being remolded in an evolutionary fashion through the gradual accumulation of custom and usage. Formal rules (specific prescriptions or proscriptions for behavior) are being superseded by more informal norms (broad standards of behavior defined in terms of rights and obligations), in a manner not unlike that of English common law—unwritten law (lex non scripta) in lieu of written or statute law (lex scripta).

The impact on governance structures can be seen at two levels: the individual state and the global system. At the state level, the dispersion of power compels governments to rethink their historical commitment to national monetary sovereignty. At the systemic level, it compounds the difficulties of bargaining on international monetary issues.

National Sovereignty

Tradition has long assigned the primary role in monetary governance to the sovereign state. As a matter of practice, governments have been assumed to enjoy a natural right of monopoly control over the issue and management of money within their borders. Ever since the seventeenth-century Peace of Westphalia, the conventions of standard political geography have celebrated the role of the nation-state, absolutely supreme within its own territory, as the basic unit of world politics. By the nineteenth century, the norm of national monetary sovereignty had become an integral part of the global governance structure. Just as political space was conceived in terms of those fixed and mutually exclusive entities we call states, currency spaces came to be identified with the separate sovereign jurisdictions where each money originated. With few exceptions, each state was expected to maintain its own exclusive territorial currency. I have labeled this the Westphalian model of monetary geography.[13]

Though never written down anywhere, the norm of monetary sovereignty was of such long standing that by the mid- to late twentieth century it had taken on the legitimacy of a formal rule. Today, however, that old tradition has been shaken by the new growth of competition among currencies across national borders, resulting from financial globalization. As currencies become increasingly deterritorialized, governments find themselves driven to reconsider their historical attachment to the Westphalian model. The monetary sovereignty norm is gradually being eroded by changes of practice and circumstance.

National monetary sovereignty clearly does have its advantages, including the privilege of seigniorage (the ability to finance public spending via money creation) and the power to manage monetary conditions. But in a world where growing numbers of societal actors can now exercise choice among diverse currencies, there are also distinct disadvantages. Most notable is the need to prioritize the goal of preserving market confidence in the value and usability of the nation's money—the "confidence game," to recall Paul Krugman's name for it.[14] The label is ironic because, as in any con game, the effort to play may prove an exercise in futility.

The dilemma is simple. To preserve confidence in its currency, a government must above all make a credible commitment to "sound" macroeconomic management, meaning a strong emphasis on low inflation and financial stability. Monetary policy must not appear to be overused for expansionary purposes; fiscal policy must not be allowed to finance deficits via the printing press. Such policy discipline—what Krugman calls "root-canal economics"—is of course by no means undesirable, as any victim of past government excesses can attest.[15] High inflation and financial instability can destroy savings, distort incentives and suppress productive investment. Conversely, if sustained, "sound" management policies may indeed successfully enhance a currency's reputation. However, there is also a distinct downside. Root-canal economics can be extremely costly in terms of lost output or higher unemployment, owing to structural deficiencies that may inhibit an economy's ability to adjust to a constrained policy environment. Experience demonstrates that tight monetary and fiscal policies can in fact turn into dismal austerity policies, depressing growth for a prolonged period.

Faced with this dilemma, governments have three options. One is to continue playing the confidence game, whatever the cost. The other two would replace a country's national currency with a regional money of some kind.[16] Currency regionalization occurs when two or more states formally share a single money or equivalent. In one variant of regionalization, countries can agree to merge their separate currencies into a new joint money, as members of EMU have done with the euro. This is currency unification, a strategy of "horizontal" regionalization.

Alternatively, any single country may unilaterally or by agreement replace its own currency with the already existing money of another country, an approach typically described as full or formal dollarization ("vertical" regionalization). Both variants involve a delegation of traditional powers away from the individual state. Monetary sovereignty is either pooled in a partnership of some sort, shifting authority to a joint institution like the ECB, or else surrendered wholly or in part to a dominant foreign power such as the United States.

Already, under the pressure of currency competition, a number of governments have opted to abandon their traditional monetary sovereignty. In 2000 Ecuador adopted America's greenback as its exclusive legal tender; a year later El Salvador followed suit. In effect, both chose to become monetary dependencies of the United States rather than fight on to sustain a money of their own. Others have established currency boards—a more limited form of vertical regionalization—or have talked seriously about a monetary union of some kind. Tentative plans have already been drawn up for currency unification in West Africa and in the Gulf region of the Middle East and are under discussion elsewhere. In the opinion of many informed observers, it is only a matter of time before the universe of moneys will be radically shrunk.[17]

In reality, of course, it is easier to talk about currency regionalization than actually to do something about it. Giving up a national currency is not easy. As I have argued elsewhere, attachments to the tradition of monetary sovereignty remain strong in most parts of the world, however costly the confidence game may be.[18] But there is no question that for many governments, the stark choice must now be faced. The shift in the balance of power between states and societal actors has unquestionably undermined the foundations of the traditional Westphalian model. As a result, a previously clear norm is now increasingly clouded with uncertainty.

International Bargaining

Much the same is happening at the systemic level, where prevailing governance structures have also been brought into question by continuing shifts in the distribution of power. As a corollary of the traditional norm of monetary sovereignty at the state level, governments have long relied on formal or informal negotiations among themselves to lay down the rules of the game at the systemic level. As far back as the Genoa Conference of 1922, the dynamics of rule-setting have centered on hard-won bargains struck among a few leading states with the capacity to cajole or coerce others into agreement. That was the scenario at the Bretton Woods Conference of 1944, which was dominated by the United States and Britain. The pattern could also be seen in the negotiations that led up to the earliest amendments of the charter of the IMF, providing for the creation of special drawing rights (negotiated in the 1960s by the Group of Ten) and ratifying a new system of flexible exchange rates (mainly the product of a 1975 agreement between France and the United States). In this respect, the geopolitics of finance was no different from the geopolitics of other issues, where power has always played a pivotal role.

But that was before so many more states gained a degree of autonomy in monetary affairs. The more governments feel insulated from outside pressure, the less likely it is that they will meekly accept the diktat of an inner circle of self-appointed leaders. Bargains made at the top will not be treated with the same respect as in the past. Existing or proposed new rules will no longer enjoy the same degree of legitimacy among states further down the hierarchy, unless these states too are incorporated into the decision-making process.

A diffusion of monetary power is nothing new, of course. The 1960s and 1970s, when US hegemony seemed to be in decline, also saw the emergence of new powers in monetary affairs. Then too there was an increase of ambiguity in governance structures, especially after the breakdown of the Bretton Woods par value system in 1971–3. But even after those troubled decades the inner circle remained remarkably small, limited essentially to the United States and its partners in the G7—as evident, for example, in the celebrated Plaza and Louvre accords of the 1980s and the management of financial crises in Mexico and East Asia in the 1990s. What is distinctive about today, by contrast, is the sheer number of states that now feel entitled to seats at the high table.

That, of course, explains why recent years have seen a proliferation of new forums designed to widen participation in global discussions. A turning point came after the Asian crisis, when broad new interest was sparked in reform of what soon came to be called the "international financial architecture." One result was the Group of Twenty finance ministers' and central bank governors' forum (G20), which was created in 1999 and now meets annually to discuss a range of economic and monetary issues. In addition to representatives of the G7 and European Union, the G20 brings to the table some dozen "systemically significant economies": Argentina, Australia, Brazil, China, India, Indonesia, Korea, Mexico, Russia, Saudi Arabia, South Africa and Turkey. A second initiative was the Financial Stability Forum (FSF), also dating from 1999, which is charged with improving the functioning of financial markets and bringing about a reduction of systemic risk. Convened twice a year, the FSF includes some 43 members representing 26 states and a variety of international financial institutions and supervisory bodies. Forums like the G20 and FSF are obviously intended to enhance the legitimacy of current reform efforts.

The same concerns also explain why so much attention is now being paid to the allocation of quotas at the IMF, which inter alia determine the distribution of voting power among the Fund's members. Many advanced economies—including especially the members of the EU—appear to be overrepresented in the Fund's voting system, while some of the larger emerging market economies are clearly underrepresented. Past quota adjustments, it is generally agreed, simply have not kept up with the transformation of the world economy. In 2006 IMF governors agreed that it was time to implement a new, "simpler and more transparent" formula to guide adjustments in the future, generating a plethora of competing proposals.[19] To date, consensus on any single approach has proved elusive—which is not at all surprising, given the zero-sum nature of the game. Any gain of voting shares for some countries must necessarily come at the expense of others. But some reallocation of quotas clearly does seem to be in the cards.

Wider participation, however, will not make rule-setting any easier. Quite the contrary, in fact. The efficiency of decision-making obviously suffers as more actors are given parts in the process. According to standard organization theory, the difficulties of negotiation actually increase exponentially, not just in proportion, with the number of parties involved. The more voices there are at the table, the greater is the temptation to smooth over unresolved differences with artful compromises and the deliberate obfuscations of classic diplomatic language. Clarity is sacrificed for the sake of avoiding the appearance of discord. Much room is left for creative interpretation.

Worse, even when some measure of agreement is achieved, little can be done about it. Apart from the IMF, none of the existing forums have any powers of direct enforcement. Bodies like the G7, G20 and FSF are essentially regularized procedures for consultation—little more than talking shops. Some advantage may be gained from the exchange of information and viewpoints that is facilitated. But wider participation, per se, does nothing to ensure that newly autonomous actors will feel obliged to compromise some part of their operational independence if it does not suit their interests. And even the enforcement powers of the IMF are limited today to just the poorest countries in the system, which remain the organization's only regular clients. The Fund's leverage rests largely on the conditions it may attach to its lending. But richer states, with their access to the global financial markets, no longer need the IMF for financing. Hence many are free to ignore Fund pronouncements, whatever the allocation of member quotas.

A case in point is provided by the Fund's recent effort to tighten up its rules for the management of exchange rates by member governments—the first revision since 1977 of the principles for what is called bilateral surveillance of currency practices.[20] Central to the revision is a new injunction urging states to avoid practices that cause "external instability." But there is little that the Fund can do if nations choose to resist. Some countries, like China (the obvious target of the new injunction), continue to maintain formal pegs that generate large trade imbalances. Others that have ostensibly abandoned pegging in favour of inflation targeting nonetheless intervene massively to manage their exchange rates, whatever the external consequences—a pattern of behaviour known as "dirty" floating. The high reserve holdings generated by today's global imbalances make dirty floating feasible for many. Only governments that lack the requisite liquidity are susceptible to IMF blandishments.

Overall, therefore, the prospect is for growing ambiguity in the system's governance structures. Whether they are part of the bargaining process or not, newly autonomous states now have more leeway to follow their own instincts. Some will undoubtedly continue to play the confidence game, at whatever cost in terms of "external stability." Others may well prefer to pool or surrender their monetary sovereignty in some degree. In effect, many governments have been freed to make up their own rules as they go along through practice and the gradual accumulation of experience.

In time, of course, patterns of behavior that originate in self-interest may lead to shared expectations (intersubjective understandings) and can eventually even become infused with normative significance. Often, what starts from a logic of consequences (a concern with material impacts) comes ultimately to rest on a logic of appropriateness (a concern with what is "right"). That kind of evolutionary process, relying on the development of informal norms rather than formal rules, is a hallmark of English common law. Increasingly, it is becoming central to international monetary governance as well.

Conclusion

The dynamics of power and governance in global finance today are indeed changing. A leaderless diffusion of power is generating greater uncertainty about the underlying rules of the game. At the state level, governments increasingly question the need for a strictly national currency. At the systemic level, governance now relies more on custom and usage, rather than intergovernmental negotiation, to define standards of behavior.

Greater ambiguity is not necessarily a bad thing, especially if it allows states and societal actors to get along without undue friction. But it does also have distinct disadvantages that cannot be ignored. Governance plainly is less tidy when effectuated through social conventions rather than formal agreements. Lex non scripta is inherently more opaque than lex scripta. Hence a wider latitude is afforded actors for strategic maneuvers that may be made at the expense of others. Outcomes may be neither as stable nor as equitable as we might wish. Crises could become more frequent or difficult to manage if more governments feel free to do their own thing, discounting disruptive externalities. Burdens of adjustment could fall disproportionately on the weakest members of the system, which have benefited least from the leaderless diffusion of power.

Can anything be done to lessen such risks? Since states remain the basic units of world politics, responsibility continues to reside with governments, which still have little choice but to try to resolve their differences through negotiation. What is needed, however, is a change of bargaining strategy to conform more comfortably to the new distribution of power. With autonomy spread more widely among actors, it is becoming increasingly fruitless to aim for specific prescriptions for behavior—what in biblical language might be called "thou shalt" types of rule. More governments are now in a position simply to ignore detailed injunctions when they wish. But it is not impractical to aim for the reverse—general "thou shalt not" types of rule that set outer limits to what might be considered acceptable. Even the most insular governments are apt to recognize that there is a common interest in keeping potential externalities within bounds. If prevailing governance structures are to retain any practical influence at all, that is the direction in which the dynamics of rule-setting must now move.

Notes

1. Susan Strange, *States and markets,* 2nd ed. (London: Pinter, 1994), p. 90.

2. Benjamin J. Cohen, "The macrofoundations of monetary power," in David M. Andrews, ed., *International monetary power* (Ithaca, NY: Cornell University Press, 2006), pp. 31–50.

3. Cohen, "Macrofoundations."

4. Robert Mundell, "The euro and the stability of the international monetary system," in Robert Mundell and Armand Cleese, eds., *The euro as a stabilizer in the international economic system* (Boston: Kluwer Academic, 2000), p. 57.

5. Benjamin J. Cohen, "The euro in a global context: challenges and capacities," in Kenneth Dyson, ed., *The euro at ten* (Oxford: Oxford University Press, 2008).

6. Benjamin J. Cohen, "Global currency rivalry: can the euro ever challenge the dollar?" *Journal of Common Market Studies* 41: 4, Sept. 2003, pp. 575–95.

7. Charles Wyplosz, "An international role for the euro?" in Jean Dermine and Pierre Hillion, eds., *European capital markets with a single currency* (New York: Oxford University Press, 1999), p. 89.

8. C. Fred Bergsten, "The euro and the dollar: toward a 'finance G-2'?" in Adam Posen, ed., *The euro at five: ready for a global role?* (Washington DC: Institute for International Economics, 2005), p. 33.

9. Jonathan Kirshner, *Currency and coercion: the political economy of international monetary power* (Princeton, NJ: Princeton University Press, 1995), p. 8.

10. Lawrence H. Summers, *The US current account deficit and the global economy* (Washington DC: Per Jacobsson Foundation, 2004).

11. Benjamin J. Cohen, *The geography of money* (Ithaca, NY: Cornell University Press, 1998).

12. David M. Andrews, "Capital mobility and state autonomy: toward a structural theory of international relations," *International Studies Quarterly* 38: 2, June 1994, pp. 193–218.

13. Cohen, *The geography of money.*

14. Paul R. Krugman, "The confidence game," *New Republic,* 5 Oct. 1998, pp. 23–5.

15. Paul R. Krugman, "Other people's money," *New York Times,* 18 July 2001, p. A23.

16. Benjamin J. Cohen, *The future of money* (Princeton, NJ: Princeton University Press, 2004).

17. Zanny M. Beddoes, "From EMU to AMU? The case for regional currencies," *Foreign Affairs* 78: 4, July 1999, pp. 8–13.

18. Cohen, *The future of money*.

19. Richard N. Cooper and Edwin M. Truman, "The IMF quota formula: linchpin of fund reform," policy brief in international economics no. PB07–1 (Washington DC: Peterson Institute for International Economics, 2007).

20. International Monetary Fund, "IMF surveillance: the 2007 decision on bilateral surveillance," fact sheet, June 2007.

PART 5

Social and Humanitarian Issues
Brian Frederking and Paul F. Diehl

INTERNATIONAL ORGANIZATIONS ARE HIGHLY AND INCREAS-
ingly active in social and humanitarian issue areas. Many goals within
this issue area (literacy, nutrition, health care, sanitation) are widely
shared. Pursuing these objectives is less controversial than those in
security or economic issue areas, and therefore support for these efforts
is generally high. For example, the World Health Organization is almost
universally applauded for its efforts at eradicating disease. The UN
High Commissioner for Refugees has twice been awarded the Nobel
Peace Prize. Some of the most effective work of international organizations takes place in this issue area. Of course, some disagreements exist:
whether to include abortion services in a global plan to reduce population growth, differing cultural perspectives about the status of women,
and whether to use war crimes tribunals to punish violations of humanitarian international law are some examples of global discord in this
issue area.

Social and humanitarian issues are also ones in which nongovernmental organizations (NGOs) have a more prominent role. NGOs do not
have the military capacity or economic strength to be major actors in
security or economic affairs. In this area, however, NGOs may have the
expertise or legitimacy that many international organizations lack.
NGOs may be able to operate without all the political constraints on
international organizations that exist in sensitive areas like human
rights. NGOs also may be able to operate more effectively on the
ground to provide aid during a wide range of humanitarian emergencies.

In Chapter 13, Paul Nelson and Ellen Dorsey investigate new forms of human rights advocacy and how this type of NGO activity is necessary for understanding global rule-making in these areas. They illustrate their argument with examples of water advocacy around the world. In Chapter 14, James Lebovic and Erik Voeten provide a quantitative analysis of whether international organizations punish human rights violators with their distribution of foreign aid. Their analysis shows that UNCHR resolutions that condemn a country for poor human rights performance are correlated with large reductions in World Bank and multilateral loan commitments. In Chapter 15, Thomas Novotny examines many aspects of global public health, including how globalization is a driving force for global health governance, the opportunities and limits for international organizations in this issue area, conceptualizing health as a human security issue, and the range of foreign policy options in a new era of global health governance.

Another innovative trend in contemporary global governance is the increased use of judicial tribunals to prosecute alleged war criminals. After the Security Council authorized ad hoc tribunals for the conflicts in Yugoslavia and Rwanda, the international community created an International Criminal Court (ICC) to punish those accused of genocide, crimes against humanity, and war crimes when national courts were either unable or unwilling to do so. In Chapter 16, Christine Chung, an ICC prosecutor, writes about both how the new court is a necessary step toward the punishment of genocide and the challenges in making the court an effective institution. Chapter 17 offers insights from Philippe Kirsch about the structure of the ICC, the cases it is pursuing, and the challenges faced by the court.

13

New Rights Advocacy in a Global Public Domain

Paul Nelson and Ellen Dorsey

THE ASCENDANCY OF MARKET-BASED, LIBERAL APPROACHES to trade, finance and development policy, and the diminishing roles of national government ownership and regulation of enterprises, are among the defining characteristics of world politics since 1980. The accompanying growth of influence by corporations has been well chronicled, as has the less powerful but significant rise of NGOs and popular movements in national and international politics.

The expanding roles of these non-state actors, and the increasing importance of decisions made in a variety of transnational fora have been summed up as the emergence of a "global public domain."[1] This is a political domain in which some—though by no means most—authoritative decisions are made in settings that cross national boundaries. This domain is "public" in a sense broader than "governmental": corporations, states, international governmental organizations and civil society organizations participate in authoritative decision-making processes. Moreover, domestic and transnational policy "spheres" blur and intermingle in trade disputes, environmental policy, and intrastate conflicts, all of which also involve states, international corporations and NGOs and citizens' movements.

"Global public domain" is an appropriately open framework by which to conceptualize changes in governance that are neither consistent nor unidirectional. While corporate interests have enjoyed success in reducing the regulatory and legal restrictions on their conduct, in some areas of public life civil society organizations appear to gain

Reprinted from *European Journal of International Relations* 13, no. 2 (2007): 187–216.
© 2007 Sage Publications. Reprinted by permission of the publisher.

prominence through their initiatives. In still other instances, states are successfully working to restore some of their discretion and authority. Rule-making to govern corporate conduct, under the rubric of corporate social responsibility, has been largely voluntary and ad hoc. One scholar notes that rules that "favor global market expansion" are widely perceived as having advanced rapidly, while those that "promote equally valid social concerns" such as "labor standards, human rights, environmental quality or poverty reduction, have not kept pace."[2]

We argue that the new rights advocacy and the full spectrum of human rights that it advances, civil and political as well as economic and social, are essential to understanding rule-making in this global public domain. One of the key characteristics of contemporary civil society activism is a dramatic increase in the application of human rights standards and strategies to economic, social and development policy issues. Despite some successes elsewhere, NGOs have been largely unable to alter the neo-liberal orientation of development finance, trade, and the regulation of monetary policy and investment.[3] This article examines the emergence of new strategies grounded in international human rights standards, strategies which represent a new approach by NGOs and which challenge widely held views of the relationship between NGOs and states.

Economic and social rights (ESC) such as the right to food, to health or the broader "right to development" have long been debated by governments, scholars and NGOs.[4] But recently these human rights have become more prominent in the agendas and strategies of some bilateral development aid donors, notably the British Department for International Development (DFID) and the Swedish International Development Agency (Sida); and of some NGOs and social movements, which have applied them to more specific policy debates, such as agrarian reform, access to essential medicines, women's reproductive health, and privatization of water supply systems. New and distinct patterns of NGO political action are emerging in advocacy on economic and social rights, as well as in other activism on economic and social policy, which we call the new rights advocacy.

We use "new rights advocacy" (NRA) to refer to advocacy on social, economic or development policy, at local, national, or international levels, which makes explicit reference to internationally recognized human rights standards. Several characteristics of the NRA are outlined in the following paragraph, but two comments on the definition are needed. First, we do not specify at what levels (national or international) NRA takes place. The advocacy explicitly draws on international standards, but it may draw on international influence to shape domestic policy choices, or on domestic initiatives to influence an international process. Second, we adopt the term "new rights advocacy" advisedly. The standards themselves are far from new. Most of the specific standards discussed here (health and food, for example) are mentioned in the Universal Declaration of Human Rights, and given legal standing in the International Covenant on Economic, Social and Cultural Rights, which entered into effect in 1976. The recent development of the "right to water" is taken up below.

What is both substantially new and significant is the nature of the advocacy that is outlined here. First, it is characterized by its explicit appeals to human rights standards, by its promotion of both civil and political human rights and economic and social human rights, and by the scope of activity and the broad range of actors whose behavior it targets. Second, it assigns accountability for the effects of economic policy in a distinctive way, attempting to develop an important if vague principle in human rights law, that responsibility for fulfilling ESC rights in some circumstances is shared by international actors and wealthy governments. Third, the NRA involves a decisive shift, compared to the established practice of civil and political human rights advocacy, in how appeals are made to international authorities to uphold those rights and in relation to governments whose duty it is to protect those rights. These features lead us to advance a substantive argument about the significance of human rights in shaping social and economic policy and the importance of NGOs in promoting economic and social human rights norms.

Theoretically, the rise of new rights advocacy challenges existing models for the relations between states, NGOs, and international authority, and clarifies the basis for rule-making in economic and social policy. Prevailing models for understanding NGOs as political actors are inspired largely by civil and political human rights and environmental advocacy, and characterize NGO advocacy as a process of building international support in order to force changes in individual states' behavior. But in a growing number of movements, especially involving economic and social rights, international actors play fundamentally different roles. Here, NGOs often work to weaken the roles of some international organizations, notably the International Monetary Fund (IMF) and the World Trade Organization (WTO), to alter the foreign and economic policies of powerful states, and to protect and broaden the options of national governments. Such advocacy only occasionally manages to win the support of G-8 governments, is unlikely in the near term to enlist the support of the United States or of the international financial institutions (IFI), yet we will argue that it provides a new and more convincing account of NGO political advocacy since the late 1990s.

This shift is momentous for human rights practice, and has important implications for how we think about the state. Many governments and human rights practitioners have historically resisted ESC rights because they are characterized as "aspirational," more subjective than civil and political human rights, and because of the difficulty of assigning accountability for ESC rights when most governments have limited control over economic conditions, and limited capacity to provide services.[5] The ascendancy and widespread application of neo-liberal economic policies intensifies this problem for ESC rights by further limiting many governments' control over economic and social conditions.

But this difficulty of assigning responsibility to a single state as sole duty bearer, usually considered a weakness of ESC rights, is being addressed by strategies that seek to transform it in practice into strength, by targeting economic actors—including rich country governments—that create barriers to the realization of specific economic and social rights in national settings. The traditional tension between international NGOs and poor country governments is altered and sometimes reversed, as NGOs support and cooperate with governments and work against the constraining effects of trade rules, economic policy conditionality, and corporate leverage.

New rights advocacy is growing in breadth and scope, and has potentially far-reaching significance. First, it calls more serious attention to ESC rights in national and international policy-making. These rights, which are legally and theoretically co-equal with civil and political guarantees such as freedom of speech, and protections against arbitrary detention and torture, have not developed the same support among powerful industrial countries, nor among NGO advocates, that civil and political human rights now enjoy. The Cold War and ideologically driven debates bifurcated the human rights system and relegated ESC rights to a secondary and "aspirational" status. The new rights advocacy challenges this relative obscurity and calls for reintegration with civil and political rights.

Second, the NRA is the first fundamental challenge to a market-dominated development framework that reshaped national economies and international trade and finance during the 1980s and 1990s. New movements are drawing on human rights standards to challenge the application of market logic to the delivery of water and basic services, to argue for the right to agrarian reform and education, and to assert the primacy of human health considerations in setting national and international policy regarding HIV/AIDS. Resistance to privatization and liberalization plans has been a feature of national politics in developing countries at least since the 1970s. New rights advocacy movements are challenging market-driven orthodoxy at the international institutions with greater political force and legitimacy than critics of structural adjustment policies have previously mustered.

Third, the new rights advocacy entails a fundamentally new understanding of accountability for the failure to meet human rights standards. In traditional civil and political rights advocacy, governments are accused of practicing arbitrary detention, torture, or discriminatory access to legal remedies, and international actors are persuaded to exert leverage, pressing the offending governments to amend policies and practices. New rights advocacy is not constrained by the sole focus on the state as duty bearer and violator of human rights, targeting many institutions, including international financial institutions (IFI), transnational corporations, trade regimes, rich country governments and poor country governments themselves, whose policies and behavior have an impact on economic and social rights and/or civil and political rights in poor countries. Advocates question the authority of international agencies and rules that weaken states' capacity to meet social and economic rights obligations. They also call upon rich countries to provide more generous and effective development assistance, invoking the provision in Article 2 of the ICESCR that establishes international co-responsibility and cooperation to meet ESC rights.[6]

Our investigation and substantiation of these claims follows in two parts. The first introduces and analyzes three distinctive features of the new rights advocacy: its challenge to market-driven development norms, its new assignment of accountability for failures in economic and social rights, and the broad range of actors—states, international organizations, corporations—that it targets. These characteristics are analyzed through a case study on the right to water and by briefer reference to other, related NGO advocacy. We conclude by outlining the implications for understanding NGOs as international political actors, their relation to states and international agencies, and the importance of ESC rights for governing in the global public domain.

The New Rights Advocacy

Development, environmental and human rights advocates are engaged in an important strain of international activity that is not sufficiently explained by contemporary International Relations, social movement or human rights literature. The new political activity draws on human rights norms to shape economic and social policy, entails a wide range of diverse organizations and issue areas, and has sparked regional and international campaigns involving grass-roots social movements and NGOs. The number and intensity of these campaigns increased rapidly in the 1990s and the first years of the new century, and focused on specifically defined issues, such as the rights to drinking water and essential medicines, rather than the broader right to food or right to development. This section first outlines the range and breadth of the initiatives; their political implications will then be analyzed through a case study on water.

The expanding interest in economic and social rights encompasses three trends: The first is the move by traditional civil and political rights NGOs to cover ESC rights, exemplified by Amnesty International's adoption in 2001 of a new mission expanding beyond its historic civil and political mandate to include work on ESC rights, or Human Rights Watch's work on HIV/AIDS or property rights for women. The second is the growth of new movements and organizations that explicitly link human needs issues to ESC rights standards, as in campaigns for essential medicines, the right to water, and women's reproductive health rights. Among the leading international NGOs making ESC rights central to their missions are the Center for Economic and Social Rights (CESR), the Center on Housing Rights and Evictions (COHRE), the Food Information and Action Network (FIAN), and the International Women's Health Coalition. These international initiatives have often been led and even challenged by national NGOs in the countries of the global South, with agendas dedicated to ESC rights.

The third trend making up the new rights advocacy is a rights-based approach (RBA) to development being adopted by existing development, environment and labor groups. International development NGOs such as CARE-USA, Oxfam, ActionAid International, and Rädda Barnen (Save the Children-Sweden) are implementing "rights-based" approaches that parallel similar moves by official development agencies including UNDP, the UN Food and Agriculture Organization (FAO) and the Swedish and British bilateral aid agencies.[7] These official development agencies' interest in rights rarely intersects with the human rights-driven advocacy campaigns. DFID and Sida are both concerned primarily with the benefit that human rights analysis of poverty and social exclusion can have for development program and project design.

NGOs have used a diverse, varied and not always consistent set of strategies as they seek out means of gaining leverage from human rights standards for economic and social policy issues. These methods include the rhetorical referencing of human rights standards to shape and frame policy debates, the application of specific standards to measure and evaluate the performance of government services or development aid projects, litigation of human rights claims before judicial and quasi-judicial bodies, and human rights education to help communities and social movements make the link between social and economic needs and human rights guaranteed by international norms and standards. These methods are often combined in issue-specific advocacy campaigns.

Education advocates, for example, have sometimes made reference to human rights guarantees in a campaign at the international level to encourage investment in guaranteeing access to universal primary education, primarily as a legitimating norm. National campaigns, on the other hand, have made the human rights guarantees more central, as in India, where advocates successfully argued for a national education policy that guarantees universal access to primary education. Advocates for African women's property rights base much of their attack on legal and cultural impediments to ownership and inheritance in the principles of non-discrimination that are enshrined in human rights agreements.

In other settings, education about human rights itself is a central strategy to realize economic and social rights. Human rights education encourages citizen groups to be aware of and to assert their rights in addressing governments and corporations. The Peoples Movement for Human Rights Education is a leading NGO in the field, and the International Women's Health Coalition supports human rights education as a means of strengthening local women's networks' ability to make the case for health services.

Human rights analysis may also be part of an effort to frame—or re-frame—an issue, to win international legitimacy for popular socio-economic struggles. Local and national advocacy for agrarian reform, for example, has broadened its support as peasant movements such as Brazil's Movimento dos Trabalhadores Rurais Sem Terra (MST) are linked to human rights-based organizations such as the Food First Information and Action Network (FIAN), which uses urgent action alerts modeled on Amnesty International's prisoner of conscience advocacy. FIAN argues that agrarian reform, which is essential to addressing rural poverty in countries with significant agricultural employment, has been betrayed by official development institutions, and makes the human right to food its basis for making the case for agrarian reform as a human rights issue.

What Is "New" About the New Rights Advocacy?

What is important about these efforts, and others like them, is the distinctly different pattern of political action involved. While the new rights advocacy borrows methods drawn from civil and political rights advocacy of the past, three major distinctions set these movements apart from the patterns outlined in existing models of NGO political action.

First, new rights advocacy addresses policy issues that are already dominated by another strong set of norms, which hold that goods and services are best delivered by markets, and that state guarantees are often inefficient, or worse. NGO campaigning against neo-liberal policies is not new, to be sure: structural adjustment plans provoked opposition, with only limited results, throughout the 1980s and 1990s. But the mobilization of human rights principles and standards against this dominant and controversial set of norms is new. Early efforts to promote civil and political rights confronted the competing norm of sovereignty, and advances in civil and political rights have often involved establishing the principle that human rights agreements give states the authority to investigate, comment on and intervene in the relations of sovereign governments and their citizens.

Human rights advocates devoted considerable political energy to winning powerful governments' cooperation in promoting civil and political rights through their foreign policies. But the core values behind civil and political rights were attractive to powerful—particularly Western—states that were being urged to constrain the sovereignty of other nations by pressuring for political reform. Economic and social rights, on the other hand, are likely to be seen as conflicting with the widely held norms of neo-liberal policy and limited government, held dear by the United States and influential international organizations.

Second, new rights advocacy establishes a different standard of accountability for failures to meet international economic and social rights. Advocates often seek to restrict, not draw on, the influence of international organizations and powerful governments, and NRA tends to involve NGOs in more complex relationships with poor country governments, relations that are sometimes adversarial, sometimes supportive.

Third, new rights advocacy involves a broad range of issues and diverse political arenas (national and international), "targets" (intergovernmental, governmental, and corporate), and partnerships (among environmental, development, human rights, women, indigenous and children's advocacy organizations). These place NGOs and social movements in a new posture as they attempt to establish the authority of human rights standards, including ESC rights, over social and economic policy-making, adding even greater complexity to the "transnational contention."[8]

This new dynamic in the emerging global public domain is illustrated by a principal social policy debate in contemporary international affairs: the privatization of water systems. The case of water illustrates characteristics of other issue campaigns, such as the campaign for access to essential medicines, for the right to agrarian reform, for women's property rights, and for the right to education. It also exemplifies the central characteristics of the new rights advocacy: the increasing specificity of campaigns related to ESC rights, their complex relations with governments and international agencies, their appeal to human rights standards as a source of leverage against norms of liberalization and privatization; and the wide range of issues, strategies, and political arenas that they address. It originates with initiatives by local social movements determined to change, or prevent changes, in state policy. Local activists use the language of rights, and international campaigns emerge, also directed at preventing international institutions or rules from blocking human rights-friendly policies.

Conflicting Norms: Markets, Human Rights, and Water

Human rights standards are being invoked and strategically deployed by advocates for guarantees of universal access to adequate supplies of safe drinking water. The human right to water is recognized in the Convention on the Elimination of All Forms of Discrimination Against Women (CEDAW, Article 14(2)(h)) and in the Convention on the Rights of the Child (Article 24), and was reinforced and given a higher profile in November 2002 when the UN Committee on Economic,

Social and Cultural Rights issued an explanatory General Comment, the fifteenth in the Treaty's history, making explicit the ICESCR's guarantee of a right to water.

Advocates of water rights, however, confront a powerful set of norms in international development and finance emphasizing market mechanisms and the benefits of economic openness and reduced government roles in the economy, norms which have been promoted influentially for more than two decades by the US government and the World Bank and International Monetary Fund. Privatization was effectively promoted by the World Bank and global water corporations including Vivendi, Suez, and other companies.[9] But market-led development, even with the now-conventional modifiers that recognize the need for "broad-based" growth, investment in human capital, good governance, and social safety nets, does not coexist comfortably with a framework for development built on guarantees of universal rights. Asserting universal rights to health, water, or education is in part a means of gaining leverage against market-based development policy.

Consider the use of human rights standards, rhetoric and strategies by advocates opposing the privatization of national and municipal water systems. At least 14 countries in sub-Saharan Africa, and numerous countries and municipalities elsewhere, are implementing or considering dramatic changes to water supply systems. Encouraged by the World Bank and/or IMF, and promoted by several large corporations specializing in water systems management, the new policies involve a shift from state-managed water provision to provision by the private sector, usually international contractors, with fees paid by end users.

There is often a good case for re-working these water systems. Many state-managed systems, while providing drinking water at little or no cost to some citizen-clients, are plagued by high administrative costs, financial losses, leakage, and inadequate coverage, especially of poor "customers." But in virtually every municipality and country where privatization has been proposed or begun, local and national resistance has been vigorous. In Ghana and Bolivia, national governments agreed in 1999 to new water delivery systems, municipal or national, managed by private contractors and financed in part by user fees. Local consumer movements, national NGOs and international NGOs have all been involved in resisting privatization and/or advancing proposals to modify fees and administration. In Ghana, the Coalition against Privatisation of Water in Ghana ("the National Coalition") objected to the government's "fast track" implementation of privatization, the lack of transparency in preparing contracts and transactions, and the perceived favoring of multinational corporations in the sale of public water utilities.

The Ghanaian campaign has succeeded in sparking international support through two mechanisms. First, the World Bank's prominent involvement in the national privatization scheme means that a set of international NGOs that focus on World Bank policy are receptive to the Ghanaian NGOs' case. Washington-based NGOs such as the Services for All and the International Water Working Group were among the earliest international critics of the Ghanaian privatization. Second, Ghanaian advocates took steps to link to international opponents of privatization, through speaking tours and by sponsoring an international fact-finding tour to Ghana.[10]

The dispute over water privatization in Cochabamba, Bolivia, has become a cause celebre of the global debates. Citizen organizations resisted a planned contract with a consortium controlled by Bechtel, Inc., which doubled water tariffs for many consumers. Extensive public protests ended with the consortium abandoning its contract to privatize Cochabamba's system, and a lawsuit by Bechtel to recover costs was dropped in January 2006. The Water Observatory's document archive provides a thorough record of social movement and NGO advocacy, and makes it possible to trace the references to economic and social rights over the course of national debate. In Ghana, Bolivia and in similar debates in South Africa, India, and elsewhere, local and national coalitions of poor people's and consumers' organizations press for free access to water and against privatization, making reference to international human rights, or to national constitutional or statutory guarantees.

The rights-based cases against privatization advanced by NGOs and human rights advocates in India and South Africa are among the most potent. In India, human rights arguments are prominent in legal and political challenges to the National Water Policy of 2002, which provided for private ownership and management of water systems. Human rights are similarly invoked in opposition to corporate use of water resources, especially by soft-drink bottlers.

In South Africa, the movement for the human right to water was galvanized by private water providers' use of pre-paid water meters on village and neighborhood pumps. These meters, which allow water to flow only to those who have paid in advance, are manufactured in South Africa and exported, and their use has sharpened the perception that privatized water systems will involve systematic violations of poor citizens' rights.

In both cases, local advocates' references to human rights have been picked up, amplified and made more systematic by NGOs working at the global level.

Through the 1990s, international support for local water movements took three primary forms: small solidarity networks with links to a country or city; anti-privatization advocates already working on privatization issues at the World Bank and IMF; and anti-corporate globalization activists led by the Canadian Blue Planet Network, concerned with global water issues. All used the language of rights, but generally without any specific reference to international agreements. For example, international coalitions mobilized individuals and organizations from five continents in support of the claim that "water is a fundamental, inalienable individual and collective right," and that "it is up to society as a whole to guarantee the right of access . . . without discrimination"[11] and calling on governments to pledge "not to privatize, trade, export water, and to exempt water from trade and investment agreements."[12] International human rights NGOs were not involved.

But the pace and intensity of human rights-related water advocacy has grown rapidly in the 2000s. Three international NGOs that have begun work on the human right to water since 2003 exemplify the dominant role of the human rights frame in the water debates. The New York-based Committee on Economic and Social Rights (CESR) advocates a human rights-based approach as the best guide to the challenges of water provision. CESR referenced human rights agreements and affirmations of the right to water in national constitutions, and proposes a standard for policy and litigation by tying the human right to water to the World Health Organization's standards of access to 20 to 40 liters of water daily, "within a reasonable distance from the household."

The International Water Working Group (IWWG), a coalition headquartered at Washington, DC-based Public Citizen, focuses its advocacy work on the IMF, World Bank, and the WTO's General Agreement on Trade in Services (GATS). Only in 2003 did IWWG begin making specific reference to water as a human right, and it has now assembled a thorough analysis of the use of prepayment water meters. Other South African and international advocacy organizations took similar positions. A flood of new reports, position papers and advocacy initiatives were launched in 2003, 2004 and 2005 by other international NGOs and networks. A major report, for example, by the WHO systematically framed water as a human rights issue.[13]

Water advocates are not alone in employing human rights-based advocacy to counter the power of market norms. HIV/AIDS advocacy,

discussed below, and some housing, education and welfare rights advocates are making similar strategic use of human rights standards and
methods. Often they do so while cooperating with poor country governments against the authority of international institutions and rules, and we
now turn to this second distinctive feature of the new rights advocacy.

Beyond the Violating State:
The Complex Politics of New Rights Advocacy

The new rights advocacy features a new approach to assigning accountability for many failures to meet ESC rights standards. While advocates
rely on international human rights norms, they are not likely to call on
international agencies or powerful governments to influence a target
government's behavior. Rather they enter into more complex and sometimes cooperative relationships with poor country governments, and
assign responsibility for the failure to fulfill rights to multiple actors,
often including powerful governments or international agencies.
Appeals to states' sovereignty, far from being used to resist or obstruct
human rights claims, here are aligned with economic and social rights
advocacy.

International norms are essential to most human rights and environmental advocacy, including advocacy of ESC rights. International
agreements on economic and social rights began with the 1948 Universal Declaration of Human Rights, but were not further specified until
the conclusion of the International Covenant on Economic, Social and
Cultural Rights (ICESCR). The ICESCR's 30 articles articulate rights
to a range of economic and social goods, many of which are further
explained by General Comments on Implementation, appended to the
Covenant by the Committee on ESC Rights of the United Nations Economic and Social Council.

The international politics of ESC rights norms and advocacy are different from those of civil and political rights. Civil and political rights
strategies tend to rely on the regulatory or diplomatic powers of G-8 governments or international agencies, and advocates devote a great deal of
political effort to winning and maintaining the support of such states.
Advocacy on economic and social rights often aims to weaken, not reinforce, the leverage of international organizations or G-8 governments. In
some cases, new rights advocacy demands an accounting of the finance,
trade and development assistance policies of G-8 countries, and their
impact on economic and social rights. Frequently, the human rights

advocates' support for poor country government initiatives means that sovereignty and human rights arguments are aligned, rather than opposed, as is often the case in civil and political human rights.

Some international agencies (notably the IFIs and WTO) and powerful governments (particularly the United States) are less friendly to ESC rights than are many poor country governments, and NGO advocates often adopt a broad, two-pronged position: that governments should retain more discretion in making choices regarding their trade and social policies; and OECD governments and international institutions should uphold their obligations for international cooperation and assistance to advance ESC rights in poor countries. This agenda implicitly broadens accountability, shifting from a sole focus on the "violating state" and assigning co-responsibility to the actors that may create obstacles for those states to the realisation of human rights in a global economy. The precedent has been set by sustained calls for rich governments to increase their support for the UN Fund to Fight Tuberculosis, Malaria and AIDS on the basis of Article 2 of the ICESCR, which sets out the international obligation for assistance.

We are not arguing that poor country governments are freed from responsibility to respect, protect and fulfill economic and social rights: international standards focus on states' duties progressively to realize those rights and to ensure that they are delivered without discrimination. The politics of human rights is now "beyond the violating state" not because states are no longer accountable for fulfilling ESC rights, but because in a global economy accountability is increasingly shared by corporations, international economic actors and—in some cases— rich donor governments.

Learning from Water: Discussion

New rights advocacy, we have argued, is leading to a larger, more influential NGO political presence, elevating the status of ESC rights in economic and social policy debates, and offering an authoritative set of principles for the governance and regulation of corporate and state actors. The water case demonstrates the new and varied roles of NGO political action, united by the application of human rights standards to social policy. It displays the variety of actors being targeted, the diversity of the institutions initiating human rights-based strategies, and the beginning of impact on policy outcomes, as well as some of the limitations of human rights-based strategies. Finally, NRA is altering popular and scholarly understanding of the contemporary human rights movement. A brief discussion of these factors follows.

The broad range of targets and political arenas targeted by the NRA—including corporations, states and international organizations—is a function both of strategic considerations and of the nature of ESC rights. Recognizing the complexity and costs of fulfilling such rights for very poor countries, the human rights covenants define governments' duty to respect, protect, and fulfill these rights in a much more qualified way than for civil and political rights, obliging governments to "take steps" to secure the rights "to the maximum of its available resources," a process known as progressive realization.

In addition to allowing for progressive realization, the ICESCR also acknowledges that the duty to fulfill ESC rights may fall on the "international community" as a whole, through the duty to provide assistance (Article 2). For the UNDP, this diffuse duty is an important link in the argument for greater international commitment to a human rights-based development assistance regime. But for advocates seeking to promote compliance with ESC human rights, the ambiguity poses a challenge, and requires an approach distinct from the appeal to international authority that often provides leverage for civil and political human rights.

The campaigns on water privatization are highly critical of the key multinational corporations involved. Water rights advocates excoriate the large multinationals that have made water systems their business, but international NGOs have done relatively little to engage the companies directly, focusing instead largely on the World Bank and IMF. By contrast, the AIDS campaign has engaged pharmaceutical companies directly and extensively. These initiatives to assert the authority of ESC rights in social and economic policy are being taken by diverse actors in the global public domain. ESC human rights norms are often being applied and clarified in situations that place them directly in conflict with intellectual property rights or other property rights. In the case of HIV/AIDS, the critical initiatives asserting the right to treatment for HIV/AIDS have been taken by a handful of governments—Brazil, India and South Africa—with powerful encouragement from social movements within their borders, and support from international NGOs and movements.

No governments have taken such clear leadership on the water privatization issue. Local and national consumer organizations and other social movements, with international NGO support, have led the outcry against privatization, and the critique of the World Bank's role. The

appeal to human rights to buttress this case began with the largely
rhetorical assertion that water is a public good and a right, not a commodity, and has now been refined and strengthened by advocacy organizations in India and South Africa, by international NGOs, and by the
UN's Committee on ESC Rights' General Comment 15.

What contributions have human rights standards, strategies, methods and analysis made to policy outcomes? Many of the most important
impacts are broad and in process: human rights advocacy, for example,
has provided protection to development, labor and environmental
activists through programs designed specifically to support and "defend
the defenders." Advocacy campaigns are in the early stages of what
may, in the end, be a successful reframing of water privatization, where
the human rights analysis of water policy has successfully entered the
mainstream of debate in international organizations.

Demonstrated impacts on policy outcomes to date have been of two
kinds: blocking policy changes at the national level, and constraining
the exercise of international power. Rights-based advocates have succeeded in blocking policy changes, in effect upholding the state's obligation to respect ESC human rights, by campaigning against certain
water privatization schemes. Also, human rights-based campaigns have
become an important source of moral suasion in the advocates' efforts
to soften the positions of the World Bank on water privatization in
Ghana and elsewhere. Water advocates have largely focused on blocking new contracts for private provision of water. To date, advocates
have been more successful in mobilizing political support by invoking
ESC rights than in using the ESC standards analytically to define the
details of policy solutions, although there is evidence of efforts in this
area by development practitioners.

Conclusions and Implications for Theory and Practice

The new rights advocacy—the expansion of traditional human rights
groups' agendas to incorporate economic and social rights, the appearance of new economic and social rights issues' campaigns and organizations, and the adoption by development organizations of rights-based
approaches—is a relatively new phenomenon. But the cases observed
here, and data available on human rights-based work on debt relief,
agrarian reform, and the rights to information and to education, provide
enough evidence to reach three early conclusions.

First, the use of human rights standards to influence social and economic policy is growing rapidly. Its practice is varied, and advocates rely heavily on the rhetoric of human rights in international circles, even as they experiment with other human rights methods—litigation, investigation and documentation, for example—and occasionally on formal regional and international human rights bodies. Detailed policy proposals explicitly grounded in human rights remain largely the domain of scholars and UN agency functionaries.

ESC rights are attracting broader attention, support, and more careful definition and operationalization, just as civil and political rights did in the 1960s, but their institutionalization is still in an early stage. Legal appeals in domestic courts to internationally codified ESC rights and formal petitions to human rights investigative bodies in the UN are still far less common than that for civil and political rights, but they are growing. As ESC rights advocates test the possibilities and the present limitations of their influence, there is evidence of a trend toward broader NGO use of the political, mobilizing, and motivational power of economic and social human rights.

Second, the principal International Relations accounts of NGO participation in international politics—in which NGOs help to bring recalcitrant states under the scrutiny of international agencies and industrial country governments—are in need of revision or supplementation. The political environment in which ESC rights advocacy takes place puts advocates in a different relation to poor country governments and to sources of political leverage in the international political arena. At times they oppose and condemn the violating state, at others they attempt to shift responsibility for violations to the international level and onto economic actors.

ESC rights advocates do sometimes "target" governments with external pressure, as in their appeals to reverse water privatization contracts, but the international pressure has come almost entirely from NGOs, social movements and the media, not from international organizations and G-8 governments. This is a new and distinct pattern of political action; rather than an appeal to norms whose resonance is stronger in international arenas than in the target government, much ESC rights advocacy appeals to human rights standards that have stronger support in the countries of the global South than among industrial country governments. It reinforces domestic sovereignty, rather than challenging it, and applies the leverage derived from international human rights to limiting or reforming the influence of international actors.

This form of NGO politics differs from the boomerang model: fulfilling economic and social rights may involve reinforcing international norms, while also calling for greater freedom for national governments and societies to set policy without reference to conditions set by international agencies. The effort to expand access to HIV/AIDS medicines in poor countries, for example, has successfully created temporary exceptions to WTO rules on intellectual property and patents, supporting the initiatives of governments such as India, South Africa and Brazil to produce cheaper generic medicines.

These advocacy strategies do not signal a wholesale reversal by NGOs, which still call for stronger international regulation of child labor, natural resource management, and labor rights. But the new rights advocacy does represent a significant shift toward a more complex and varied relationship with poor country governments, often strategically supporting and cooperating with national authorities. One effect of this changing pattern is that NGO advocates are likely to have to learn to work without US government cooperation. The United States' aggressive, if inconsistent, support of some environmental and civil and political human rights reforms is unlikely to extend to rights-based claims to social services, access to land, or water, where the Scandinavian and British governments' development agencies have been more sympathetic.

The third theme—the one on which conclusions are most difficult— is the assessment of the new rights advocacy's impact. Has the NRA decisively affected policy outcomes, and what role have human rights-based strategies played in those outcomes? Advocacy on economic and social policy to date has not gathered the record of successes that is often attributed to advocates of civil and political rights. Human rights claims and strategies have played a part in pressuring, blocking and modifying planned water privatization schemes in several countries. Human rights support has been a part of the growth of land occupation movements in Brazil, the Philippines, and parts of Central America.

ESC advocates' greatest challenge may be that the rights they advocate confront well-established norms of a market-oriented development paradigm, against which NGO advocates had little success in the 1980s and 1990s. Research is needed to test the impact of ESC rights over the coming decade by monitoring the strategies and impact of advocacy, especially on issues that directly confront norms of liberalization, privatization, and free trade. Whether such advocacy strategies can succeed, and to what extent, without significant support from the US government or the most influential international organizations, remains to be seen. The answer is, perhaps, even more strongly dependent on whether significant constituencies can be built globally, than in the case of civil and political rights four decades ago. The record of human rights-based advocacy on social and economic policy suggests that broad and diverse configurations of participants can be expected. Human rights-based approaches to social and economic policy, with their capacity to bring together broad coalitions and to bring NGOs and poor country governments into cooperative arrangements, now figure largely in the construction of broad-based governance processes in the global public domain.

Notes

1. Ruggie, John G. (2004) "Reconstituting the Global Public Domain— Issues, Actors and Practices," *European Journal of International Relations* 10(4): 499–531.

2. Ruggie 2004: 511.

3. O'Brien, Robert, Anne Marie Goetz, Jan Aart Scholte and Marc Williams (2000) *Contesting Global Governance*. Cambridge: Cambridge University Press; Nelson, Paul (1996) "Internationalising Economic and Environmental Policy: Transnational NGO Networks and the World Bank's Expanding Influence," *Millennium* 25(3): 605–33.

4. Sengupta, A. (2000) "Realizing the Right to Development," *Development and Change* 31: 553–78.

5. Korey, William (1998) *NGOs and the Universal Declaration of Human Rights: A Curious Grapevine*. New York: St. Martin's Press; Alston, Philip (1994) "Economic and Social Rights," in L. Henkin and J. Hargrove (eds.) *Human Rights: An Agenda for the Next Century*, pp. 137–66.

6. Jochnick, Chris (1999) "Confronting the Impunity of Non-State Actors: New Fields for the Promotion of Human Rights," *Human Rights Quarterly* 21(1): 56–79.

7. Nelson, Paul and Ellen Dorsey (2003) "At the Nexus of Human Rights and Development: New Methods and Strategies of Global NGOs," *World Development* 31(12): 2013–26.

8. Tarrow, Sidney (2005) *The New Transnational Activism*. Cambridge: Cambridge University Press.

9. Goldman, Michael (2005) *Imperial Nature: The World Bank and Struggles for Social Justice in the Age of Globalization*. New Haven, CT: Yale University Press.

10. Amenga-Etego, Rudolf and Sara Grusky (2005) "The New Face of Conditionalities: The World Bank and Water Privatization in Ghana," in David A. McDonald and Greg Ruiters (eds.) *The Age of Commodity: Water Privatization in Southern Africa*. London: Earthscan, p. 285.

11. Global Committee for the Water Contract (1998) "The Water Manifesto: The Right to Life," at http://www.f1boat.com/99/watermanifesto.html; accessed on 14 May 2004.http://www.waterobservatory.org/library/uploaded files/Accra_ Declaration_On_The_Right_To_Water_The.htm.

12. Blue Planet Project (2001) "The Treaty Initiative to Share and Protect the Global Commons," 14 June 2001, at http://www.waterobservatory.org/; accessed on 21 January 2003.

13. World Health Organization (2003) "Right to Water." http://www.who .int/water_sanitation_health/rtwrev.pdf.

14

The Cost of Shame: International Organizations and Foreign Aid in the Punishing of Human Rights Violators

James H. Lebovic and Erik Voeten

HOW AND WHEN DOES THE INTERNATIONAL COMMUNITY PUNish violators of international human rights norms? Certainly, deposed rulers and their accomplices must account, at times, for their barbarous conduct in office. This is apparent in the prosecution of Saddam Hussein in Iraq, Slobodan Milosovic in the former Yugoslavia, and other alleged war criminals by international or hybrid tribunals. There is little evidence, however, that mechanisms are in place to hold governments accountable routinely and consistently for ongoing violations and to give violators reasons to improve their records. Global international human rights treaties lack teeth and rely upon weak normative pressures for enforcement.[1] Governments do not appear to receive substantial material benefits, such as economic assistance, for adhering to rights norms, or experience costs in lost benefits for violating them. Research suggests that the strategic relationship between a donor and recipient and, to a lesser extent, the economic needs of the recipient account for the flow of aid, and that human rights abuses are a modest, negative predictor of bilateral allocations for only some donor countries.[2]

Existing findings pertain only to a direct relationship between assistance and rights practices. Yet, states might punish human rights violators indirectly by passing the task to international organizations (IOs) that are not under pressure to preserve strategic relationships with rights

Reprinted from *Journal of Peace Research* 46, no. 1 (2009): 79–98. © 2009 Sage Publications. Reprinted by permission of the publisher.

abusers. This is a possible result if: (1) multilateral aid institutions want to consider these abuses, and (2) multilateral aid institutions can bypass restrictions on evaluating the political character of potential recipients. We speculate that both conditions apply. Specifically, we argue that a multilateral aid institution might selectively reduce aid when receiving signals from the international community that certain human rights violators are politically acceptable targets. Such signals are provided by public votes in IOs, in this case the United Nations Commission on Human Rights (UNCHR). "Shaming" in the UNCHR through resolutions that explicitly criticized a government for its human rights record provided substantive information about rights abuses and gave political cover for liberal multilateral aid institutions seeking to sanction human rights violators. The result was a reduction in multilateral—but not bilateral—aid received by targets of public UNCHR resolutions.

Admittedly, we invite controversy by arguing that multilateral aid-granting institutions that promote the policy preferences of Western industrial states take guidance from an institution, like the UNCHR, that was notorious for its biased handling of rights abuses throughout the Cold War and post–Cold War periods. The UNCHR was formally disbanded in 2006 after a decades-long history that provoked charges that members were more interested in protecting themselves and their allies and hurting enemies than in punishing rights abuses. Our response is twofold. First, we concede that politics influenced commission behavior; in fact, our argument requires a widely held perception that UNCHR resolutions were politically motivated (i.e., some abusers avoided punishment and other states received relatively severe sanctions, at least partially for political reasons). We also assume, however, that some states—Burma, South Africa under a white minority government, Cambodia under Pol Pot, and Iraq under Saddam Hussein, to name but a few—became political outcasts within the international community in no small measure because these states were abusive. The targeting by the commission of these states signaled effectively that they were "safe targets" for material and non-material sanctions by other institutions, dispatched at their discretion. An earlier study substantiates the assumptions that UNCHR resolutions were motivated by both political factors and actual human rights violations.[3] Second, we do not assume that donor institutions methodically monitored the actions of the UNCHR or that its resolutions were important in a formal or legalistic sense. We assume only that these resolutions articulate global political realities that are gleaned, as well, from other (perhaps less formal) international sources. We remain open to the possibility, however, that these resolutions damaged the reputations of the targeted countries and increased their susceptibility to punishment.

In this article, we focus on two IOs—the UNCHR, the UN's main body for sanctioning countries for their human rights abuses, until it was replaced by the Human Rights Council in 2006, and the World Bank. In principle, our theory applies to all international financial institutions that might take domestic human rights violations into account but are politically constrained from doing so. We focus on the World Bank because it is the largest global multilateral aid institution devoted to development aid, a liberal institution (given weighted voting that favors Western, industrialized countries), and attentive to human rights and legal institutions within participating countries, compared with other global international financial institutions such as the International Monetary Fund. Indeed, the World Bank is under increasing pressure to consider the political character of recipient governments despite explicit prohibitions from doing so in the Bank's Articles of Agreement.

We organize this article as follows. First, we present the theory behind our arguments and the plausible roles of the World Bank and the UNCHR in punishing rights abuses. Second, we present descriptive evidence for our main hypotheses using cross-sectional time-series data on aggregate bilateral, multilateral, and World Bank aid commitments from 1979 to 2002. During this period, the UNCHR became increasingly active and employed diverse mechanisms to sanction a wide variety of countries. Third, we subject our hypotheses to rigorous tests with multiple regression analysis. We conclude that the support for our propositions is considerable and robust with respect to alternative model specifications and estimating techniques. The evidence supports prior findings that "objective" measures of human rights have no robust effect on aid allocation and shows further that UNCHR resolutions have no impact on aggregate bilateral aid. The evidence establishes, however, that these resolutions have a substantial effect on multilateral aid and World Bank aid.

Human Rights Norms, Aid Giving, and IOs

Evidence abounds that governments internalize human rights norms by incorporating them into their own domestic rights practices.[4] Yet, the social stigma of violating human rights norms is obviously insufficient to prevent widespread rights abuses, and many governments sign and ratify human rights treaties and then routinely violate them.[5] Therefore, it is helpful to study the mechanisms that states employ to reward compliance and sanction non-compliance with given rights standards, as well as the obstacles that impede the effective use of these mechanisms.

One plausible mechanism, in this regard, is bilateral aid. Scholars have long studied the extent to which donor countries condition their aid allocations on the human rights and democratic practices of potential recipients. Most empirical studies on the subject focus on US foreign aid with mixed results.[6] In general, they reveal that aid is more sensitive to a country's political and civil liberties than personal integrity rights and that economic aid, more than military aid, is influenced by rights considerations. The significance of these effects is not robust, though, to method, period, and location. Studies on a broad range of donors also indicate that despite their self-proclaimed commitment to human rights, aid allocations are largely based on the political objectives of donors and, less so, on the economic needs of recipients and/or their rights practices.[7] It appears, then, that aid is used to reward countries for their economic (e.g., trade), historical (e.g., colonial ties), political (e.g., UN voting), and military relevance (e.g., security ties) to the donor, rather than to reward or punish these countries for their domestic human rights performances.

These findings do not necessarily imply that donor governments are indifferent to the human rights practices of aid recipients. Instead, a weak relationship (at best) between human rights indicators and governmental aid flows might simply reflect the difficulties of implementing bilateral punishment strategies. If bilateral aid to a country serves strategic purposes, then donor governments prefer some other government or institution to punish that country for its human rights violations. Doing otherwise could result in lost opportunities to sustain or build a relationship with an important country and competitive disadvantages relative to other donors that are willing to aid the violator to claim a valuable market, raw material source, or military prize, such as a base or port. Thus, donor governments might hide behind the policies and procedures of (somewhat non-transparent) international institutions by allowing them to perform a "laundering" function.

These institutional deference strategies are impaired, however, by the limited mandates of multilateral aid organizations. The World Bank's Articles of Agreement, for example, forbid interference in the political affairs of its members and consideration of the "political character" of recipient governments. Public challenges to this posture incite fierce resistance. A case in point is the 2006 decision by the executive board of the Bank to oversee its corruption policy, after then-President Paul Wolfowitz admitted publicly that he had withheld more than $1 billion in aid to countries on suspicions of corruption. This obviously uncompromising response is rooted in realistic fears that an anti-corruption campaign will lead to growing Bank intrusions into politics within aid-recipient countries. Indeed, Wolfowitz linked the fight against corruption to the building of "transparent and accountable institutions"— and these, in turn, to democracy-building (e.g., a free press and independent judiciary)—within candidate countries.[8]

Still, the overall reaction within the Bank speaks more to Wolfowitz's stylistic affront to World Bank practices, and a general wariness about Wolfowitz's motives, than to an institutional aversion to considering a country's political practices when dispersing aid. Wolfowitz was tainted by his lingering association with the (unilateralist and unpopular global policies of the) Bush administration, and he only increased internal suspicions with his selective accusations of corruption that appeared to target countries on the outs with the administration. Wolfowitz's offense was apparently that his actions were public and (at best) ad hoc—that he broke a consensual norm in decision making, failed to live by established and transparent criteria, and, in consequence, alienated potential state supporters within the Bank, including traditional US allies. The reality is that political criteria are politically sensitive, by definition, and preferably introduced into funding decisions with caution to avoid opening the Bank to charges of bias. Participants must feel comfortable that the targeted countries are worthy of punishment and that the use of political criteria will not set precedents that politicize—and maybe paralyze—the institution.

In practice, political considerations—and human rights, in particular—had come to shape the World Bank's aid granting criteria well before Wolfowitz's appointment, for the following reasons. First, the Bank staff, which has considerable power in recommending projects, has acted within the leeway allowed by an absence of clear guidelines on what constitutes the "economic" and the "political." Second, the World Bank has assessed how its programs and policies affect societies, cultures, minorities, and genders, with an expansion in the number of global treaties that govern the rights of these groups and concerted efforts by nongovernmental organizations (NGOs) to push their agendas upon intergovernmental institutions. The refocusing has been institutionalized through the installation of specific Bank divisions that address these matters. Third, the World Bank's economists have recognized that the economic aspects of policies, programs, and projects cannot be considered apart from their political dimensions. Consequentially, the Bank has increased its efforts to measure good governance and now publishes rankings of its aid recipients on various aspects of good governance, including human rights.

Whereas the Bank focused traditionally on infrastructure, it now devotes more than half of its lending to human development and legal and institutional reforms. The expected return depends critically upon the domestic political and social character of a country. Important, too, is that the Bank has increased its collaboration with the UN High Commissioner for Human Rights, which led to the formation of a Work Group on Human Rights headed by general counsel Roberto Dañino. He argued that changing legal understandings of the protections of sovereignty and changing beliefs about the relation between human rights and economic development require a broader interpretation of the limits imposed by the Bank's Articles of Agreement.

Although the World Bank has allegedly denied aid to countries like Kenya and Malawi specifically because of their rights practices, the Bank must be sensitive to political constraints. We suggest that UNCHR resolutions that publicly chastised countries for their human rights abuses provided relevant signals to the Bank staff. These resolutions conveyed information about human rights violations and the political opposition to the abusers within the international community. Thus, we suggest that UNCHR resolutions were informative—not despite, but, at least partially, because of the politics involved in commission decisions.

The UNCHR served for over half a century as the principal UN organ for promoting global respect for human rights, with a mandate to scrutinize rights practices and enforce an ever-growing number of rights treaties. Each spring, more than 3,000 delegates from governments and NGOs congregated in Geneva to attend the commission's six-week regular session. With the diverse membership of the commission, its deliberations and sanctioning votes were often controversial, and certainly political. Given profound differences in outlook and interests among its members, the commission focused on principle throughout much of its early history and confined its specific efforts to symbolic cases—notably, Israel, South Africa, and Chile. This led one scholar to conclude that the commission was biased against pro-US and in favor of left-leaning regimes.[9] By the 1980s, the commission had acquired several devices, of varying severity, for expressing displeasure with a country's rights practices and, by the end of the Cold War, the commission was liberally employing all of these instruments. The UNCHR held hearings, appointed investigators, and with its most powerful tool, passed public resolutions that officially, loudly, and unequivocally condemned a large variety of countries for their purported abuses.

During our period of analysis, the UNCHR examined the human rights records of 92 countries at least once, reprimanded 62 countries at least once, and adopted public resolutions criticizing the human rights records of 34 different countries, many on multiple occasions. Through these resolutions, the commission continued to engage in selective sanctioning votes that included the frequent targeting of Israel to the neglect of major rights abusers such as China. Indeed, concerns about questionable voting and the human rights records of some of the UNCHR's members led the UN Secretary General to call for disbanding the commission, resulting in negotiations for a replacement body, which culminated in the creation of the Human Rights Council in June 2006. Nevertheless, politics was not the only source of commission behavior even in the Cold War years. One statistical analysis concluded that politics mattered in targeting and punishment by the UNCHR but so did increasingly a variety of other factors that do not fit comfortably with a realist account.[10] These factors include whether potential targets have committed formally to major rights treaties, the rights practices of these countries, and their participation within the international community (i.e., various IOs).

Thus, multilateral aid organizations might have looked to the UNCHR to identify rights abusers that were punishable with impunity. We assume that the World Bank was peculiarly attentive to the international standing of a country with respect to its human rights practices, given the Bank's well-documented liberal bias, attention to the domestic practices of recipient governments, and desire to avoid contentious decisions. At the same time, we do not believe that the World Bank or other multilateral institutions distributed aid in response to the more impartial rights assessments of NGOs, such as Amnesty International. If our arguments hold, such judgments affected aid receipts indirectly by helping shape a political consensus that certain violators deserve punishment. We thus test the following hypotheses:

H1: Countries publicly sanctioned by the UNCHR experience reduced multilateral aid allocations, especially World Bank loans.

H2: Countries publicly sanctioned by the UNCHR do not experience reduced bilateral aid allocations.

H3: Assessments of human rights violations have no direct effect on multilateral aid allocations.

Theoretically, this argument fits most comfortably within the liberal institutionalist framework. It suggests that IOs help governments address two dilemmas—the first, a coordinative dilemma and, the second, a collaborative one. With respect to coordination, political institutions render judgments that serve as a focal point, that is, widely accepted opinions that a transgression should be punished.[11] With respect to collaboration, IOs (multilateral aid institutions) help governments cooperate when they have strong incentives to defect.

Shaming and Aid: Preliminary Patterns

The OECD's International Development Statistics is the source for our aid data. Our main dependent variables are total official development aid (ODA), commitments from OECD countries (bilateral aid), multilateral institutions, and the World Bank, in 2004 US dollars. We focus on commitments because these are tied most proximately to decisions by governments and IOs to reward or punish the actions of governments.

The sample includes all countries identified as "developing countries" by the OECD in the 1979–2002 period. As is common in studies of aid allocation, we exclude Egypt and Israel from the analysis to acknowledge the unique aid trajectory and amounts for these countries. This leaves us with 118 developing countries. Our main independent variable is the adoption of a public UNCHR resolution. We expect that a UNCHR resolution in year t–1 will produce a drop in aid the next year. Thus, we collect data on public UNCHR resolutions from 1978–2001. In this period, UNCHR adopted resolutions targeting 31 different developing countries.

Figure 14.1 plots the average commitment of aid (per capita) to countries that were and were not condemned by a public UNCHR resolution in the preceding year. The graphs show that, on average, developing countries subject to a UNCHR resolution received less than half the World Bank commitments of countries that were not accorded this treatment. Similarly, total multilateral ODA commitments were almost half those for countries subjected to UNCHR shaming. There was no notable difference, however, in the bilateral aid commitments received by countries that were, and were not, singled out by the UNCHR. This

Figure 14.1   Bilateral and Multilateral Aid per Capita for Developing
              Countries With and Without a Public UNCHR Resolution

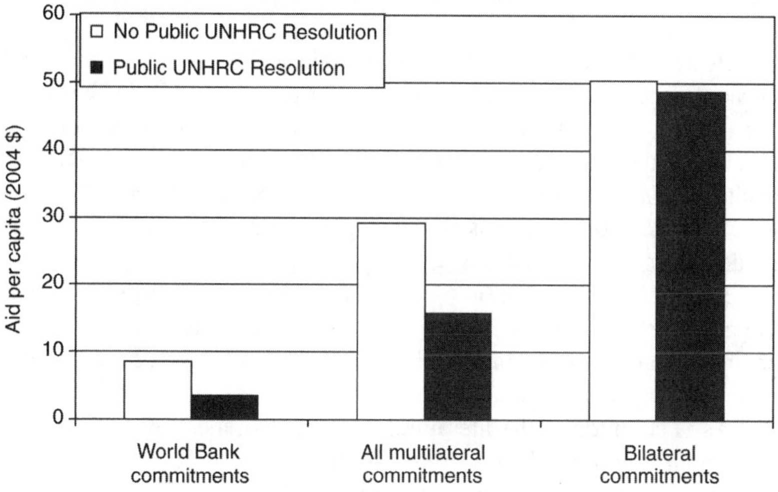

evidence is only suggestive and does not control for several confound-
ing factors. For that reason, we turn to the estimation of multiple regression models.

Multiple Regression Analysis

In this section, we present the control variables for our multiple regression analysis, the statistical model that we estimate, and the resulting
model estimates. The effects of UNCHR resolutions on aid could easily
be conflated with the effects of the human rights performance for a
given country and year, as judged by a more impartial source. Because
human rights performance can affect both the probability of a UNCHR
resolution and aid levels, our models include the widely used "Political
Terror Scale" (PTS) based on Amnesty International reports. Countries
are ranked for their physical integrity rights on a five-point scale, where
countries with low values exhibit little or no political terror and countries with high values experience regular terror and abuse. We also
include Freedom House civil liberty scores in our model. Freedom
House yearly assigns scores to countries on a seven-point scale, where
low scores (1) indicate the most free countries and high scores (7) the
least free countries. These two indicators measure quite distinct aspects

of a country's human rights record, both theoretically and empirically. Countries subject to UNCHR resolutions had somewhat worse human rights records than countries that were not subject to such resolutions in a given year.

Because the literature suggests that aid levels are need-based and because poorer countries might be inviting targets for UNCHR resolutions, we control for a potential spurious relationship by incorporating into the model a measure of economic need—the natural log of GDP per capita in 2004 dollars, drawn from International Development Statistics. A similar logic informs our decision to include population in our model. Given a potential bias against countries with large populations in per capita aid distribution (e.g., India receives large amounts of aid but not in proportion to its large population) and a plausible bias (for or against) large countries in the UN sanctioning process, we include the natural log of total population in the model.

As is common in the literature, we include a measure of vote correspondence with the United States in the UN General Assembly. This variable measures how much a country's foreign policy orientation coincides with that of the United States and, indirectly, Western countries more generally. This variable is a useful control because Western countries, as influential participants in the World Bank and other large multilateral aid organizations, might promote their alignments with multilateral aid and because UN voting is a known correlate of UNCHR sanctioning behavior.

In addition, we include two control variables measuring the strategic standing of potential recipients. First, involvement in armed conflict may make a country more susceptible to UNCHR condemnation (as shown in Table 14.1) and may reduce the country's supply of aid, at least from multilateral sources. Multilateral institutions generally distribute aid for specific projects which are less likely to succeed in countries that are actively involved in armed conflict either internally or externally (as resources are diverted toward the military, economic disruptions occur, infrastructures suffer, and populations are dislocated). We therefore include a dummy variable that takes the value 1 if a state is involved in an armed conflict.

Second, we include a measure of a country's material capabilities— based on the Correlates of War's Composite Indicator of National Capability (CINC). This is a composite indicator of military expenditure, military personnel, energy consumption, iron and steel production, urban population, and total population. If aid is determined by strategic

Table 14.1   Descriptive Statistics

	Full Sample		Only World Bank Countries	
	UNCHR	No UNCHR	UNCHR	No UNCHR
Ln (bilateral aid per capita)	2.83	3.08	3.18	3.35
	(1.61)	(1.23)	(1.11)	(1.03)
Ln (multilateral aid per capita)	1.73	2.38	2.27	2.74
	(1.46)	(1.39)	(1.44)	(1.27)
Ln (World Bank aid per capita)	—	—	0.47	1.23
	—	—	(1.01)	(1.31)
Ln (GDP per capita)	6.68	6.75	6.50	6.26
	(1.15)	(1.20)	(0.92)	(0.82)
Ln (population)	16.09	15.84	15.68	16.00
	(1.52)	(1.60)	(1.55)	(1.59)
PTS (1–5 scale)	3.88	2.72	3.80	2.78
	(1.11)	(1.04)	(1.10)	(1.00)
Civil liberties (7-point scale)	5.32	4.62	5.33	4.66
	(1.41)	(1.49)	(1.22)	(1.43)
Agreement with USA	0.37	0.35	0.37	0.35
	(0.15)	(0.12)	(0.12)	(0.12)
War	0.60	0.25	0.47	0.27
	(0.49)	(0.43)	(0.50)	(0.44)
Capabilities	0.02	0.02	0.01	0.03
	(0.02)	(0.08)	(0.01)	(0.09)
N	156	2,168	95	1,453

Note: Entries are mean values; standard deviations in parentheses.

concerns, we would expect that stronger countries receive more aid; moreover, if UNCHR shaming is political, we expect that, compared to weaker states, powerful states are more likely to escape UNCHR resolutions. Finally, we include orthogonal quadratic temporal trends. This controls for across-the-board fluctuations in levels of aid-giving.

Results

Table 14.2 presents the results of the random and fixed effects regressions. A number of conclusions emerge. First, there is virtually no evidence in the models that the human rights record of a country directly affects its aid receipts. The coefficients on both the level of, and changes in, domestic physical integrity rights are negatively signed, as expected, in most regressions. Yet, only short-term changes in physical rights abuses reach conventional levels of statistical significance, and only in the analysis of bilateral aid receipts. (Similar results are obtained from models that employ only one of the two rights indicators.) As with

Table 14.2 Random and Fixed Effects MLE Regressions on Logged Aid per Capita, 1979–2002

	Bilateral		All Multilateral		World Bank	
	RE	FE	RE	FE	RE	FE
Lagged dependent variable	0.553	.448	0.437	0.328	0.167	−.089
	(25.51)**	(16.58)**	(19.35)**	(11.31)**	(6.04)**	(2.49)*
UNCHR Resolution	−0.03	−.064	−0.301	−.280	−0.423	−.280
	(0.51)	(1.03)	(3.84)**	(3.04)**	(3.02)**	(2.15)*
Δ PTS	−0.037	−.039	0.016	.009	−0.018	−.025
	(2.20)*	(2.37)*	(0.71)	(0.41)	(0.46)	(0.63)
PTS_{t-1}	−0.018	−.023	0.017	.007	−0.041	−.051
	(0.96)	(1.25)	(0.69)	(0.29)	(0.96)	(1.16)
Δ Civil liberties	−0.015	−.007	0.003	.008	0.004	.002
	(0.80)	(0.04)	(0.10)	(0.31)	(0.08)	(0.05)
Civil liberties$_{t-1}$	−0.02	−.008	−.019	−.011	0.042	0.032
	(1.6)	(0.55)	(1.17)	(0.55)	(1.49)	(.09)
Ln (GDP per capita$_{t-1}$)	−0.107	−.051	−0.33	−.196	−0.475	−.270
	(4.26)**	(1.29)	(11.72)**	(3.30)**	(7.69)**	(2.80)**
Ln (population$_{t-1}$)	−0.162	−.873	−0.298	−1.18	−0.089	.192
	(5.23)**	(4.09)**	(9.73)**	(3.88)**	(1.85)	(0.33)
Agreement with USA$_{t-1}$	−0.123	−.328	0.261	.307	1.11	.521
	(0.85)	(2.13)*	(1.36)	(1.30)	(3.25)**	(1.44)
War	−0.088	−.103	−.110	−.110	−0.219	−.212
	(2.54)*	(3.07)**	(2.38)*	(2.33)*	(2.77)**	(2.60)**
Capabilities	−0.759	−1.59	0.096	2.518	−1.131	−3.13
	(1.25)	(0.85)	(0.17)	(1.50)	(1.36)	(1.56)
Time (1st spline)	−0.005	.001	−0.003	.005	0.011	.002
	(4.41)**	(0.47)	(1.89)	(1.10)	(4.16)**	(0.21)
Time (2nd spline)	.00	0.000	.000	.000	0.001	0.000
	(0.54)	(0.72)	(2.51)*	(2.70)**	(3.08)**	(2.02)*
Constant	4.903	16.15	8.288	21.53	5.122	−.257
	(8.66)**	(4.59)**	(14.08)**	(4.99)***	(5.65)**	(0.03)
Observations	2,324	2,324	2,308	2,308	1,548	1,548
Number of countries	118	118	118	118	84	84
LR chi^2	1108.44**		767.39**		126.33**	
R-squared (overall)		0.473		0.455		0.210

Notes: * significant at 5% level; ** significant at 1% level (two-tailed tests).
Absolute value of *z*-statistics in parentheses for random effects regressions; *t*-statistics for fixed effects (based on robust standard errors).

previous analyses, we detect no consistent evidence, then, that human rights abuses consistently affect aid receipts and no evidence that human rights abuses influence multilateral aid receipts. Simply put, it appears that violations generally go unpunished. This result is consistent with prior findings in the literature.

Second, public UNCHR resolutions do not have a significant negative impact on overall bilateral aid commitments. This also holds when we analyze only US aid disbursements. Nevertheless, public UNCHR resolutions significantly—and greatly—affect World Bank aid and multilateral aid. The results from the random effects model imply that a

UNCHR resolution is associated with an average per capita reduction in multilateral aid of 35%, holding other variables at their means and modes. The linkage between UNCHR resolutions and World Bank aid is even greater—a resolution is tied to a 52% reduction in average per capita World Bank commitments. The fixed effects estimates are somewhat smaller, suggesting a 32% reduction in aid per capita from both the World Bank and all multilateral sources. Together, these findings provide strong support for our hypotheses. It appears that a negative UNCHR resolution is associated with a drop by roughly one-third in overall multilateral and World Bank aid, but not in bilateral aid.

The results for the other variables in the model also deserve recognition. Supporting prior research, these indicate that aid receipts are stable, that poorer countries receive more aid per capita than wealthier countries, and that more-populated countries receive less aid than less-populated countries on a per capita basis. Also, participation in armed conflict is shown to have a significant negative effect on aid receipts, especially World Bank aid. Although there is little evidence that aid flows disproportionately to countries with superior materiel (military) capabilities, countries in the World Bank sample appear to Bretton Woods institutions are beholden to benefit from a US geopolitical affiliation, as measured by UNGA vote correspondence. Thus, World Bank aid patterns are especially sensitive to the political influence of the United States and its Western allies. This finding fits our assumption that Bretton Woods institutions are beholden to liberal states.

Conclusions

The statistical analysis provides strong evidence that UNCHR resolutions that condemn a country for poor human rights performance are correlated with large reductions in World Bank and multilateral loan commitments, but have no impact on bilateral aid allocations. Instead, bilateral aid responds mildly to short-term changes in levels of civil rights. These findings have a number of interesting implications for the broader literature in international relations.

First, they shed light on whether public shaming votes in international organizations actually "matter." This issue was addressed heretofore with the circumstantial evidence that countries would not exert energy in shaming, and defending against it, if such actions carried no weight. A more convincing case is built around the practical consequences of these sanctioning votes, as they affect donor allocation patterns. We account for this finding, in theoretical terms, by arguing that public votes communicate information about actual norms violations and political preferences within the international community. This information can be useful to other IOs, such as the World Bank, that make consequential decisions under constraints imposed by the preferences of their political principals.

Second, the findings contribute to the large literature on material consequences that governments experience for failing to live up to human rights standards. This literature has focused mostly on bilateral aid or trade relationships and has reduced the role of IOs, at least by implication, to persuading or socializing donors to design their aid policies around the human rights practices of potential recipients. We argue that governments often do not have the incentives to punish norm violators bilaterally, even if these governments would prefer, in the abstract, to punish rights abuses. This gives governments incentives to delegate the enforcement of human rights norms to multilateral institutions, such as the World Bank—this is an important point, because prior research suggests that states might soften their abusive practices with the right foreign incentives, for example, preferential trade agreements.[12]

Our findings are interesting, too, because the World Bank is not generally believed to engage in human rights norms enforcement. Although the World Bank is under considerable pressure from NGOs and governments to take human rights and other social/political factors into consideration when making policy, project, and programmatic decisions, and has adjusted its staff and priorities accordingly, it must also defer to the preferences of its principals. UN resolutions denouncing the human rights performance of an individual government provide a strong signal that project applications by that government can and should be evaluated with admonition. These signals are likely less important for the commission's actions per se than what they represent—a glimpse or culmination of a larger political process through which countries are marginalized in international politics. By the time the UNCHR acts decisively against alleged violators, they could be well along in the process of global shaming. Notable, for instance, is that the commission contended with some cases (e.g., Israel) because they were symbolic cases and acted, then, in response to world opinion as much as to reinforce that opinion. Regardless, the implication remains that, in an important sense, multilateral institutions bolstered their interventions by ensuring that they had adequate international political support and, thus, that the World Bank acted as a selective enforcer of international human rights norms.

Notes

1. Hafner-Burton, Emilie & Kiyoteru Tsutsui, 2005. "Human Rights Practices in a Globalizing World: The Paradox of Empty Promises," *American Journal of Sociology* 110(5): 1373–1411; Hafner-Burton, Emilie & Kiyoteru Tsutsui, 2007. "Justice Lost! The Failure of International Human Rights Law to Matter Where Needed Most," *Journal of Peace Research* 44(4): 407–425.

2. Alesina, Alberto & David Dollar, 2000. "Who Gives Foreign Aid to Whom and Why?" *Journal of Economic Growth* 5(1): 33–63. Alesina, Alberto & Beatrice Weder, 2002. "Do Corrupt Governments Receive Less Foreign Aid?" *American Economic Review* 92(4): 1126–1137. Lebovic, James H., 1988. "National Interests and US Foreign Aid: The Carter and Reagan Years," *Journal of Peace Research* 25(2): 115–135. Lebovic, James H., 2005. "Donor Positioning: Development Assistance from the U.S., Japan, France, Germany, and Britain," *Political Research Quarterly* 58(1): 119–126. Neumayer, Eric, 2003c. *The Pattern of Aid Giving: The Impact of Good Governance on Development Finance.* London: Routledge.

3. Lebovic, James H. & Erik Voeten, 2006. "The Politics of Shame: The Condemnation of Country Human Rights Practices in the UNCHR," *International Studies Quarterly* 50(4): 861–888.

4. Risse, Thomas & Kathryn Sikkink, 1999. "The Socialization of International Human Rights Norms into Domestic Practices: Introduction," in Thomas Risse, Stephen C. Ropp & Kathryn Sikkink, eds., *The Power of Human Rights.* New York: Cambridge University Press (1–38).

5. Hathaway, Oona A., 2002. "Do Human Rights Treaties Make a Difference?" *Yale Law Journal* 111(8): 1935–2042.

6. Apodaca, Clair & Michael Stohl, 1999. "United States Human Rights Policy and Foreign Assistance," *International Studies Quarterly* 43(1): 185–198. Carleton, David & Michael Stohl, 1987. "The Role of Human Rights in US Foreign Assistance Policy: A Critique and Reappraisal," *American Journal of Political Science* 31(4): 1002–1018. Cingranelli, David L. & Thomas E. Pasquarello, 1985. "Human Rights Practices and the Distribution of U.S. Foreign Aid to Latin American Countries," *American Journal of Political Science* 29(3): 539–563. Meernik, James, Eric L. Krueger & Steven C. Poe, 1998. "Testing Models of U.S. Foreign Policy: Foreign Aid During and After the Cold War," *Journal of Politics* 60(1): 63–85.

7. Carey, Sabine C., 2007. "European Aid: Human Rights Versus Bureaucratic Inertia?" *Journal of Peace Research* 44(4): 447–464. Neumayer, Eric, 2003. "Is Respect for Human Rights Rewarded? An Analysis of Total Bilateral and Multilateral Aid Flows," *Human Rights Quarterly* 25(2): 510–527. Schraeder, Peter J., Steven W. Hook & Bruce Taylor, 1998. "Clarifying the For-

eign Aid Puzzle: A Comparison of American, Japanese, French, and Swedish Aid Flows," *World Politics* 50(2): 294–323.

8. Wolfowitz, Paul, 2006. "Good Governance and Development: A Time for Action," Jakarta, Indonesia, 11 April (http://go.worldbank.org/ HKMUDLHE10).

9. Donnelly, Jack, 1988. "Human Rights at the United Nations 1955–1985: The Question of Bias," *International Studies Quarterly* 32(3): 275–303.

10. Lebovic, James H. & Erik Voeten, 2006. "The Politics of Shame: The Condemnation of Country Human Rights Practices in the UNCHR," *International Studies Quarterly* 50(4): 861–888.

11. Weingast, Barry R., 1997. "The Political Foundations of Democracy and the Rule of the Law," *American Political Science Review* 91(2): 245–263. Voeten, Erik, 2005. "The Political Origins of the United Nations Security Council's Ability to Legitimize the Use of Force," *International Organization* 59(3): 527–557.

12. Hafner-Burton, Emilie & Kiyoteru Tsutsui, 2005. "Human Rights Practices in a Globalizing World: The Paradox of Empty Promises," *American Journal of Sociology* 110(5): 1373–1411.

15

Global Governance and Public Health Security in the 21st Century

Thomas E. Novotny

GOVERNANCE IS NOT THE SAME AS GOVERNMENT; RATHER, IT is a broader concept necessary to address the complex issues of a globalized world, a world where sovereign nations cannot individually respond to problems that span national borders. In health, global governance is changing in response to the globalization of diseases, the shifting power structures of government, the concern for security in a politically unstable world, the weakening of international organizations, and the increasing roles of civil society and the commercial sector in global health. Global health governance is necessary for society to "steer" itself to achieve common goals. It involves rules, norms, principles, and procedures to structure cooperation, and it is effective only with the agreement and compliance of both governors and the governed.[1]

In December 2004, the United Nations issued "A More Secure World," a follow-up report to the Millennium Summit, where commitments to global cooperation were made in response to several major health and development challenges.[2] This report emphasized the need to achieve the Millennium Development Goals (Table 15.1), with a focus on health and biological security.

The focus of the U.N. report extends to the social determinants of health (especially poverty and economic inequities), infectious diseases, and environmental degradation. Although sovereign states are

Reprinted from *California Western International Law Journal* 38, no. 1 (2007): 19–40. © 2007 California Western University. Reprinted by permission of the publisher.

Table 15.1   The United Nations Millennium Development Goals for 2015

1. Eradicate extreme poverty and hunger;
2. Achieve universal primary education;
3. Promote gender equality and empower women;
4. Reduce child mortality;
5. Improve maternal health;
6. Combat HIV/AIDS, malaria and other diseases;
7. Ensure environmental sustainability; and
8. Develop a global partnership for development.

the front line in dealing with health threats, the report emphasized that no state can stand wholly alone and that collective strategies, collective institutions, and a sense of collective responsibility are indispensable in addressing the global health challenges of the twenty-first century. Indeed, governments have begun to align themselves in new agreements such as in the 2007 Oslo Declaration, wherein the Ministers of Foreign Affairs (not of Health) of Brazil, France, Indonesia, Norway, Senegal, South Africa, and Thailand recognized the need for new forms of governance to support development, equity, peace, and security.[3]

With the growth of civil society and the enormous new funding for global health from the private sector, new concepts of governance involving non-state actors are needed. Not all of this assistance has been unconditionally accepted, and may in fact present significant complications in global health governance.[4] In addition, academia has seen the growth of training, research, and service programs in global health that respond to concerns about social justice and emerging global health threats.[5] Health professionals and students throughout the world feel a need to respond to these challenges, and there is now a clear challenge to join health and foreign policy disciplines together in preparing the next generation of global health professionals.

This essay addresses the following issues related to global governance and public health security in the twenty-first century:

- Globalization as a driving force for global governance in health;
- Opportunities and limits for multinational actions on global health;
- Health as a human security issue; and
- Foreign policy options in the new era of global health governance.

Globalization as a Driving Force
for Global Governance in Health

Globalization refers to a broad range of issues regarding the movement of information, goods, and services through print and electronic media and trade liberalization, and to the movement of people through migration and global travel. Much also has been written on the global effects of environmental degradation, population growth, and economic disparity. In addition, the pace of scientific development has accelerated, with both negative and positive implications for global health. Concerns for health transcend national borders, and sovereign nations must have a global approach to assure health security for their citizens. In 1997, the Board on International Health of the U.S. National Academy of Sciences' Institute of Medicine described how the United States must protect its own people, improve its economy, and advance its international interests through engagement in global health.[6] Further, the board affirmed that all developed countries can benefit similarly through active and coherent cooperation. This approach may represent enlightened self-interest, but it also asserts a set of humanitarian goals and moral values for foreign policy.

International labor movements, deepening economic disparities, political strife, and loss of sustainable agricultural resources have dramatically increased the movement of people across national borders, perhaps causing as many as one million transits per day. In addition, the rapidity of global travel, combined with the growth of the global population, permits human contact around the world in a matter of hours compared with a matter of months a century ago. Health of domestic populations may be threatened by emerging infectious diseases, drug-resistant pathogens, contaminated food supplies, chemical and biologic attacks, and even by the cross-border advertising and marketing of harmful substances such as tobacco and alcohol. Even though health is ultimately the responsibility of sovereign nations, the protection of domestic populations now demands international cooperation and invigorated global governance to support such cooperation.[7]

The global health community now extends far beyond government. It includes: private or commercial entities (multinational corporations); academia; non-governmental organizations such as private foundations, humanitarian groups, and advocacy organizations; multilateral organizations such as the World Health Organization (WHO), the World Bank, and the U.N. development agencies; and bilateral aid structures such as the U.S. Agency for International Development, the Swedish International Development Agency, and the Japan International Cooperation Agency. Given this panoply of players, a state-centric approach to health is inadequate given the new financial resources for global health and cross-border nature of today's public health challenges.

Indeed, private-public partnerships now abound (examples include the STOP TB Initiative; the Multilateral Initiative on Malaria; and the Global Fund for AIDS, TB and Malaria). These initiatives are largely uncoordinated and are directed at specific high-profile diseases rather than at health infrastructure development or public health in general. They are in large part fueled by huge infusions of cash from charitable institutions such as the Bill and Melinda Gates Foundation, which had provided $6.6 billion for global health programs as of 2006. In addition, the World Bank is now the largest multinational health development agency, providing an average of $2 billion per year for health programs.[8] The World Bank embraced health as a major development issue beginning in the late 1980s, and solidified its leadership (some say at the expense of the WHO) with its 1993 World Development Report. This report proved influential on Gates and others who turned their attention to global health.

Fidler developed a useful model to display the complexity of global governance in today's world.[9] He differentiates international from global: international agreements occur between nations, and global interactions include all the other non-state and multinational organizations (Figure 15.1). One might ask, just how do these myriad actors fit together in common purpose for global health? Do the multilateral organizations provide sufficient governance structure to coordinate, govern, and monitor the activities of these actors? What is the role of the state in this governance scheme?

Opportunities and Limits for Multinational Actions on Global Health

Fidler has asserted that legal systems provide the core architecture for governance, and a strong legal and structural framework in global health is increasingly important given the current institutional chaos. Although traditionally recognized as the primary multinational global health agency, the WHO lost much of its strength under limits imposed by major nations and the increasing influence of the World Bank in the

Figure 15.1   A Schematic of Global Health Governance

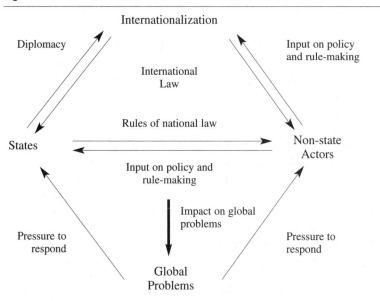

Source: David Fidler, Global Health Governance: Overview of the Role of International Law in Protecting and Promoting Global Public Health (Key Issues in Global Health Governance Discussion Paper No. 3, at 47, May 2002) at 9.

1980s. In addition, the WHO had little interest in international law, since most international agreements were perceived to be outside its competency. These agreements included environmental treaties (such as the Kyoto Protocol on Greenhouse Gases), trade agreements (such as the General Agreement on Tariffs and Trade), and labor law (under the International Labour Organization (ILO)). However, given the new complexities, the WHO is arguably more important than ever to global health governance, and it has tried to regain much of its purpose under recent reforms brought by Director Generals Gro Harlan Brundtland and J. W. Lee.

Although the constitution of the WHO recognizes the role of law in national public health, its core mission is to provide standards, practices, and technical recommendations for collaborative accomplishment of agreed-upon public health goals. Usually, these take the form of nonbinding, consensus-based resolutions (so-called "soft law") promulgated by the World Health Assembly (WHA) during its annual May meeting of member states. In addition, the WHO may develop binding legal agreements in the form of treaties among the member states. Two legal mechanisms—the International Health Regulations and the Framework Convention on Tobacco Control—are now in place under Article 23 of the WHO constitution, which authorizes the development and implementation of such agreements by the member states. In fact, these two legal structures may have been developed because of the observed failures of public health governance among sovereign states. Whether these structures succeed in their purpose, however, depends on national enforcement of the binding obligations within them. International legal structures are necessary but not sufficient for global health governance; the state is still the entity responsible for assuring compliance. For example, a recent case showed the potential weaknesses in the IHRs: an individual infected with multi-drug resistant tuberculosis traveled across several borders on several different commercial airlines before being appropriately quarantined. This was a test of the revised IHRs, and in this case, enforcement proved almost impossible, with deficiencies at several levels.[10] Additional national and multinational commitments are going to be necessary to fully implement the IHRs.

In addition, non-state actors are increasingly involved in the work of the WHO. This involvement may be through official recognition status, which permits groups having common interests with the WHO to speak at the WHA but not to vote on resolutions or governance issues. Such officially recognized groups may also be invited by the WHO Secretariat to provide commentary, consultation, or even text for resolutions to be considered by the WHA. On the negative side, another set of non-state actors may provide challenges to WHO governance. These include private entities that might attempt to influence both WHO staff and the officially recognized WHO affiliates. These entities may engage in political lobbying that may not be transparent and may even subvert WHO programs. One notable example is the effort of transnational tobacco corporations to obstruct the work of the WHO; this was exposed by a WHO Expert Committee in 2000, at the beginning of negotiations of the Framework Convention on Tobacco Control.[11]

International law has been established in several areas of global concern: environmental change, humanitarian needs, human rights, bioethics, arms control, labor issues, and trade agreements. Clearly, many of these areas include health issues, but are grounded in intergovernmental organizations other than the WHO (e.g., the ILO and the World Trade Organization [WTO]). One major, recent development under the leadership of the WHO is the revision of the International Health Regulations (IHRs).

The International Health Regulations

Communicable disease concerns drove the development of health regulations beginning with quarantine as far back as the fifteenth century. In the nineteenth century, sanitary treaties (e.g., the International Sanitary Conference of 1851) and then various Sanitary Bureaus regulated trade, goods, and the movement of people in order to control communicable diseases. The intent here was to sustain trade and commerce across borders, not necessarily to assure the health of populations. It was only later, in the context of humanitarianism and human rights, that such legal agreements addressed health issues directly.

The IHRs were established in 1969 to provide maximum protection against the international spread of disease and to assure minimal interference with world travel and trade. Initially, they focused only on yellow fever, cholera, plague, and smallpox. The WHO member states were the signatories to this agreement, which was implemented not as a direct treaty negotiation, but as a consensus process through the WHA. In 2005, the IHRs were revised by the WHO to focus on expanded public health risks of urgent international importance, taking into account international trade law and trade agreements related to disease prevention and control. These became active in June 2007, and the IHRs now cover emerging infections such as Severe Acute Respiratory Syndrome (SARS), tuberculosis, and a new human influenza virus. They also cover cross-border threats that arise from public health emergencies such as chemical spills, leaks and environmental dumping, or nuclear melt-downs. Of critical importance in the IHRs is the inclusion of rules on global disease surveillance under the existing Global Outbreak Alert and Response System.[12] IHRs 2005 requires countries to improve international surveillance and reporting mechanisms for public health events and to strengthen their national surveillance and response capacities. Under the IHRs, member states must harmonize their national policies, laws, practices, and regulatory actions to comply.

Other International Laws

International environmental laws address air pollution, biological diversity, ozone depletion, and climate change, generally under a framework treaty process. This is a formally negotiated general agreement that usually includes additional protocols to which the signatory parties may agree (or not agree) as legally binding obligations.

The International Covenant on Economic, Social, and Cultural Rights includes issues related to mental health, infectious diseases, and other conditions. It affirms a goal of the highest attainable standard of physical and mental health, the basis for the 1978 WHO declaration (commonly known as the "Declaration of Alma Ata") to achieve "health for all," as a human right. This Declaration presciently advocated for an intersectoral and multidimensional approach to health and development, including the increased involvement of civil society and education. The WHO recently reaffirmed its commitment to "health for all" through twenty-one health targets for the twenty-first century.[13]

The Framework Convention on Tobacco Control

Non-communicable diseases (NCDs) account for sixty percent of the fifty-six million annual global deaths. Deaths from NCDs will continue to increase with the aging of the global population and the spreading of risk factors such as smoking, poor diets, and obesity.[14] NCDs are generally ignored in the IHRs, but other legal structures address them in the context of occupational health and safety, narcotic and psychotropic drug abuse, and environmental health. In 1999, the WHO began deliberations on the Framework Convention on Tobacco Control (FCTC), an agreement that contains general obligations and sets forth diplomatic channels to develop more specific binding protocols similar to the environmental frameworks mentioned above. The FCTC aims to harmonize national efforts to reduce tobacco use as a trans-border health problem. To date, 168 countries have signed the FCTC, and of these, 147 have ratified it (notably missing from this list is the United States). The FCTC focuses on demand reduction strategies such as clean indoor air legislation, advertising restrictions, package labeling, and improved cessation services, as well as supply reduction issues related to tobacco smuggling and agriculture.

The spread of the tobacco epidemic is exacerbated by a variety of complex factors with cross-border effects including trade liberalization, direct foreign investment, global marketing, promotion and sponsorship, and the international movement of contraband and counterfeit cigarettes. Because of the complexities of the tobacco epidemic, the FCTC was a major breakthrough in global health governance. With the infusion of new moneys from the philanthropic community (including Bloomberg and Gates), the WHO and the member states that signed the FCTC may have an historic opportunity to control a truly cross-border

NCDs risk. A unique feature of the FCTC's negotiating process was the purposeful inclusion of non-state actors in the deliberations. In fact, extraordinary attention has been paid by these non-state groups to the day-to-day process of treaty negotiation. The continued engagement among states, multilateral organizations, and civil society in such efforts may be an important new governance direction for global health in the twenty-first century.

Limits and Challenges to the WHO

The WHO must address increased complexities in management and new governance structures. The WHO also recognizes the influence of donors, the World Bank, and new foreign policy strategies of the Organization for Economic Co-operation and Development (OECD) countries on global health development. For example, the Global Fund for AIDS, TB, and Malaria (GFATM) is one of the new governance structures outside the authority of the WHO. The GFATM has an executive director who answers to a board consisting of representatives of donor and recipient governments, non-governmental organizations, the private sector (including businesses and foundations), and affected communities. The WHO has an AIDS division that may provide specific technical recommendations, but the GFATM decides what, where, and when funding is supplied to national programs. Neither the state recipient nor the WHO is held accountable for any assistance provided by the GFATM. Clearly, such a structure is a challenge to the traditional global health governance of the WHO.

Indeed, the WHO has expanded beyond its reliance on Ministries of Health to include public and private sector actors through new consultation mechanisms and increased collaboration with the World Bank at the country level.[15] With the ability to mobilize large financial resources, World Bank loans for health programs and research activities significantly surpass WHO program budgets. Nevertheless, the WHO has been trying to maintain its role as a chief technical resource for member states.

One last important point to make about the WHO and other U.N. organizations concerns the influence of member states and donor agencies on WHO work programs. The WHO's $3.3 billion operating budget for 2007 is comprised of country assessments (28%) and voluntary contributions (72%). The WHO has authority only over the direction of the regular budget, and thus must heed the influence of voluntary contributors for the majority of its work program. In general, these voluntary contributions are directed to specific issues, and they may also have political or policy contingencies that supersede independent governance by the WHO. One particularly troublesome contingency is the Helms-Biden Agreement for Payment of Arrears to the United Nations. In essence, this 1998 agreement "not only imposed conditions on the payment of arrears but also added new conditions to the payment of current US obligations to the UN regular budget, peacekeeping operations, and three UN specialized agencies (World Health Organization, Food and Agriculture Organization and International Labor Organizations)."[16] Specifically, the agreement calls for a zero nominal growth budget for the WHO, wherein the regular budget must stay the same each year. Thus, the WHO must respond to the conditionalities of extra-budgetary sources mentioned above (now at 72% of the total WHO budget).

International technical assistance still is provided directly by the WHO and other multinational health organizations; however, much of this assistance is now financed through extra-budgetary contributions, as described above. Such contributions are usually accompanied by conditionalities, where donor priorities, politics, and values are imposed on recipient entities. This situation raises concerns about how agencies such as the WHO may accomplish their core missions. Large countries such as the United States, as well as foundations, tend to mandate performance guidelines from multinational organizations, including measurable outcomes and narrowly targeted objectives. These all resonate with corporate-like governing boards, but these conditionalities make it difficult to govern recipient organizations, which are made up of member states. Further complexity is added at the country level for ministries and non-governmental organizations that must cope with both the largesse provided and their own organizational cultures and limited absorptive capacities.

The WHO depends on the participation, budgetary support, and multinational commitment of its member states. In the recent past, the United States severely criticized the WHO and other U.N. organizations, despite playing a major role in their establishment after World War II. Some of this criticism may have been justified, but the WHO is still the primary governance structure through which global health may be engaged by member states. Now, in the twenty-first century, it is clear that there is an increasing mandate for growing multinationalism, engaging with non-state actors, and strengthening U.N. organizations that serve the interests of global health. Further, these actions really serve the sovereign responsibility of nations to protect the health of their own people. The changing shape of global health governance calls for increased consideration of how all the various pieces fit together. Clearly, the WHO responded to these considerations beginning in the late 1990s by forming new partnerships, stakeholder alliances, and targeted multilateral programs such as STOP TB, Roll Back Malaria, and the Global Alliance for Vaccines and Immunization. It will be important for member states to support and strengthen the work of the WHO as the most important mechanism for global health governance in the twenty-first century.

Health as a Human Security Issue

Beginning in the 1990s, significant attention developed towards global health threats in the United States and elsewhere. The previously cited America's Vital Interest in Global Health,[17] along with popular literature and news of new viral threats such as West Nile, Ebola, and SARS, led agencies such as the U.S. Center for Disease Control and Prevention and the Institute of Medicine to develop specific strategies to control emerging and re-emerging infectious disease threats. The global HIV/AIDS epidemic was described as a threat to international security, which led to significantly increased funding and resources dedicated to the low-income countries that bear the majority of the HIV/AIDS disease burden. The significance of this threat and that of other infectious diseases was reaffirmed in a report by the Council on Foreign Relations, emphasizing that "the security of the most affluent state can be held hostage to the ability of the poorest state to contain an emerging disease."[18]

The WHO also joined the call to improve global health security. In 2007, World Health Day was dedicated to International Health Security. In Invest in Health, Build a Safer Future, an official issues paper, the WHO asserted the need for coordinated action and cooperation among and within governments, the private sector, civil society, media, and individuals.[19] The paper argued for capacity-building in developing countries, the support of multiple stakeholders, and global preparedness for infectious disease emergencies. In addition, the WHO highlighted the need to develop public health infrastructure as a global public good, with increased political goodwill and financial commitment to improve health security. Trade also was addressed as a component of health security, with attention given to providing drugs and services necessary to contain various global health threats. Other areas of concern for health security include humanitarian assistance and donor coordination; chemical, radioactive, and biological terror threats; and environmental and climate changes that affect health.

In Invest in Health, Build a Safer Future, the IHRs were emphasized as a key tool to support international health security, with prompt reporting of disease outbreaks and collaboration among countries and networks for disease control. The WHO has increased technical capacity to monitor infectious and other disease threats as they are reported, and increased support to member states to help them develop surveillance capacity, laboratory backup, and communication among public health agencies. Finally, Invest in Health, Build a Safer Future specifically addressed the need to strengthen health systems as the "bedrock" of international health security. According to the paper, governments are key in this process, but multinational organizations, the private sector, and civil society are all stakeholders in this challenge as well.[20] For example, the Bill and Melinda Gates Foundation has provided substantial support for public health network development through academia and public health institutes across the globe. The foundation's $20 million grant to the International Association of National Public Health Institutes will provide concrete tools for improving public health infrastructure and health security internationally through academic leadership and advocacy. Additional attention must be paid to governmental health system development, particularly in public health areas, which is essential to global health collaborative efforts.

There has also been increased attention by the global health community for physical security against violence, the threat of violence, and the resultant injury, death, psychological harm, and impaired development opportunities.[21] Security is an essential requirement for health development, and personal security is therefore seen as a human right in this context. To achieve this sense of security, the health sector, as well as the defense, foreign policy, and finance sectors, must be involved to form a nexus of necessity for defense. Armed violence, displacement of populations, natural and man-made disasters, and poverty are concerns for global health security and a challenge to global governance structures. Clearly, human security demands cooperation across unfamiliar sectoral boundaries. Traditionally, security was a more national concern, but now, human security at the global level is rooted in the idea that security for all is linked to the physical and economic insecurity of even the most marginalized populations and distant, unstable political entities.[22]

Finally, health security is dependent on sustainable development. This means that global health governance must focus on the underlying determinants of health, including economic inequities, environmental degradation and disasters, and, in particular, social determinants of health. Many of these determinants fall outside the health sector and are related to "engines in society that generate and distribute power, wealth and risk."[23] Economic asymmetry is inextricably linked to ill-health, including both infectious disease and NCD conditions. In response to this concern, the WHO established the Commission on Social Determinants of Health. This commission will review not only existing knowledge, but also will engage debate and promote global policies that may reduce inequalities in health within and among countries. This may be the most significant challenge to global health governance among all challenges presented in this essay. Health and economic inequity solutions will involve major shifts in national priorities as well as investments in poverty reduction and health development. Indeed, three of the eight Millennium Development Goals address specific health issues: reducing mortality of children under age five, reducing maternal mortality, and reversing the spread of communicable diseases such as HIV/AIDS, malaria, and TB. The other goals are also critical to health development. These goals address education, gender equality, poverty reduction, and global partnerships. The U.N. has recognized these goals and the security concerns created by the social determinants of health. The security of nation states now depends more than ever on shared responsibilities, international cooperation, and improved accountability of all stakeholders, including attention by these stakeholders to the underlying determinants of health across sectors.

Foreign Policy Options in the New Era of Global Health Governance

Given the rise in importance of global health, several important countries now include health as a key element of foreign policy.[24] Global health is rooted in national security concerns, as discussed above, and is rooted also in the increasing global concern for social justice and equity. Hence, a new field of health diplomacy is emerging. This new field of diplomacy is based more on altruism, human rights, and human security than concerns for the preservation of commerce, mobility, and power traditionally engaged through foreign policy.[25]

There are several examples of health as foreign policy worthy of discussion. In the United Kingdom, the central government's Department of Health is developing a government-wide strategy to support global health.[26] The strategy will bring the U.K.'s foreign policy leadership, international development agency, and trade and investment policies to bear directly on global health. This initiative follows on the human rights agreements that the United Kingdom has signed. It covers the availability of health care, health promotion and protection, safe water, adequate sanitation, and occupational and environmental concerns germane to health. It also recognizes the need to engage across multiple sectors of the U.K. government to respond to persistent and emerging global health threats, both to the United Kingdom and globally.

Switzerland proposed an agreement among its Federal Councilors (cabinet) to assure policy coherence among multiple administrative services active in global health.[27] This mapping of global health across government sectors established new mechanisms of coordination for a national global health strategy. This agreement includes domestic strategies relevant to international agreements and cooperation, international assistance on development, and policy activities in other relevant sectors (such as trade). Brazil has involved its diplomats, trade negotiators, and health ministry in purposeful ways as national entities to support global health strategies. Most notably, Brazil's national HIV/AIDS policy required actions at the 2001 WTO conference in Doha, Qatar, to assure that health was the primary concern in discussions of pharmaceutical intellectual property rights. Further, Brazilian diplomats led the FCTC negotiation process, involving cross-governmental policy consistence to be able to sign and support this health treaty.

The European Union has increasingly asserted that the health of its people requires new processes and channels to engage all elements of society in the response to global health needs. European Foundations Centre has created the European Partnership for Global Health to raise awareness and utilize the bridge between governments provided by the EU structure.[28] Global health will likely now become a policy priority for the EU, with a European approach to governance and health equity.

In March 2007, the Ministers of Foreign Affairs of Brazil, France, Indonesia, Norway, Senegal, South Africa, and Thailand issued a joint statement to broaden the scope of foreign policy to recognize health as one of the most important, but often neglected, policy issues.[29] They committed to an "Agenda for Action" involving collective approaches and emphasizing commitment to health and development as prerequisites to global security. Collaborative actions included: using health as a defining lens for foreign policy, developing a "roadmap" in preparation for large-scale disasters and emergencies, strengthening the U.N. agencies to coordinate approaches to global health security, and identifying gaps in surveillance, outbreak investigation, and disease control.

Finally, the United States may now have opportunities to support health as a major component of foreign policy. Beginning with the President's Emergency Plan for AIDS Relief (PEPFAR) in 2003,[30] substantial funds were devoted to international cooperation on HIV/AIDS. These started with a $15 billion, five-year commitment, tied to several political objectives, now expanding to a proposed $30 billion overall commitment. Legislation has been proposed to carve out of this significant funding source an innovative program to support global health diplomacy. The legislation follows on the heels of Healers Abroad: Americans Responding to the Human Resource Crisis in HIV/AIDS, a report issued by the Institute of Medicine that called for the establishment of a Global Health Corps to help with manpower shortages, training needs, and responses to HIV/AIDS, TB, and malaria. This health corps would serve as an important outlet for global engagement by U.S. health professionals, initially focusing on target countries and diseases mandated by PEPFAR, but expanding in scope to support international collaboration and global service.[31] Given the extensive negative feelings about recent U.S. foreign policies in the Middle East and elsewhere, a positive program of global health engagement might provide an opportunity for the United States to support true international cooperation and provide leadership. The human resources are needed, but what is needed more is an outlet for public diplomacy by health professionals in U.S. foreign policy.

Conclusion

Global health has gained significant momentum through an expanded roster of partners, funding sources, and policy developments. Along with the disease challenges of globalization, this momentum has created new opportunities and challenges for governance structures. What is clear is that the sovereign state cannot protect the health and security of its domestic population without engaging globally and collaborating with other state entities, multinational organizations, the private sector, and non-governmental health groups. Health is a cross-cutting issue in foreign policy. Governments increasingly recognize they must prioritize health as a source of international security and develop coherent policies at the international as well as the national level. The twenty-first century is unfolding with health at the forefront of the U.N.'s global concerns, and, we may hope for critical new advances in global cooperation in health and development that will support a more cohesive and peaceful global community.

Notes

1. Kent Buse & Kelley Lee, *Business and Global Health Governance* (Key Issues in Global Health Governance Discussion Paper No. 5, at 14, Dec. 2005).

2. The Secretary-General, *A More Secure World: Our Shared Responsibility,* Report of the High-level Panel on Threats, Challenges and Change, P 57, U.N. Doc A/59/565 (Dec. 2, 2004) [hereinafter A More Secure World].

3. Oslo Ministerial Declaration, Global Health: A Pressing Foreign Policy Issue of Our Time, 369 Lancet 1373–78 (2007).

4. Laurie Garrett, The Challenge of Global Health, 86 Foreign Aff. 14, 14 (2007).

5. Thomas E. Novotny, Education and Careers in Global Health, in *Understanding Global Health* 318–19 (William H. Markle et al., eds., 2007).

6. America's Vital Interest in Global Health: Protecting Our People, Enhancing Our Economy, and Advancing Our International Interests 4 (Bd. on Int'l Health, Inst. of Med. 1997) [hereinafter Vital Interest].

7. David Fidler, Global Health Governance: Overview of the Role of International Law in Protecting and Promoting Global Public Health (Key Issues in Global Health Governance Discussion Paper No. 3, at 47, May 2002.

8. Garrett, supra note 4, at 14.

9. Fidler, supra note 7, at 9.

10. William H. Markel et al., Extensively Drug-Resistant Tuberculosis: An Isolation Order, Public Health Powers, and a Global Crisis, 298 J. Am. Med. Ass'n 83–86 (2007).

11. Thomas Zeltner et al., World Health Organization, Tobacco Control Activities at the World Health Organization: Report of the Committee of Experts on Tobacco Industry Documents (2000).

12. Global Outbreak Alert and Response System, http://www.who.int/csr/outbreaknetwork/en (last visited Oct. 4, 2007).

13. World Health Organization, Health-for-all Policy for the Twenty-first Century art. 1, WHO Doc. A51/5 (May 11, 1998).

14. Derek Yach et al., The Global Burden of Chronic Diseases: Overcoming Impediments to Prevention and Control, 291 J. Am. Med. Ass'n 2616, 2616 (2004).

15. Richard Dodgson et al., Global Health Governance: A Conceptual Review (Key Issues in Global Health Governance Discussion Paper No. 1, at 12, Feb. 2002).

16. Steven A. Dimoff, The Helms-Biden Agreement: An Analysis of Proposed Conditions Affecting U.S. Assessed Contributions to the United Nations, UNA-USA, May 1998, http://www.unausa.org/site/pp.aspx?c=fvKRI8MPJpF&bl=475009.

17. Vital Interest, supra note 13.

18. Laurie Garrett, Council on Foreign Rel., HIV and National Security: Where are the Links? 12 (2005), p. 55.

19. World Health Org., Issues Paper: Invest in Health, Build a Safer Future 2 (2007), http://www.who.int/world-health-day/2007/issues paper/en/index.html.

20. Id. at 2.

21. Robin Coupland, Security, Insecurity and Health, 85 Bull. of WHO 181, 181 (2007).

22. Daniele Anastasion, The Role of Health in a Security-Obsessed World, SAIS Rev. 175, 175–76 (2004).

23. Ronald Labonte & Ted Schrecker, Foreign Policy Matters: A Normative View of the G8 and Population Health, 85 Bull. of WHO 185, 185 (2007).

24. Rebecca Katz & Daniel A. Singer, Health and Security in Foreign Policy, 85 Bull. of WHO 233, 233–34 (2007).

25. Mary Robinson, The Value of a Human Rights Perspective in Health and Foreign Policy, 85 Bull. of WHO 241, 241–42 (2007).

26. Liam Donaldson & Nicholas Banatvala, Health Is Global: Proposals for a U.K. Government-wide Strategy, 369 Lancet 857, 857 (2007).

27. Ilona Kickbusch et al., Global Health Diplomacy: The Need for New Perspectives, Strategic Approaches and Skills in Global Health, 85 Bull. of WHO 230 (2007).

28. European Perspectives on Global Health: A Policy Glossary 5 (Ilona Kickbusch & Graham Lister, eds., 2006.

29. Foreign Policy Taking Up the Challenges of Global Health: Agenda for Action, http://www.norvege.no/policy/peace/peace/helse+og+utenrikspolitkk+-+Agenda+for+Action.htm (last visited Nov. 29, 2007).

30. President's Emergency Plan for AIDS Relief, http://www.pepfar.gov.

31. Fitzhugh Mullan, Responding to the Global HIV/AIDS Crisis: A Peace Corps for Health, 297 J. Am. Med. Ass'n 744, 744 (2007).

16

The Punishment and Prevention of Genocide: The International Criminal Court as a Benchmark of Progress and Need

Christine H. Chung

SIXTY YEARS AGO, THE DRAFTERS OF THE GENOCIDE CONVEN-tion envisioned the creation of an "international judicial organ" that would be available to try individuals accused of committing genocide and other crimes under international law. Article VI of the Convention itself specified the possibility that persons charged with genocide be tried by such "international penal tribunal as may have jurisdiction" by agreement of contracting States.[1] Today, following decades of a difficult "birthing" process, the permanent international criminal tribunal antic-ipated by the drafters of that Convention—the International Criminal Court (ICC)—has been in operation for nearly five years. The ICC has issued eleven arrest warrants relating to war crimes and crimes against humanity committed during three of the gravest ongoing conflicts in the world: in the Darfur region of the Sudan, in northern Uganda, and in the Democratic Republic of Congo (DRC). . . .

A handful of years are a slim record upon which to begin reaching any conclusions. Still, in the spirit of commemorating the negotiation and adoption of the Genocide Convention, this article offers observa-tions on the manner in which the earliest operations of the "international judicial organ" foreseen by the Convention drafters demonstrate and

Reprinted from *Case Western Reserve Journal of International Law* 40, no. 1 (2008): 227–243. © 2008 Case Western Reserve University. Reprinted by permission of the publisher.

underscore: (1) progress in the mission of punishing and preventing genocide and other crimes of international concern, and (2) the difficulties and next challenges in accomplishing the Genocide Convention's objectives.

Progress

On the progress front, the ICC has begun fulfilling at least three core aims of the Genocide Convention drafters.

Strengthening of the International Rule of Law

Most fundamentally, the ICC represents and fosters international consensus supporting a rule of law that defines genocide and other mass atrocities as crimes condemned by the civilized world. The Genocide Convention expressed an agreement among States that genocide is a crime under international law and obligated ratifying States to adopt domestic legislation criminalizing genocide, as defined in the Convention. Nearly fifty years after the adoption of the Convention, in signing the treaty at Rome that created the ICC, States again reached consensus that genocide is a crime, under the same definition set forth in the Convention.[2] The signatory States also placed war crimes and crimes against humanity within the ICC's jurisdiction, judging that these crimes, like genocide, were among "the most serious crimes of concern to the international community as a whole."[3] The growing number of countries that continue to ratify the Rome Statute—over 100 countries—represents the continuing commitment to a rule of law that criminalizes genocide, as well as an expanded consensus that war crimes and crimes against humanity are also crimes of international concern. As with the Genocide Convention, ICC ratification serves as a catalyst for harmonizing domestic standards to an international rule of law, because States that ratify the Rome Statute often also adopt ICC definitions of crimes in their domestic legislation.

The building of the consensus expressed by the Genocide Convention grows in at least three dimensions via the ICC ratification process. First, there is the fact that through joining the ICC, additional countries have accepted the norm that genocide and other mass atrocities are indeed crimes deserving of international judgment and denunciation. Japan, which recently joined the ICC, is one of eighteen countries that never ratified the Genocide Convention, but have elected to ratify the Rome Statute

Second, through ratification of the Rome Statute, States bind themselves to enforce the international rule of law within their own borders and agree that, if they fail, the ICC may intervene.[4] This simple commitment represents a huge innovation. Like Odysseus, who bound himself to the mast in anticipation of hearing the Sirens, States that join the ICC have foreseen the possibility of their own frailty and have committed themselves to the fail-safe remedy. Member States pledge to support the permanent international criminal court in its work by means of an international cooperation network. The States also express, through the 128 articles of the Rome Statute, consensus upon the specific procedures, standards, and cooperation mechanisms by which perpetrators of genocide, crimes against humanity, and war crimes should be brought to justice under universal standards of fairness. The Rome Statute, in short, creates both a court and an international criminal justice system.

Finally, the ICC's existence simultaneously strengthens the instrument that will always constitute the primary "line of defense" against genocide and other crimes under international law—domestic punishment of those crimes. The Genocide Convention recognized that the operations of any international judicial organ must be complementary to the enforcement efforts of States. The ICC, likewise, complements national enforcement mechanisms in that it possesses authority to act only when States are "unwilling" or "unable" to do so. By its existence and operations, however, the ICC raises the bar of domestic accountability, even while pursuing international prosecutions. For example, knowledge that the ICC was ready to exercise its jurisdiction created the incentive for the then-transitional government of the DRC to invite an investigation into crimes committed in that country which otherwise would have escaped scrutiny. The DRC government self-referred the investigation of crimes allegedly committed in the DRC to the ICC after ICC Prosecutor Luis Moreno-Ocampo made public statements that he was prepared to use *proprio motu* powers to initiate an investigation.[5]

The spread of the domestic enactment of ICC standards also strengthens State enforcement. In the United Kingdom, the International Criminal Court Act of 2001, which was enacted in connection with the ratification of the Rome Statute, became the basis for military charges brought in 2005 against soldiers in the British Army for allegedly committing war crimes against civilian prisoners in Iraq. In the Netherlands, Dutch prosecutors publicly identified statements in which the Prosecutor of the ICC had encouraged the investigation of the "criminal business" of war, as motivation for two domestic prosecutions relating to war crimes and human rights abuses in the Middle East and Africa: one in which a Dutch businessman was charged with furnishing chemicals to Saddam Hussein, and another in which another Dutch citizen was alleged to have provided support, including militia, to Charles Taylor.

The Systematic Review of Allegations of Genocide and Other Mass Atrocities

A second area of progress that the drafters of the Genocide Convention might identify from the existence and operation of the ICC is the circumstance that there exists for the first time a judicial entity that systematically reviews allegations of mass atrocities to identify situations for investigation and prosecution. One wonders if the Convention drafters would have been gratified or horrified to learn that the ICC Office of the Prosecutor has received thousands of communications and referrals in its first years of operation—from individuals, organizations, and nations in over one hundred countries—recommending investigation and prosecution of atrocities allegedly committed around the world. The achievement is that the ICC now reviews each of these communications and referrals. It determines whether the communications and referrals contain allegations deserving further investigation under the legal standards adopted in the Rome Statute and thus representing, at a minimum, the consensus of the member States of the ICC. As a result of this legal analysis, and of further culling based on its mandate of focusing upon the gravest crimes, the ICC has selected some situations for investigation (thus far, in the DRC, in northern Uganda, in the Darfur region of the Sudan, and in the Central African Republic), while declining others (e.g., in Venezuela and Iraq).

It is impossible, of course, to achieve perfect consensus about which investigations and prosecutions should be accepted or declined. The advance is that a worldwide clearinghouse for the evaluation of allegations of genocide, war crimes, and crimes against humanity, is operational. Further, the evaluation proceeds under known legal standards, to permit an examination of the merits of the decisions ultimately made.

Prevention of Genocide and Other Mass Crimes

A final area in which the negotiators of the Genocide Convention might view progress in fulfilling their long-term objectives is the ICC's effort to advance the most difficult aim of the Genocide Convention: the prevention of genocide. In each of the first three investigations it opened, the Office of the Prosecutor undertook to carry out investigation and prosecution in the midst of an ongoing conflict that qualified as one of the worst in the world. In doing so, the Office of the Prosecutor opened itself to every possible complication that accompanies an attempt to carry on a criminal investigation in the middle of a war. These include, most notably, the struggles of conducting field investigations within the war zone, of providing adequate protection to victims and witnesses within that zone, and of keeping ICC field staff safe. In the most extreme case, in Darfur, the Prosecutor decided not to conduct any investigations in Darfur itself because of the danger to victims and witnesses.[6] The perceived benefit of each of the early ICC interventions— a benefit outweighing the disadvantages—was the possibility of maximizing the opportunity to have a preventive effect on the conflict, rather than letting the violence run its course before attempting to punish the perpetrators of past atrocities.

An important qualification is that the Office of the Prosecutor did not target crimes committed as part of ongoing conflicts because of any unrealistic expectation that the ICC, in and of itself, can end violence through its interventions. Rather, it was hoped that by being prompt in pursuing its mandate of seeking accountability and naming perpetrators, the ICC could maximize the prospect that States and other parties could capitalize upon the ICC intervention to aid in ending the conflicts and deterring further crimes.

As might be expected, each situation has been unique and the progress has been varied. In Darfur, where the violence has been the most intense, the Sudanese government has resisted any type of international intervention and State actors are among the alleged perpetrators. It was never anticipated that the ICC intervention would, in itself, end the violence, and no effort thus far—whether in the realm of peacekeeping, negotiation, or enforcement—has curbed that conflict. Nonetheless, as is described below, the international community may be neglecting an important opportunity by failing to press for execution of the ICC arrest warrants naming Sudanese nationals and thereby potentially to deter current and future perpetrators in Darfur. In Uganda, the issuance of ICC warrants of arrest appears to have had a strong positive effect. The warrants of arrest naming the top leadership of the Lord's Resistance Army (LRA) are seen to have motivated that leadership to enter into negotiations to end the twenty-year war that the LRA had been waging against the Ugandan government. Whether the LRA leadership will face arrest and accountability remains unclear, but an undoubted benefit flowing from the ICC intervention is that hundreds of thousands of refugees from the war are now returning to their homes, croplands, and schools after spending years living in camps for the internally displaced.

The foregoing suggests just a few of the ways in which the most recent instrument of international justice—the ICC—represents the truly significant gains that have been made, since the Genocide Convention was adopted, in pursuing and fulfilling the mission of punishing and preventing genocide and other mass atrocities. Certainly, there is much to suggest that the drafters of the Genocide Convention would have been impressed that States, albeit after six additional decades of discussion of the need to punish crimes under international law, reached the breadth and depth of consensus reflected in the Rome Statute. The fact that the ICC is now fully operational, despite all of the difficulties during negotiations and efforts to frustrate implementation of the Rome Statute,[7] represents the fulfillment of the fundamental aspiration of the Genocide Convention: that an "international judicial organ" be vested by States with the authority to try perpetrators of crimes against mankind.

Need

ICC operations to date also underscore the difficulties and challenges of seeking accountability for the world's worst crimes. It is not a difficult exercise to identify the failures and shortcomings in ongoing efforts to punish and deter perpetrators of the world's gravest crimes. Still, examining what the ICC has been able to do in its first years—and what it has not done or cannot do—sharpens the exercise. This is because the ICC, since the inception of the idea for such a court, has shouldered the highest expectations of those who support accountability for crimes under international law. It lives in the hopes and imaginations of many as the ultimate instrument of justice. At the same time, the ICC was never intended, nor designed to be, a cure-all instrument. The limitations on its authority, as well as its powers, were carefully drawn and agreed upon by the States at Rome.

The result has been that even in its first years of operation, and despite the not inconsiderable achievements of the ICC to date, an "expectations gap" has been revealed—a space between what observers aspire for the ICC to do and what the ICC has accomplished or attempted. Analyzing the gap, and the degree to which expectations about the ICC are realistic, begins to suggest the next set of challenges for enforcing an international rule of law. Two challenges bear consideration, particularly in light of the preoccupations and aspirations of those who negotiated and drafted the Genocide Convention. These challenges are to continue to build a truly global system of justice, based in complementarity, and to muster and strengthen the political will necessary to make that system effective in combating impunity.

Strengthening of a Global System of Accountability

First, the ICC has served to emphasize that real progress in the fight against impunity will come through deepening and reinforcing a truly global system of accountability, rather than reliance on the latest instrument or "international judicial organ." Some aspects of the ICC's design—its permanence and theoretically global jurisdiction—can promote an expectation that the ICC will rapidly bring justice to numerous perpetrators of mass crimes. The degree of selectivity with which the ICC has proceeded thus far—ten persons named in warrants of arrest in four massive conflicts—should serve to moderate any such expectation.

Over time, the ICC will be able to increase its volume of cases, but an important outer limit exists: the ICC, like every internationalized tribunal before it, will never have the capacity to investigate and prosecute more than a small fraction of the perpetrators who fall into the category of the "most responsible." States determine the budgets of internationalized courts and it is both rational and likely that States will not fund more than a limited number of representative prosecutions in any single judicial organ. In the ICC's case, the member States approve the anticipated number of situations and trials during the budgeting process, and thus the workload of the Court and the number of cases it can commence are regulated—not by the Prosecutor or the judges—but by the funders.

The State funders' requirements can be stringent. In the case of Darfur, the investigation was referred to the ICC by the exceptional measure of a U.N. Security Council Resolution. The Security Council resolution that referred the Darfur investigation, after stating the Security Council's decision and urging all States to cooperate fully in assisting the ICC, simultaneously provided that none of the expenses of the Darfur investigation would be borne by the United Nations or offset by means other than voluntary contributions by States. Funding constraints also mean that occurrences that are common in law enforcement can trigger budgeting crises. For example, when co-defendants are arrested separately, and separate trials follow, the resource drain correspondingly can double, and the next prosecutorial priority may be crowded out.

The lesson is that the perspective of the States, and the scale of the undertaking they are willing to support, must temper expectations and planning in the ongoing fight against impunity. So far, the ICC has opened investigations arising from four vast and distinct conflicts, based on a smaller budget than the current budgets of the ICTY or ICTR. If one accepts that the ICC's resources are unlikely to be increased by multiples in upcoming years, one must also accept that the ICC is unlikely to pursue anything near the number of prosecutions, in any one situation, that the ICTY or ICTR achieved. As a matter of political reality, and to maximize its unique impact, the ICC must spread its work across numerous different situations, but within each situation focus more stringently on the most responsible perpetrators.

The more promising solution to the inevitable and persistent "impunity gap" is to use the work of the ICC to reinforce the global system of justice, rather than expecting the ICC to grow into an assembly line. The Genocide Convention itself suggests this solution because it recognized that the efforts of any "international judicial organ" should supplement those of other competent courts. In 1948, the only available alternative was a competent tribunal in the State in which the crimes were committed. Sixty years later, and likely beyond the imaginings of the Genocide Convention drafters, there is a menu of judicial mechanisms to bring perpetrators of genocide and other crimes under international law to justice. The *ad hoc* tribunals have tried cases, including cases of genocide, arising from the conflicts in Yugoslavia and Rwanda, hybrid tribunals are operating in Sierra Leone and Cambodia, and domestic prosecutions of alleged war criminals and violators of human rights—such as the prosecutions of Augusto Pinochet and Alberto Fujimori—are gaining in number and credibility. Initiatives have expanded well beyond any single "international judicial organ," and they share, in addition to a common mission, a growing body of law and experience.

The challenge therefore is to build the complementarity advocated in the Genocide Convention and the Rome Statute: to strengthen the global system of justice by maximizing the effectiveness and impact of the efforts of the combination of judicial organs addressing crimes under international law. Each component of the system is already reinforcing the others, and the objectives of punishment and prevention are best served by actively promoting this reinforcement. The scope, quality, and effectiveness of domestic enforcement work are enhanced by the growth and acceptance of international criminal law standards. Proceedings conducted by the ICC and other internationalized tribunals provide starting points and blueprints for proceedings involving perpetrators in the same conflicts who are tried domestically. The ICC can serve as a strong advocate of the international rule of law, as well as a global monitor of non-compliance, making it easier to prioritize and divide the seemingly limitless work of devising and implementing remedies, including the work of prosecuting violators.

The suggestion is not that all judicial instruments will work equally well. The constant factor, from 1948 to date, is the vastness of impunity and the impossibility of reaching all perpetrators. What has changed, through the robust growth of initiatives to enforce the international rule of law, is the opportunity and responsibility to evaluate and compare outcomes, and to be active and strategic in promoting the combination of remedies that can best advance the objective.

Constancy in Political Will

The second challenge in preventing and punishing genocide and other mass crimes, as further exposed by the early operations of the ICC, is the ultimate dependence of the success of each anti-impunity instrument—including the ICC—upon the political will of States. The Genocide Convention both reflected a compact among States to combat genocide and diagnosed that any success in combating the "odious scourge of genocide" would depend on continuing "international cooperation" furnished by States. It can indeed seem a dull truism to declare that mass atrocities can only be prevented and punished through State cooperation and action. But again, the ICC experience is instructive because the expectation seems to have been that this new, permanent "judicial organ" would somehow magically circumvent the hardest problem of mobilizing sufficient will (on the part of States in particular) to compel alleged perpetrators to be brought to justice.

The most conspicuous ICC-related example of the hard reality that State support will always determine the success or failure of an effort to bring accountability is the following circumstance: the ICC has obtained the arrest of only one individual who has been named in an ICC warrant of arrest who was not previously in State custody. Of the three individuals currently in detention at The Hague, only Mathieu Ngudjolo Chui, a former DRC militia leader, was arrested following issuance of an ICC arrest warrant. Thomas Lubanga Dyilo and Germain Katanga were transferred into ICC custody following domestic detention in the DRC. Seven alleged perpetrators—including all of the individuals charged in the course of the Darfur and Uganda investigations—remain at large. These include two Sudanese nationals named in warrants of arrest in April 2007: Ahmad Mohammad Harun, the former Minister of State for the Interior in the Government of Sudan and the alleged orchestrator of the arming and funding of Arab Militia in Darfur, and Ali Muhammad Ali Abd-Al Rahman (known as Ali Kushayb), an alleged Janjaweed militia leader. Also named in as-yet-unexecuted warrants of arrest are Joseph Kony, the leader of the LRA, and three other top LRA commanders, Vincent Otti, Okot Odhiambo, and Dominic Ongwen. Bosco Ntaganda, a co-defendant of Lubanga Dyilo, is at liberty and remains an active and high-ranking militia leader in the DRC.

The misperception is that the ICC is the party responsible for executing these arrests and for moving the Darfur and Uganda cases past the pre-trial stage. The fact is that the ICC, by conscious design, was never given a police force or authority to arrest. Rather, the States, via the Rome Statute, retained this responsibility. This means that the mission of rendering punishment for atrocities—at the ICC as at any other judicial mechanism—cannot move forward absent state support in furtherance of investigations and cases.

The history and status of the ICC's intervention in Darfur illustrates the division of responsibilities and the continued centrality of the issue of political will. The Security Council's referral of the situation in Darfur to the ICC for investigation in March 2005 was an achievement in expressing an international consensus that the perpetrators of the horrific violence and crimes in Darfur should be held accountable. When, in April 2007, the ICC issued the arrest warrants, those warrants named individuals squarely within the power of the Sudanese government to turn over. Harun is currently serving as the Minister of Humanitarian Affairs, and Kushayb, according to the Sudanese government, was made to face domestic charges proceedings, of which he was reportedly acquitted. The Sudanese government has stated repeatedly that it will surrender no Sudanese national to the ICC's jurisdiction.

The question is now by what mechanism will Harun or Kushayb—or for that matter any other individuals who might be named in any warrants relating to the atrocities in Darfur—be brought to face justice? What steps, if any, will be taken to enforce U.N. Security Council Resolution 1593, which both referred the situation in Darfur for ICC investigation and obligated the Sudanese government to cooperate "fully" in the ICC's investigation? Will States and the Security Council accept the stalemate between the ICC and the Sudanese government? The resolution to all of these questions, and therefore the success of the overall objective of bringing accountability in Darfur, lies not in the hands of the ICC, but within the power of the Sudanese government and the international community.

In Uganda, the question is also whether sufficient resolve exists or can be galvanized in furtherance of the mandate to bring justice. The remarkable achievement of a permanent end to violence in Northern Uganda may soon be realized, but nearly three years after issuance of warrants of arrest naming the top LRA leadership, the leadership remains at large, and progress toward the aim of accountability is at a standstill. Joseph Kony and other LRA leaders continue to deny having perpetrated any crimes and to refuse to release abducted women and children. These leaders have offered peace only at the price of obtaining immunity from ICC prosecution.

The point is that even the advent of new and potentially powerful mechanisms for promoting accountability will not obviate the need to continue tackling the hardest and most eternal problem: that of generating the political will within the international community to bring perpetrators to justice. Whether the perpetrator is Radovan Karadic, or Ahmad Harun, or Joseph Kony, an inability to arrest, as just one example, utterly frustrates the core objective of punishing crimes under international law. It renders theoretical any goal of rendering judgments or meting out punishment.

The difficulty of galvanizing international support for arrests and prosecutions cannot be equated, however, to a lack of progress in the war against impunity. Each judicial organ that embarks on the mission of bringing accountability adds another instrument that can exert moral authority, and thus promote consensus that perpetrators should be brought to account. The power of exposing violence to be criminal under an international rule of law, and of naming perpetrators, cannot be underestimated. The ICC, because it stands as a representative of 106 States, should be the institution most capable of exerting moral suasion resulting in State action. Still, if States, fail to provide the support necessary to advance the cases commenced in the ICC, they will face questions about the depth of their commitment to the goal of actually ending impunity.

The challenge is for all actors who play a strong role in advocating accountability for crimes against mankind—States, the United Nation, regional organizations, civil society, the media, and grassroots organizations—to exert the maximum possible pressure on States to perform their responsibilities of supporting international and domestic mechanisms for protecting populations. It is vital that, at a minimum, the international community carry through criminal justice initiatives that it has directly prioritized or commenced, such as in Darfur. It is also critical that States fulfill obligations of cooperation they have undertaken with respect to the punishment of crimes under international law, by treaty, or by any other means.

The alternative—of permitting these obligations to remain unfulfilled or half-fulfilled—can only diminish the rule of law. It is predictable, for example, that it might be more difficult to muster the will to arrest an alleged perpetrator than to agree in principle to do so. States cannot neglect a treaty obligation to effectuate arrest, however, simply because a Court has specified alleged perpetrators, by exercising independent judgment. The Prosecutor of the ICC has reported that in reaction to the warrants of arrest issued in the Darfur situation, certain States or stakeholders in the ICC urged him to target lower level perpetrators who might be easier to arrest than ministers of state or militia leaders. The choice is starkly presented: (1) to send a message that powerful perpetrators, at a minimum, can expect impunity, despite the expressed resolve of the U.N. Security Council that punishment be meted; or (2) to find the will and the means to execute the arrest warrants, and thereby reinforce the deterrent effect of the ICC, for perpetrators at all levels of responsibility. No court will pursue precisely the investigations and cases that the States might agree upon or prefer, and it is precisely this circumstance that will compel States to evaluate the advantages and disadvantages of either supporting judicial decision-making as a matter of principle, or of appearing to make politically expedient selections on a case by case basis.

Conclusion

The Genocide Convention referenced, very much as a prospect for the future, a single "international judicial organ" that would render judgment regarding the most serious crime of international concern, genocide. Sixty years later, it seems that the drafters' aspirations of advancement were simultaneously too modest and too lofty. Today, there exists a network of judicial mechanisms, domestic and internationalized, for punishing and deterring crimes, including genocide, under international law. This network is fully engaged in strengthening an international rule of law by, among other things, punishing crimes and perpetrators who, in prior times, would never have faced justice. At the same time, the ability of courts to render judgments and impose punishment for the gravest of crimes, even in the case of the Court which fulfilled the hope of an "international judicial organ," remains firmly tied to the will and power of States to compel the perpetrators of those crimes to be brought to court. Each advance in the ongoing mission of fighting impunity necessitates recreating the momentous achievement of sixty years ago: compelling and expressing a consensus that the civilized world finds certain crimes utterly repugnant to humanity and therefore necessary to punish and eliminate.

Notes

1. Convention on the Prevention and Punishment of the Crime of Genocide, art. 6, Dec. 9, 1948, 102 Stat. 3045, 78 U.N.T.S. 277 [hereinafter *Genocide Convention*].

2. Compare *Genocide Convention,* at art. 2, with Rome Statute of the International Criminal Court, art. 6, July 17, 1998, 2187 U.N.T.S. 90, 37 I.L.M. 1002 (entered into force July 1, 2002) [hereinafter *Rome Statute*]. Crimes against humanity and war crimes are placed within the jurisdiction of the ICC in the Rome Statute at articles 7 and 8, respectively. *Id.*

3. See *Rome Statute,* supra note 2, at art. 5.

4. See *Rome Statute,* supra note 2, at art. 17 (providing that a case can only be deemed admissible, and thus susceptible of prosecution by the ICC, if a State which otherwise would have jurisdiction is "unwilling or unable" to prosecute it).

5. See Luis Moreno-Ocampo, *The International Criminal Court: Seeking Global Justice,* 40 CASE W. RES. J. INT'L L. 215 (2008). Under the Rome Statute, the Prosecutor may initiate an investigation but if he or she does so, the judges of a Pre-Trial Chamber must also authorize the investigation. See *Rome Statute,* supra note 2, at art. 15. Investigations may also be commenced by means of referral by a State Party, or referral by the U.N Security Council. See *id.* at arts. 13, 14.

6. See The Office of the Prosecutor of the Int'l Criminal Court, *Third Report of the Prosecutor of the International Criminal Court to the U.N. Security Council Pursuant to UNSCR 1593,* at 2 (June 14, 2006), available at http://www.icc-cpi.int/library/cases/OTP_ReportUNSC_3-Darfur_English.pdf.

7. The most well-known opposition has come from the U.S. government, which passed legislation forbidding the cooperation of governmental agencies with the ICC, and so-called Article 98 agreements, conditioning the ability of other governments to receive U.S. aid upon agreement not to surrender to the ICC any U.S. national named in an ICC arrest warrant. See American Service-members' Protection Act of 2002, 22 U.S.C. § 7421-7433 (2007).

17

The Role of the International Criminal Court in Enforcing International Criminal Law

Philippe Kirsch

FOR EXPERTS ON HUMAN RIGHTS IT IS CLEAR THAT THE PROTECtion of individuals from violations of human rights and humanitarian law requires appropriate mechanisms to enforce the law. For decades, international law lacked sufficient mechanisms to hold individuals accountable for the most serious international crimes. Naturally, like any other crimes, punishment for grave breaches of the Geneva Conventions or for violations of the Genocide Convention or the customary law of war crimes and crimes against humanity depended primarily on national courts. The problem is that it is precisely when the most serious crimes were committed that national courts were least willing or able to act because of widespread or systematic violence or because of involvement of agents of the State in the commission of crimes. If you look at the past to the best known historical events of that kind—Nazi Germany, Rwanda, the former Yugoslavia, Cambodia—the governments themselves or their agents were involved in the commission of those crimes. And so the failures of national courts in these contexts protected perpetrators with impunity. To prevent impunity in those situations, it is necessary to enforce international justice when national systems are unwilling or unable to act.

The first actions taken by the international community were to create ad hoc tribunals in such situations. The first tribunals were, of

Originally published in *American University International Law Review* 22 (2007): 539–547. © 2007 American University. Reprinted by permission of the publisher.

course, those of Nuremberg and Tokyo after World War II. Then, more recently, the United Nations set up tribunals for Rwanda and the former Yugoslavia. These tribunals were extremely important. They were pioneers. They showed that international justice could work, but they all possessed several limitations.

One is that only a few States participated in their creation. The Nuremberg and Tokyo tribunals were set up by the victorious Allied powers after World War II, and the Rwanda and Yugoslavia tribunals were created by the Security Council. There are also other limitations. Ad hoc tribunals are limited to specific geographic locations. They respond primarily to events in the past. Their establishment involves extensive costs and delays. Last but not least, their creation depended, every time, on the political will of the international community at the time. And so in some cases there was action; in some cases there was nothing. As a result, their ability to punish perpetrators of international crimes and to deter future perpetrators has been limited. Eventually, a permanent truly international court was necessary to respond to the most serious international crimes and to overcome the limitations of the ad hoc tribunals.

In the summer of 1998, the U.N. General Assembly convened the Rome Conference to fill this essential need by establishing the ICC. In creating the ICC, States were particularly concerned with guaranteeing the Court's underlying legitimacy. Unlike the ad hoc tribunals, the ICC is the first and only tribunal that was created by an international treaty, which enabled all States to participate in its creation. All States were invited to participate in the negotiations of the statute and the vast majority—160—did so. There was a genuine effort to seek wide agreement among States without compromising the key values and objectives behind a fair and impartial court. Efforts towards universal acceptance were largely achieved. Eventually, on July 17, 1998, the Statute was approved by 120 States.

After the Rome Conference, a Preparatory Commission met for over three and a half years. It was charged with developing the Court's subsidiary instruments, notably, the Rules of Procedure and Evidence and the Elements of Crimes. It should be noted that the Rules of Procedure and Evidence for every other international criminal tribunal were developed by the judges in those tribunals. In the case of the ICC, they were developed by the States, again because States wanted to ensure that the system underlying the operation of the ICC would be as tight as possible. But it is clear that since the ICC would have prospective jurisdiction over then unknown situations, it was impossible for the States to know what exactly the ICC would deal with. Therefore it was absolutely vital for States to ensure that the ICC would be a purely judicial court.

Out of the desire to ensure as wide acceptance as possible, all decisions taken by the Preparatory Commission were taken by consensus—by general agreement. That included the adoption of both the Rules of Procedure and Evidence and the Elements of Crimes. By this method of consensus, the Preparatory Commission contributed significantly to international support for the Court.

At the end of 2000, the deadline for signature of the Rome Statute, 139 States had signed the Statute, which was about twenty more than those that had voted for the Statute in 1998. This is a unique case in the history of a treaty negotiation. Normally what happens is that you vote for an instrument at the time of the conference because it is easier and then forget about it because that is also easier. In the case of the ICC, the momentum to have a functioning Court in place was such that the number of signatures was higher than the number of votes at the conference.

In the eight years since the adoption of the Rome Statute, 102 countries representing broad geographical diversity have ratified or acceded to the Statute. It is a very good pace for a treaty establishing an international institution, in particular an international institution that requires considerable modifications in the legislation of States that have ratified the Statute.

The Features of the International Criminal Court

A common misperception about the Court is that the ICC has universal jurisdiction. Its jurisdiction is limited to crimes committed on the territory of or by nationals of States which have voluntarily consented to its jurisdiction. These bases of jurisdiction—territory of the crime and the nationality of the perpetrator—are the most firmly established bases of criminal jurisdiction.

The Court's jurisdictional regime recognizes the special role of the Security Council in maintaining peace and security. Under the Statute, the Security Council may refer situations to the Court so that it no longer has to create ad hoc tribunals as it did for the former Yugoslavia and Rwanda. The Security Council has already used this power when it referred the situation in Darfur, Sudan, to the Court—Sudan not being a Party to the Rome Statute. The Security Council, acting under Chapter

VII of the U.N. Charter, may also defer an investigation or a prosecution for a period of one year.

The Court's jurisdiction is also limited temporally. It has jurisdiction only over events since its Statute entered into force on July 1, 2002. No crime committed before that time can be dealt with by the ICC.

The Court's subject matter jurisdiction covers the most serious international crimes. In that sense, although obviously the ICC deals with the most serious violations of human rights, it is not a human rights court in the traditional sense. It is a criminal court that is limited to genocide, crimes against humanity, and war crimes. The crimes contained in the Statute are well established in customary and conventional international law as well as national laws.

The Statute also provides that the Court has jurisdiction over the crime of aggression, but the Court will not exercise this jurisdiction until both a definition of aggression, and conditions for the exercise of jurisdiction are agreed upon. This has to happen through an amendment to the Statute, agreed to by the States Parties. Such amendment could occur at the earliest at a review conference to be held in 2009. Aggression was seen by many States as a symbolic crime—a crime that certainly was central to proceedings after World War II. It was a general view among States that if aggression were not committed, many other crimes would not be committed and therefore aggression had to be part of the Statute. However, there was no agreement on how aggression should be defined and there was certainly no agreement how to move from a declaration of aggression by States as an act covered by public international law to proceedings covering individuals having been involved in their crimes under international criminal law.

Even where the Court has jurisdiction, it will not necessarily act. This is the fundamental point that has to be understood about the ICC. The ICC is a court of last resort. It is intended to act only when national courts are unwilling or unable to carry out genuine proceedings. This is known as the principle of complementarity. Under this principle, a case will be inadmissible if it is being or has been investigated or prosecuted by a State with jurisdiction. In addition, a case will be inadmissible if it is not of sufficient gravity to justify action by the Court.

There is an exception under the principle of complementarity where the Court may act. This is when the State is unwilling or unable genuinely to carry out the investigation or prosecution. For example, if proceedings were undertaken solely to shield a person from criminal responsibility—and that can take different forms, which are indeed spelled out in the Statute—or if the proceedings were carried out in a manner inconsistent with an intent to bring the person to justice.

It follows from the concern of States to ensure that the Court would be a purely judicial institution and would act in a purely judicial way, that the guarantee of a fair trial and protection of the rights of the accused have paramount importance before the ICC. The Statute incorporates the fundamental provisions of the rights of the accused or the rights of the accused and due process common to national and international legal systems.

A particular feature of the ICC, which is different again from ad hoc tribunals, is the treatment given to victims. Victims have of course participated in other international proceedings, but largely as witnesses for the prosecutor or for the defense. In the case of the ICC, victims may participate in proceedings even when not called as witnesses. The Court also has the power to order reparations to victims including restitution, compensation, and rehabilitation. The ICC has the obligation to take into account the particular interests of victims of violence against women and children.

The International Criminal Court Today

Three States Parties have referred situations occurring on their own territories to the Court and in addition the Security Council has referred the situation in Darfur, Sudan, a non–State Party. After analyzing the referrals for jurisdiction and admissibility, the Prosecutor began investigations in three situations: Uganda, the Democratic Republic of the Congo, and Darfur, Sudan. The Prosecutor is also monitoring five other situations.

In March 2008, the first wanted person was surrendered to the Court. Mr. Thomas Lubanga Dyilo, a national of the Democratic Republic of the Congo, is alleged to have committed war crimes; namely, conscripting and enlisting children under the age of 15 and using them to participate actively in hostilities. The confirmation of charges against Mr. Lubanga is scheduled for September and if the charges are confirmed, the trial will begin thereafter.

Arrest warrants have also been issued in the situation in Uganda for five members of the Lord's Resistance Army, including its leader Joseph Kony. In that case, the alleged crimes against humanity and war crimes contained in the warrants include sexual enslavement, rape, intentionally attacking civilians, and the forced enlistment of child soldiers. The arrest warrants were initially issued under seal because of concerns about the security of victims and witnesses. The warrants were only made public once the Pre-Trial Chamber was satisfied that the Court had taken adequate measures to ensure security.

This illustrates a major difference between the ICC and other international tribunals, which by and large were dealing with crimes that had been committed in the past in the course of conflicts that were over. The ICC deals with crimes that continue to be committed in the course of conflicts that are ongoing. As a result, the ICC faces many challenges in particular in relation to its field activities and security.

The Future of the International Criminal Court

Finally, I would like to turn to what we can expect from the Court and from the wider system of international justice in the future. As investigations and trials proceed, the Court of course recognizes that it has the primary responsibility to demonstrate its credibility in practice through fair, impartial and efficient proceedings consistent with due process and proper administration of justice.

But the Court will never be able to end impunity alone. Its success will depend upon the support and commitment of States, international organizations, and civil society. The Court is complementary, as I said, to national jurisdictions and States will continue to have the primary responsibility to investigate and prosecute crimes—the Court being, as I said, only a court of last resort. There will be situations where national systems do not work properly or are unable to work. Because the Court's jurisdiction is limited to nationals and territories of States Parties, continued ratification of the Statute is essential to the Court having a truly global reach.

When the Court does act, it will require cooperation from States at all stages of the proceedings, such as by executing arrest warrants, providing evidence, and enforcing sentences of the convicted. Cooperation is absolutely crucial. For example, without sufficient support in arresting and surrendering persons, there can be no trials. Not only the States where crimes were committed or wanted persons are located can help, but all States in a position to provide cooperation can assist the Court. What States wanted when they created the ICC was a strong judicial institution, but not an institution that had at its disposal the normal tools of any national court. The ICC has no army. The ICC has no police. That's what States wanted, and—having wanted that system—now States need to cooperate with the Court to ensure that the system works.

International organizations also provide critical support for the Court. The support of the United Nations is particularly important in this regard. The United Nations and the Court cooperate on a regular basis, both in our field activities and our institutional relations. In October, 2004, the Secretary General of the United Nations and I concluded a relationship agreement, which was later supplemented by an agreement with the U.N. Mission in the Democratic Republic of Congo.

The Court is also developing its cooperation with regional organizations. In April, the Court entered into a cooperation agreement with the European Union. We hope to do the same with the African Union in the near future. There is also a role for cooperation by the Organization of American States ("OAS"). The OAS has been a strong proponent of the Court. Court officials, including myself, have participated in a number of meetings of the OAS.

Then we come to non-governmental organizations ("NGOs") and civil society more broadly, which are also instrumental to the work of the Court. NGOs have played a large role in urging ratification of the Statute. They have assisted States in developing legislation implementing the Rome Statute. Local NGOs may possess knowledge which is directly relevant to the Court's work in the field. NGOs also continue to have a critical role in disseminating information about and building awareness of the ICC.

Academic institutions have a particularly important role in relation to the Court. It is my experience, truly, that ignorance is one of the biggest obstacles to the success of the Court. Often, opposition to the Court is based on misconceptions which can be easily avoided. I believe that the more people understand the Court, the more it will be accepted. Of course, for that to happen there needs to be a dialogue. If there is no dialogue, the chances of mutual understanding are much lower.

In conclusion, I would say that the creation of the ICC was a truly historic achievement, more than fifty years in the making, but its creation was only the beginning. The Court now stands as a permanent institution capable of punishing perpetrators of the worst offenses known to humankind. Indeed, as early as 2004, the U.N. Secretary General stated that the Court "was already having an important impact by putting would-be violators on notice that impunity is not assured and serving as a catalyst for enacting national laws against the gravest international crimes."[1] Indeed, we at the Court who have a system of monitoring media reports on issues of international criminal justice and a fairly broad set of related issues do know how much notice is taken of the Court in many situations— some situations which are already under the jurisdiction of the Court and many other situations elsewhere.

To be fully effective, we must continue our efforts to ensure that the Court has the support necessary to dispense justice as fairly and efficiently as possible. If there is only one thing that you should retain from this piece, it is that the Court will do whatever it can to be as credible as possible, but that it will only succeed with concrete, tangible support.

Note

1. The Secretary-General, Report of the Secretary-General on the Rule of Law and Transitional Justice in Conflict and Post-Conflict Societies, ¶ 49, delivered to the Security Council, U.N. Doc. S/2004/616 (Aug. 3, 2004).

PART 6

International Organizations and the Future

Paul F. Diehl and Brian Frederking

WE BEGAN THIS BOOK BY NOTING THE DIFFERENT VIEWS OF international organizations. In the preceding chapters, we saw evidence to support both the realist and the idealist viewpoints. As a conclusion to the book, we look broadly at the potential of international organizations in global governance. The debate on the utility of international organizations is similar to national debates about the proper size and functions of government; this often includes a juxtaposition of government solutions against a reliance on other mechanisms such as the free market.

However one judges international organizations, there is always room for improvement. Various proposals for reform abound. The proposal from a blue-ribbon panel in late 2004 to "reform" the United Nations was only one in a string of efforts. In Chapter 18, Edward Luck reviews the multitude of UN reform proposals over the past half-century, including some whose ideas have led to significant changes in the way that body operates. Still, it is clear from his review and the lessons that he draws from them that UN reform is likely to fall short of the most ambitious plans and trigger even more calls for change in the future.

Finally, in Chapter 19, Campbell Craig analyzes the argument that the current condition of security interdependence may inevitably lead to some sort of world government. Craig provides a fitting conclusion to this collection by analyzing the arguments for and against this seemingly radical idea.

18

Reforming the United Nations: Lessons from a History of Progress

Edward C. Luck

THE NEVER-ENDING QUEST FOR REFORM, FOR IMPROVING the functioning of the United Nations, has been an integral part of the life of the world body since its earliest days. Indeed, one of the more controversial issues at the UN founding conference in San Francisco during spring 1945 was how the process of amending its Charter should be structured and when a general review conference of its provisions should be called.[1] Those delegations unhappy with some of the compromises reached in San Francisco, especially concerning the inequities of the veto power granted the "big five" permanent members (P-5) of the Security Council, wanted to schedule a general review relatively soon and to make the hurdles to amendment relatively low. The Soviet Union and, to a lesser extent, the other "big five" powers, on the other hand, naturally preferred to keep the barriers to Charter change relatively high.

On a more operational level, the UN had barely passed its second birthday before members of the U.S. Congress started to call for sweeping reforms of UN finance and administration. In October 1947 the Senate Expenditures Committee launched a study that found serious problems of overlap, duplication of effort, weak coordination, proliferating mandates and programs, and overly generous compensation of staff within the infant but rapidly growing UN system.[2] Similar complaints have been voiced countless times since.

Through the years, scores of independent commissions, governmental studies, and scholars have put forward literally hundreds of proposals

Reprinted from *The United Nations,* edited by Jean Krasno, pp. 359–397. © 2004 Lynne Rienner Publishers. Reprinted by permission of the publisher.

aimed at making the world body work better, decide more fairly, modify its mandate, or operate more efficiently. Not to be left behind by the reform bandwagon, successive Secretaries-General and units of the Secretariat have engaged in frequent, if episodic, bouts of self-examination and self-criticism, offering their own reform agendas.

What explains this apparently irresistible impulse for reforming the United Nations? Six factors suggest themselves:

1. Public institutions depend on recurring processes of criticism, reassessment, change, and renewal to retain their relevance and vitality. Reform is a sign of institutional health and dynamism, not a penalty for bad behavior.

2. Highly complex, decentralized, and multifaceted institutions, like the UN system, offer more targets for criticism and more opportunities for change. The temptation to tinker with the United Nations is only magnified by its high visibility, symbolic aura, and broad agenda.

3. The diversity of UN membership and the ambitious nature of its mandates make it highly likely that some constituencies will be seriously disappointed with its power-sharing arrangements and/or its accomplishments at any point in time. Persistent disappointment or feelings of disenfranchisement have often led to calls for reform.

4. As the world changes, so do the politics of the UN and the priorities of its Member States. In looking to the UN to fulfill new mandates that exceed its capacities, influential nongovernmental organizations (NGOs) often look to structural innovations or to the creation of new bodies to close the gap between expectations and capabilities. In both cases, proposals for reform usually follow.

5. Critics keep calling for reform in part because the United Nations has been so slow in delivering it. As the major powers hoped in San Francisco, formal institutional and structural reforms have proven hard to achieve in the UN system. The concerns about UN management and finance voiced by Congress in the late 1940s, moreover, were echoed a half-century later in the late 1990s.

6. The universality of the UN has fueled a dual pattern on the intergovernmental level: frequent calls for change by one Member State or group, followed by blocking moves by others with divergent interests or perspectives. At times, it seems as if every Member State is in favor of some sort of reform, but their individual notions of what this should entail differ so markedly as to make consensus on the direction reform should take hard to achieve.

These dynamics ensure almost continuous attention to the reform agenda, but much slower progress on the intergovernmental than Secretariat plane. If gauged by the sheer quantity of deliberations, debates, studies, and resolutions devoted to it, reform has become one of the enduring pastimes and primary products of the UN system. For example, from 1995 to 1997, the General Assembly was consumed with no less than five working groups on different aspects of reform, its president was engrossed in developing his own reform package, the Security Council reviewed its working methods, the Economic and Social Council (ECOSOC) adopted new procedures for relating to NGOs, and the new Secretary-General offered a comprehensive, if generally modest, plan for Secretariat reform. Before the dust had settled from these battles, the U.S.-led drive to have the Member State assessment scales revised took center stage in the Assembly from 1998 to 2000. And in September 2002, a reform study led by the Deputy Secretary-General called for aligning activities with the priorities voiced in the Millennium Declaration, trimming reporting, improving coordination, streamlining the budgeting process, and improving human resource management.

The hardest reforms to achieve, of course, are those entailing amendments to the UN Charter. As noted above, after a good deal of divisive debate, the big five managed at San Francisco to set the political bar quite high for any modifications of the Charter. Contending that their unity was key to making the new body more successful at securing the peace than its predecessor, the League of Nations, the five insisted on their having individual vetoes over amendments to the Charter. As a result, Article 108 stipulates:

> Amendments to the present Charter shall come into force for all Members of the United Nations when they have been adopted by a vote of two thirds of the members of the General Assembly and ratified in accordance with their respective constitutional processes by two thirds of the Members of the United Nations, including the permanent members of the Security Council.

Some of the other delegations not only objected to the inequity of these provisions but also fretted that those Member States in the minority opposing a particular amendment were given no recourse. Unlike the League Covenant, the Charter offers no mechanism for a dissatisfied member to withdraw from the UN—a practice that had disabled the League in the years preceding World War II. As a gesture toward these concerns, Article 109 offers the possibility of convening a general conference to review the Charter. While a number of delegations at San Francisco expected this to take place within the Organization's first decade, the polarization of the membership during the Cold War years made this look like an unpromising course.[3]

As discussed in the next section, the Charter has been amended only three times in over half a century. The Security Council has been enlarged once and the Economic and Social Council twice. The last of these moves took place almost three decades ago. So, while much of the public debate on reform continues to focus on possible Charter amendments, such as further expanding and diversifying the composition of the Security Council, in practice this has proved to be difficult to accomplish. Much of the action, instead, has occurred below this level and often with little publicity. The rules of procedure for the Security Council, the General Assembly, and ECOSOC have repeatedly been modified, as have their rosters of subsidiary bodies.[4] The latter, naturally, have been more prone to expansion to meet new priorities than to contraction as old mandates fade. The relationships among UN bodies have provided material for successive waves of reform aimed at greater coordination, coherence, or even unity of purpose among the UN's many and disparate pieces. The activities of one principal organ, the Trusteeship Council, were suspended when the task of eliminating it from the Charter appeared too ambitious.[5] Financial, administrative, and personnel matters have been the target of so many reform and retrenchment campaigns through the years that some wags in the Secretariat have suggested that the most useful reform would be to declare a moratorium on introspection and reform so that the UN's workers could get back to their assigned tasks. More serious, the dizzying diversity of initiatives and proposals labeled "reform" has led to some reflective inquiries about the proper meaning of the term.[6]

In theory, it would be analytically cleaner to adopt a relatively narrow and rigorous definition, such as the following: reform is the purposeful act of modifying the structure, composition, decisionmaking procedures, working methods, funding, or staffing of an institution in order to enhance its efficiency and/or effectiveness in advancing its core goals and principles. In terms of the UN, this would encompass those steps intended to make the Organization more efficient, more effective, and/or more capable of fulfilling the purposes laid out in Article 1 of its Charter, consistent with the principles expressed in Article 2.

In practice, however, many other endeavors have also been called "reform" by one party or another in the world body; in this field, as in others, the seemingly irresistible impulse at the UN to expand the definition and scope of basic terms until they begin to lose their meaning, as well as their analytical value, is much in evidence. Reform has taken on so many guises through the years as to be almost unrecognizable. When there appears to be political momentum behind a reform exercise, various delegations are quick to repackage some of their favorite perennial hobbyhorses as innovative reform measures. Few Member States, for example, are reticent about claiming that measures to reduce their assessments or to increase their voice in the organization qualify as essential reforms that would make the United Nations both more effective and more equitable. Seen in that context, of course, what looks like reform to one national delegation may appear regressive to others. At other points, when the term "reform" has taken on negative connotations, there has been a reticence to label reform measures by their real name. It was telling, for example, that during the intergovernmental deliberations of the late 1990s none of the five reform working groups established in the General Assembly had the term included in their elongated and carefully negotiated titles.[7] Clearly the notion of reform is more popular with larger and richer delegations than with others these days.

Another unsettled question—whether reform should encompass changes in what the UN does, for example, in its mandates and priorities, or only modifications in its administration, budgeting, financing, structure, and decisionmaking methods—also directly affects the scope of the concept. Judging from the titles and mandates of the five reform working groups in the General Assembly referred to above, it would seem that some believe that adjustments in programmatic substance should be included, as well as steps related to structure and procedures. In addition to the more traditional areas of Security Council, financial, and management reform, there were also working groups on an agenda for peace and an agenda for development that ranged over most of the UN's extensive substantive interests.

Reform was not treated as an abstract phenomenon, but rather as one of the potential tools for strengthening the Organization's capacities for dealing with specific issue areas.[8] Given this context, it is understandable why the United Nations has not sought to develop a single definition of reform that would be acceptable to all or most of the Member States. Such an undertaking might well prove as frustrating, controversial, and time-consuming as the decades-long attempts to negotiate universal definitions for terms such as "aggression" or "terrorism."

The first step toward understanding the twisting course of UN reform efforts through the years and the confusing maze of reform proposals that have been put forward is to bear in mind the fundamentally political nature of the United Nations. Within the UN context, even seemingly routine matters of administration, personnel, and finance have a way of assuming a political character, should one group of Member States or another come to perceive potential slights to their interests, stature, or priorities. To put it crudely, much of the reform debate, at its basest level, is a struggle over political turf, over who is perceived to gain or lose influence within the Organization if the proposed changes are enacted or implemented. One of the most frequently voiced questions in UN corridors during the late 1990s reform exercise was: "Reform for what purpose?" To gain support, the answers needed to be on two levels: substantive and political. Even if the goal of a particular proposal was to enhance efficiency, to some it mattered a good deal in which priority areas these efficiencies were to be carried out, who headed those programs, and whether the balance of attention and resources vis-à-vis other priorities would be affected. In short, much of the reform debate has been about three things: who makes decisions, who implements them, and who pays. If these political questions are settled, then international cooperation on moving the reform agenda will most assuredly flourish.

Who Decides? Reforming the UN's Intergovernmental Organs

For the UN's first three decades, reform of its intergovernmental bodies was largely a question of numbers. How large should ECOSOC and the Security Council be to represent properly the UN's rapidly growing membership?[9] What should the balance be between different geographical or ideological groups of states? In other words, who decides? For the past two-plus decades, however, the emphasis has shifted. While debates about numbers and names have continued without agreement, the action in terms of reform progress has moved to matters of working methods and of relations with other organs and with civil society.

The key "Who decides?" questions have become: "How are decisions reached, including whether there should be limitations on the use of the veto in the Security Council?" and "Who is consulted along the way, even if the formal composition of these bodies has not changed?"

During the 1950s and 1960s, one of the UN's cardinal achievements was to serve as midwife to the decolonization process. With the resulting influx of newly independent Member States, the ranks of UN members swelled from 51 in 1945 to 114 in 1963 (compared to 191 in

2003). Though only three African and three Asian countries were among the founders at San Francisco, by the early 1960s more than half of the Member States came from those two regions.[10] In 1956, after 20 new Member States were admitted to the UN over the two previous years, the calls for enlarging the two Councils came into the open. The original "gentlemen's agreement" on the geographical distribution of nonpermanent seats in the Security Council could no longer hold, since Latin America and Europe increasingly appeared to be "overrepresented" and the new majority "underrepresented." Unresolved squabbles over the six nonpermanent seats led to the constitutionally questionable practice of dividing a two-year term between countries from different regions. At one point, the Soviet Union favored redistributing the existing six nonpermanent seats, a step that would not have required Charter amendment. But this would have entailed a major sacrifice on the part of the West-leaning nations of Latin America and Europe, something Washington opposed.

The expansion of ECOSOC, in contrast, appeared to be a simpler and less consequential step. One-third of its eighteen members were elected each year for three-year terms, with each member having a single vote and equal rights. Not only were there no permanent members or vetoes in ECOSOC, but its mandate avoided core security issues, its primary task was coordination not policy, and its decisions were only recommendations, with none of the binding character of Security Council decisions under Chapter VII.[11] So as early as 1956, U.S. representatives acknowledged that both Councils should eventually be enlarged and suggested that the initial focus be on ECOSOC expansion.[12]

The developing countries, on the other hand, were especially keen on having a louder voice in the Security Council, which had become increasingly active in dispute resolution and peacekeeping efforts in the developing world. Some complained that their second-class status in the world body seemed to mirror the colonial status that they had recently struggled to overcome. For example, the heads of state of the members of the new Organization of African Unity (OAU), at their founding meeting in 1963, made this the topic of their very first joint summit resolution. In this context, and given their competition for influence in what was then known as the "Third World," neither Washington nor Moscow wanted to be the first to oppose openly the growing campaign for enlargement, whatever their actual misgivings.[13]

The expansion debate came to a head at the eighteenth General Assembly session in fall 1963.[14] Despite the building momentum, there was no consensus during the Assembly debate on either the need for an immediate expansion or the dimensions and voting rules of the enlarged bodies. On the final day of the session, none of the P-5—all of whose ratifications would be needed for formal amendment—voted in favor of the resolution to expand ECOSOC, and only China, of the five, voted for the resolution to expand the Security Council. During the debates preceding the votes, all P-5 members had called, in one form or another, for more time and further consultation before action was taken.

Nevertheless, on December 17, 1963, the General Assembly passed resolutions 1990 (XVIII) and 1991 (XVIII), the latter for the first time calling for amendments to the UN Charter. The first resolution, which passed 111 votes to none, enlarged the General Assembly's gate-keeping General Committee to permit fuller representation of the new African and Asian members. The second resolution was divided into two parts, each subject to its own roll call vote. Part A, to expand the Security Council from eleven to fifteen members, to increase the majority required from seven to nine, and to specify the geographical distribution of the ten nonpermanent members, was adopted by a vote of 97 to 11, with 4 abstentions. Those opposed included France and the Soviet bloc, while the United States and the UK were among those abstaining. Part B, which passed 96 to 11, with 4 abstentions, enlarged ECOSOC from eighteen to twenty-seven members and indicated the geographical breakdown of the nine new members. The only difference in the voting pattern was that the Republic of China shifted from an affirmative vote in Part A to an abstention on Part B, dealing with ECOSOC, a body on which it had been denied a seat in recent years. Adding a note of urgency, both parts called on the Member States to ratify the amendments by September 1, 1965, less than two years away.

Following the Assembly vote, the expansion bandwagon inexorably gathered momentum. Of the P-5, the Soviet Union was the first to reverse course and to ratify the amendments (followed, of course, by the rest of the Soviet bloc). By the time the U.S. Senate Foreign Relations Committee held hearings on this question in late April 1965, the United Kingdom had also announced its intention to ratify the alterations in the Charter, and 65 of the required 76 Member State ratifications had already been completed. When the Senate gave its consent to ratification in June, France had added its intention to ratify, and 71 of the 76 required ratifications were in hand. Though none of the permanent members had voted for both amendments in the General Assembly, within nineteen months all had overcome their reservations and ratified them.

The reasons for this remarkable about-face could be instructive for future efforts to amend the Charter. In theory, because of the need to attain ratification by all P-5 members, the amendment process is ultimately subject to a veto by any of them, including a pocket veto in which one or more of them simply fail to act. In practice, however, this step can be invoked only after at least a two-thirds majority of the Member States have expressed support for the amendment through their votes in the Assembly and possibly through their national ratification processes. So, in terms of the politics of the UN, the costs of vetoing a proposed Charter amendment can be quite high, and this has never been done once an amendment has cleared the Assembly. The political costs are disproportionately high, of course, if one permanent member has to cast a lonely veto, so there is a premium on cooperation among the five.

Cold War politics and the lack of coordination among the five were not the only explanations for this historic reversal. The UN's precarious financial position also contributed. In the early 1960s, the United Nations was in the midst of a severe financial and constitutional crisis, brought on by the refusals of the Soviet Union, France, and some developing countries to pay their assessments for the UN's first two large-scale peacekeeping operations, in the Congo and the Middle East, despite the decision of the International Court of Justice that they were required to do so. Washington and most Western capitals were very concerned with rallying the support of developing countries on these questions. The Article 19 crisis reached its boiling point in 1964, when the Soviet Union threatened to quit the UN, the United States pushed to have Moscow denied its vote in the General Assembly under Article 19 of the Charter for its accumulated arrears, and as a result, voting was suspended in the Assembly session that fall.[15] For those capitals concerned about preserving the fiscal and political integrity of the UN—and in those days Washington was in the front ranks—this was no time to veto reforms sought so fervently by the developing-country majority.

Then, as now, the dominant argument for expansion of both Councils was equity, not performance in fulfilling their august missions. In their statements before the Senate Foreign Relations Committee on this matter, none of the Johnson administration witnesses raised cautions about whether the expanded Councils would be better equipped to carry out their missions effectively, or whether due regard would be paid to the first Charter qualification for Security Council membership: the Member State's contribution to the maintenance of international peace and security.[16] Nor, in turn, did any of the committee members ask such pointed questions about the effects of the amendments during the public hearings, which ranged over a wide spectrum of UN and foreign policy matters. On the floor of the House, several representatives spoke in favor of the amendments and none raised these issues.[17] Prior to giving its consent to ratification virtually without dissent, by a 71-0 vote, the Senate held a perfunctory debate on the floor.[18] Only Strom Thurmond, the conservative Republican from South Carolina, spoke against the measure.[19] So, with ringing words of endorsement from the Johnson administration and a unanimous vote by the Senate, the United States acceded to the proposition that bigger is better in terms of UN fora.

A scant six years later, with this precedent firmly in place, the United States put forward a package of ECOSOC reform measures that included a substantial enlargement.[20] Many developing countries wanted to go further and faster, proposing a doubling of the size of ECOSOC, from twenty-seven to fifty-four members. In opposing this step, the French representative complained that the General Assembly had not "devoted as much time to this problem as it did 10 years ago, the last time the membership of the Economic and Social Council was enlarged."[21] Arguing that the Council's "authority is not necessarily a function of the size of its membership and the distribution of seats among regions," he suggested that already "the number of seats is too large."[22] Along similar lines, the Soviet delegate stressed that "the belief that the work of the Council can be improved solely through enlargement and through corresponding changes in the United Nations Charter is unfounded."[23] The United States, however, had accepted the principle of proportional growth in ECOSOC to parallel the proliferation of UN members, which reached 135—well beyond State Department predictions—by the end of 1973, the year the second expansion of ECOSOC came into force.[24] When the question of doubling the membership of ECOSOC came to a head in 1971, first in ECOSOC and then in the General Assembly, on both occasions the United States was the only P-5 member to vote in favor.[25] In terms of ratification, however, the United States was the last of the P-5 (including China) to complete the process, with the others deciding once again not to resist the international political tide. With the deposit of the U.S. ratification on September 24, 1973, this second expansion of ECOSOC, the last Charter amendment to be accomplished, came into force.

Calls for ECOSOC reform, of course, hardly subsided with this second increment to its membership. Indeed, many Member States went along with the two expansion steps on the assumption that they would be followed by measures to enhance ECOSOC's working methods, to

bolster its capacity to coordinate systemwide programs, and to rationalize its structure.[26] By the early 1970s, it had become increasingly apparent that the UN system was failing to fulfill the expectations of Member States—from the North as well as the South—in the realm of
economic and social development, despite the fact that some four-fifths
of its outlays then went to such programs.[27] A group of high-level
experts, appointed by the Secretary-General under a mandate from the
General Assembly, concluded in 1975 that the revitalization of
ECOSOC would be one of the keys to more effective global policymaking.[28] Their report urged ECOSOC to adopt a biennial calendar, with a
series of short subject-oriented sessions, a one-week ministerial session,
and annual reviews of program budgets, medium-term plans, and operational activities. It stressed the utility of the Council establishing small
negotiating groups to facilitate the search for common ground on key
economic issues, as well as initiating consultations at an early stage
with the most affected states on each issue. In addition, the report identified steps to raise the level of participation in ECOSOC sessions and
called on the Council to assume the responsibilities of many of its subsidiary bodies.

A number of UN-sponsored and independent studies have proposed
even more sweeping reorganizations of ECOSOC.[29] Some would
enlarge it further, while others would eliminate it altogether or divide it
in two. Several have advocated the creation of a smaller executive body
to set priorities and negotiate key issues, and most urge that the specialized agencies be made more subservient to the Council. Some of the
more modest reform proposals have been realized—the institution of a
high-level segment, shorter sessions, a somewhat more theme-oriented
agenda, and greater use of panels of independent experts on selected
issues—but there has been no agreement among the Member States on
a more fundamental restructuring. One area where ECOSOC has been
somewhat more innovative, however, is in recasting and clarifying the
rules for the engagement of NGOs in the work of the UN.[30] In this
respect, ECOSOC reform progress compares favorably to that of the
General Assembly, which has resisted the adoption of new rules for
NGO access.

In retrospect, however, the effects of ECOSOC expansion appear to
have been mixed at best. As some developing countries have gained a
stronger sense of ownership of the Council, developed countries on the
whole have been more prone to question its relevance and effectiveness.[31]
In part because of its unwieldy size—too big for serious negotiation and
too small to represent the membership as a whole—ECOSOC has been

the target of repeated reform campaigns during the 1970s, 1980s, and 1990s. It is not evident, moreover, that ECOSOC has found it any easier to coordinate the disparate and decentralized pieces of the UN system as it has itself grown larger and more diverse. After all, ECOSOC's powers have not expanded appreciably, its decisions remain only recommendations, it is still subservient to the Assembly on political questions, and the specialized agencies and the Bretton Woods institutions (the World Bank and the International Monetary Fund [IMF]) as always have their own political and financial constituencies, charters, and governing bodies. For these and similar constitutional reasons, the enlargement of ECOSOC has been irrelevant to addressing that body's core weaknesses.

Though they were linked in the package of Charter amendments that came into force in 1965, the efforts to reform ECOSOC and the Security Council have followed quite distinct paths since then. The Security Council, for instance, has not undergone a second tranche of expansion. Yet the pressures for enlarging the Security Council, at least judging by the public expressions of Member State policies, have been far greater than has been the case for ECOSOC. But then, of course, so too has been the resistance to tinkering with a body charged with such awesome security responsibilities. The mixed results of ECOSOC expansion are often cited as reasons not to enlarge the Council. The end of the Cold War, moreover, has had a far more profound effect on the debate over changes in the Security Council than in ECOSOC. On the one hand, the Council was rejuvenated as East-West divisions began to fade and the scope of its possible actions grew dramatically. Its new-found activism led some to declare that there had been nothing wrong with its structure and working methods, only a lack of political will, and that if there was nothing amiss in its performance, then there was no need to fix it. On the other hand, once the Council was freed of its Cold War shackles, it appeared to become, more than ever, the most dynamic and consequential piece of the system. The attractiveness of becoming a member rose, as did the stigma of being excluded from this inequitable and, some said, anachronistic club. In the consensus-driven atmosphere of this new era, moreover, the casting of vetoes came to appear decidedly out of step with the tenor of the times.

In 1993 the General Assembly convened the "Open-Ended Working Group on the Question of Equitable Representation and Increase in the Membership of the Security Council and Other Matters Related to the Security Council," a body whose very title embodied the complexities, uncertainties, and general awkwardness of its mandate. It divided its task into two clusters: one on membership, including expansion, the veto, and voting; the second on enhancing transparency through improved working methods and decisionmaking processes. While the first cluster has attracted far more public attention and Member State rhetoric, the second has spurred the greater progress.[32] By 2003 the 191 members of the General Assembly had not been able to come close to agreement on any Council reform package. But their high-profile debate has encouraged the Security Council to take a number of parallel steps on the second cluster working methods.

As the pace and profile of Security Council activities rose during the 1990s, a series of modifications in its working methods were adopted.[33] Among these were the following:

• Under the Arria formula, a member of the Council invites the others to meet with one or more independent experts for a candid exchange of views on a pressing issue before the Council. This innovative practice, which permits more direct input from civil society and encourages Council members to reflect on the complexities of the choices facing them, has proven quite popular, as have more formal meetings with agency heads and others with knowledge of developments in the field.

• The Council has also participated in a number of retreats, away from headquarters, with the Secretary-General, other UN officials, and sometimes leading independent experts.

• Council members have undertaken a number of missions to visit areas where developments are of particular interest or concern to the Council. This has allowed much more extensive contact with government officials, NGOs, and UN personnel on the ground in regions of crisis.

• The Council has met a number of times over the past decade at either the foreign minister or summit level.

• To assist transparency and accountability, it has become common practice for the president of the Council to brief nonmembers, and often the press, on the results of informal (private) consultations.

• Tentative forecasts and the provisional agendas for the Council's upcoming work are now provided regularly to nonmembers, as are provisional draft resolutions.

• Consultations among Security Council members and troop contributors, along with key Secretariat officials, are now held on a more regular basis.

While acknowledging the progress that has been made on the second cluster, most Member States contend that it has not gone nearly far enough. The ten nonpermanent members of the Security Council called for the institutionalization of the steps that had been taken, for taking several of them further, and for more public meetings and fewer informal consultations.[34] It is questionable, however, whether all of the transparency and reporting measures called for would result in a more efficient or effective Security Council. The bulk of the negotiations among the members are bound to be carried out in private, and the public sessions of the Council have become opportunities largely for restating official positions and for public rationalizations. Even nonmembers of the Council frequently complain of the number and repetitiveness of the speeches given in the formal, public sessions. While it would aid accountability to require states to explain why they cast each veto, and the Council could be more forthcoming in its reports to the General Assembly, excessively detailed or frequent reporting could make it that much harder for an already overburdened Council to devote sufficient time and attention to its wide-ranging substantive work.

The first cluster has proven more problematic. Most distinct, the volume of complaints about the veto privilege of the P-5, a point of contention since the founding conference in San Francisco, seemed to rise precipitously during the 1990s.[35] Most of the other 186 Member States, as well as numerous scholars and blue ribbon commissions, have criticized the veto provision for being inequitable, undemocratic, and debilitating to the capacity of the Council to fulfill its core responsibility for the maintenance of international peace and security. Others, however, have stressed that the principle of unanimity among the major powers was central to the conception of the UN, and that principle has permitted it not only to survive the tensions of the Cold War, but also to play a role in helping to resolve them.

The veto controversy has complicated progress on the array of first-cluster issues in several ways:

• Since Article 108 gives the permanent members a veto over Charter amendments, they can trump any efforts to weaken formally their veto power.
• Those seeking to expand the number and geographical spread of the permanent members face a dilemma: Should additional permanent members, in the name of equity, be given the very veto power that critics claim is so debilitating to the work of the Council? Wouldn't a Council with eight or ten permanent members be even more restricted in terms of where it could act, and wouldn't the common denominator for Council action be even lower in most cases?[36]

• Alternative formulas for coping with the veto dilemma raise additional concerns. A number of delegations criticized the proposal by Ismail Razali, when he was president of the General Assembly in 1997, to add five permanent members without veto power because they said it would add a third layer to the Council hierarchy.[37] Asking the current permanent members to exercise greater restraint in their use of the veto, for example, by restricting it to matters under Chapter VII of the Charter, offers no guarantees and sets a precedent of calling on selected Member States to relinquish rights given them under the Charter.[38]

• Divisive questions about which states should have the veto have exacerbated splits within each region about which local states should be on the Council, especially since most security threats come from within one's own region, not from afar. Moreover, there is no provision in the Charter suggesting that one Member State may or should represent the interests and positions of others, neighbors or not.

So, while the General Assembly working group has made progress on narrowing differences over the size of a reformed Council, there has been little agreement either about names or about vetoes.

In sum, though it has now been almost thirty years since the Assembly last voted to amend the Charter, in retrospect, the three Charter amendments did make participation in the Security Council and ECOSOC accessible to more Member States, more of the time. They made some accommodation, if not full places, at the decisionmaking table for the scores of new members. They demonstrated a degree of flexibility, for example, some willingness to adapt to changing circumstances. But clearly they did not address the root shortcomings of either body, nor quench the public's thirst for stronger tools and machinery for dealing with the world's persistent security, economic, and social problems. Indeed, the fact that the only Charter revisions that have proven capable of sparking wide support among the members have been those to increase the size of limited membership bodies has also served to fuel skepticism about whether Charter reform is the best route to a stronger and more effective United Nations.

Who Implements? Coordination and Management

Though lacking the high drama of the debates over who decides, the question of implementation—how the mandates agreed upon by the intergovernmental bodies are to be carried out—has generated sustained attention since the UN's infancy. At its opening session in London, Arthur H. Vandenberg, the influential Republican senator who led the administrative and financial committee in both San Francisco and London, warned his colleagues against mistaking "pomp for power" and letting their aspirations for the United Nations "outrun its resources."[39] The next year, in November 1946, he wrote to Secretary of State James Byrnes that the specialized agencies "are being created entirely too rapidly and too ambitiously."[40] The following year, as noted above, the U.S. Senate initiated its first critical review of UN management and administration. The problems identified—overlap, duplication, coordination, proliferation of papers and mandates, and staff competence and compensation—have formed the core of the reform agenda ever since, in part because such challenges are common in, perhaps endemic to, complex multilateral organizations.

International bodies may properly be assessed first and foremost by what they stand for and seek to accomplish, the things determined by their constitutions and principal intergovernmental decisionmaking bodies. Yet over time, the most stinging rebukes are often about their failure to perform, about the gaps between their high purposes and meager capacities to carry them out. It has been to this second set of challenges, to narrowing the implementation gap, that most of the UN's internal reform efforts have been devoted.

From early on, two characteristics of the UN system underlined the value of developing effective practices and/or mechanisms for coordination: one was the interdisciplinary and multisectoral nature of many of the key issues on the international agenda, and the other was the complex and horizontally segmented mix of agencies, funds, and programs that composed the "system." The whole, it seemed, often acted as less than the sum of its parts. The Charter, in Articles 57 and 63, called on ECOSOC to "enter into agreements" with the various specialized agencies, several of which predated the world body, so as to bring them "into relationship with the United Nations." ECOSOC was asked to coordinate their activities "through consultations and recommendations," while Article 64 gave ECOSOC permission to seek reports from the agencies. Nowhere in the Charter, however, is there any suggestion that ECOSOC would have any binding power over them.

In practice, of course, a number of the agencies had their own boards, bylaws, mandates, and funding sources, giving them every reason to maintain a substantial degree of independence from the General Assembly, which lacked budgetary authority over them (Article 17[3] of the Charter). Since the major donor countries were members of most of these agencies, they could, if they worked together, enforce substantial discipline and coherence on the pieces of the system. But this would have required a degree of coordination among national ministries and within capitals that was only occasionally achieved. According to the 1948 Senate review, "a considerable portion of the problem of coordination seems to be due to the failure of national governments to achieve coordination in their own policy formulation. As a result, various departments of government often tend toward an autonomous handling of relationships with specific international organizations."[41] Within the UN system, weaknesses in program coordination were compounded by an inability to set and maintain clear priorities. . . .

Of course, the Member States, with their disparate interests and priorities, have been as much or more to blame as the Secretariat for the proliferation of mandates and the mismatch between ambitions and resources, problems that continue to plague the world body. To be fair, however, at times the various agencies and programs have managed to pull together to respond to emergencies and special opportunities with a sense of common purpose. When the goal is clearly articulated by the Secretary-General and the Member States pull together, so do the programs and agencies. On the whole, though, the highly decentralized nature of the system and its resistance to integrative reforms have tended to fuel perceptions of institutional disarray and fragmentation.

No one has more pungently described the malady or more painstakingly detailed possible remedies than Sir Robert Jackson, a former high-ranking international civil servant from Australia who had been tapped in 1968 by the United Nations Development Programme (UNDP) to carry out a "study of the capacity of the United Nations system to carry out an expanded development program."[42] Unlike the more pessimistic premises of recent reforms, which have been identified with cost and post retrenchments, this assessment was undertaken at a time of rapid growth in development funding through multilateral channels. The challenge was not whether the world body could do more with less, but whether the UN could handle another doubling of its development programs in the course of a few years time.

Sir Robert and his small team of researchers produced a report of almost 600 pages, laying out a detailed plan for restructuring the way the UN goes about assisting the development process. Yet it was a few unvarnished comments in the report's foreword about the shortcomings of the existing arrangements that gained the study almost instantaneous notoriety around the world. Sir Robert noted that he had been left with two strong impressions: one positive, one negative. On the plus side, he was "convinced that technical co-operation and pre-investment are one of the most effective ways of assisting the developing countries in achieving economic and social progress. I believe the United Nations, despite its present limitations, has demonstrated conclusively that it is the ideal instrument for the job."[43] There was, according to Sir Robert, "an unprecedented opportunity to revitalize the United Nations development system. Yet he doubted that the governments of the world could grasp this chance given "the great inertia of this elaborate administrative structure which no one, it seems, can change. Yet change is now imperative."

The UN development "machine," in Sir Robert's view, had evolved into "probably the most complex organization in the world." He pointed out that "about thirty separate governing bodies" tried to exercise control over different pieces of the administrative machine, yet "at the headquarters level, there is no real 'Headpiece,' no central coordinating organization which could exercise effective control." He luridly described the "administrative tentacle" that ran down to a vast complex of regional, subregional, and field offices in over ninety developing countries. Governments could not control the process, and "the machine is incapable of intelligently controlling itself." As a result, "unmanageable in the strictest sense of the word," the machine "is becoming slower and more unwieldy, like some prehistoric monster." While praising the largely good work of UNDP, he concluded that management lapses and structural shortcomings had permitted about 20 percent of the programs to qualify as "deadwood," or "nonessential projects."

He had surmised, moreover, that his preferred solution was not politically feasible: "In theory, complete control of the machine would require the consolidation of all of the component parts—the United Nations and the Specialized Agencies—into a single organization, which is not within the realms of possibility." Movement in this direction, even restructuring UNDP into "a strong central coordinating organization," would be resisted, he feared, by UN officials, by agencies that had "become the equivalent of principalities," and by those national ministries that tend to take positions in UN agencies that conflict with their "government's policies toward the UN system as a whole."

An alternative way to reform the machine without amending the Charter, in his view, "would be to centralize the budgets of all of the Specialized Agencies and bring them under effective coordinated control in ECOSOC. Then you really would see opposition to change! That battle was fought out when I was at Lake Success in the early days and the supporters of the sectoral approach won the day." Moreover, the UN system had become "a disproportionately old and bureaucratic organization," plagued with a pervasive sense of "negativism." Based on his consultations, Sir Robert had concluded that the "UN system has more than its fair share of 'experts' in the art of describing how things cannot be done."

For all of his doubts, Sir Robert saw some rays of light ahead. He urged his readers to reflect on how much the developing countries had already achieved, on the advances of science and technology, on the growing interdependence of nations, on the principles the General Assembly had articulated for relations between the UN and the Third World, and on the complementary roles that had been carved out for UNDP and the specialized agencies. With greater funds and top-flight managerial talent, he argued, a great deal could be accomplished given these favorable conditions. "The sheer force of political circumstances," he concluded, "will compel governments to act sooner or later."

The study emphasized the importance of clarifying and defining the respective roles of the various pieces of the system. "The World Bank Group should be the chief arm of the UN system in the field of capital investment, while UNDP should perform the same function for basic technical co-operation and pre-investment." UNDP should serve "as the hub of the UN development system," coordinating the efforts of the specialized agencies and other UN operational programs at the country level through UNDP resident representatives; at headquarters through a new program policy staff, four regional bureaus, and a technical advisory panel; and at the highest interagency level through the replacement of the Inter-Agency Consultative Board (IACB) with a more powerful Policy Coordination Committee. The specialized agencies would serve both as executing agents for projects contracted with UNDP and as technical advisers in their respective fields of expertise, but "UNDP would assume full responsibility for all development activities carried out under its aegis, and with its funds, irrespective of which agency or other institution expedited a particular programme or project on its behalf."[44] Therefore, the agencies would have to be accountable to the administrator of the UNDP for these projects, just as he would be accountable to governments and to the UNDP Governing Council.

Following the suggested reorganization of UNDP, the study urged consideration of the merger of the governing bodies of the World Food

Programme (WFP), the UN Children's Fund (UNICEF), and UNDP. Calling for a decentralization of line authority within UNDP, the report recommended a strengthening of the role of the resident representatives, an enhancement of the authority of the administrator, and a focus on policymaking by the Governing Council. To facilitate a more decentralized apparatus, the report also stressed the need to upgrade the quality of the Secretariat, especially the resident representatives, and to improve communications throughout the system.[45]

While much of Sir Robert's plan depended on establishing this more integrated organizational structure, in many ways the operational heart of his vision centered on the institution of country-based programming and a "UN Development Cooperation Cycle."[46] The latter would consist of five phases: country program and annual review; formulation and appraisal of projects; implementation; evaluation; and follow-up. The country program would be prepared by the recipient government and the UNDP resident representative, hopefully with the participation of the agencies and in association with the World Bank, and then submitted to the UNDP Governing Council for approval. This process would provide each developing country with "a comprehensive view of the total cooperation it might expect from the UN development system during the whole period of its national development plan." For developed countries, it would provide an overview of the use of resources, facilitate forward planning, and permit bilateral and multilateral programs to be harmonized country by country.

Much of the thrust of Jackson's vision has been implemented, some at that point and some over time. But the core dilemmas that he identified have not disappeared. In particular, though his proposed combination of central authority and country-based programming has its attractions, it does not eliminate the possibility of disputes between the priorities of field-level and headquarters-level decisionmaking. This tension between centralization and decentralization has plagued UN reform efforts from the organization's early days.[47]

Because the Secretary-General lacks the power either of the purse or of appointment in dealing with the specialized agencies and the Bretton Woods institutions, he must rely on persuasion, personality, and indirect appeals to publics and Member States to give a sense of direction and coherence to the system as a whole.[48] Some Secretaries-General, and Kofi Annan has set an especially good example, are better at pulling the disparate pieces of the system together than others have been. More fundamentally, the capacity of the Member States to set and hold priorities has been markedly episodic. Divisions or indifference among the Member States, in turn, provide ample opportunities for agency heads to engage in splitting tactics or to pursue independent agendas. As a 1987 blue ribbon commission convened by the United Nations Association of the United States of America (UNA-USA) put it, the system's potential for interdisciplinary analysis and integrated implementation efforts has been hampered by the fact that "there is no center at the center of the U.N. system."[49]

The next wave of social and economic restructuring, undertaken between 1974 and 1977, unfolded in a much less propitious political context than had Jackson's capacity study a few years before.[50] The early 1970s saw growing strains between developed and developing countries on a host of economic, energy, trade, and financial questions of a bilateral, regional, and global nature. While solutions to problems of the magnitude of the oil crisis far transcended the bounds of the UN system, the world body, with its broad-based membership, became the favorite forum for the countries of the South to raise their concerns about the equity of the existing economic and political system. Through their numbers in the one-nation, one-vote General Assembly, the developing countries sought to codify a series of principles, targets, and procedures that would define a new set of global economic relationships. In this larger political context, the question of UN reform took on a more intense and divisive meaning in terms of the control, direction, and priorities of UN bodies. Amid calls by the developing countries for a new international economic order (NIEO), in 1974 the General Assembly (resolution 3343 [XXIX]) asked the Secretary-General to appoint a group of experts to prepare "a study containing proposals on structural changes within the UN system so as to make it fully capable of dealing with problems of international economic co-operation in a comprehensive manner." With Professor Richard N. Gardner of Columbia University as its rapporteur, the group of experts reached a consensus on a broad-ranging report in only four months of deliberations during the first half of 1975.

The experts' report acknowledged that "no amount of restructuring can replace the political will of Member States to discharge their obligations under Article 56 of the Charter."[51] It stressed that the group viewed efficiencies and financial economies at best as secondary factors in its deliberations, though they expected that some of their recommendations could lead to staff reductions and budgetary savings. Of higher priority to the group was the need to bring much greater coherence to the planning, programming, and budgetary processes of the UN system. According to the report, at that point, of the almost $1.5 billion expended annually by the system, less than one-quarter was covered by the regular budget, one-quarter by fifteen largely autonomous specialized agencies, one-quarter by UNDP, and one-quarter by voluntary contributions. Recognizing that this arrangement made policy direction and priority-setting that much more problematic, the experts called for a series of steps to make the budgetary and programmatic reporting of the various pieces of the system at least sufficiently compatible to permit the possibility of cross-sectoral planning and monitoring.

The proposed innovation that attracted the most attention was for the creation of the post of director-general for development and international economic cooperation, to be placed above agency heads and undersecretaries-general, as the second highest official in the world body. The director-general would be supported by two deputy directors-general, one for research and policy and the other to head a new United Nations development authority. While the director-general could not exercise authority over the relatively autonomous specialized agencies, he or she would be in charge of interagency coordination and operational activities and would chair a new interagency advisory committee on economic cooperation and development. It was suggested that the post be occupied by "a national of a developing country at least during those years when the post of Secretary-General is occupied by a developed country."[52]

The report also advocated the consolidation of all of the funds for technical assistance and preinvestment activities—except for those of UNICEF—into a new UN development authority. In a politically charged recommendation on a matter of high priority to the capitals of both developed and developing countries, the group urged that the weighted voting systems in the IMF and World Bank be revised "to reflect the new balance of economic power and the legitimate interest of developing countries in a greater voice in the operation" of those institutions.[53] The report did not specify how this should be done, and in any case the General Assembly has no authority over the Bretton Woods institutions and the specialized agencies. Though the experts from around the world had managed to reach a consensus on a shared vision in short order, the same could not be said either of the Member States or of the heads of the various parts of the UN system. Though welcoming some aspects of the report, the West cautioned against any changes that might worsen the unstable North-South political dynamic of the time or weaken its control of the Bretton Woods institutions. The East opposed steps that would entail Charter amendment or additional costs. The Group of 77 (G-77) lacked a coherent view, other than placing a higher priority on the achievement of the NIEO and on expanding the authority of the General Assembly than on restructuring the system. Wary of the implications of greater institutional integration, the G-77 preferred to stress the need for a third expansion of ECOSOC.[54]

Finally, on December 20, 1977, more than three years after the economic and social restructuring exercise was launched with the mandating of the group of experts, the General Assembly, without vote, endorsed a substantially weakened version of the Group's proposals (resolution 32/197). The parallels also included measures to rationalize the work of the Second and Third Committees, to biennialize the agenda of ECOSOC, to institute shorter and more frequent subject-oriented sessions of ECOSOC over the course of the year, to hold periodic sessions of the Council at the ministerial level, and to have the Council "assume to the maximum extent possible direct responsibility for performing the functions of its subsidiary bodies." Lost, however, was the experts' core notion of small negotiating groups in both bodies on key economic issues. Instead, the Assembly predictably called for the consideration of ways to enable all Member States to participate in the work of the Council and to make "the Council fully representative." The idea of facilitating agreement through the convening of smaller groups of states on an ad hoc basis, for all of its appeal to logic, simply cut across the grain of the current political dynamics at a time of continuing North-South struggles over an array of macroeconomic issues.

Though the post of director-general survived the negotiating process, it was stripped of the authority and support structures that would have allowed it to be a powerful new locus for policy coordination and advocacy within the system. The two new deputy director-general posts were not established, none of the existing undersecretary-general posts were eliminated, the funds were not consolidated into a UN development authority, and their governing boards were not merged. The resolution called for greater uniformity in financial and administrative procedures and extolled UNDP's country-based programming process, but essentially the director-general was superimposed on the existing highly decentralized structure, without the authority to reshape or redirect it. Kenneth Dadzie, the Ghanian chairman of the Ad Hoc Committee, was appointed to be the first director-general. Though widely liked, he had little real power and was never fully accepted by the Secretary-General.

Over the years, the post came to be seen at best as marginally useful at moving these issues within the Secretariat, and at worst as a high-level appendage with little influence. Fourteen years later, in a sweeping gesture of unilaterally imposed reform, incoming Secretary-General Boutros Boutros-Ghali unceremoniously included the position of director-general as one of a list of eighteen high-level posts he was abolishing "to redress the fragmentation which existed in the Secretariat" and "to consolidate and streamline the Organization's activities into well-defined functional categories."[55]

Nevertheless, below the intergovernmental level, the efforts to bolster the system's capacity for coherent implementation of mandates have continued. The Joint Inspection Unit (JIU) has undertaken a number of assessments of how these efforts have been faring or might be enhanced. For example, a 1999 JIU report reviewed the history of steps to strengthen the Administrative Committee on Coordination (ACC), and called for further modifications, including of its name.[56] Established by ECOSOC in 1946 (resolution 13 [III]), the ACC was the only forum that convened the executive heads of all of the Organizations of the UN system, under the chairmanship of the Secretary-General, to focus on questions of coordination and crosscutting policy issues. While its effectiveness had varied with the personalities involved, its agenda had become increasingly substantive in recent years. In 2000 the name of the ACC was changed to the Chief Executives Board (CEB) and the responsibilities for coordination were divided into a High-Level Committee on Management (HCLM) and a High-Level Committee on Programmes (HLCP).

Achieving greater unity of purpose was a central theme of Secretary-General Kofi Annan's 1997 reform plan. Earlier that year, he organized four sectoral executive committees to bring together all relevant departments, funds, and programs under the headings of peace and security, the UN Development Group, humanitarian affairs, and economic and social issues.[57] He established a senior management group to act as a sort of cabinet on management issues, and a strategic planning unit to identify and assess crosscutting issues and trends. He also asked the General Assembly to establish the post of Deputy Secretary-General to address, among other things, questions that "cross functional sectors and Secretariat units."[58] While seeking to improve communication and the sense of common purpose at headquarters level, the Secretary-General also recognized the value in delegating authority and initiatives to the country level for operational development and humanitarian programs. In this regard, he called for "decentralization of decision-making at the country level and consolidation of the UN's presence under 'one flag.'"[59] Consolidations were undertaken to create a single Department of Economic and Social Affairs and a unified office to combat crime, drugs, and terrorism in Vienna.

While these steps have modified in significant ways the internal workings of the United Nations, they have had relatively little impact either on the way intergovernmental decisions are made or on the way others perceive the world body. As Kofi Annan has often pointed out, reform is a process, not an event. In closing his reform report, he captured these points nicely:

> to an organization as large and complex as the United Nations, reform necessarily consists not of one or two simple actions but a multitude of tasks that amount to a major agenda that must be pursued over time. But the world will not measure the reform process by the number of items on the agenda, by how many more or fewer activities are undertaken, or how many committees are formed or disbanded. The Organization will be judged, rightly, by the impact all these efforts have on the poor, the hungry, the sick and the threatened—the peoples of the world whom the United Nations exists to serve.[60]

Who Pays? Assessments, Finance, and Budgeting

. . . The UN Charter is quite explicit about who decides on other matters; however, when it comes to revenues and outlays, the Charter has relatively little to say, leaving these core matters to be determined by the Member States over time. According to Article 17:

1. The General Assembly should consider and approve the budget of the Organization.
2. The expenses of the Organization shall be borne by the Members as apportioned by the General Assembly.

Article 18(2) lists "budgeting questions" as among those "important questions" requiring "a two-thirds majority of the members present and voting." The skeletal nature of these provisions did not reflect a downplaying of the potential importance of these issues at the San Francisco founding conference or the preparatory meetings that led up to it. Rather, it was widely believed that open debates on finance and burden sharing would become so contentious and divisive as to threaten the sense of unity and common purpose the founding members were seeking to achieve.[61] Recognizing how acutely political questions of outlays and assessments would be, moreover, the founders of the world body felt it best to let the answers be adjusted periodically according to the ebb and flow of political power and economic means among the Member States over time. Thus, in seeking to postpone or finesse the issue, they ensured that finance would be a hardy perennial on the reform agenda for years to come.

No doubt, the most highly charged issue has been the assessment scale, which determines the relative burden borne by each member for financing the UN's regular budget and, since the late 1950s, its peacekeeping operations.[62] Other than assigning the task of apportionment to the Assembly, the Charter provides neither a mechanism nor a set of principles by which this determination should be made. These tasks were assigned in 1945 to an expert committee on contributions, which encountered politically turbulent seas when it sought to lay down both a set of criteria and its initial recommendations for the percentage assessments for each Member State.[63]

The capacity to pay has been the underlying principle for assessing states. Yet as more and more developing nations with very low capacities to pay joined the UN, placing more demands on the Organization, the United States began to complain. As Jeane Kirkpatrick testified before the Senate Committee on Governmental Affairs in May 1985, soon after she stepped down from the post of UN Permanent Representative: "The countries who pay the bills do not have the votes, and the countries who have the votes do not pay the bill. . . . The countries which contribute more than 85 percent of the U.N. budget regularly vote against that budget, but are unable to prevent its increases because the countries who pay less than 10 percent of the U.N. budget have the votes."[64] . . .

Fair or not, these arguments found a ready audience in Congress. Finding that the UN and its specialized agencies "have not paid sufficient attention in the development of their budgets to the views of the member governments who are major financial contributors," in August 1985 Congress passed the Kassebaum-Solomon Amendment as part of the Foreign Relations Authorization Act for fiscal years 1986 and 1987.[65] It precluded for fiscal year 1987 and beyond payment of assessed contributions of over 20 percent to the UN or any of its specialized agencies—which meant the withholding of 20 percent of the

U.S. contribution—until they adopted weighted voting on budgetary matters "proportionate to the contribution of each such member state." In seeking to assert greater control by the major contributors over spending, Republican senator Nancy Kassebaum insisted that her aim was to strengthen, not weaken, the world body.[66] Putting their intent more bluntly, her cosponsor, the veteran Republican representative Gerald Solomon of New York, later remarked that "the way to get the attention of a mule is to hit him in the head with a 2x4. The way to get the attention of the United Nations was to pass the Kassebaum-Solomon amendment."[67]

The worsening financial crisis and the growing U.S. withholdings gave the UN's fortieth General Assembly session a markedly somber cast. After weeks of sharp debate, much of it directed toward U.S. withholding tactics, the Assembly agreed to establish a group of eighteen experts, though with a limited mandate, as most developing countries preferred. The group's purpose was to conduct a thorough review of the administrative and financial matters of the United Nations, with a view to identifying measures for further improving the efficiency of its administrative and financial functioning, which would

• contribute to strengthening its effectiveness in dealing with political, economic, and social issues; and
• submit to the General Assembly, before the opening of its forty-first session, a report containing the observations and recommendations of the Group.[68]

The experts were to stick to questions of efficiency and to avoid political matters, such as the relative priority of security and economic/social questions in the work of the UN.[69]

Meanwhile, Secretary-General Pérez de Cuéllar and his top managers had been undertaking a review of possible personnel and spending cuts in parallel to the deliberations of the Group of 18. In January and March of 1986, the Secretary-General announced two series of economy measures, such as reductions in travel, consultants, overtime, recruitment, promotions, benefits, and maintenance. While not eliminating any mandated posts or activities, these initial steps produced an estimated $30 million in savings.[70] Department heads were asked to identify how an additional 10 percent reduction in outlays could be achieved, if required. Deeper cuts and more far-reaching reforms, however, would require action by the Member States, since they are responsible for setting program mandates and priorities. So the Secretary-General asked the General Assembly to resume its fortieth session in late April 1986 to consider further economies to ease the worsening financial crisis. In the end, the Assembly, despite the considerable reluctance of many developing countries, adopted the Secretary-General's interim package of austerity measures with the caveat that "no project or programme for which there was a legislative mandate would be eliminated if adequate financial resources were available."[71]

The Group of 18 had only six months to try to forge a consensus on matters on which the Member States were deeply divided. It soon became painfully obvious that there was little chance of the group reaching agreement on a proposal for a new scale of assessments, something the Secretary-General had urged them to examine.[72] Reportedly, the U.S. expert in the group rebuffed suggestions by some of the other members that the possibility of lowering the U.S. assessment rate, as had been proposed by Olaf Palme and others, be considered in their deliberations.[73] Likewise, questions relating to the elimination of marginal intergovernmental bodies, to a restructuring of the UN's programs, or to recasting priorities among activities and budget line items also proved too divisive to be tackled. The group's report acknowledged problems of duplication and insufficient coordination of agendas and programs, but stated that the group did not have time to undertake an in-depth review, which "should be entrusted to an intergovernmental body."[74] The group likewise called for a streamlining of the machinery for interagency coordination, but failed to specify how this should be done (recommendations 9–13). It urged reductions in the number and duration of conferences, and in documentation, travel costs, and conference facilities (recommendations 1–7, 38). To improve the monitoring, evaluation, and inspection of UN activities, the group recommended an upgrading of the Joint Inspection Unit, a broadening of its mandate, amid closer coordination and a clearer division of labor between the JIU and external auditors (recommendations 63–67).

As seems perennially to be the case with intergovernmental bodies, the one target the Member States can readily agree to criticize is the Secretariat.[75] In this respect, the group's report was both specific and far-reaching. Noting that the number of posts funded through the UN regular budget had grown more than sevenfold in forty years, from 1,546 in 1946 to 11,423 in 1986, the report devoted two full chapters to Secretariat-related questions. Of greater concern to coherent management than these aggregate numbers was that the structure was "both too top-heavy and too complex," with twenty-eight posts at the Under-Secretary-General level and twenty-nine posts at the Assistant Secretary-General level under the regular budget, plus an additional seven and twenty-three, respectively, financed through extrabudgetary sources.[76] The experts thus called for a 15 percent reduction in the overall number of regular budget posts and a deeper 25 percent cut in Under-Secretary-General and Assistant Secretary-General regular budget posts, both to be achieved within a three-year period (recommendation 15). They also proposed a consolidation of the political departments, a review of those devoted to economic and social affairs, a streamlining of administration, and a review of public information activities, though these recommendations were mostly expressed in general terms (recommendations 16–40).

While the Group of 18 report, which included a consensus-based decisionmaking process, was generally well received, many delegations were wary of institutionalizing a U.S. financial veto over the UN's budget and programs, which would be the result of the consensus requirement. Delegations did not want to appear to buckle in the face of U.S. financial and political pressure. The developing countries, in particular, seemed far less concerned about Secretariat retrenchment than about how their own voice and influence in the United Nations might be affected by modification in the procedures for intergovernmental decisionmaking. The one-nation, one-vote rule mattered to them in terms of both principle and national interest. This sensitivity was especially apparent in the question of budgeting, the one area in which the Charter permits the Assembly to make binding decisions on its own accord.

Yet on December 19, 1986, a weary Assembly approved by consensus resolution 41/213, calling for implementation of the agreed upon proposals of the Group of 18 and of a new consensus-based planning, programming, and budgeting process. Three factors helped to turn the tide. First, throughout the fall, the financial straits of the UN had grown more desperate. According to UN officials, the Organization, which opened 1986 with a $240 million deficit, had since depleted its contingency funds and exhausted ways of shifting funds among different accounts, leaving it increasingly vulnerable to financial pressures imposed by Member State withholdings.[77] At the end of October, the Secretary-General terminated ten top officials, while maintaining the cuts and freezes announced earlier in the year. There was growing talk of "payless paydays" if the United States—and other countries—did not make substantial additional payments before year's end.[78] Second, top U.S. officials and legislators began to make a positive linkage between UN reform and congressional restraint, contending that together they could produce a more effective and sounder world body.[79] The U.S. administration lobbied key capitals in the developing world on the value of consensus-based decisionmaking, including sending an envoy with this message from Washington to selected capitals in Africa in early December—seen as the key to moving the process in New York.[80] Third, in New York, the president of the General Assembly, Humayun Rasheed Choudhury of Bangladesh, helped shape a diplomatically worded description of the new budget process that would be relatively inoffensive to all parties.

Despite Choudhury's reassuring language, many delegations wanted an opinion from the UN Legal Counsel that these provisions would not undermine Article 18 of the Charter, which stipulates that "each member of the General Assembly shall have one vote" and that "important questions," including budgetary ones, require a two-thirds majority. The Counsel's opinion, included as Annex II of the resolution, found that "these draft proposals read separately or together do not in any way prejudice the provisions of Article 18 of the Charter of the United Nations or of the relevant rules of procedure of the General Assembly giving effect to that Article."[81]

With all of the horse-trading, however, opinions were divided about whether the multilateral negotiations had produced a mouse or something of historic proportions. Maurice Bertrand, a member of the group and a former JIU inspector, was skeptical. In his view, the resolution "defined the process of decision-making regarding the size and content of the programme budget so obscurely that everyone could declare himself satisfied but nothing was really settled."[82] As U.S. Permanent Representative Vernon Walters acknowledged, "we got most of what we wanted and so did nearly everyone else."[83] But he also claimed that "what has been done here is something really historic. We have gotten the things that the United States intended."[84] Based on these results, he said that he would urge Congress to repeal the Kassebaum-Solomon Amendment and to appropriate the full U.S-assessed contribution to the world body. Yet critics could argue that very little had changed, given the option to resort to voting if consensus fails. On the other hand, while the new process fell well short of weighted voting, the emphasis had shifted toward the presumption that consensus was the preferred way to determine the size and shape of the budget. The new system, however, offered no guarantees. Small contributors, as well as large ones, could conceivably prevent the attainment of a consensus in the Committee for Programme and Coordination (CPC). While traditionally the P-5 had regularly been elected to the CPC, there was no formal rule requiring that the United States or any of the others be seated.[85] Even if the CPC reached a consensus, the Assembly retained its prerogative to accept, modify, or reject those recommendations. As President Choudhury asserted, the new mechanism would depend on a tacit agreement between the big contributors and the developing countries, as well as on Congress's willingness to provide sustained financial support.[86] In the State Department's view, the new system would change relationships and assumptions among the Member States:

> This process has the effect of reducing the ability of the numerical majority to dictate decisions about the size and use of UN resources. If the resort to majority power cannot simply be assumed, real compromise becomes essential. Trade-offs must be achieved between minority and majority viewpoints, involving the exchange and modification of tangible interests. That is why the reform program budget decision-making process is so significant.[87]

More bluntly, Assistant Secretary of State Alan Keyes cautioned that the United States would consider further funding cuts down the road if the CPC failed to maintain a consensus. The hesitant steps toward implementing the 1986 reforms were monitored closely by Congress and the Reagan administration. The week after the General Assembly in 1987 decided to expand the CPC membership from twenty-one to thirty-four, Congress enacted legislation placing new conditions on U.S. payments to the UN, this time geared to the implementation of the provisions of resolution 41/213.[88] Though a range of assessments could be heard in Washington about the degree of progress being made in carrying out these provisions, over the course of 1988 the Reagan administration seemed to gain greater confidence that UN reform, on balance, was moving forward. The Secretary-General had not yet reached the 15 percent personnel cut targeted for the end of 1989, but he appeared to be closing in on that goal.[89] The 1988–1989 budget estimates were revised modestly upward, but with the United States joining the consensus because the additional outlays related to UN peacekeeping operations in Afghanistan and the Western Sahara, which the United States strongly supported. These add-ons were termed by the U.S. delegation as ones that were "critically important" or would "strengthen the Organization," unlike ones in earlier years that "were marginally useful, and, in some cases, politically divisive." Though the 41/213 procedures had not yet been fully operationalized, the United States was pleased with the way the 1990–1991 budget outline had been developed and, again, joined in the consensus approval of it.

More fundamentally, the larger political context within which relations with the UN had been viewed was changing in important ways. The Soviet Union had agreed to withdraw its forces from Afghanistan, and Mikhail Gorbachev was bringing "new thinking" to Soviet domestic and foreign policy. The prospects and utility of UN peacekeeping operations were rising in Washington's strategic calculations. In the U.S. presidential election campaign, both candidates pledged to repay U.S. arrears to the world body. On the eve of the president's final speech to the General Assembly, the White House announced its decision to authorize the release of outstanding 1988 dues and to develop a multi-year plan to pay back the accumulated arrears.[90]

These years of crisis in U.S.-UN relations produced a number of intriguing ironies and lessons for the process of UN reform and renewal. Most striking was the metamorphosis in Reagan administration attitudes toward, and perceptions of, the UN. The question of reform played a major role in this transformation, at first seeming to confirm the widely held assumption that the Organization would never change and later, after resolution 41/213, fueling a sense that the world body had been somehow transformed into a far more effective and promising vehicle. Positive developments in the larger political atmosphere mattered a great deal in the end, boosting both reform and U.S.-UN relations. By the latter stages of the second Reagan term, U.S. officials seemed inclined to see the reform glass as half full, when earlier it appeared at best as half empty. The ultimate irony was that the Reagan team had left office and the United States was committed to full funding and to repaying the arrears before the supposedly pivotal consensus-based budgeting mechanism was fully realized in December 1989.[91] Ultimately, it required carrots, as well as sticks, to accomplish durable fiscal reform.

The progress of the 1980s hardly satiated the financial reform agenda and the debate was rekindled in the 1990s. Indeed, it took the terrorist attacks on the United States of September 11, 2001, and mounting pressure from the Bush administration for the House finally to vote to pay the arrears to the UN body (and for the Senate to confirm John Negroponte as the U.S. Permanent Representative to the UN, after some nine months of waiting). To those hoping for a promising new chapter in U.S. relations with the United Nations or an end to the squabbles over dues and assessments, these developments could not offer much encouragement.

Conclusion

As this historical review makes abundantly clear, the process of institutional change at the UN works in subtle, complex, and uneven ways. The dual phenomena of reform and adaptation have not been widely studied and are not well understood.[92] Some of the following lessons, drawn from this review, are consistent with prevalent assumptions, but others seem counterintuitive.

1. Reform does not come easily to the UN system. The Secretary-General has little leverage, the system is diffuse, and the Member States are rarely united behind specific reform goals. Any number of reform initiatives have fizzled because the sponsors lacked the time, patience, political capital, or commitment to see the process through to the end.

2. On the other hand, the process of reform is a constant. Big waves of high-visibility initiatives may only come every five to seven years, but less publicized and less contentious tinkering closer to the surface never seems to cease. In the UN, as the premier multilateral political entity, a premium is put on consultative processes. At times, process seems more important than results, while at other times process *is* the desired result.

3. Those unaware of the history of reform may indeed be condemned to repeat it. Since conditions change, it may make sense to test the waters again from time to time with proposals that have been tried before. But a lot of time and aggravation can be saved by learning the history first, especially because the UN is such a precedent-dependent institution. Delegations that are uncertain or reluctant to press forward on a particular initiative can be counted on to recite their version of the history of past efforts and steps on that subject.

4. The key to UN reform, in that sense, may lie less in trying to be innovative than in understanding why past initiatives have failed and how the strategies and tactics for achieving them could be improved. Scholars and commissions thus might utilize their time more productively in thinking through how to advance existing proposals than in developing new ones that have little chance of implementation.

5. More study is needed of how scholars and commissions have helped to shape the UN reform process.[93] In a few of the cases addressed here, such as the Jackson capacity study, the Group of 18, the Razali plan, and Kofi Annan's July 1997 package, there have been direct, creative, and productive interactions between idea producers from civil society and the official reform processes. In each case, of course, the independent voice is sought by those actors who believe that this expert input will help to bolster their case for or against a particular step. In turn, the perspectives, values, and positions of official actors may well have been shaped to some extent by what scholars and blue ribbon commissions had been saying and/or writing. At the same time, however, it is striking how often the reform debates have proceeded with only modest or marginal input from civil society, which is readily excluded from these processes and which tends to gravitate to less technical and tedious topics. Though they took place at the height of the clamor for greater NGO access to UN proceedings, the five General Assembly working groups established during the mid-1990s largely operated behind closed doors and interacted regularly with only a handful of enterprising NGO representatives.

6. When it comes to moving an agenda for reform in the UN, it is not always clear where power dwells (or who, if anyone, is in charge). In the 1960s, none of the P-5 voted for the expansion of both ECOSOC and the Security Council, yet all eventually found it easier to go along with the tide for expansion. In the 1990s, by contrast, their mere ambivalence helped to foster doubts and divisions among the rest of the membership regarding enlarging the Security Council. Through dues withholding, the United States has been able to achieve some of its financial goals, but has less to show in terms of structural, institutional, or programmatic change. And to the extent that financial leverage matters, the United States has worked hard to ensure that it has less and less of this dwindling asset at the UN. Some Secretaries-General, moreover, have been far more adept than others at playing their modest reform cards.

7. Change happens even if reform doesn't. The UN is highly adaptable to changing world conditions. Sometimes formal reform follows (it never leads). When reform fails to keep pace with changing needs or conditions, entrepreneurial UN officials, Member States, and civil society representatives are all adept at circumventing the rules and procedures to get things done. Given the often glacial pace of institutional reform, it is not surprising that through the years more and more fund-

ing and programmatic initiatives have avoided the regular budget and scrutiny by the Assembly, finding voluntary and ad hoc routes instead.

8. The course of reform tends to be decidedly unpredictable. Rarely does a reform wave end up where its initiators expected. Sometimes the detour takes place at the negotiating stage, sometimes during implementation. Given the number and diversity of players in the UN community, as well as the episodic nature of the engagement of national leaders in these matters, it is very difficult to map the political course reform initiatives are likely to take. They invite free-riding, empty gestures, and a playing to domestic audiences along the way.

9. As this review has demonstrated, the temptation to mistake modest and short-term adjustments for epochal change has proven irresistible time and again. Unfortunately, such repeated overselling of reform accomplishments has tended to undermine support for reform in two ways: it has led to overly high expectations and resulting disillusionment with the whole enterprise; and it has too often made the best the enemy of the good, encouraging flashy proposals that squeeze out sound but incremental ones.

Where do these lessons leave us in terms of future prospects? . . . In terms of historical lessons, perhaps the most important is also the most obvious: UN reform has an unusually full and rich history. The impulse to improve the workings of the world body has been present since San Francisco. It ebbs and flows, of course, but it keeps coming back. The tensions, divisions, and distasteful compromises of the last reform drive have left delegations, officials, specialists, and even private foundations with a mighty anti-reform hangover. In UN circles, congressional withholdings have given reform a bad name. But a lot of parties have also been left with a sense of incomplete agendas and unfulfilled ambitions. Very few delegations, in particular, got what they wanted out. As this chapter documents, the pace of UN reform has become markedly skewed. There have been repeated incremental refinements to the UN's response to the question, "Who implements?" Likewise, the struggle over "Who pays?" never ends. The most disgruntled party, the United States, has been forcing its will on the rest and getting results. Others are deeply resentful of its tactics, but can live with the results. There has been no new answer, however, to the core question of "Who decides?" for the past three decades. The ongoing debate about Security Council reform, in particular, increasingly revolves around complaints about the inequity of the current system.

The question of "Who decides?" raises a related dilemma: Should the goal of UN reform be to make its decisionmaking processes more reflective of the membership as a whole or more in line with the prevailing balance of power and capacity outside of its halls? Clearly, most Member States, in calling for democratization, equity, and transparency, have the former in mind. The founders, as noted earlier, recognized this dilemma and sought, in the creation of an Assembly and a Council, to have it both ways. Today, however, the question is more pointed because of the growing imbalance of power in the real world outside. The United States has not only built an unrivaled power position, including importantly in the projection of military force, but has also shown a growing willingness to go it alone on a number of issues of great concern to the rest of the membership. The latter, in turn, have begun to see multilateral organization as a way of discouraging or even countering the unilateral instincts of the United States. It is frequently said, as well, that the UN is an organization for smaller countries and should be restructured to reflect this. . . . [The question of U.S. power and influence within the world body, it seems, will become the subtext for much of the debate about what kind of a UN the world will need in the future: one that constrains or multiplies U.S. power?] . . . In terms of the "Who implements?" issues, the only ones over which the Secretary-General can exercise decisive influence, the possibility of slippage is always present. So too are pressures to create new posts and increase spending, especially after so many years of relative austerity. The next Secretary-General will have some big shoes to fill, since it is never easy to succeed a popular leader. The political dilemmas noted above, moreover, suggest that the dual task of political management and institutional management will be merged in a most challenging way. But after all, in the United Nations, reform has always been about politics. This is what history teaches us.

Notes

1. Ruth B. Russell, *A History of the United Nations Charter: The Role of the United States 1940–45* (Washington, D.C.: Brookings Institution, 1958), pp. 742–749.

2. Senate Committee on Expenditures in the Executive Departments, *United States Relations with International Organizations,* 80th Congress, 2nd sess., 1948, Senate Report 1757, pp. 11–19.

3. For ideas for a 1995 review conference, see Francis O. Wilcox and Carl M. Marcy, *Proposals for Changes in the United Nations* (Washington, D.C.: Brookings Institution, 1955).

4. Sidney D. Bailey and Sam Daws, *The Procedure of the UN Security Council,* 3rd ed. (Oxford: Oxford University Press, 1998).

5. See A/49/1, para. 46, and A/50/1, para. 69. For a proposal to revive and reorient the Trusteeship Council, see Kofi Annan, Report of the Secretary-General, *Renewing the United Nations: A Programme for Reform,* A/51/950, July 7, 1997, paras. 84–85, 282; Note by the Secretary-General, *United Nations Reform: Measures and Proposals: A New Concept of Trusteeship,* A/52/849, March 31, 1998; and Report of the Secretary-General, *United Nations Reform: Measures and Proposals, Environment and Human Settlements,* A/53/463, October 6, 1998, para. 61 and recommendation 24(b).

6. For example, see W. Andy Knight, *A Changing United Nations: Multilateral Evolution and the Quest for Global Governance* (New York: Palgrave, 2000), pp. 41–50.

7. The five groups included the Open-Ended Working Group on the Question of Equitable Representation and Increase in Membership of the Security Council and Other Matters Related to the Security Council; the Ad Hoc Open-Ended Working Group of the General Assembly on an Agenda for Development; and the High-Level Open-Ended Working Group on the Strengthening of the United Nations System.

8. See, for example, the so-called Brahimi Report, on UN peace operations. A/55/305, August 21, 2000.

9. Of the UN's four principal intergovernmental organs, this review focuses on the two that have been the targets of the most reform attention: the Economic and Social Council and the Security Council. For the results of the latest drive to improve the General Assembly's performance, achieved by the Strengthening Working Group in 1997, see *Report of the Open-Ended High-Level Working Group on the Strengthening of the United Nations System,* A/51/24, July 18, 1997.

10. This count of founding members deletes Australia, New Zealand, and several countries of the Middle East.

11. One of the few studies of ECOSOC was by Walter R. Sharp, *The United Nations Economic and Social Council* (New York: Columbia University Press, 1969).

12. Report by the President to the Congress for the Year 1963, *U.S. Participation in the U.N.,* Department of State (Washington, D.C.: U.S. Government Printing Office, 1964, pp. 143–161.

13. Nikolai Fedorenko, the Soviet Permanent Representative to the United Nations, to the Special Political Committee on December 10, 1963, A/SPC/96, pp. 1–9.

14. See A/PV.1285, December 17, 1963, pp. 6–17; A/5487, September 4, 1963, pp. 1–4; and A/5502, July 16, 1962–July 15, 1963, pp. 95–96.

15. Edward C. Luck, *Mixed Messages: American Politics and International Organization, 1919–1999* (Washington, D.C.: Brookings Institution Press, 1999), pp. 233–238.

16. But see U.S. Senate Committee on Foreign Relations, *Hearings on United Nations Charter Amendments,* 89th Congress, 1st sess., 1965 (Washington, D.C.: U.S. Government Printing Office, 1965), no. 89-51678-1, p. 22.

17. U.S. House of Representatives, *Congressional Record,* 89th Congress, 1st sess., 1965, vol. III, pt. 7 (Washington, D.C.: U.S. Government Printing Office, 1965), pp. 8713–8716.

18. U.S. Senate, *Congressional Record,* 89th Congress, 1st sess., 1965, vol. III, pt. 9 (Washington, D.C.: U.S. Government Printing Office, 1965), pp. 12547–12559.

19. Ibid., pp. 12548–12549.

20. Report by the President to the Congress for the Year 1971, *U.S. Participation in the U.N.* (Washington, D.C.: U.S. Government Printing Office, 1972), pp. 134–136.

21. A/PV.2026, p. 1.

22. Ibid., pp. 1–2.

23. Ibid., p. 3.

24. Statement of Martin F. Herz, acting assistant secretary of state, Bureau of International Organization Affairs, to the Senate Foreign Relations Committee, July 24, 1973, reproduced as an appendix in the committee's report, *Amendment to Article 61 of the Charter of the United Nations,* July 26, 1973, 93rd Congress, 1st sess., Executive Report no. 93-9, pp. 2–4.

25. See *Report of the Economic and Social Council on the Work of Its Fiftieth and Fifty-first Sessions, General Assembly, Official Records: Twenty-sixth Session, Supplement no. 3* (A/8403), pp. 9–13. See also A/PV.2026, p. 2. China was not a member of ECOSOC and was absent for the Assembly vote.

26. Ronald I. Meltzer, "Restructuring the United Nations System: Institutional Reform Efforts in the Context of North-South Relations," *International Organization* 32, no. 4 (Autumn 1978), pp. 993–1018.

27. Report of the Group of Experts on the Structure of the United Nations System, *A New United Nations Structure for Global Economic Co-operation,* E/AC.62.9 (New York: United Nations, 1975), p. 1.

28. Ibid., pp. 13–19.

29. Sir Robert G. A. Jackson, *A Study of the Capacity of the United Nations Development System,* vols. 1–2, DP/5 (Geneva: United Nations, 1969); Peter J. Fromuth, ed., *A Successor Vision: The United Nations of Tomorrow* (New York: United Nations Association of the United States of America, 1988); Independent Working Group on the Future of the United Nations, *The United Nations in Its Second Half-Century: The Report of the Independent Working Group on the Future of the United Nations* (New York: Yale University/Ford Foundation, 1995); Commission on Global Governance, *Our Global Neighborhood* (New York: Oxford University Press, 1995); South Centre, *For a Strong and Democratic United Nations: A South Perspective of UN Reform* (Geneva: South Centre, 1996); and South Centre, *The Economic Role of the United Nations* (Dar-es-Salaam and Geneva: South Centre, 1992).

30. ECOSOC, resolution 1996/31, July 25, 1996. Also see the NGLS Roundup of November 1996, available at www.globalpolicy.org/ngos/docs96/review.htm.

31. Maurice Bertrand, *Some Reflections on Reform of the United Nations,* Joint Inspection Unit, JIU/REP/85/9 (Geneva: United Nations, 1985), p. 59.

32. See GA/9945, November 1, 2001; GA/9692 and GA/9693, December 20, 1999; and A/[49-55]/47 (1994 to 2000).

33. See Note by the President of the Security Council, S/2002/603 and A/AC/247/1996/CRP.4.

34. Memorandum by the Elected Members on Transparency in the Security Council, December 22, 1997, www.globalpolicy.org/security/docs/memo 1297.htm.

35. Russell, *History of the United Nations Charter,* pp. 713–749.

36. As the Commission on Global Governance phrased it, "to add more permanent members and give them a veto would be regression, not reform." *Our Global Neighborhood* (New York: Oxford University Press, 1995), p. 239.

37. The Razali plan can be found at www.globalpolicy.org/security/ reform/raz497.htm.

38. Razali called for such restraint, as did the Independent Working Group on the Future of the United Nations in *The United Nations in Its Second Half-Century,* p. 16.

39. Arthur H. Vandenberg Jr., ed., *The Private Papers of Senator Vandenberg* (Boston: Houghton Mifflin, 1952), pp. 238–239.

40. U.S. Department of State, *Foreign Relations of the United States, 1946,* vol. 1, *General: The United Nations* (Washington, D.C.: U.S. Government Printing Office, 1972), p. 494.

41. Senate Committee on Expenditures, *United States Relations,* pp. 16–18.

42. UNDP, *Progress Report by the Administrator to the Governing Council,* May 9, 1968, DP/L.79, p. 2.

43. Jackson, *Capacity Study,* vol. 1, pp. ii–x, 10, 21, 34–36, 49.

44. Ibid., vol. 2, pp. 302, 329, 335–337.

45. Ibid.; see vol. 2, chaps. 8 (pp. 339–372) and 6 (pp. 215–278) respectively.

46. Ibid., vol. 1, pp. 25–29.

47. Johan Kaufmann, "The Capacity of the United Nations Development Program: The Jackson Report," *International Organization* 25, no.1 (Winter 1971), p. 946.

48. This was lamented in the 1948 Senate report. Senate Committee on Expenditures, *United States Relations,* p. 18.

49. Fromuth, *Successor Vision,* p. xx.

50. Rosemary Righter, *Utopia Lost: The United Nations and World Order* (New York: Twentieth Century Fund, 1995), pp. 155–184.

51. Report of the Group of Experts on the Structure of the United Nations System, *New United Nations Structure,* p. 1.

52. Ibid., p. 23.

53. Ibid., pp. 56–57.

54. *Contributions by the Executive Heads of the Organization of the United Nations System,* A/AC.179/16, October 20, 1977, and *Note by the Secretary-General,* A/AC.179/6, April 15, 1976.

55. A/46/882, February 21, 1992, and A/C.5/47/2, June 2, 1993. Ironically, by that point the last few incumbents of the post of director-general had been French nationals, so the goal of making this a high-level post for developing-country nationals was not being served in any case.

56. E/1999/L.61, December 15, 1999.

57. For a listing of these units, see Annan, *Renewing the United Nations,* p. 31.

58. Ibid., p. 17, para. 38.

59. Ibid., p. 6, plus p. 20, paras. 49–51. For the rationale and workings of the new UN Development Group and other aspects of development cooperation, see pp. 49–56, paras. 46–169 and actions 9–11.

60. Ibid., p. 90, para. 283.

61. J. David Singer, *Financing International Organization: The United Nations Budget Process* (The Hague: M. Nijhoff, 1961), pp. 122–123; and Russell, *History of the United Nations Charter,* pp. 62–63.

62. While voluntary payments for particular agencies, programs, or trust funds have grown very substantially over time, they have not proven nearly so controversial as assessments either in UN fora or in capitals.

63. For a more detailed account of these early debates, see Singer, *Financing International Organization,* pp. 122–146.

64. *U.S. Financial and Political Involvement in the United Nations,* 99th Congress, 1st sess., 1985 (Washington, D.C.: U.S. Government Printing Office, 1985), p. 6.

65. Section 143 of Public Law 99-93 (H.R. 2068), August 16, 1985.

66. See U.S. Congress, *Congressional Record,* 99th Congress, 1st sess., 1985, vol. 131, pt. 11 (Washington, D.C.: U.S. Government Printing Office, 1985), pp. 14937–14940. Also see U.S. House of Representatives, *Congressional Record,* May 8, 1985, 99th Congress, 1st sess., vol. 131, pt. 8 (Washington, D.C.: U.S. Government Printing Office, 1985), pp. 11096–11098.

67. House Subcommittee on Human Rights and International Organizations and Subcommittee on International Operations, Committee on Foreign Affairs, *Recent Developments in the United Nations System,* 100th Congress, 2nd sess., 1988 (Washington, D.C.: U.S. Government Printing Office, 1988), no. 88-H381-61, p. 66.

68. Subparagraphs 2(a)–2(b) of resolution 40/237, December 18, 1985.

69. See A/40/PV.121, pp. 7–8, 16, 27, 41.

70. See Tapio Kanninen, *Leadership and Reform: The Secretary-General and the UN Financial Crisis of the Late 1980s* (The Hague: Kluwer Law International, 1995), pp. 44–45; and A/40/1102, pp. 5–8, paras. 15–31.

71. Subparagraph (c) of resolution 40/572, and A/40/1102 and its addenda.

72. Tapio Kanninen, *Leadership and Reform,* p. 51. The Secretary-General called for a reduction in the U.S. assessment to 15 or 20 percent and for the five permanent members to pay "more or less the same amount." Elaine Sciolino, "U.N. Chief Suggests U.S. Contribution Be Cut," *New York Times,* April 29, 1986.

73. Kanninen, *Leadership,* p. 73.

74. *Report of the High-Level Intergovernmental Experts to Review the Efficiency of the Administrative and Financial Functioning of the United*

Nations, A/41/49, p. 4, para. 19. Also see p. 7, para. 22, and recommendation 8, pp. 7–8.

75. Maurice Bertrand, *The Third Generation World Organization* (Dordrecht, Netherlands: M. Nijhoff, 1989), p. 111.

76. A/41/49, pp. 1, 10.

77. Michael J. Berlin, "U.N. Adopts Agreement to Trim Costs; Weighted Voting, Staff Cuts Approved," *Washington Post,* December 20, 1986.

78. Don Shannon, "State Department to Lobby Congress for U.N. Budget," *Los Angeles Times,* September 15, 1986; and James F. Clarity, Milt Freudenheim, and Katherine Roberts, "U.N.'s Bloated Bottom Line," *New York Times,* August 24, 1986.

79. See Alan L. Keyes, "Why Imperil U.N. Reform?" *New York Times,* September 25, 1986; José S. Sorzano, "The Congress Is Not 'Bashing' the UN," *Christian Science Monitor,* August 19, 1986; and Dante B. Fascell, "Enough U.N.-Bashing," *New York Times,* September 19, 1986.

80. The United States circulated a UNA-USA report that proposed a similar consensus-based budgeting mechanism and that was signed by four African leaders, a Latin American foreign minister, and Senator Kassebaum, among others. See United Nations Management and Decision-Making Project, *U.N. Leadership: The Roles of the Secretary-General and the Member States* (New York: UNA-USA, December 1986).

81. A/41/PV.102, pp. 7–8.

82. Bertrand, *Third Generation,* p. 115.

83. Quoted in Elaine Sciolino, "U.N. Assembly Favors Plan to Alter the Budget Process," *New York Times,* December 20, 1986.

84. "Walters Says U.S. Should Restore U.N. Dues," *New York Times,* December 21, 1986.

85. The CPC was established by ECOSOC as a subsidiary body by resolution 920 (XXXIV) of 1962. Also see ECOSOC resolutions 1171 (XLI) of 1966, and 2008 (LX) of 1976. It serves as the principal subsidiary body of both ECOSOC and the General Assembly for planning, programming, and coordination. Its members are nominated by the Council and elected by the Assembly for three-year terms, according to a formula for equitable geographical distribution.

86. Berlin, "U.N. Adopts Agreement."

87. *United States Participation in the UN* (Washington, D.C.: U.S. Government Printing Office, 1986), p. 306.

88. Public Law 100-204, sec. 143, December 22, 1987, Foreign Relations Authorization Act, fiscal years 1988 and 1989. In essence, Congress—a full year after the passage of 41/213—decided to ease one condition but to add two new ones before the United Nations could receive full funding.

89. Report by the President to the Congress for the Year 1988, *United States Participation in the UN* (Washington, D.C.: U.S. Government Printing Office, 1989), pp. 305–306, 309, 310.

90. Elaine Sciolino, "Reagan, in Switch, Says U.S. Will Pay Old U.N. Dues," *New York Times,* September 14, 1988; and Lou Cannon, "U.S. to Pay Dues, Debt to U.N.; White House Offers Olive Branch, Praise for Fiscal Reforms," *Washington Post,* September 14, 1988.

91. See U.S. statement, A/44/PV.84, pp. 17–21.

92. But see Knight, *Changing United Nations,* and Kanninen, *Leadership and Reform.*

93. Edward C. Luck, "Blue Ribbon Power: Independent Commissions and UN Reform," *International Studies Perspectives,* no. 1 (2000): 89–104.

19

The Resurgent Idea of World Government

Campbell Craig

THE IDEA OF WORLD GOVERNMENT IS RETURNING TO THE
mainstream of scholarly thinking about international relations. Univer-
sities in North America and Europe now routinely advertise for positions in "global governance," a term that few would have heard of a
decade ago. Chapters on cosmopolitanism and governance appear in
many current international relations (IR) textbooks. Leading scholars
are wrestling with the topic, including Alexander Wendt, perhaps now
America's most influential IR theorist, who has recently suggested that
a world government is simply "inevitable."[1] While some scholars envision a more formal world state, and others argue for a much looser system of "global governance," it is probably safe to say that the growing
number of works on this topic can be grouped together into the broader
category of "world government"—a school of thought that supports the
creation of international authority (or authorities) that can tackle the
global problems that nation-states currently cannot.

It is not, of course, a new idea. Dreaming of a world without war,
or of government without tyranny, idealists have advocated some kind
of world or universal state since the classical period. The Italian poet
Dante viewed world government as a kind of utopia. The Dutch scholar
Hugo Grotius, often regarded as the founder of international law,
believed in the eventual formation of a world government to enforce it.
The notion interested many visionary thinkers in the late nineteenth and
early twentieth centuries, including H. G. Wells and Aldous Huxley. In
1942 the one-time Republican presidential candidate Wendell Willkie

Reprinted from *Ethics and International Affairs* 22, no. 2 (2008): 133–142. © 2008
Blackwell Publishers. Reprinted by permission of the publisher.

published a famous book on the topic, *One World*. And after the Second World War, the specter of atomic war moved many prominent American scholars and activists, including Albert Einstein, the University of Chicago president Robert Hutchins, and the columnist Dorothy Thompson, to advocate an immediate world state—not so much out of idealistic dreams but because only such a state, they believed, could prevent a third world war fought with the weapons that had just obliterated Hiroshima and Nagasaki. The campaign continued until as late as 1950, when the popular magazine *Reader's Digest* serialized a book by the world-government advocate Emery Reves, while at the same time the Senate Subcommittee on Foreign Relations was considering several motions to urge the Truman administration to adopt a policy of world federalism.[2] In fact, to this day the World Federalist Movement—an international NGO founded in 1947 and recognized by the United Nations—boasts a membership of 30,000 to 50,000 worldwide.

By the 1950s, however, serious talk of world government had largely disappeared. The failure of the Baruch Plan to establish international control over atomic weaponry in late 1946 signaled its demise, for it cleared the way (as the plan's authors quietly intended) for the United States and the Soviet Union to continue apace with their respective atomic projects. What state would place its trust in a world government when there were sovereign nations that possessed, or could soon possess, atomic bombs?[3]

Certainly, neither the United States nor the Soviet Union was willing to do so, and once the two states committed themselves to the international rivalry that became known as the Cold War, the impossibility of true global government became obvious and the campaign in favor of it diminished. Even after the invention of thermonuclear weaponry and intercontinental missiles in the late 1950s, a technological development that threatened to destroy all of humanity, few voices in the West (it was never an issue in the Soviet bloc, at least until Gorbachev) were raised to demand a new kind of government that could somehow eliminate this danger. There were some exceptions: a surprising one was the common conclusion reached by the two American realists Reinhold Niebuhr and Hans Morgenthau, who deduced around 1960 that the "nuclear revolution" had made a world state logically necessary. But how to achieve one when the United States and the Soviet Union would never agree to it? Niebuhr and Morgenthau had no answer to this question. The British philosopher Bertrand Russell, however, did: the antinuclear activist once argued that, since his preferred solution of total disarmament was not going to occur, the nuclear revolution had made global government immediately necessary and, thus, the only way to achieve it was to wage war on the USSR. There was a perverse logic to this, but we can be thankful that his demands were not heeded.

The end of the Cold War, together with the emergence of various intractable global problems, has spurred the resurgence of writing about world government. In this essay I will introduce three themes that appear frequently in this writing: how the "collective action problem" lies behind many of the current global crises; the debate between those who support a softer form of "governance" and those who look toward a full-fledged world state; and the fundamental question of whether world government is possible, and whether it is even desirable.

The Intensifying Dangers of International Anarchy

Certainly, one of the most evident failures of the nation-state system in recent years has been its inability to deal successfully with problems that endanger much or most of the world's population. As the world has become more globalized—economically integrated and culturally interconnected—individual countries have become increasingly averse to dealing with international problems that are not caused by any single state and cannot be fixed even by the focused efforts of individual governments. Political scientists refer to this quandary as the "collective action problem," by which they mean the dilemma that emerges when several actors have an interest in eradicating a problem that harms all of them, but when each would prefer that someone else do the dirty work of solving it. If everyone benefits more or less equally from the problem's solution, but only the actor that addresses it pays the costs, then all are likely to want to "free ride" on the other's efforts. The result is that no one tackles the problem, and everyone suffers.

Several such collective action problems dominate much of international politics today, and scholars of course debate their importance and relevance to world government. Nevertheless, a few obvious ones stand out, notably the imminent danger of climate change, the difficulty of addressing terrorism, and the complex task of humanitarian intervention. All of these are commonly (though not universally) regarded as serious problems in need of urgent solutions, and in each case powerful states have repeatedly demonstrated that they would prefer that somebody else solve them.

The solution to the collective action problem has long been known: it requires the establishment of some kind of authoritative regime that can organize common solutions to common problems and spread out the costs fairly. This is why many scholars and activists concerned with acute global problems support some form of world government. These advocates are not so naïve as to believe that such a system would put an effortless end to global warming, terrorism, or human rights atrocities, just as even the most effective national governments have not eradicated pollution or crime. The central argument in favor of a world-government approach to the problems of globalization is not that it would easily solve these problems, but that it is the only entity that can solve them.

A less newsworthy issue, but one more central to many advocates of world government, is the persistent possibility of a third world war in which the use of megaton thermonuclear weaponry could destroy most of the human race. During the Cold War, nuclear conflict was averted by the specter of mutual assured destruction (MAD)—the recognition by the United States and the Soviet Union that a war between them would destroy them both. To be sure, this grim form of deterrence could well obtain in future international orders, but it is unwise to regard the Cold War as a promising model for future international politics. It is not at all certain that international politics is destined to return to a stable bipolar order, such as prevailed during the second half of the Cold War, but even if this does happen, there is no guarantee that nuclear deterrence would work as well as it did during the second half of the twentieth century. It is well to remember that the two sides came close to nuclear blows during the Cuban crisis, and this was over a relatively small issue that did not bear upon the basic security of either state. As Martin Amis has written, the problem with nuclear deterrence is that "it can't last out the necessary time span, which is roughly between now and the death of the sun."[4] As long as interstate politics continue, we cannot rule out that in some future conflict a warning system will fail, a leader will panic, governments will refuse to back down, a third party will provoke a response—indeed, there are any number of scenarios under which deterrence could fail and thermonuclear war could occur.

It is possible that the United States, if not other nations, can fight against the thermonuclear dilemma with technology. By constructing an anti–ballistic missile (ABM) system, America could perhaps defend itself from a nuclear attack. Also, and more ominously, the United

States may be on the verge of deploying an offensive nuclear capability so advanced that it could launch a first strike against a nuclear adversary and disarm it completely.[5] But these are weak reeds. As things currently stand, an ABM system remains acutely vulnerable to inexpensive decoy tactics, jamming, and the simple response of building more missiles. The first-strike option is even more questionable: an aggressive or terrified United States could launch a nuclear war against a major adversary, but no American leader could be sure that every enemy weapon would be destroyed, making the acute risks of initiating such a war (unless a full-scale enemy thermonuclear attack was imminent and certain) likely to outweigh the benefits. Technology is unlikely to solve the nuclear dilemma.

Theorists considering world government regard the thermonuclear dilemma as particularly salient because it epitomizes the dangers of the continuation of the interstate system. As long as sovereign nations continue to possess nuclear arsenals, nuclear war is possible, and the only apparent way to put a permanent end to this possibility is to develop some kind of world government, an entity with sufficient power to stop states—not to mention subnational groups—from acquiring nuclear arsenals and waging war with them.

Global Governance Versus a World State

Scholars nevertheless disagree whether an informal, loose form of governance is sufficient, or whether a more formal world state is necessary. Supporters of global governance argue that the unique dangers created by globalization can be solved by a gradual strengthening of existing international institutions and organizations, making the imposition of a full-blown world state unnecessary. Anthony McGrew, a leading scholar of globalization in the British academy, where support for global governance is particularly pronounced, suggests that global problems can be effectively dealt with by liberal international agencies, such as the World Trade Organization; nongovernmental organizations, such as Greenpeace and Doctors Without Borders; and security bodies, such as the U.N. Security Council. McGrew argues that the key is to grant increased and more formal powers to such institutions and organizations, ultimately giving them greater effectiveness and influence on the international stage than nation-states. Another British scholar, David Held, stresses the importance of making international institutions accountable

402 INTERNATIONAL ORGANIZATIONS AND THE FUTURE

to democratic controls. Held maintains that the world's population must have a direct say in the composition and policies of increasingly powerful international bodies.[6] Held, along with others who insist on greater democratic oversight of global institutions, worries that the current "democratic deficit" afflicting existing international bodies, such as the International Monetary Fund and the U.N. Security Council, could become far worse as they acquire and wield greater and greater power.

The European Union is often offered as a model of what could happen at the international level. Gradually, once-hostile European states have cooperated to develop forms of transnational governance without subjecting themselves to the convulsive and possibly violent task of creating a European state. Nations that might refuse to accept the formation of a dominant state have nevertheless readily accepted the establishment of institutions and bureaucracies that slowly create transnational political bonds and reduce their own sovereignty. True, the process of establishing the European Union has been unsure and—for those who want to see a stronger political union—remains incomplete, but it has taken place, and in a peaceful manner. A similar process at the international level, contend advocates of global integration, would constitute a practical way to establish global government.

Theorists who believe that a more formal world state is necessary do not necessarily disagree with the logic of global governance: it is difficult to dispute the claim that the gradual creation of supranational institutions is likely to be more feasible and peaceful than the imposition of a true world state. The "key problem" for the governance argument, however, as Alexander Wendt writes, is "unauthorized violence by rogue Great Powers."[7] As long as sovereign states continue to exist under a system of governance, in other words, there is nothing to prevent them from using violence to disrupt the international peace for their own purposes. The European Union has created forms of transnational governance, but decision-making in the areas of security and defense is still the prerogative of its member states. Thus, the EU remains effectively powerless to stop violence undertaken by one of its own members (such as Britain's involvement in the Iraq war), not to mention war waged by other nations even in its own backyard (such as in Bosnia and Herzegovina). Until this problem is solved, world-state advocates argue, any global order will be too fragile to endure. Sooner or later a sovereign state will wage war, and the inability of a regime of global governance to stop it will deprive it of authority and legitimacy. International politics would then revert to the old state system.

In "Why a World State Is Inevitable," Wendt argues that a formal world state—by which he means a truly new sovereign political entity, with constitutional authority over all nations—will naturally evolve as peoples and nations come to realize that they cannot obtain true independence, or what Wendt calls "recognition," without one. In other words, the advent of global technologies and weaponry present weaker societies with an emerging choice between subjugation to powerful states and globalized forces or participation in an authentic world government; a world state would not threaten distinct national cultures, as pluralist scholars have argued, but rather it is the only entity that can preserve them. Wendt sees this as a teleological phenomenon, by which he means that the logic of globalization and the struggle by all cultures and societies for recognition are bound to lead to a world state whether it is sought or not. Such a state, Wendt argues, would not need to be particularly centralized or hierarchical; as long as it could prevent sovereign states from waging war, it could permit local cultures, traditions, and politics to continue.[8] But a looser system of governance would not be enough, because societies that seek recognition could not trust it to protect them from powerful states seeking domination.

Daniel Deudney's recent book, *Bounding Power*, provides the fullest and most creative vision yet of formal world government in our age.[9] Deudney argues that the driving force behind world government is the fact that international war has become too dangerous. Unified by a common interest in avoiding nuclear extermination, states have the ability to come together in much the same way as tribes and fiefdoms have in the past when advances in military technology made conflict among them suicidal. Unlike Wendt, Deudney does not see this as an inevitability: states may well choose to tolerate interstate anarchy, even though it will sooner or later result in a nuclear war. But Deudney is also optimistic that a world government created for the purpose of avoiding such a war can be small, decentralized, and liberal. In *Bounding Power*, he develops an elaborate case for the establishment of a world republic, based upon the same premise of restraining and diffusing power that motivated the founders of the American republic in the late eighteenth century.

World-state theorists such as Wendt and Deudney stress the danger that advocates of more global governance often downplay: the risk that ambitious sovereign states will be unrestrained by international institutions and agencies, even unprecedentedly powerful ones, and wage war for traditional reasons of power and profit. For Wendt, military conflict of this sort will simply push along the inevitable process of world-state formation, as societies and peoples recognize that a return to interstate anarchy will only unleash more such wars, while a world government will put an end to them and so guarantee their cultural independence. Deudney is less hopeful here. Military conflict in our age can well mean thermonuclear war, an event that could put an end to the pursuit of meaningful human independence and of the kind of world government that would respect it.

Is a World Government Possible?

The initial argument against a world state, and even a coherent system of global governance, is the one that anyone can see immediately: it is impractical. How could nations of radically different ideologies and cultures agree upon one common political authority? But the "impracticality" argument disregards historical experience. The history of state formation from the days of city-states to the present era is precisely the history of warring groups with different ideologies and cultures coming together under a larger entity. While the European Union is not at all yet a state, who would not have been denounced as insane for predicting a political and economic union among France, Germany, and other European states seventy years ago? For that matter, how "practical" would it have seemed forty years ago to foresee the peaceful end of the Cold War? As Deudney argues, smaller political units have always merged into larger ones when technology has made the violence among them unsustainable. The surprising thing, he maintains, would be if this did not happen at the planetary level.

The more important objections to world government posit not that it is impractical but that it is unnecessary and even undesirable. According to one such argument, the world should be governed not by a genuinely international authority but rather by the United States: a Pax Americana.[10] This school of thought stresses two main points: that such authority could more readily come into being without the violent convulsions that would likely accompany genuine world-state formation; and, as neoconservative writers particularly stress, that a world run by the United States would be preferable to a genuinely transnational world government given the superiority of American political, economic, and cultural institutions.

The case against Pax Americana, however, can be boiled down to one word: Iraq. The war in Iraq has shown that military operations undertaken by individual nation-states lead, as they have always done, to nationalist and tribal reactions against the aggressor that pay no heed to larger claims of superior or inferior civilizations. The disaster in Iraq has emboldened other revisionist states and groups to defy American will, caused erstwhile allies and friends of the United States to question its intentions and competence, and at the same time soured the American people on future adventures against states that do not overtly threaten them. In conceiving and executing its war in Iraq, it would have been difficult for the Bush administration to undermine the project of Pax Americana more effectively had it tried to do so. The United States could choose in future to rally other states behind it if it can persuade them of a global threat that must be vanquished. But, as Wendt implies, to do that successfully is effectively to begin the process of world-state formation.

Another objection to world government was first identified by Immanuel Kant. In articulating a plan for perpetual peace, Kant stopped short of advocating a world state, for fear that the state could become tyrannical. In a world of several nation-states, a tyranny can be removed by other states or overthrown from within. At least it could be possible for oppressed citizens of that state to flee to less repressive countries. But a sovereign world government could be invulnerable to such measures. It could not be defeated by an external political rival; those who would overthrow it from within would have nowhere to hide, no one to support them from the outside. Kant concluded that these dangers overrode the permanent peace that could be had with world government, and he ended up advocating instead a confederation of sovereign, commercial states.

One can raise two points in response to Kant's deeply important concern. First, he wrote in the eighteenth century, when the specter of war was not omnicidal and the planet did not face such global crises as climate change and transnational terrorism. International politics as usual was not as dangerous an alternative to his vision of perpetual peace as it potentially is today. Second, as Deudney argues, there is one central reason to believe that a world government could avoid the temptations of tyranny and actually exist as a small, federal authority rather than a global leviathan.[11] This is the indisputable fact that—barring extraterrestrial invasion—a world government would have no need for a policy of external security. States often become increasingly tyrannical as they use external threats to justify internal repression and authoritarian policies. These threats, whether real or imagined, have throughout history and to the present day been used by leaders to justify massive taxation, conscription, martial law, and the suppression of dissent. But no world government could plausibly make such demands.

Will the world-government movement become a potent political force, or will it fade away as it did in the late 1940s? To a degree the answer to this question depends on the near-term future of international politics. If the United States alters its foreign policy and moves to manage the unipolar world more magnanimously, or, alternatively, if a new power (such as China) arises quickly to balance American power and instigate a new Cold War, the movement could fade. So, too, if existing international organizations somehow succeed in ameliorating climate change, fighting terrorism, and preventing humanitarian crises and other global problems. On the other hand, if the United States continues to pursue a Pax Americana, or if the transnational problems worsen, the movement could become a serious international cause.

These considerations aside, as Reinhold Niebuhr, Hans Morgenthau, and others discerned during the height of the Cold War, the deepest argument for world government—the specter of global nuclear war—will endure as long as sovereign nation-states continue to deploy nuclear weaponry. Whatever occurs over the near-term future, that fact is not going away. The great distinction between the international system prevailing in Niebuhr and Morgenthau's day and the system in our own time is that the chances of attaining some form of world government have been radically enhanced by the end of the Cold War and the emergence of a unipolar order. This condition, however, will not last forever.

Notes

1. Alexander Wendt, "Why a World State Is Inevitable," *European Journal of International Relations* 9, no. 4 (2003): 491–542. For a more extensive discussion of new scholarship on world government, see especially Catherine Lu, "World Government," in Edward N. Zalta, ed., *The Stanford Encyclopedia of Philosophy* (Winter 2006 Edition); available at plato.stanford.edu/entries/world-government/.

2. See Paul Boyer, *By the Bomb's Early Light: American Thought and Culture at the Dawn of the Atomic Age* (New York: Pantheon, 1985); and Luis Cabrera, "Introduction," in Cabrera, ed., *Global Government/Global Governance,* forthcoming.

3. Campbell Craig and Sergey Radchenko, *The Atomic Bomb and the Origins of the Cold War* (New Haven, Conn.: Yale University Press, 2008).

4. Martin Amis, *Einstein's Monsters* (London: Jonathan Cape, 1987), pp. 16–17.

5. Keir Lieber and Daryl Press, "The End of MAD?: The Nuclear Dimension of U.S. Primacy," *International Security* 30, no. 4 (2006): 7–44. Lieber and Press do not advocate an American first strike against a potential aggressor; they simply argue that the United States has developed a capability to do so.

6. For an overview of McGrew's and Held's positions, see Anthony McGrew and David Held, eds., *Governing Globalization* (London: Polity, 2002), chaps. 13 and 15. Also see Andrew Hurrell, *On Global Order* (New York: Oxford University Press, 2007). American scholars in favor of global governance include Richard Falk, *On Humane Governance* (University Park: Pennsylvania State University Press, 1995); and Anne-Marie Slaughter, *A New World Order* (Princeton, N.J.: Princeton University Press, 2005). For an innovative treatment of the problem of global democracy, see Luis Cabrera, *Political Theory of Global Justice: A Cosmopolitan Case for the World State* (London: Routledge, 2004).

7. See Wendt, "Why a World State Is Inevitable," p. 506.

8. Ibid., especially pp. 507–10 and 514–16. For the argument that world government would threaten cultural pluralism, see Michael Walzer, *Arguing About War* (New Haven, Conn.: Yale University Press, 2004).

9. Daniel H. Deudney, *Bounding Power: Republican Security Theory from the Polis to the Global Village* (Princeton, N.J.: Princeton University Press, 2006).

10. For example, Niall Ferguson, *Colossus: The Rise and Fall of the American Empire* (New York: Penguin, 2004).

11. Deudney, *Bounding Power,* esp. chap. 6 and conclusion.

Index

About the Book

THE POLITICS OF GLOBAL GOVERNANCE HELPS STUDENTS OF international organizations understand the major themes, theories, and approaches central to the subject. The fourth edition of this widely used anthology has been thoroughly updated with fourteen new essays to reflect the current concerns of the global system. Peacekeeping and collective security, finance and trade, and social and humanitarian issues are among the key topics covered.

The editors' section introductions underscore the importance of the essays, which have been selected not only for their relevance but also for their accessibility.

Paul F. Diehl is Henning Larsen Professor of Political Science and University Distinguished Teacher/Scholar at the University of Illinois at Urbana-Champaign, where he also serves as director of the Correlates of War Project. His recent publications include *Evaluating Peace Operations* (with Daniel Druckman) and *The Scourge of War: New Extension of an Old Problem.* **Brian Frederking** is associate professor of political science at McKendree University. He is author of *The United States and the Security Council: Collective Security Since the Cold War* and *Resolving Security Dilemmas: A Constructivist Explanation of the INF Treaty.*